William A. Kaplin

The Law of
Higher Education

Legal Implications of
Administrative Decision Making

 Jossey-Bass Publishers
San Francisco • Washington • London • 1978

THE LAW OF HIGHER EDUCATION
Legal Implications of Administrative Decision Making
by William A. Kaplin

Copyright © 1978 by: Jossey-Bass, Inc., Publishers
433 California Street
San Francisco, California 94104

&

Jossey-Bass Limited
28 Banner Street
London EC1Y 8QE

Library of Congress Catalogue Card Number LC 78-62571

International Standard Book Number ISBN 0-87589-378-3

Manufactured in the United States of America

JACKET DESIGN BY WILLI BAUM

FIRST EDITION

Code 7829

The Jossey-Bass Series
in Higher Education

Preface

The law has arrived on the campus—sometimes it has been a beacon, other times a blanket of ground fog. But even in its murkiness the law has not come "on little cat feet," like Carl Sandburg's "Fog"; nor has it sat silently on its haunches; nor will it soon move on. It has come noisily and sometimes has stumbled. And even in its imperfections the law has spoken forcefully and meaningfully to the higher education community and will continue to do so.

The Law of Higher Education is written for administrators and legal counsel who deal with the multitudes of new challenges and complexities that arise from the law's presence on campus and for students and observers of higher education and law who desire to explore the intersection of these two disciplines. In this book, *higher education* is considered broadly and covers all *postsecondary* education—from the large state university to the small private

liberal arts college, from the graduate and professional school to
the community college and vocational and technical institution,
from the traditional campus-based program to the innovative off-
campus or multistate program. For persons dealing with all or part
of this universe, as specialists or as generalists, this book is
intended to provide an analytical text, a practical guide, a ready
reference, and a research resource. To be equally usable by
administrators and legal counsel, the text avoids legal jargon and
technicalities when possible and explains them when used.
Footnotes throughout the book are designed primarily to provide
additional technical analysis and research resources for legal
counsel.

Chapter One provides a framework for understanding and
integrating what is presented in subsequent chapters and a
perspective for dealing with future legal developments. Chapters
Two through Four discuss legal concepts and issues affecting the
internal relationships among the various members of the campus
community and address the law's impact on particular roles,
functions, and responsibilities of postsecondary administrators.
Chapters Five through Seven are concerned with the postsecondary
institution's external relationships with local, state, and federal
government and examine broad questions of governmental power
and process that cut across all the internal relationships and
administrative functions considered in Chapters Two through
Four. These chapters also discuss particular legal issues arising
from the institution's dealings with government agencies and
identify connections to the issues explored in the earlier chapters.
In each instance, the issues in Chapters Five through Seven involve
a particular level of government, while the issues in Chapters Two
through Four involve a particular institutional relationship or
administrative function regardless of what level(s) of government
may have an impact on it. Chapter Eight also deals with the
institution's external relationships—not to government but to the
private educational accrediting agencies. Although these agencies
are part of the larger academic community and are themselves
monitored by government, the institution's relationships with
them in some respects parallel those with government agencies.
The mixture creates an interesting, concluding perspective from

which to view the developing relationship between education and law.

Each chapter ends with a selected annotated bibliography. Readers can use the sources listed to extend the discussion of particular issues presented in the chapter, to explore issues not treated in the chapter, to obtain additional practical guidance in dealing with the chapter's issues, to keep up to date on later developments, or to discover resources for research. Other sources pertaining to particular questions are cited occasionally in the text, and footnotes contain additional legal resources, primarily for lawyers. Court decisions, statutes, and administrative regulations are cited throughout the text. The citation form generally follows *A Uniform System of Citation,* 12th ed. (Harvard Law Review Association, 1976), and the legal resources that the citations refer to are explained in Chapter One, Sections 1.3.2 to 1.3.5. The appendix contains an abridged version of the United States Constitution.

Some precautions on using the book are in order. The legal analyses and suggestions, of necessity, are general: they are not adapted to the law of any particular state or to the circumstances prevailing at any particular postsecondary institution. Thus the book is not a substitute for the advice of legal counsel, for further research into primary legal resources, or for individualized study of each legal problem's specific circumstances. Nor is the book necessarily the latest word on the law. There is a saying among lawyers that "the law must be stable but it cannot stand still," and the law is moving especially fast in its applications to postsecondary education. Thus administrators and counsel will want to keep abreast of ongoing developments concerning the issues in this book. Various aids exist for this purpose. The selected annotated bibliographies in this book list various loose-leaf services and newsletters that report periodically on legal developments in particular areas. Footnotes to the text cite *American Law Reports* (A.L.R.) annotations—lawyers' research tools on particular subjects that are updated periodically with recent cases. In addition, the following resources will be useful.

For frequent information on a wide range of legal developments: (1) *School Law News,* biweekly news service of

Capitol Publications, Washington, D.C.; (2) *College Law Digest,* bimonthly report on cases filed or decided, recent periodical commentary, and other legal developments, published by the National Association of College and University Attorneys (NACUA), Washington, D.C.; and (3) *School Law Reporter,* bimonthly abstracts of recent cases published by the National Organization on Legal Problems of Education (NOLPE), Topeka, Kansas.

For extended analytical commentary: (1) *Journal of College and University Law,* published quarterly by NACUA and focusing exclusively on postsecondary education; and (2) *Journal of Law and Education,* covering elementary and secondary as well as postsecondary education and published quarterly by Jefferson Lawbook Company, Cincinnati, Ohio.

For information on federal legislative and administrative developments and related information: (1) *Business Officer,* a monthly magazine published by the National Association of College and University Business Officers (NACUBO) and available only to NACUBO members; (2) *Special Reports,* a newsletter especially for attorneys, published several times annually by NACUA and available only to NACUA members; (3) *Higher Education and National Affairs,* a newsletter published weekly by the American Council on Education (ACE), Washington, D.C.; and (4) *College and University Reports,* a loose-leaf service updated periodically and supplemented with weekly reports on current developments, published by Commerce Clearing House, Chicago, Illinois.

For general news reporting that includes substantial coverage of legal developments: (1) *The Chronicle of Higher Education,* published weekly by Editorial Projects for Education, Washington, D.C.; and (2) *Higher Education Daily,* published every weekday by Capitol Publications.

Institutions should give serious and continuing consideration to the ways they use legal counsel to deal with the law. There are several different organizational arrangements by which institutions can obtain legal counsel. State institutions are often served by the state attorney general's office. Working relationships may vary with the state and the campus. In general, administrators should seek to have services centralized in one or a small number of assistant attorney generals who devote all or the bulk of their time to the institution and become thoroughly familiar with its operations.

Many larger colleges and universities now employ their own in-house staff counsel. Such an arrangement has the advantage of providing daily coordinated services of resident counsel acclimated to the particular needs and problems of the institution. Though staff counsel can become specialists in postsecondary education law, they normally will not have the time or exposure to become expert in all the specialty areas (such as labor law, tax law, patent law, or litigation) with which institutions must deal. Thus these institutions may sometimes retain a private law firm for special problems.

Other institutions, large and small, may retain one or more private law firms to provide legal services. This arrangement has the advantage of increasing the number of attorneys with particular expertise available for the variety of problems that confront institutions. A potential disadvantage is that no one attorney will be conversant with the full range of the institution's needs and problems nor be on call daily for early participation in administrative decision making. Administrators of institutions depending on private firms may thus want to ensure that at least one lawyer is generally familiar with and involved in the institution's affairs and regularly available for consultation even on routine matters.

Regardless of the organizational arrangement chosen, administrators and counsel will have to face a number of questions in forging working relationships. Which institutional administrators will have direct access to counsel? To whom will counsel report? Will there be any particular procedure to follow in obtaining legal advice? Will counsel be expected to routinely review institutional policy statements, contracts, and major decisions? What kinds of correspondence or documents should be cleared by counsel before they are issued? Will counsel advise only administrators, or will he or she also be available to recognized faculty or student organizations or committees, or perhaps to other members of the university community on certain matters?

Besides these questions, there will be more subtle questions about counsel's role. Broadly stated, counsel's function is to identify, define, and provide options for resolving legal problems. But there are two basic ways to perform this function: through *preventive* law or through *treatment* law. Preventive law involves a continual setting of the legal parameters within which administrators should operate in order to avoid litigation or disputes with government agencies. Counsel identifies the legal consequences of proposed actions; pinpoints the range of alternatives for resolving problems and the legal risks of each alternative; sensitizes administrators to legal issues and the importance of recognizing them early; helps the institution devise its own internal grievance mechanisms for resolving legal disputes; does legal health "check-ups" by periodically reviewing institutional regulations, policies, forms, and practices; and determines the impact of new or proposed laws and regulations, and new court decisions, on institutional operations.

Treatment law focuses on actual challenges to institutional practices and on affirmative legal steps by the institution to protect its interests. When suit is filed against the institution, or litigation is threatened; when a government agency cites the institution for noncompliance with its regulations; when the institution needs formal permission of a government agency to undertake a proposed course of action; when the institution wishes to sue some other party—then treatment law operates. The goal is to resolve the specific legal problem at hand.

Treatment law today is indispensable to the functioning of a postsecondary institution, and virtually all institutions have such legal service. Preventive law is not so readily accepted, although it becomes increasingly valuable as the presence of the law on campus increases. Institutions using or considering the use of preventive law face some difficult questions. To what extent will administrators and counsel give priority to the practice of preventive law? What working arrangements will assure that administrators are alert to incipient legal problems and that counsel is involved in institutional decision making at an early stage? What degree of autonomy will counsel have to influence institutional decision making, and what authority will counsel have to halt legally unwise institutional action?

For discussion of such questions and of legal counsel's role, see J. R. Beale, "Delivery of Legal Services to Institutions of Higher Education," 2 *J. of College and University Law* 5 (1974); R. Bickel, "The Role of College or University Legal Counsel," 3 *J. of Law and Education* 73 (1974); J. Corbally, Jr., "University Counsel—Scope and Mission," 2 *J. of College and University Law* 1 (1974); N. Epstein, "The Use and Misuse of College and University Counsel," 45 *J. of Higher Education* 635 (1974); H. Orentlicher, "The Role of College or University Legal Counsel: An Added Dimension," 4 *J. of Law and Education* 511 (1974); and R. Sensenbrenner, "University Counselor: Lore, Logic and Logistics," 2 *J. of College and University Law* 13 (1974).

The hope of this book is to provide a base for the debate concerning law's role on campus; for improved understanding between law and academia; and for effective relationships between administrators and counsel. The challenge of our age is not to get the law off the campus; it is there to stay. The challenge is to make law more a beacon and less a fog. The challenge is for law and higher education to accommodate one another, preserving the best values of each for the mutual benefit of both. Just as academia benefits from the understanding and respect of the legal community, so law benefits from the understanding and respect of academia.

Washington, D.C.   WILLIAM A. KAPLIN
August 1978

Acknowledgments

Many, many people have helped in the preparation of *The Law of Higher Education*. Peter Wolff, executive director of the National Association of College and University Attorneys, was first. He encouraged the writing of this book, helped get the project started, and gave continuing moral support along the way.

Various sections of the book were reviewed by colleagues at the Columbus School of Law, Catholic University of America: Louis Barracato, Nancy Duff Campbell, Jane Dolkart, Roger Hartley (whose own recent book *Labor Relations Law in the Private Sector* gave him an excellent base for reviewing collective bargaining discussions), Michael O'Keefe, Ralph Rohner, William Taylor (director of the law school's Center for National Policy Review), and Harvey Zuckman (whose recent book *Mass Communications Law* gave him an excellent base for reviewing discussions of the student press).

Harold Jenkins and Steven Schatken of the U.S. Department

of Health, Education, and Welfare's Office of General Counsel reviewed sections of the book dealing with federal aid programs. Ronald Pugsley of USOE and C. William Tayler, a private practitioner in Washington, D.C., reviewed Chapter Eight. James Wilson, chief counsel for the University of Washington, reviewed a section of Chapter Three. Ira Lobel, labor relations specialist with the Federal Mediation and Conciliation Service, also reviewed a section of Chapter Three; and Michael Sorgen, counsel to the Oakland Unified School District, reviewed much of Chapter Four.

My law student research assistants during this period were invariably helpful: Joan DeLise (who served longest and set a high standard for others), James DeMarce, Nancy Finkbeiner, Lisa Newell, Anne Hermann, Michael Nugent, Russell Frank, and Janice D'Amato.

Joseph Coudon, assistant to the dean at the law school, consistently performed his magic in assuring that support services were available without hassle. Nancy Freil, faculty office manager, consistently made sure that typing and xeroxing were done on schedule, and did excellent work preparing much of the manuscript herself. Ava McClure also did a great deal of the typing, always promptly and accommodatingly. Mary Stock Kelly did efficient emergency typing during the biggest crunch period. John Valeri, Patrick Petit, and Craig Parker of the law library staff were always ready to help, on a moment's notice, with my library needs.

Finally, I save the greatest thanks for my parents, Joan and Al Kaplin, whose faith, encouragement, and love mark this book and my life.

The Author

⋈⋈⋈⋈⋈⋈⋈⋈⋈⋈⋈⋈

WILLIAM A. KAPLIN is a law professor at the Catholic University of America in Washington, D.C., and the editor of the *Journal of College and University Law*. A frequent consultant in the field of education law and policy, he was a visiting professor at Cornell University's School of Law (1975). In addition to writing numerous articles and reports in this field, Kaplin is a coauthor of *State, School, and Family: Cases and Materials on Law and Education* (with M. Sorgen, P. Duffy, and E. Margolin, 1973).

William Kaplin received his bachelor's degree in political science from the University of Rochester (1964) and the doctor of law degree with distinction from Cornell University (1967), where he was editor-in-chief of the *Cornell Law Review*. He then worked with a Washington, D.C., law firm, served as a law clerk at the U.S. Court of Appeals for the District of Columbia circuit, and was an attorney in the education division of the U.S. Department of Health, Education, and Welfare before joining the Catholic University law faculty.

Kaplin enjoys escaping from professional pursuits to be with his children, Colleen and Keith, and to strum his guitar, make soups and omelettes, and follow Atlantic Coast Conference basketball.

Contents

░░░░░░░░░░░░░░░░░░░░░░░░░░░░░░░░░

Chapter I

❦❦❦❦❦❦❦❦❦❦❦❦

Overview

of Postsecondary

Education Law

Sec. 1.1. How Far the Law Reaches and How Loud It Speaks:
Some Illustrative Cases

With increasing frequency, disputes that arise on campuses
across America end not on campus but in court. For example,
several years ago, when an instructor in childhood education at a
West Coast college began bringing her infant daughter to the
campus during working hours, the college's board of trustees
passed a resolution forbidding employees to bring children on
campus. The instructor was subsequently suspended for violating
the rule, even though students cared for her child whenever she was
engaged in teaching or counseling. She appealed her suspension

1

through the college's internal review processes, and she threatened to go to court if her appeal failed.

At about the same time, a journalism instructor at a New Jersey community college was dismissed from her position three days before she was to have received tenure. She had written an editorial for the campus newspaper critical of the college president and accusing the chairman of the board of trustees of a conflict of interest regarding the college's purchase of teaching equipment from a firm headed by his nephew. She sued the president and various trustees, arguing that her dismissal was in retaliation for her exercise of constitutionally protected rights of speech and press. The court agreed; it held her dismissal invalid under the First Amendment. Victory for this instructor was sweet: The trial court ordered that she be reinstated with full back pay and awarded her damages of $80 thousand. Of that amount, $70 thousand was in punitive damages to be paid not from the college's coffers but from the pockets of the president and six of the trustees. The appellate court affirmed the victory but took away some of the sweetness: It reduced the damage award to $5 thousand eliminating all punitive damages except for $25 hundred against the college president (*Endress* v. *Brookdale Community College,* 144 N.J. Super. 109, 364 A.2d 1080 (1976)).

Not only faculty members appear more often in court; students, too, make their way to court more frequently, such as those from a Connecticut college who wished to form a campus chapter of Students for a Democratic Society. They reached the U.S. Supreme Court in 1972 and successfully challenged the institution's denial of official recognition to their group. (See Section 4.8.1.) Even applicants for admission are becoming litigants, especially with the claim of reverse discrimination. In 1971 a rejected law school applicant sued officials of the University of Washington on such a claim in the *DeFunis* case, and before the university eventually prevailed, there was a state court trial, a lengthy state court appellate opinion issued in 1973, a U.S. Supreme Court decision in 1974, and a follow-up decision of the state supreme court in 1975. Later a rejected medical school applicant raised the same issues in the *Bakke* case, and, amidst extensive national publicity and debate, the U.S. Supreme Court again heard the argument. (See Section 4.2.5.)

Nor are students, faculty members, and their institutions the only litigants. The private accrediting associations that accredit postsecondary institutions and programs are being sued. In the most celebrated case, Marjorie Webster Junior College, a proprietary college, successfully challenged its exclusion from eligibility for accreditation by the Middle States Association of Colleges and Secondary Schools in a ten-week federal court trial in 1969, only to have the decision reversed on appeal a year later. (See Section 8.2.2.) Unions and professional associations representing faculty members or other university employees are also involved in litigation, and government agencies themselves are increasingly becoming parties to suits involving postsecondary education, both as plaintiffs seeking to enforce their laws in court and as defendants sued for enforcing their laws erroneously or refusing to enforce them at all.

As judicial business has thus expanded, so has the use of administrative agencies as alternative forums for airing legal disputes. Postsecondary institutions may now find themselves not only in court but also before the federal Equal Employment Opportunity Commission, the National Labor Relations Board, the administrative law judges of the U.S. Department of Health, Education, and Welfare (HEW), state licensing or approval boards, state public employment commissions and civil service commissions, state or local human relations commissions, local zoning boards, and other quasi-judicial bodies at all levels of government. Proceedings can be quite complex, and the legal sanctions which these agencies may invoke can be quite substantial.

Paralleling these developments has been an increase in the forums for dispute resolution created by private organizations and associations involved in postsecondary governance. Thus, besides appearing before courts and administrative agencies, postsecondary institutions may become involved in grievance procedures of faculty and staff unions, hearings of accrediting agencies on the accreditation status of institutional programs, probation hearings of athletic conferences, and censure proceedings of the American Association of University Professors. Similarly, postsecondary institutions are themselves creating new internal processes for resolving legal disputes (see Sections 3.5.3 and 4.13), such as faculty grievance committees, student judiciaries, procedures for challenging the content of education records (see Section 4.12.1), and grievance procedures for handling Title IX sex discrimination complaints (see Section 7.4.7).

In all, the number and kind of contacts between the law and postsecondary educational administration have grown remarkably in recent years. Law has become an indispensable consideration in the daily professional lives of postsecondary administrators at all levels. The trend continues.

Sec. 1.2. Evolution of the Law Relating to Postsecondary Education

Traditionally, the law's relationship to postsecondary (or higher) education was much different from what it is now. There were few legal requirements relating to the educational administrator's functions, and they were not a major factor in most administrative decisions. The higher education world, moreover, tended to think of itself as removed from and perhaps above the world of law and lawyers. The roots of this traditional separation between academia and law are several.

Higher education was often viewed as a unique enterprise which could regulate itself through reliance on tradition and consensual agreement. It operated best by operating autonomously, and it thrived on the privacy which autonomy afforded. Academia, in short, was like a Victorian gentlemen's club whose sacred precincts were not to be profaned by the involvement of outside agents in its internal governance.

Not only was the academic environment perceived as private; it was also thought to be delicate and complex. An outsider would, almost by definition, be ignorant of the special arrangements and sensitivities underpinning this environment. And lawyers and judges as a group, at least in the early days, were clearly outsiders. Law schools did not become an established part of American higher education until the early twentieth century, and the older tradition of "reading law" (studying and working in a practitioner's office) persisted for many years afterward. Lawyers, moreover, were often perceived as representatives of the crass world of business and industry, or as representatives of the political world, or as mere pettifoggers scratching for a fee. Interference by such outsiders was considered by academia to be destructive of the understandings and mutual trust which must prevail in its world.

The special higher education environment was also thought to support a special virtue and ability in its personnel. The faculties and administrators (often themselves respected scholars) had knowledge and training far beyond that of the general populace, and they were charged with the guardianship of knowledge for future generations. Theirs was a special mission pursued with special expertise—and often at a considerable financial sacrifice. The combination spawned the perception that ill-will and personal bias were strangers to academia and that outside monitoring of its affairs was therefore largely unnecessary.

The law to a remarkable extent reflected and reinforced such attitudes. Federal and state governments generally avoided exten-sive regulation of higher education. Legislatures and administra-tive agencies imposed few legal obligations on institutions and provided few official channels through which their activities could be legally challenged. What legal oversight existed was generally centered in the courts.

And the judiciary was also deferential to higher education. In matters concerning students, courts found refuge in the in loco parentis doctrine borrowed from early English common law. In placing the educational institution in the parents' shoes, the doctrine permitted the institution to exert almost untrammeled authority over students' lives:

> College authorities stand in loco parentis concern-ing the physical and moral welfare and mental training of the pupils, and we are unable to see why, to that end, they may not make any rule or regulation for the government or betterment of their pupils that a parent could for the same purpose. Whether the rules or regulations are wise or their aims worthy is a matter left solely to the discretion of the authorities or parents, as the case may be, and, in the exercise of that discretion, the courts are not disposed to interfere, unless the rules and aims are unlawful or against public policy [*Gott* v. *Beria College*, 156 Ky. 376, 161 S.W. 204, 206 (1913)].

Nor could students lay claim to constitutional rights in the higher education environment. In private education the U.S. Constitution had no application (see Section 1.4.2); and in the public realm, in cases such as *Hamilton* v. *Regents of the University of California,* 293 U.S. 245 (1934), which upheld an order that student conscientious objectors must take military training as a condition of attending the institution, courts accepted the proposition that attendance at a public postsecondary institution was a privilege and not a right. Being a "privilege," attendance could constitutionally be extended and was subject to termination on whatever conditions the institution determined were in its and the students' best interests. Occasionally courts did consider students to have some contract rights under an express or implied contractual relation with the institution. But as in *Anthony* v. *Syracuse University,* 224 App. Div. 487, 231 N.Y.S. 435 (1928), where the institution was upheld in dismissing a student without assigning a reason but apparently because she was not "a typical Syracuse girl," contract law provided little meaningful recourse for students. The institution was given virtually unlimited power to dictate the contract terms, and the contract, once made, was construed heavily in the institution's favor.

Similar judicial deference prevailed in the institution's relationship with faculty members. While an employment relationship substituted here for in loco parentis, it focused far more on judgments of senior faculty members and experienced administrators than on the formalities of written employment contracts. Courts considered academic judgments regarding appointment, promotion, and tenure to be expert judgments suitably governed by the complex traditions of the academic world. Judges did not possess the special skill needed to review such judgments, nor, without glaring evidence to the contrary, could they presume that nonacademic considerations might play a part in such processes. Furthermore, in private institutions, faculty members, like students, could assert no constitutional rights against the institution, since the Constitution had no application to private activity. And in public institutions, the judicial view was that employment, somewhat like student attendance, was a privilege and not a right. Thus as far as the Constitution was concerned, employment could also be extended or terminated on whatever grounds the institution considered appropriate.

As further support for these judicial hands-off attitudes, higher education institutions also enjoyed immunity from a broad range of lawsuits alleging negligence or other torts. For public institutions this protection arose from the governmental immunity doctrine, which shielded state and local governments and their instrumentalities from legal liability for their sovereign acts. For private institutions a comparable result was reached under the charitable immunity doctrine, which shielded charitable organizations from legal liability that would divert their funds from the purposes for which they were intended. (See Sections 2.3.1 and 2.3.2.)

Traditionally, then, the immunity doctrines substantially limited the range of suits maintainable against higher educational institutions. And because of the judicial attitudes discussed above, the chances of victory in suits against either the institution or its officers and employees were slim. Reinforcing these legal limitations was a practical limitation on litigation: Before free legal services were available, few of the likely plaintiffs—faculty members, administrators, and students—had enough money to sue.

In the past generation, however, events and changing circumstances have worked a revolution in the relationship between academia and the law. The federal government and state governments have become heavily involved in postsecondary education, creating many new legal requirements and new forums for raising legal challenges. Students, teachers, other employees, and outsiders have become more willing and more able to sue postsecondary institutions and their officials. Courts have become more willing to entertain such suits on their merits and to offer relief from certain institutional actions.

The most obvious and perhaps most significant change to occur since World War II has been the dramatic increase in the number, size, and diversity of postsecondary institutions. But beyond the obvious point that more people and institutions produce more litigation is the crucial fact of the changed character of the academic population itself. (See, for example, K. P. Cross,

Beyond the Open Door: New Students to Higher Education
(Jossey-Bass, 1971).) The G.I. Bill expansions of the late forties and
early fifties, and the "baby boom" expansion of the sixties, brought
large numbers of new students, faculty members, and administrative personnel into the educational process. In 1940 there were
approximately one and a half million degree students enrolled in
institutions of higher education; by 1955 the figure had grown to
more than two and a half million and by 1965 to more than five
and a half million. The expanding pool of persons seeking
postsecondary education prompted the growth of new educational
institutions and programs, as well as new methods for delivering
educational services. Great increases in federal aid for both students
and institutions further stimulated these developments.

As new social, economic, and ethnic groups entered this
broadened world of postsecondary education, the traditional
processes of selection, admission, and academic acculturation
began to break down. Because of the changed job opportunities
and rapid promotion processes occasioned by rapid growth, many
of the new academics did not have sufficient time to learn the old
rules. Others were hostile to traditional attitudes and values
because they perceived them as part of a process which had
excluded their group or race or sex from access to academic success
in earlier days. For others in new settings such as junior and
community colleges, technical institutes, and work experience
programs, the traditional trappings of academia simply did not fit.

For many of the new students as well, older patterns of
deference to tradition and authority became a thing of the past—
perhaps an irrelevant or even consciously repudiated past. The
emergence of the student-veteran, the loosening of the "lock-step"
pattern of educational preparation which led students directly from
high school to college to graduate work, and finally the lowered
age of majority combined to make the in loco parentis relationship
between institution and student less and less tenable. The notion
that attendance was a privilege seemed an irrelevant nicety in an
increasingly credentialized society. To many students higher
education became an economic or professional necessity, and some,
such as the G.I. Bill veterans, had cause to view it as an earned
right.

As a broader and larger cross-section of the world passed through postsecondary education's gates, institutions became more tied to the outside world. Governmental allocations and foundation support covered a larger share of institutional budgets, making it more difficult to maintain the autonomy and self-sufficiency afforded by large endowments. Competition for money, students, and outstanding faculty members focused institutional attentions outward. As institutions engaged increasingly in government research projects, as large state universities grew and became more dependent on annual state legislative appropriations, and as federal and state governments increasingly paid tuition bills through scholarship and loan programs, postsecondary education lost much of its isolation from the political process. Social and political movements became a more integral part of campus life, not the least of which was the civil rights movement. And with the civil rights movement, as well as with most other outside influences that converged on postsecondary institutions, the law came also.

Sec. 1.3. Sources of Postsecondary Education Law

The modern law of postsecondary education is no longer simply a product of what the courts say, or refuse to say, about education problems. The modern law comes from a variety of sources, as set out in this section.

1.3.1. Federal and state constitutions. Constitutions are the fundamental source for determining the nature and extent of governmental powers. Constitutions are also the fundamental source of the individual rights guarantees which limit the powers of governments and protect citizens generally, including members of the academic community. The federal Constitution, set forth in abridged form in the Appendix, is by far the most prominent and important source of individual liberties. The First Amendment protections for speech, press, and religion are often litigated in major court cases involving postsecondary institutions, as are the Fourth Amendment protection against unreasonable searches and seizures and the Fourteenth Amendment guarantees of due process and equal protection. As explained in Section 1.4, these federal constitutional provisions apply differently to public and private institutions.

The federal Constitution has no provision which specifically refers to education. State constitutions, however, often have specific provisions establishing state colleges and universities or state college and university systems, and occasionally community college systems. State constitutions may also have provisions establishing a state department of education or other governing authority with some responsibility for postsecondary education. (See Section 6.2.)

The federal Constitution is the highest legal authority that exists. No other law, either state or federal, may conflict with its provisions. Thus, although a state constitution is the highest state law authority, and all state statutes and other state laws must be consistent with it, any of its provisions which conflict with the federal Constitution will be subject to invalidation by the courts.

1.3.2. Statutes. Statutes are enacted both by states and by the federal government. Ordinances, which are in effect local statutes, are enacted by local legislative bodies such as county and city councils. While laws at all three levels may refer specifically to postsecondary education or postsecondary institutions, the greatest amount of such specific legislation is written by the states. Examples include laws establishing and regulating state postsecondary institutions or systems, laws creating statewide coordinating councils for postsecondary education, and laws providing for the licensure of postsecondary institutions. (See Sections 6.2 and 6.3.) At the federal level, the major examples of such specific legislation are the federal grant-in-aid statutes, such as the Higher Education Act of 1965 (see Section 7.3). At all three levels, there is also a considerable amount of legislation which applies to postsecondary institutions in common with other entities within the jurisdiction —for example, the federal tax laws and civil rights laws (see Sections 7.2.8 and 7.4), state human rights laws and corporation laws (see Section 6.5), and local zoning laws and property tax laws (see Sections 5.2 and 5.3). All these state and federal statutes and local ordinances, as stated earlier, are subject to the higher constitutional authorities.

Federal statutes, for the most part, are collected and codified in the *United States Code* (U.S.C.) or *United States Code Annotated* (U.S.C.A.). State statutes are similarly gathered in a state codification that will be available in many law libraries. Local ordinances are usually collected in local ordinance books, but those may be difficult to locate and may not be organized as systematically as state and federal codifications. Local ordinance books may also be considerably out of date, and state codes sometimes have that problem as well. In order to be sure that the statutory law on a particular point is up to date, one must check what are called the session or slip laws of the jurisdiction for the current year or sometimes the preceding year.

1.3.3. Administrative rules and regulations. The most rapidly expanding source of postsecondary education law is the directives of state and federal administrative agencies. The number and size of these bodies are increasing, and the number and complexity of their regulations are easily keeping pace. In recent years the rules applicable to postsecondary institutions, especially those issued at the federal level, have often generated controversy in the education world, which must negotiate a substantial regulatory maze in order to be eligible for federal grant programs or to receive federal contracts.

Although such regulations often have the status of law and are therefore as binding as a statute would be, they do not always have such status. Thus it is important that administrators check with legal counsel when problems arise in order to determine the exact status. Every rule or regulation issued by an administrative agency, whether state or federal, must be within the scope of the authority delegated to that agency by its enabling statutes. Any rule or regulation which is not authorized by the relevant statutes is subject to invalidation by a court. And, like the statutes and ordinances referred to earlier, administrative rules and regulations must also comply with and be consistent with applicable state and federal constitutional provisions.

The regulations and rules of federal administrative agencies are published upon enactment in the *Federal Register* (Fed. Reg.), and regulations from the *Federal Register* are eventually codified in the *Code of Federal Regulations* (C.F.R.). Those that are not published in the *Federal Register* usually do not have the status of law. State administrative agencies have various ways of publicizing their rules and regulations, sometimes in government publications comparable to the *Federal Register* or the *Code of Federal Regulations.* Generally speaking, however, administrative rules and regulations are harder to find and less likely to be codified at the state level than at the federal level.

1.3.4. Administrative adjudications. Besides promulgating rules and regulations (called rulemaking), administrative agencies often also have the authority to consider and make decisions in particular disputes involving particular parties (called adjudication). The extent of an administrative agency's adjudicatory authority, as well as its rulemaking powers, depends on the relevant statutes which establish and empower the agency. An agency's adjudicatory decisions must be consistent with its own rules and regulations and with any applicable statutory or constitutional provision. Legal questions concerning the validity of an adjudicatory decision are usually reviewable in the courts. Examples of such decisions at the federal level would include a National Labor Relations Board decision on an unfair labor practice charge or, in another area, an HEW decision on whether to terminate funds to a federal grantee for noncompliance with statutory or regulatory requirements. Examples at the state level would include the determination of a state human relations commission on a complaint charging violation of individual rights, or the decision of a state workers' compensation board in a workers' compensation benefit case. Administrative agencies may or may not officially publish compilations of their adjudicatory decisions. Agencies without official compilations may informally compile and issue their opinions; other agencies may simply file opinions in their internal files or distribute them in a limited way. It can often be a difficult problem for counsel to determine what all the relevant adjudicatory precedents are within an agency.

1.3.5. Case law. Every year the state and federal courts reach decisions in hundreds of cases involving postsecondary education. Opinions are issued and published for many of these decisions. Many more decisions are reached and opinions rendered each year in cases which do not involve postsecondary education but do elucidate important established legal principles with potential application to postsecondary education. In this latter group is a

large body of elementary and secondary education cases. (See, for
example, the *Wood* v. *Strickland* case in Section 2.4.3 and the *Goss*
v. *Lopez* case in Section 4.6.) But it is a mistake to uncritically
apply elementary/secondary precedents to postsecondary education. Differences in the structures, missions, and clienteles of these
levels of education may make precedents from one level inapplicable to the other or may require that the precedent's application be
modified to account for the differences. In *Lansdale* v. *Tyler Junior
College*, 470 F.2d 659 (5th Cir. 1972), for instance, the court
considered the applicability to postsecondary education of a prior
precedent permitting high schools to regulate the length of
students' hair. The court refused to extend the precedent. As one
judge explained:

> [T]he college campus marks the appropriate bound-
> ary where the public institution can no longer assert that
> the regulation of . . . [hair length] is reasonably related to
> the fostering or encouraging of education. . . .
> There are a number of factors which support the
> proposition that the point between high school and college
> is the place where the line should be drawn. . . . That place
> is the point in the student's process of maturity where he
> usually comes within the ambit of the Twenty-Sixth
> Amendment and the Selective Service Act, where he often
> leaves home for dormitory life, and where the educational
> institution ceases to deal with him through parents and
> guardians . . . .
> [T]he majority holds today that as a matter of law
> the college campus is the line of demarcation where the
> weight of the student's maturity, as compared with the
> institution's modified role in his education, tips the scales
> in favor of the individual and marks the boundary of the
> area within which a student's hirsute adornment becomes
> constitutionally irrelevant to the pursuit of educational
> activities [470 F.2d at 662–64].

Conversely, in *Cary* v. *Adams-Arapahoe School Board*, 427 F.
Supp. 945 (D. Colo., 1977), the court considered whether academic
freedom precedents from postsecondary education were applicable
to high school education. After exploring "the role of elementary
and secondary public education in the United States" and finding
parallels between the missions of high school and postsecondary
education, the court decided "[i]t would be inappropriate to

conclude that academic freedom is required only in the colleges and universities."

A court's decision has the effect of binding precedent only within its own jurisdiction. Thus, at the state level, a particular decision may be binding either on the entire state or only on some subdivision of the state, depending on the court's jurisdiction. At the federal level, the decision may be binding within a particular district or region of the country, in the case of the United States District Court and United States Courts of Appeals, while decisions of the United States Supreme Court are binding precedent throughout the country. Since the Supreme Court's decisions are the supreme law of the land, they bind all lower federal courts as well as all state courts, even the highest court of the state.

Court decisions may interpret state or federal statutes or the rules or regulations of state or federal administrative agencies. In order to understand the meaning of such statutes, rules, and regulations, it is important to understand the case law which has construed them. Court decisions may also construe the meaning of federal or state constitutional provisions, and sometimes determine the constitutionality of particular statutes or rules and regulations under particular provisions of state or federal constitutions. A statute or rule or regulation that is found to be unconstitutional because it conflicts with a constitutional provision is void and no longer enforceable by the courts. Sometimes courts issue opinions that interpret neither a statute, nor an administrative rule or regulation, nor a constitutional provision. In breach of contract disputes or tort litigation, for instance, the only precedents the court utilizes are those the courts have created themselves. These decisions create what is commonly called American "common law." Common law, in short, is judge-made law rather than law which originates from constitutions or from legislatures or administrative agencies.

The important opinions of state and federal courts are published periodically and collected in bound volumes available in most law libraries. For state court decisions, besides each state's official reports, there is the National Reporter System, a series of regional case reports comprising the (1) *Atlantic Reporter* (cited "A." or "A.2d"), (2) *Northeastern Reporter* (cited "N.E." or

"N.E.2d"), (3) *Northwestern Reporter* (cited "N.W." or "N.W.2d"), (4) *Pacific Reporter* (cited "P." or "P.2d"), (5) *Southeastern Reporter* (cited "S.E." or "S.E.2d"), and (6) *Southern Reporter* (cited "So." or "So.2d"). Each regional reporter publishes opinions of the courts within that particular region. There are also special reporters in the National Reporter System for the states of New York (the *New York Supplement,* cited "N.Y. Supp." or "N.Y.S.2d") and California (the *California Reporter,* cited "Cal. Rptr."). In the federal system, United States Supreme Court opinions are published in the *United States Reports* (cited "U.S."), the official reporter, as well as in two unofficial reporters, the *Supreme Court Reporter* (cited "S. Ct.") and the *United States Supreme Courts Reports—Lawyer's Edition* (cited "L. Ed." or "L.Ed.2d"). Opinions of the United States Courts of Appeals are published in the *Federal Reporter* (cited "Fed." or "F.2d"), and United States District Court opinions are published in the *Federal Supplement* (cited "F. Supp.").

1.3.6. Institutional rules and regulations. The rules and regulations promulgated by individual institutions are also a source of postsecondary education law. These rules and regulations are subject to all the other sources of law listed above and must be consistent with all the legal requirements of those other sources that apply to the particular institution and to the subject matter of the rule or regulation. Courts may consider some institutional rules and regulations to be part of the faculty-institution contract or the student-institution contract (see Section 1.3.7), in which case these rules and regulations are enforceable by contract actions in the courts. Some rules and regulations of public institutions may also be legally enforceable as administrative regulations (see Section 1.3.3) of a government agency. Even where such rules are not legally enforceable by courts or outside agencies, a postsecondary institution will likely want to follow and enforce them internally to achieve fairness and consistency in its dealings with the campus community.

Institutional rules and regulations may establish certain adjudicatory bodies within the institution which have the authority to resolve particular disputes. When such decision-making bodies operate within the scope of their authority under institutional rules and regulations, their decisions also become part of the governing law within the institution. Insofar as courts are concerned, these decisions may also compose part of the faculty-institution or student-institution contract, at least in the sense that they become part of the applicable custom and usage (see Section 1.3.8) within the institution.

 1.3.7. Institutional contracts. Postsecondary institutions have contractual relationships of various kinds with faculties (see Sections 3.1 and 3.2); staffs; students (Section 4.1); and outside parties such as government agencies, construction firms, or other institutions. These contracts create binding legal arrangements between the contracting parties, enforceable by either party in case of the other's breach. In this sense a contract is a source of law governing a particular subject matter and relationship. When a question arises concerning a subject matter or relationship covered by a contract, the first legal source to consult is usually the contract terms.

 Contracts, especially with faculty members and students, may incorporate some institutional rules and regulations (see Section 1.3.6), so that they become part of the contract terms. Contracts are interpreted and enforced according to the common law of contracts (Section 1.3.5) and any applicable statute or administrative rule or regulation (Sections 1.3.2 and 1.3.3). They may also be interpreted with reference to academic custom and usage (Section 1.3.8).

 1.3.8. Academic custom and usage. This category, by far the most amorphous source of postsecondary education law, comprises the particular established practices and understandings within particular institutions. It differs from institutional rules and regulations (see Section 1.3.6) in that it is not necessarily a written source of law and, even if written, is far more informal; custom and usage may be found, for instance, in policy statements from speeches, internal memoranda, and other such documentation within the institution.

 This source of postsecondary education law, sometimes called "campus common law," is important within particular institutions because it helps define what the various members of the academic community expect of each other as well as of the institution itself. Whenever the institution has internal decision-making processes such as a faculty grievance process or a student disciplinary procedure, campus common law can be an important guide for decision making. In this sense campus common law does not displace formal institutional rules and regulations but supplements them, helping the decision maker and the parties in situations where rules and regulations are ambiguous or do not exist for the particular point at issue. Academic custom and usage is also important in another, and broader, sense: It can supplement contractual understandings between the institution and its faculty and between the institution and its students. Whenever the terms of such contractual relationship are unclear, courts may look to academic custom and usage in order to interpret the terms of the contract. The U.S. Supreme Court recently put its imprimatur on this role of academic custom and usage in *Perry* v. *Sindermann*, 408 U.S. 593 (1972). In analyzing a professor's claim that he was entitled to continued employment at the institution, the Court explained:

> [T]he law of contracts in most, if not all, jurisdictions long has employed a process by which agreements, though not formalized in writing, may be "implied." 3 Corbin on Contracts, secs. 561–672A. Explicit contractual provisions may be supplemented by other agreements implied from "the promisor's words and conduct in the light of the surrounding circumstances." *Id.*, at sec. 562. And, "[t]he meaning of [the promisor's] words and acts is found by relating them to the usage of the past." *Ibid.*
>
> A teacher, like the respondent, who has held his position for a number of years, might be able to show from the circumstances of this service—and from other relevant facts—that he has a legitimate claim of entitlement to job tenure. Just as this Court has found there to be a "common law of a particular industry or of a particular plant" that may supplement a collective-bargaining agreement, *United Steelworks* v. *Warrior & Gulf Nav. Co.*, 363 U.S. 574, 579, 80 S. Ct. 1347, 1351, 4 L.Ed.2d 1409 (1960), so there may be an unwritten "common law" in a particular university that certain employees shall have the equivalent of tenure [408 U.S. at 602].

Sindermann was a constitutional due process case, and

academic custom and usage was relevant to determining whether
the professor had a "property interest" in continued employment
which would entitle him to a hearing prior to nonrenewal. (See
Section 3.5.2.) Academic custom and usage is also important in
contract cases where courts, arbitrators, or grievance committees
must interpret provisions of the faculty-institution contract (see
Sections 3.1 and 3.2) or student-institution contract (see Section
4.1). In *Strank* v. *Mercy Hospital of Johnstown*, 383 Pa. 54, 117
A.2d 697 (1955), a student nurse who had been dismissed from
nursing school sought to require the school to award her transfer
credits for the two years' work she had successfully completed. The
student alleged that she had "oral arrangements with the school at
the time she entered, later confirmed in part by writing and carried
out by both parties for a period of two years, . . . [and] that these
arrangements and understandings imposed upon defendant the
legal duty to give her proper credits for work completed." When
the school argued that the court had no jurisdiction over such a
claim, the court responded: "[Courts] have jurisdiction . . . for the
enforcement of obligations whether arising under express contracts, written or oral, or implied contracts, including those in
which a duty may have resulted from long recognized and
established customs and usages, as in this case, perhaps, between
an educational institution and its students" (117 A.2d at 698).
Faculty members may make similar contract claims relying on
academic custom and usage, as, for example, in *Lewis* v. *Salem
Academy and College*, 23 N.Car. App. 122, 208 S.E.2d 404 (1974),
where the court considered but rejected the plaintiff's claim that
under campus custom and usage he was entitled to teach to age
seventy. Custom and usage is also relevant in implementing faculty
collective bargaining agreements (see the *Sindermann* quotation
above in this subsection), and such agreements may explicitly
provide that they are not intended to override "past practices" of
the institution.

Sec. 1.4. The Public-Private Dichotomy

1.4.1. Background. Historically, higher education has roots
in both the public and private sectors, although the strength of
each one's influence has varied over time. Sometimes following and

sometimes leading this historical development, the law has tended to support and reflect the fundamental dichotomy between public and private education.

A forerunner of the present university was the Christian seminary. Yale was an early example. Dartmouth began as a school to teach Christianity to the Indians. Similar schools sprang up throughout the colonies. Though often established through private charitable trusts, they were also chartered by the colony, received some financial support from the colony, and were subject to its regulation. Thus colonial colleges were often a mixture of public and private activity. The nineteenth century witnessed a gradual decline in governmental involvement with sectarian schools. As states began to establish their own institutions, the public-private dichotomy emerged. (See D. Tewksbury, *The Founding of American Colleges and Universities Before the Civil War* (Anchor Books, 1965).) In recent years this dichotomy has again been fading as state and federal governments provide increasingly larger amounts of financial support to private institutions, many of which are now secular. In 1973, for instance, approximately 14 percent of the income of public higher education came from the federal government, while the corresponding figure for private higher education was 18.3 percent (J. Greene (ed.), *Standard Education Almanac* 1973/74, Table 24 (Marquis, 1973)).

Despite the fact that attending private institutions has always been more expensive than going to public institutions, private higher education has been a vital and influential force in American intellectual history. The private school can cater to special interests that a public one often cannot serve because of legal or political constraints. Private education thus draws strength from "the very possibility of doing something different than government can do, of creating an institution free to make choices government cannot—even seemingly arbitrary ones—without having to provide a justification that will be examined in a court of law" (H. Friendly, *The Dartmouth College Case and the Public-Private Penumbra* 30 (Humanities Research Center, University of Texas, 1969)).

Though modern-day private institutions are not always free from examination "in a court of law," the law often does treat public and private institutions differently. These differences will

20

underlie much of the discussion in this book. They are critically important in assessing the law's impact on the roles of particular institutions and the duties of their administrators.

In theory, the law protects private institutions to some extent from state control of their operations, whereas public institutions are usually subject to the plenary authority of the government which creates them. Government can alter, enlarge, or completely abolish its public institutions, but since the famous *Dartmouth College* case, 17 U.S. 518 (1819), private schools have been spared any governmental encroachment that impairs their own charters of incorporation. In that case, the U.S. Supreme Court turned back New Hampshire's attempt to assume control of Dartmouth by finding such action to violate the Constitution's contract clause. (But see *Berea College* v. *Kentucky*, 211 U.S. 45 (1908).) Subsequently in three other landmarks, *Meyer* v. *Nebraska*, 262 U.S. 390 (1923), *Pierce* v. *Society of Sisters*, 268 U.S. 510 (1925), and *Farrington* v. *Tokushige*, 273 U.S. 284 (1927), the Supreme Court used the due process clause to strike down unreasonable governmental interference with teaching and learning in private schools.

In practice, however, government does retain substantial authority to regulate private education. But whether for legal, political, or policy reasons, state governments usually regulate private institutions less than they regulate public institutions. The federal government, on the other hand, has tended to apply its regulations comparably to both public and private institutions or, bowing to considerations of federalism, has regulated private institutions while leaving public institutions to the states.

In addition to these differences in regulatory patterns, the law makes a second and more pervasive distinction between public and private institutions: Public institutions and their officers are fully subject to the constraints of the federal Constitution, whereas private institutions and their officers are not. Because the Constitution was designed to limit only the exercise of government power, it does not prohibit private individuals or corporations from impinging on such freedoms as free speech, equal protection, and due process. Thus, *insofar as the federal Constitution is concerned,* a private university can engage in private acts of discrimination, prohibit student protests, or expel a student without affording the procedural safeguards that a public university is constitutionally required to provide.

Indeed, this distinction can be crucial even within a single university. In *Powe* v. *Miles*, 407 F.2d 73 (2d Cir. 1968), seven Alfred University students had been suspended for engaging in protest activities which disrupted an ROTC ceremony. Four of the students attended Alfred's Liberal Arts College, while the remaining three were students at the Ceramics College. The state of New York had contracted with Alfred to establish the Ceramics College, and a New York statute specifically stated that the disciplinary acts of the university were the acts of the state with respect to Ceramics students. The court found that the dean's action suspending the Ceramics students was "state action" but the suspension of the Liberal Arts students was not. Thus, the court ruled that the dean was required to afford the Ceramics students due process but was not required to follow any constitutional dictates in suspending the Liberal Arts students, even though both groups of students had engaged in the same course of conduct.

1.4.2. The state action doctrine. As *Powe* makes clear, before a court will apply constitutional guarantees of individual rights to a postsecondary institution, it must first determine that the institution's action is "state (governmental) action." Although this determination is essentially a matter of distinguishing public from private institutions, or the public part of an institution from the private part, these distinctions do not necessarily depend on traditional notions of public or private. Because of varying patterns of governmental assistance and involvement, a continuum exists ranging from the obvious public school (such as the tax-supported state university) to the obvious private school (such as the religious seminary). The large gray area between these extremes provides a continuing source of debate about how far the government must be involved before a "private" institution may be considered "public" under the Constitution.

Though government funding is often a central consideration, much more than money is involved in a state action determination. Courts and commentators have dissected the state action concept in many different ways, but at heart essentially three approaches have emerged for attributing state action to an ostensibly private entity. When the private entity either (a) acts as an agent of government in performing a particular task government has delegated to it (the delegated power theory), or (b) performs a function which is generally considered to be the responsibility of government (the public function theory), or (c) obtains substantial resources, prestige, or encouragement from its contacts with government (the government contacts theory), its actions may be considered state action subject to constitutional constraints.

The first theory, delegated power, was relied on in the *Powe* v. *Miles* case (discussed above), where the court found that New York State had delegated authority to Alfred to operate a state ceramics school at the university. This same court also considered the delegated power theory in *Wahba* v. *New York University*, 492 F.2d 96 (2d Cir. 1974), in which a research professor had been fired from a governmentally funded research project. But here the court refused to find that the firing was state action because the government did not exercise any managerial control over the project. This focus on state involvement *in addition to funding* has assumed increasing importance in state action law. In *Greenya* v. *George Washington University*, 512 F.2d 556 (D.C. Cir. 1975), for instance, the university had a contract with the Navy to provide instruction at the U.S. Naval School of Hospital Administration. When the university fired a teacher assigned to teach in this program, he argued state action on the basis that he had been teaching government employees at government facilities—essentially a delegated power theory. But the court rejected the argument on grounds similar to those in *Wahba:*

> [Plaintiff] was always under the supervision and control of university officials, and . . . he maintained no contractual relations with the Navy. Nothing in the record indicates that the Navy had any right to say who would be hired to teach the English course. Neither does the record indicate that the Navy had anything whatsoever to do with the failure to renew appellant's contract. Appellant was merely the employee of an independent contractor who was

providing educational services to the Navy [512 F.2d at 561–62].

The second, public function, theory has generally not been a basis for finding state action in education cases. Though the issue has often been raised, courts have recognized that education has substantial roots in the private sector and cannot be considered a solely public function. In the *Greenya* case above, for instance, the court simply remarked: "[W]e have considered whether higher education constitutes 'state action' because it is a 'public function' as that term has been developed . . . and have concluded that it is not. . . . [E]ducation . . . has never been a state monopoly in the United States."

It is the third theory, the government contacts theory, which has had the greatest workout in postsecondary education cases. Although this theory is closely related to the delegated power theory, it focuses on less formal and particularized relationships between government and private entities. As the U.S. Supreme Court noted in the landmark *Burton* v. *Wilmington Parking Authority* case, 365 U.S. 715, 722 (1961), "Only by sifting facts and weighing circumstances can the nonobvious involvement of the State in private conduct be attributed its true significance." The search is not for state involvement with the private institution generally but involvement in the particular activity which gives rise to the law suit.[1]

The *Greenya* case above also illustrates the government contacts theory. In challenging his termination by the university, the plaintiff sought to base state action not only on the government's contract with the university (see above) but also on

---

[1]The U.S. Supreme Court appears to have nailed this point down in *Jackson* v. *Metropolitan Edison Co.*, 419 U.S. 345 (1974), where it rejected the petitioner's state action argument because "there was no . . . [state] imprimatur placed on the practice of . . . [the private entity] about which petitioner complains," and the state "has not put its own weight on the side of the . . . practice by ordering it." *Id.* at 357. Such a showing of state involvement in the precise activity challenged may not be required, however, in race discrimination cases; see *Norwood* v. *Harrison*, 413 U.S. 455 (1973), and the cases discussed later in this section. See also note 2.

the government's general support for the university. The court quickly affirmed that neither the grant of a corporate charter nor the grant of tax-exempt status is sufficient to constitute state action. It then reached the same conclusion regarding federal funding of certain university programs and capital expenditures. Government funding, in the court's view, would not amount to state action unless and until the conditions placed on such funding "become so all pervasive that the government has become, in effect, a joint venturer in the recipient's enterprise."[2]

In *Rackin* v. *University of Pennsylvania*, 386 F. Supp. 992 (E.D. Pa. 1974), on the other hand, the court did find state action using the government contacts theory. The case was brought by a female English professor who claimed she was denied tenure and the opportunity to teach in her specialty solely on the basis of sex. In determining that "the Commonwealth has so far insinuated itself into a position of interdependence with the University that it must be recognized as a joint participant in the challenged activity," the court relied on many factors:

> Each participant enjoys the mutual benefits derived from their relationship. The Commonwealth, by aiding the University, has enabled the residents of Pennsylvania to continue to take advantage of the multitude of opportunities available from a major university. Commonwealth funds, on the other hand, in the form of less expensive and rent-free educational facilities for the University's primary learning centers, annual appropriations, tax exemptions, scholarships, and research projects are filtered throughout the entire University to all facets of the educational process. If the source were to run dry, the University's operations and status would suffer irreparably to the point where it could no longer compete as an educational institution of

[2]*Greenya* at 561. The "joint venturer" concept comes from the *Burton* case, cited above, where the Court concluded that "the State has so far insinuated itself into a position of interdependence with . . . [defendant] that it must be recognized as a joint participant in the challenged activity." 365 U.S. at 725. See also *Moose Lodge* v. *Irvis*, 407 U.S. 163, at 176–77 (1972). When the state is so substantially involved in the whole of the private entity's activities as to be considered a joint venturer, courts will normally not require proof that it was involved in the particular activity challenged in the lawsuit. Compare note 1 earlier.

national prominence. The Commonwealth, in effect, maintains a stranglehold on the University and therefore potentially has significant input into University policies.

The University has not remained impervious to this reality as evidenced by its varying admission standards for Pennsylvania residents in the Schools of Dental Medicine, Veterinary Medicine, Medicine; acceptance of Senatorial Scholarships; and reducing tuition for Pennsylvania residents. . . . [W]e doubt that the University would ever make major policy decisions without looking over its shoulder to gauge the attitude of its omnipresent informal partner [386 F. Supp. at 1004–05].

While *Rackin* was never appealed and its result would likely be questioned by some other courts adopting more restrictive views of state action, the case does demonstrate, as well as any that has been decided, the complex interplay of factors that may become involved in a state action determination.

There is another major complexity important to state action law under each of the three theories: Courts appear more likely to find state action in race discrimination cases than in any other kind of case. In both the *Wahba* and *Greenya* cases above, the courts specifically noted as part of their reasoning processes that race discrimination was not involved. In *Williams* v. *Howard University*, 528 F.2d 658 (D.C. Cir. 1976), where the plaintiff alleged both race discrimination and procedural due process violations, the court distinguished between the two claims; it held federal funding an insufficient basis for state action as to the due process claim but indicated that "the allegation of substantial federal funding would be enough to demonstrate governmental action as to . . . [the] claim of racial discrimination."

In *Weise* v. *Syracuse University*, 522 F.2d 397 (2d Cir. 1975), the court recognizes this same "double standard" in state action cases and extends it in part to claims of sex discrimination. The plaintiffs were two women, one a rejected faculty applicant and the other a terminated faculty member, who claimed the university had discriminated against them solely on the basis of sex. In remanding the case to the trial court, the court of appeals explained the significance of both race and sex discrimination in state action cases:

If our concern in this case were with discipline and
the First Amendment, the alleged indicia of state action—
funding and regulation—would most likely be insufficient.
. . . [But as the] conduct complained of becomes more
offensive, and as the nature of the dispute becomes more
amenable to resolution by a court, the more appropriate it
is to subject the issue to judicial scrutiny. . . . Class-based
discrimination is perhaps the practice most fundamentally
opposed to the stuff of which our national heritage is
composed, and by far the most evil form of discrimination
has been that based on race. It should hardly be surprising,
then, that in race discrimination cases courts have been
particularly vigilant in requiring the states to avoid support
of otherwise private discrimination, and that where the
conduct has been less offensive, a greater degree of tolerance
has been shown. . . . [I]t is not necessary to put sex
discrimination into the same hole as race discrimination.
. . . It is enough to note that the conduct here alleged—
invidious class-based discrimination on account of sex—
would appear . . . to be more offensive than the disciplinary
steps taken in prior cases [522 F.2d at 405–06].

State action, in sum, is a complex area of law. Because of its
technical and still-developing nature, postsecondary administrators
should rely particularly heavily on legal counsel for guidance.
State action questions most often arise in the context of litigation,
and to date private postsecondary institutions have won many
more state action cases than they have lost.[3] Nevertheless,
administrators of private institutions should keep the state action

[3]There are, however, a number of cases where a "private"
postsecondary institution has been found to be engaged in state action in
all or some part of its operations. In addition to the *Powe, Rackin,* and
Weise cases discussed in the text above, see *Pennsylvania* v. *Board of
Directors of City Trusts of Philadelphia,* 353 U.S. 230 (1957) (the Girard
College Case); *Braden* v. *Univ. of Pittsburgh,* 552 F.2d 948 (3d Cir. 1977)
(upholding trial court denial of motion to dismiss for want of state action);
Hammond v. *Univ. of Tampa,* 344 F.2d 951 (5th Cir. 1965); *Klain* v. *Penn.
State Univ.,* 434 F. Supp. 574 (M.D. Pa. 1977); *Isaacs* v. *Bd. Trustees of
Temple Univ.,* 385 F. Supp. 473 (E.D. Pa. 1974); *King* v. *Conservatorio de
Musica de Puerto Rico,* 378 F. Supp. 746 (D.P.R. 1974); *Buckton* v. *NCAA
and Boston Univ.,* 366 F. Supp. 1152 (D. Mass. 1973); *Belk* v. *Chancellor of
Washington Univ.,* 336 F. Supp. 45 (E.D. Mo. 1970); *Ryan* v. *Hofstra
Univ.,* 67 Misc.2d 651, 324 N.Y.S.2d 964 (1971).

concept in mind in all major dealings with government: Could your institution's relationships with government subject it to a state action determination in some future litigation? As a policy matter, is the institution hospitable to the consequences of a state action determination, that is, being bound by the Constitution?

1.4.3. Other bases for legal rights in private institutions. The inapplicability of the federal Constitution to private schools does not necessarily mean that students, faculty members, and other members of the private school community have no legal rights assertable against the school. There are other sources for individual rights which may resemble those found in the Constitution.

The federal government and, to a lesser extent, state governments have increasingly created statutory rights enforceable against private institutions, particularly in the discrimination area. The federal Title VII prohibition on employment discrimination (42 U.S.C. secs. 2000e *et seq.*, discussed in Section 3.3.2.1), applicable generally to public and private employment relationships, is a prominent example. The Title VI race discrimination law (42 U.S.C. secs. 2000d *et seq.*) and the Title IX sex discrimination law (20 U.S.C. secs. 1681 *et seq.*) (see Section 7.4), applicable to federal aid recipients, are other major examples. Such sources provide a large body of nondiscrimination law which parallels and in some ways is more protective than the equal protection principles derived from the 14th Amendment. For example, see *Lau* v. *Nichols*, 414 U.S. 563 (1974) (Chinese speaking students denied equal educational opportunity under Title VI).

Beyond such statutory rights, several common law theories for protecting individual rights in private postsecondary institutions have been advanced. Most prominent by far is the contract theory under which students and faculty members are said to have a contractual relationship with the private school. Express or implied contract terms establish legal rights which can be enforced in court should the contract be breached. Although the theory is a useful one that has been referred to in a number of cases (see Sections 3.1 and 4.1), most courts agree that the contract law of the commercial world cannot be imported wholesale into the academic environment. The theory must thus be applied with sensitivity to academic customs and usages. Moreover, the theory's usefulness may be quite limited. The "terms" of the "contract" may be difficult to identify, particularly in the case of students. (To what extent, for instance, is the college catalogue a source of contract terms?) The terms, once identified, may be too vague or ambiguous to enforce. Or the contract may be so barren of content or so one-sided in favor of the institution as to be an insignificant source of individual rights.

Despite its shortcomings, the contract theory is likely to gain importance in future years. As it becomes increasingly clear that the bulk of private institutions can escape the tentacles of the state action doctrine, alternative theories for establishing individual rights will be increasingly tested. With the lowering of the age of majority, postsecondary students will have a capacity to contract under state law which many previously did not have. In what is becoming the age of the consumer, students will increasingly be encouraged to import consumer rights into postsecondary education. And in an age of collective negotiation, faculties may increasingly rely on a contract model for ordering employment relationships on campus. (See Section 3.2.)

Such developments can affect both public and private institutions, although state law may place additional restrictions on contract authority in the public sphere. While contract concepts can of course limit the authority of the institution, they should not be seen only as a burr in the administrator's side. They can also be used creatively to provide order and fairness in institutional affairs and to create internal grievance procedures which encourage in-house rather than judicial resolution of problems. Administrators thus should be sensitive to both the problems and the potentials of contract concepts in the postsecondary environment.

Sec. 1.5. Religion and the Public-Private Dichotomy

It is clear that, under the establishment clause of the First Amendment, public institutions must maintain a neutral stance regarding religious beliefs and activities; they must, in other words, maintain religious neutrality. Public institutions may neither favor or support one religion over another nor favor or support religion over nonreligion. Thus, for instance, public schools have been prohibited from using an official nondenominational prayer (*Engel* v. *Vitale*, 370 U.S. 421 (1962)) and from prescribing the reading of verses from the Bible at the opening of each school day (*Abington School Dist.* v. *Schemmp*, 374 U.S. 203 (1963)).

The First Amendment contains two "religion" clauses, the first prohibiting government from "establishing" religion and the second protecting individuals' "free exercise" of religion from governmental interference. Although the two clauses have a common objective of ensuring governmental "neutrality," they pursue it in different ways. As the Supreme Court explained in *Abington School Dist.* v. *Schemmp*, 374 U.S. 203, 222-23 (1963):

> The wholesome "neutrality" of which this Court's cases speak thus stems from a recognition of the teaching of history that powerful sects or groups might bring about a fusion of governmental and religious functions or a concert or dependency of one upon the other to the end that official support of the State or Federal Government would be placed behind the tenets of one or of all orthodoxies. This the Establishment Clause prohibits. And a further reason for neutrality is found in the Free Exercise Clause, which recognizes the value of religious training, teaching, and observance and, more particularly, the right of every person to freely choose his own course with reference thereto, free of any compulsion from the state. This the Free Exercise Clause guarantees. . . . The distinction between the two clauses is apparent—a violation of the Free Exercise Clause is predicated on coercion, whereas the Establishment Clause violation need not be so attended.

Neutrality, however, does not necessarily require a public institution to prohibit all religious activity on campus. If a rigidly observed policy of neutrality would discriminate against campus organizations with religious purposes or impinge on an individual's right to "free exercise" of religion, the institution may be permitted—sometimes required—to allow some religion on campus. The difficulty of delineating neutrality in such contexts is illustrated by *Keegan* v. *University of Delaware*, 349 A.2d 14 (Del. 1975). The university had banned all religious worship services from campus facilities. The plaintiffs contended that this policy was unconstitutional as applied to students' religious services in the commons areas of campus dormitories. The court first asked whether the university could permit religious worship in the commons area without violating the establishment clause:

> [W]e hold that the University cannot support its absolute ban of all religious worship on the theory that, without such a ban, University policy allowing all student groups, including religious groups, free access to dormitory commons areas would necessarily violate the Establishment Clause. The Establishment cases decided by the United States Supreme Court indicate that neutrality is the safe harbor in which to avoid First Amendment violations: neutral "accommodation" of religion is permitted, . . . while "promotion" and "advancement" of religion are not. . . . University policy without the worship ban could be neutral towards religion and could have the primary effect of advancing education by allowing students to meet together in the commons room of their dormitory to exchange ideas and share mutual interests. If any religious group or religion is accommodated or benefited thereby, such accommodation or benefit is purely incidental, and would not, in our judgment, violate the Establishment Clause. . . . The commons room is already provided for the benefits of students. It is not a dedication of the space to promote religious interests [349 A.2d at 16].

Then the court asked whether the university was constitutionally *required* by the free exercise clause to make the commons area available for students' religious worship:

> The only activity proscribed by the regulation is worship. . . . The commons area is already provided for student use and there is no request here that separate religious facilities be established. The area in question is a residence hall where students naturally assemble with their friends for many purposes. Religion, at least in part, is historically a communal exercise.
> It may be that every class division involving religion would not constitute a burden in the Constitutional sense on the free exercise of religion. . . . It may be that this case

> can be viewed as the mere denial of an economic benefit.
> Indeed, it can be argued, as it has been, that the question is
> whether the University must permit the students to worship
> on University property. But, in terms of religious liberty,
> the question is better put, in our judgment, from the
> perspective of the individual student. Can the University
> prohibit student worship in a commons area of a University
> dormitory which is provided for student use and in which
> the University permits every other student activity? It is
> apparent to us that such a regulation impedes the
> observance of religion [349 A.2d at 17, 18].

The court in *Keegan* thus holds not only that the university could
permit the religious services but also that the university was
required to do so by the free exercise clause.[4]

A private institution's position under the establishment and
free exercise clauses differs markedly from that of a public
institution. Private institutions have no obligation of neutrality
under the establishment clause. Moreover, the religious beliefs and
practices of private institutions are affirmatively protected from
government interference by the free exercise clause. The establishment clause does become important to private institutions,
however, when government—federal, state, or local—undertakes to
provide financial or other support for private education. If the
school receiving support is church-related, the question arises
whether government support for the school is also government
support for religion. If it is, such support would violate the
establishment clause because government would have departed
from its position of neutrality.

Two 1971 cases decided by the Supreme Court provide the
basis for the modern law on government support for church-related
schools. *Lemon* v. *Kurtzman*, 403 U.S. 602 (1971), invalidated two
state programs providing aid for church-related elementary and
secondary schools. *Tilton* v. *Richardson*, 403 U.S. 672 (1971), held

---

[4]The starting point for the court's establishment clause analysis in
Keegan was the three-pronged test set out in *Lemon* v. *Kurtzman*, 403 U.S.
602 (1971), and discussed later in this section. This test applies both to
situations where public institutions support allegedly religious activity
and to situations, as described below, where government supports allegedly
religious activity in private institutions.

constitutional a federal aid program providing construction grants
to higher education institutions, including those that are church-
related. In deciding the cases the Court developed a three-pronged
test for determining when a government support program passes
muster under the establishment clause:

> First, the statute must have a secular legislative
> purpose; second, its principal or primary effect must be one
> that neither advances nor inhibits religion . . . ; finally, the
> statute must not foster "an excessive government entangle-
> ment with religion" [403 U.S. at 612–13].

The first prong (purpose) has proved easy to meet and has not been
of major significance in subsequent cases. But the second two
prongs (effect and entanglement) have been both very important
and very difficult to apply in particular cases. The Court's major
explanation of "effect" came in *Hunt* v. *McNair*, 413 U.S. 734
(1973):

> Aid normally may be thought to have a primary
> effect of advancing religion when it flows to an institution
> in which religion is so pervasive that a substantial portion
> of its functions are subsumed in the religious mission or
> when it funds a specifically religious activity in an
> otherwise substantially secular setting [413 U.S. at 753].

Its major explanation of "entanglement" appeared in the *Lemon*
case:

> In order to determine whether the government
> entanglement with religion is excessive, we must examine
> (1) the character and purposes of the institutions which are
> benefited, (2) the nature of the aid that the State provides,
> and (3) the resulting relationship between the government
> and the religious authority [403 U.S. at 615].

Three Supreme Court cases have applied this complex three-
pronged test to church-related postsecondary institutions. In each
case the aid program passed the test. *Tilton*, above, the first case,
approved the federal construction grant program by a narrow 5-4

vote. In the second case, *Hunt* v. *McNair,* above, the Court, by a 6-3 vote, sustained a state program which assisted colleges, including church-related colleges, by issuing revenue bonds for their construction projects. The third case is *Roemer* v. *Board of Public Works,* 426 U.S. 736 (1976), where the Court, by a 5-4 vote, upheld Maryland's program of general support grants to private, including church-related, colleges. Though there were strong dissents in each case, and though a majority of the Court could agree on an opinion only in *Hunt,* the cases nevertheless suggest that a wide range of postsecondary support programs can be devised compatibly with the establishment clause and that a wide range of church-related institutions can be eligible to receive government support. The *Roemer* case is the most revealing. There the Court refused to find that the grants given a group of church-related schools constituted support for religion—even though the funds were granted annually and could be put to a wide range of uses, and even though the schools had church representatives on their governing boards, employed Roman Catholic chaplains, held Roman Catholic religious exercises, required students to take religion or theology classes taught primarily by Roman Catholic clerics, made some hiring decisions for theology departments partly on the basis of religious considerations, and began some classes with prayers.

Though the cases have been quite hospitable to government support programs for postsecondary education, administrators of church-related institutions should still be most sensitive to establishment clause issues. Since the cases have been decided by close votes, with great disagreement among the justices in their reasoning, the law has not yet settled. Thus, administrators should exercise great care in using government funds (certainly, for instance, they should not be used to build a chapel or purchase religious texts for a divinity school) and should keep in mind that, at some point, religious influences within the institution can still jeopardize government funding. In addition, state constitutions or the statutes creating the funding programs may contain clauses which restrict government support for church-related institutions more vigorously than the establishment clause does.

Selected Annotated Bibliography

General

The College Administrator and the Courts (College Administration Pub., 1977, plus periodic supp.) is a basic casebook written for administrators that briefs and discusses leading court cases. The first chapter introduces the legal system and sources of law. Other chapters discuss the role of counsel, distinctions between public and private colleges, and the state action concept. Updated quarterly.

Sec. 1.2 (Evolution of the Law Relating to Postsecondary Education)

1. Metzger, W., Kadish, S., DeBardeleben, A., and Bloustein, E., *Dimensions of Academic Freedom* (U. Illinois Press, 1969), is a series of papers presenting historical, legal, and administrative perspectives on academic freedom's evolution; considers the changing nature of the university, its professors and students, and changes in the university's internal and external commitments.
2. Van Alstyne, W., "The Demise of the Right-Privilege Distinction in Constitutional Law," 81 *Harvard L. Rev.* 1439 (1968), provides a historical and analytical review of the rise and fall of the right-privilege distinction; includes discussion of several postsecondary education cases to demonstrate that the pursuit of state postsecondary education opportunities and jobs is no longer a "privilege" to which constitutional rights do not attach.

Sec. 1.3 (Sources of Postsecondary Education Law)

1. Bakken, G., "Campus Common Law," 5 *J. of Law and Education* 201 (1976), is a theoretical overview of custom and usage as a source of postsecondary education law; emphasizes the impact of custom and usage on faculty rights and responsibilities.

2. Farnsworth, E. A., *An Introduction to the Legal System of the United States* (Oceana, corrected 1st ed., 1975), is an introductory text emphasizing the fundamentals of the American legal system. Written for the layperson.

Sec. 1.4 (The Public-Private Dichotomy)

1. Beach, J.,"Fundamental Fairness in Search of a Legal Rationale in Private College Student Discipline and Expulsions," 2 *J. of College and University Law* 65 (1974), analyzes the theories and problems encountered in fairly applying the law to private institutions. Emphasis is on students' rights, but the analysis is helpful in understanding the public-private distinction in general.

2. Faccenda, P., and Ross, K., "Constitutional and Statutory Regulations of Private Colleges and Universities, 9 *Valparaiso University L. Rev.* 539 (1975), is an overview of the ways in which private institutions are subjected to federal constitutional and regulatory requirements; draws distinctions between public and private institutions. Written primarily for administrators with footnotes designed for counsel.

3. Howard, A. E. D., *State Aid to Private Higher Education* (Michie, 1977), is a comprehensive treatment of state aid programs in each of the fifty states, as well as a general national overview. Provides legal analysis of state and federal constitutional law, historical developments, and descriptive information on aid programs; emphasizes church-state issues, such as those discussed in Section 1.5 of this chapter.

4. O'Neil, R., "Private Universities and Public Law," 19 *Buffalo L. Rev.* 155 (1969), discusses the philosophical and legal distinctions between public and private universities. The author treats the "state action" concept as an artificial barrier in modern constitutional law and provides a framework for analysis of state action issues.

Sec. 1.5 (Religion and the Public-Private Dichotomy)

1. Smith, M., "Emerging Consequences of Financing Private Colleges with Public Money," 9 *Valparaiso University L. Rev.* 561 (1975), provides a legal and policy analysis of govern-

ment subsidies for private postsecondary institutions; discusses the U.S. Supreme Court decisions in *Tilton* v. *Richardson* and *Hunt* v. *McNair* as well as important state court decisions. Useful resource for both laypersons and legal counsel.

2. Underwood, J., "Permissible Entanglement Under the Establishment Clause," 25 *Emory L. J.* 17 (1976), provides an analysis of U.S. Supreme Court attitudes concerning government entanglement with religion; includes extended discussion of *Hunt* v. *McNair*. Primarily for legal counsel.

Chapter II

❧❧❧❧❧❧❧❧❧❧❧❧❧❧❧❧❧❧

The College
and Trustees,
Administrators,
and Agents

Sec. 2.1. The Question of Authority

T rustees, officers, and administrators of postsecondary institutions
—public or private—can take only those actions and make only
those decisions which they have authority to take or make. Acting
or deciding without authority to do so can have legal consequences
both for the responsible individual and for the institution. It is

thus critical, from a legal standpoint, for administrators to understand and adhere to the scope and limits of their authority and that of other institutional functionaries with whom they deal. Such sensitivity to authority questions will also normally be good administrative practice, since it can contribute order and structure to institutional governance and make the governance system more understandable, accessible, and accountable to those who deal with it.

Authority generally originates from some fundamental legal source which establishes the institution as a legal entity. For a public institution, the source is usually the constitution or statutes of the state (see Section 6.2), while for a private institution it is usually articles of incorporation, sometimes in combination with some form of state license. (See Section 6.3.) This source, though fundamental, is only the starting point for legal analysis of authority questions. To be fully understood and utilized, an institution's fundamental authority must be construed and implemented in light of all the sources of law described in Section 1.3. For public institutions, state administrative law (administrative procedure acts or similar statutes; court decisions) and agency law (court decisions) provide the backdrop against which authority is construed and implemented; for private institutions, state corporation or trust law (statutes; court decisions) and agency law (court decisions) are the bases. Authority is particularized and dispersed (delegated) to institutional officers, employees, and organizations by institutional rules and regulations and the institution's employment contracts and, for public institutions, by administrative regulations of the state education boards or agencies. Gaps and ambiguities in authority may be filled in by resort to custom and usage at the institution. And authority may be limited by individual rights guarantees of federal and state constitutions (see especially Sections 3.5 and 3.6 and Sections 4.4 through 4.10) and by federal and state statutes and administrative regulations or adjudications (see especially Sections 6.3 and 6.5 and Sections 7.2 and 7.4).

There are several generic types of authority. As explained in *Brown* v. *Wichita State University* (Section 2.3.2), authority may be either *express, implied,* or *apparent.* Express authority is that which is found within the plain meaning of a written grant of authority. Implied authority is that which is necessary or appropriate for exercising express authority and can therefore be inferred from the express authority. Apparent authority is not actual authority at all; the term is used to describe the situation where someone acting for the institution induces a belief in other persons that authority exists when in fact it does not. Administrators should avoid this appearance of authority and should not rely on apparent authority as a basis for acting, because the institution may be held liable, under the doctrine of "estoppel," for resultant harm to persons who rely to their detriment on an appearance of authority. (See Section 2.2.2.) When an institutional officer or employee does mistakenly act without authority, the action can sometimes be corrected through "ratification" by the board of trustees or other officer or employee who does have authority to undertake the act in question. (See Section 2.2.2.)

One other type of authority is occasionally referred to in the postsecondary context: *inherent* authority. In *Morris* v. *Nowotny*, 323 S.W.2d 301 (Tex. 1959), for instance, the court remarked that the statutes establishing the University of Texas "imply the power and if they do not so imply then the power is inherent in University officials to maintain proper order and decorum on the premises of the University." And in *Esteban* v. *Central Missouri State College*, 415 F.2d 1077 (8th Cir. 1969), the court held that the college had "inherent authority to maintain order and to discipline students." The inherent authority concept is often loosely used in judicial opinions and has no clear definition. Sometimes courts appear to apply the phrase to what is really a very broad construction of the institution's implied powers. In *Goldberg* v. *Regents of the University of California*, 57 Cal. Rptr. 463 (Ct. App. 1967), the court found broad disciplinary authority over students to be implicit in the state constitution's grant of power to the university, but then called that authority "inherent." Other times inherent authority is clearly distinct from implied authority and exists not because of any written words but rather because, given the nature of postsecondary education, it would not be sensible for the institution to be without authority in some particular circumstance. In all, inherent authority is an elusive concept of

uncertain stature and questionable value, and it is a slender reed to
rely on to justify actions and decisions. If administrators need
broader authority, it will be sounder to seek counsel's help in
construing implied authority more broadly than to rely on
inherent authority.

The law is not clear on how broadly or narrowly authority
should be construed in the postsecondary context. To some extent
the answer will vary from state to state and, within a state, may
depend on whether the institution is established by the state
constitution, by state statutes, or by articles of incorporation.
Although authority issues have been addressed in judicial opinions, such as those discussed in Section 2.2, analysis is sometimes
cursory and authority problems are sometimes overlooked. There is
debate among courts and commentators about whether postsecondary institutions should be subject to traditional legal principles
for construing authority or whether such principles should be
applied in a more flexible, less demanding, way that takes into
account the unique characteristics of postsecondary education.
Given the uncertainty, administrators should rely when possible on
express rather than implied or inherent authority and should seek
clarity in statements of express authority, in order to avoid leaving
authority questions to the vagaries of judicial interpretation. To
the extent institutional needs require greater flexibility and
generality in statements of authority, administrators should consult
legal counsel to determine how much breadth and flexibility the
courts of the state would permit in construing the various types of
authority.

Miscalculations of the institution's authority, or the authority of particular officers or employees, can have various adverse
legal consequences. The institution's ability to enforce or accept
the fruits of its actions may depend on its authority to act. For
public institutions, for instance, unauthorized acts may be
invalidated in courts or administrative agencies under the *ultra
vires* doctrine of administrative law. For private institutions a
similar result occasionally can be reached under corporation law.

When the unauthorized act is a failure to follow institutional regulations and the institution is public (see Section 1.4.2),
courts will sometimes hold that the act violated procedural due

process. In *Escobar* v. *State University of New York/College at Old Westbury*, 427 F. Supp. 850 (E.D. N.Y. 1977), a student sought to enjoin the college from suspending him or taking any further disciplinary action against him. The student had been disciplined by the Judicial Review Committee acting under the college's "Code of Community Conduct." After the college president learned of the disciplinary action, he rejected it and imposed more severe penalties on the student. The president purported to act under "The Rules of Public Order" adopted by the Board of Trustees of the State University of New York rather than under the college code. The court found that the president had violated the rules and enjoined enforcement of his decision:

> [E]ven if we assume the President had power to belatedly invoke the Rules, it is clear that he did not properly exercise that power, since he did not follow the requirements of the Rules themselves. The charges he made against the plaintiff were included in the same document which set forth the plaintiff's suspension and the terms for his possible readmission. Contrary to the Rules, the President did not convene the Hearing Committee, did not give notice of any hearing, and received no report from the Hearing Committee. There is no authority in either the Rules or the Code for substituting the hearing before the Code's Judicial Review Committee for the one required to be held before the Rule's Hearing Committee. . . .
>
> Of course, not every deviation from a university's regulations constitutes a deprivation of due process. . . . But where, as here, an offending student has been formally charged under the college's disciplinary code, has been subjected to a hearing, has been officially sentenced, and has commenced compliance with that sentence, it is a denial of due process of law for the chief administrative officer to step in, conduct his own in camera review of the student's record, and impose a different punishment without complying with any of the procedures which have been formally established for the college. Here the President simply brushed aside the college's formal regulations and procedures and, without specific authority, imposed a punishment of greater severity than determined by the hearing panel, a result directly contrary to the Code's appeal provisions [427 F. Supp. at 858].

For both public and private institutions, an unauthorized act violating institutional regulations may also be invalidated as a breach of an express or implied contract with students or the faculty. *Lyons* v. *Salve Regina College,* 422 F. Supp. 1354 (D.R.I. 1976), reversed, 565 F.2d 200 (1st Cir. 1977), involved a student who had received an F grade in a required nursing course because she had been absent from several classes and clinical sessions. After the student appealed the grade under the college's published "Grade Appeal Process," the Grade Appeal Committee voted that the student receive an Incomplete rather than an F. Characterizing the committee's action as a recommendation rather than a final decision, the associate dean overruled the committee, and the student was dismissed from the nursing program.

The parties agreed that the Grade Appeal Process was part of the terms of a contract between them. Though the Grade Appeal Committee's determination was termed a "recommendation" in the college's publications, the lower court found that, as the parties understood the process, the recommendation was to be binding on the associate dean. The associate dean's overruling of the committee was therefore unauthorized and constituted a breach of contract. The lower court ordered the college to change the student's grade to an Incomplete and reinstate her in the nursing program. While the appellate court reversed, it did not disavow the contract theory of authority. Instead, it found that the committee's determination was not intended to be binding on the associate dean and that the dean therefore had not exceeded his authority in overruling the committee.

Authority questions are also central to a determination of various questions concerning liability for harm to third parties. The institution's tort liability may depend on whether the officer or employee committing the tort was acting within the scope of his authority. (See Section 2.3.1.) The institution's contract liability may depend on whether the officer or employee entering the contract was authorized to do so (Section 2.3.2). And under the estoppel doctrine, both the institution and the individual may be liable where the institution or individual had apparent authority to act (Section 2.2.2).

These various legal ramifications, along with the relationship between authority questions and good administrative practice, underscore the importance for postsecondary administrators of understanding the scope of the institution's authority and its system for delegating authority among its officers, employees, and organizations. The authority of the institution and its constituent parts should be organized and documented with the assistance of legal counsel. The organization and delegation of authority should be made generally available to the campus community so that persons with questions or grievances can know where to turn for assistance. Delegations should be reviewed periodically to determine whether they accurately reflect actual practice within the institution and reflect an appropriate balance of specificity and flexibility. Where a gap in authority is found, or an unnecessary overlap or ambiguity, it should be corrected. Where questions concerning the permissible scope of authority are uncovered, legal counsel should be consulted.

Similarly, administrators should understand the scope of their own authority and that of the officers, employees, and organizations with whom they deal. They should understand where their authority comes from and which higher-level administrators may review or modify their acts and decisions. They should attempt to resolve unnecessary gaps or ambiguities in their authority. They should consider what part of their authority may and should be subdelegated to lower-level administrators and what checks or limitations should be placed on those delegations. And they should attempt to assure that their authority is adequately understood by those members of the campus community with whom they deal.

Sec. 2.2. Sources and Scope of Authority

The following discussion illustrates particular kinds of legal challenges which may be made to the authority of various functionaries within postsecondary institutions. Although the discussion reflects general concepts and issues critical to an understanding of authority in the postsecondary context, the specific legal principles which courts apply to particular challenges to authority may vary from state to state.

2.2.1. Trustees. In public institutions the authority of trustees is defined and limited by the state statutes, and sometimes constitutional provisions, which create trustee boards for individual institutions. Such laws generally confer power on the board itself as an entity separate from its individual members. Individual trustees generally have authority to act only when doing so on behalf of the board, pursuant to some board bylaw, resolution, or other delegation of authority from the board. Other state laws, such as conflict of interest laws or ethics codes, may place obligations on individual board members as well as on the board itself.

In *First Equity Corporation of Florida* v. *Utah State University,* 544 P.2d 887 (Utah 1975), a state court examined the Utah constitution and laws to determine whether the board had authority to authorize the assistant vice president of finance to invest in common stock on behalf of the university. The board had general control and supervision "of all appropriations made by the Territory for the support" of the school (Compiled Laws of Utah sec. 1855 (1888)), and the university had authority to handle its own financial affairs under the supervision of the board (The Higher Education Act of 1969, Utah Code Ann. sec. 53-48-10(5)). The court held, however, that these provisions did not give the university unlimited authority to encumber public funds:

> Whether or not the grant of a "general control" of "all appropriations" and the right to "handle its own financial affairs" grant unrestricted power to invest is answered by *The University of Utah* v. *Board of Examiners of the State of Utah* [4 Utah 2d 408, 295 P.2d 348 (1956)] case. After quoting Sections 1 and 2 of Article X of the Constitution, which mandates the Legislature to provide for the maintenance of the University of Utah and USU, the Court states:
>
> > Would it be contended by the University that under Article X, Section 1, it might compel the Legislature to appropriate money the University considers essential? Is it contended that the demands of the University are not subject to constitutional debt limits? If so, respondent would have the power to destroy the solvency of the State and all other insti-

tutions by demands beyond the power of the State to meet.

The Court then quotes in full Sections 5 and 7 of Article X of the Constitution, which provides, respectively, that the proceeds of the sale of land reserved by Congress for the University of Utah shall constitute permanent funds of the State, and that all public school funds shall be guaranteed by the State against loss or diversion. Then the Court concludes:

> It is inconceivable that the framers of the Constitution in light of the provisions of Sections 1, 5, and 7 of Article X and the provision as to debt limitations intended to place the University above the only controls available for the people of this State as to the property, management and government of the University. We are unable to reconcile respondent's position that the University has a blank check as to all its funds with no preaudit and no restraint under the provisions of the Constitution requiring the state to safely invest and hold the dedicated funds and making the State guarantor of the public school funds against loss or diversion. To hold that respondent has free and uncontrolled custody and use of its property and funds while making the State guarantee said funds against loss or diversion is inconceivable. We believe the framers of the Constitution intended no such result [544 P.2d at 890].

Because of this state constitutional limitation regarding finances, and the absence of any "specific authorizing grant" of investment power under the state statutes, the court held that the board did not have authority to purchase the particular type of stock involved. The board therefore could not authorize the assistant vice-president or any other agent to make the purchases.

In *Feldman* v. *Regents of the University of New Mexico*, 88 N.Mex. 392, 540 P.2d 872 (1975), the head football coach at the university sued the regents for discharging him during the term of his contract. According to New Mexico law the regents had "power to remove any officer connected with the university when in their judgment the interests require it" (N. Mex. Stat. Ann. sec. 73-25-9). The regents relied on the statute as sufficient authority for dismissing the coach. In ruling on the regents' motion for summary judgment, the state courts refused to approve the dismissal under this statute. The courts reasoned that additional information was needed to determine whether the coach was an "officer" or an "employee" of the institution, since the statute would not authorize his discharge if he were in the latter category.

In private institutions, the authority of institutional trustees is defined and limited by the institution's corporate charter (articles of incorporation) and the state corporation laws under which charters are issued. As in public institutions, the power generally lodges in the trustee board as an entity separate from its individual members. But charter provisions, corporate bylaws, or board resolutions may delegate authority to individual trustees or trustee committees to act for the board in certain situations. Moreover, general state corporate law or trust law may place affirmative obligations on individual board members to act fairly and responsibly in protecting the institution's resources and interests.

The Missouri case of *Burnett* v. *Barnes*, 546 S.W.2d 744 (Mo. 1977), illustrates how the authority of a private institution's board of trustees may be limited by the institution's articles of incorporation. In *Burnett* the Missouri state courts determined that the Board of Trustees of the Kansas City College of Osteopathic Medicine (a membership corporation) did not have authority to amend the bylaws to eliminate membership in the corporation. The Missouri General Not-For-Profit Corporation Law gave the trustees power "to make and alter bylaws not inconsistent with its articles of incorporation or with the laws of this state" (Mo. Rev. Stat. sec. 355.090). The institution's original Articles of Agreement and its subsequent Articles of Acceptance each referred to the admission of new members to the corporation. On the basis of these two references, the courts concluded that the board's power to amend the bylaws was limited by the institution's articles of incorporation to matters that did not eliminate membership.

The "Sibley Hospital Case" or *Stern* case, *Stern* v. *Lucy Webb Hayes National Training School for Deaconnesses and Missionaries*, 381 F. Supp. 1003 (D.D.C. 1974), delineates the authority of a private charitable corporation's trustees regarding financial matters. Though the case concerns a hospital, the standards set out by the court are clearly transferable to private educational institutions. *Stern* is the first reported opinion to comprehensively review the obligations of the trustees of private charitable corporations and to set out guidelines for trustee involvement in financial dealings. The court's decision to analyze the trustees' standard of duty in terms of corporate law, rather than trust law, apparently reflects the evolving trend in the law.

The plaintiffs represented patients of Sibley Hospital, a nonprofit charitable corporation in the District of Columbia and the principal concern of the Lucy Webb Hayes National Training School. Nine members of the hospital's board of trustees were among the named defendants. The plaintiffs charged that the defendant trustees "conspired to enrich themselves and certain financial institutions with which they were affiliated [and which were also named as defendants] by favoring those institutions in financial dealings with the hospital, and that they breached their fiduciary duties of care and loyalty in the management of Sibley's funds." The Court examined evidence of the relationships between the defendant trustees and the defendant institutions. Although most of the hospital's funds were deposited in the defendant institutions, the funds were controlled and managed almost exclusively from the early 1950s until 1972 by a deceased trustee, without the active involvement of any of the defendant trustees.

The court concluded that the plaintiffs had not established a conspiracy but had established serious breaches of duty by the trustees. According to the court, the trustees owed a duty to the institution comparable to that owed by the directors of a business corporation:

1. Mismanagement

Both trustees and corporate directors are liable for losses occasioned by their negligent mismanagement of investments. However, the degree of care required appears to differ in many jurisdictions. A trustee is uniformly held to a high standard of care and will be held liable for simple negligence, while a director must often have committed "gross negligence" or otherwise be guilty of more than mere mistakes of judgment.

This distinction may amount to little more than a recognition of the fact that corporate directors have many areas of responsibility, while the traditional trustee is often charged only with the management of the trust funds and can therefore be expected to devote more time and expertise to that task. Since the board members of most large charitable corporations fall within the corporate rather than the trust model, being charged with the operation of ongoing businesses, it has been said that they should only be held to the less stringent corporate standard of care. More specifically, directors of charitable corporations are required to exercise ordinary and reasonable care in the performance of their duties, exhibiting honesty and good faith.

2. Nonmanagement

Plaintiffs allege that the individual defendants failed to supervise the management of Hospital investments or even to attend meetings of the committees charged with such supervision. Trustees are particularly vulnerable to such a charge, because they not only have an affirmative duty to "maximize the trust income by prudent investment," but they may not delegate that duty, even to a committee of their fellow trustees. A corporate director, on the other hand, may delegate his investment responsibility to fellow directors, corporate officers, or even outsiders, but he must continue to exercise general supervision over the activities of his delegates. Once again, the rule for charitable corporations is closer to the traditional corporate rule: directors should at least be permitted to delegate investment decisions to a committee of board members, so long as all directors assume the responsibility for supervising such committees by periodically scrutinizing their work.

Total abdication of the supervisory role, however, is improper even under traditional corporate principles. A director who fails to acquire the information necessary to supervise investment policy or consistently fails even to attend the meetings at which such policies are considered has violated his fiduciary duty to the corporation. . . .

3. Self-Dealing

Under District of Columbia Law, neither trustees nor corporate directors are absolutely barred from placing funds under their control into a bank having an interlocking directorship with their own institution. In both cases, however, such transactions will be subjected to the closest scrutiny to determine whether or not the duty of loyalty has been violated. A deliberate conspiracy among trustees or Board members to enrich the interlocking bank at the expense of the trust or corporation would, for example, constitute such a breach and render the conspirators liable for any losses. In the absence of clear evidence of wrongdoing, however, the courts appear to have used different standards to determine whether or not relief is appropriate, depending again on the legal relationship involved. Trustees may be found guilty of a breach of trust even for mere negligence in the maintenance of accounts in banks with which they are associated, while corporate directors are generally only required to show "entire fairness" to the corporation and "full disclosure" of the potential conflict of interest to the Board.

Most courts apply the less stringent corporate rule to charitable corporations in this area as well [381 F. Supp. at 1013-15 (footnotes omitted)].

On the basis of these principles, the court created explicit guidelines for the future conduct of trustees in financial matters:

[T]he Court holds that a director or so-called trustee of a charitable hospital organized under the Non-Profit Corporation Act of the District of Columbia (D.C. Code sec. 29-1001 *et seq.*) is in default of his fiduciary duty to manage the fiscal and investment affairs of the hospital if it has been shown by a preponderance of the evidence that:

(1) While assigned to a particular committee of the Board having general financial or investment responsibility under the bylaws of the corporation, he has failed to use due diligence in supervising the actions of those officers, employees, or outside experts to whom the responsibility for making day-to-day financial or investment decisions has been delegated; or

(2) he knowingly permitted the hospital to enter

into a business transaction with himself or with any corporation, partnership, or association in which he then had a substantial interest or held a position as trustee, director, general manager, or principal officer without having previously informed the persons charged with approving that transaction of his interest or position and of any significant reasons, unknown to or not fully appreciated by such persons, why the transaction might not be in the best interests of the hospital; or

(3) except as required by the preceding paragraph, he actively participated in or voted in favor of a decision by the Board or any committee or subcommittee thereof to transact business with himself or with any corporation, partnership, or association in which he then had a substantial interest or held a position as trustee, director, general manager or principal officer; or

(4) he otherwise failed to perform his duties honestly, in good faith, and with a reasonable amount of diligence and care [381 F. Supp. at 1015].

2.2.2. Other officers and administrators. The authority of the highest ranking officers and administrators of postsecondary institutions may occasionally be set out in statutes or state board regulations (for public institutions) or in corporate charters (for private institutions). But more often even the highest ranking officers and employees, and almost always the lower-ranking ones, derive their authority not directly from statute, state board regulation, or charter but rather from subdelegation by the institution's board of trustees. The lower the administrator in the administrative hierarchy, the greater the likelihood of subsubdelegation, that is, subdelegation of authority from the board of trustees to an officer or administrator who in turn subdelegates part of this authority to some other administrator.

Silverman v. *University of Colorado*, 555 P.2d 1155 (Colo. 1976), illustrates the subdelegation of authority. A terminated assistant professor claimed that her termination constituted a breach of contract. In December 1972, the associate dean of the professor's school wrote the professor that she would be reappointed for 1973–74 if certain federal funding was renewed and if the professor's peers recommended reappointment. The professor claimed that, although both conditions were fulfilled, the school did not renew her contract, thus violating the December 1972 letter. The trial court held for the university, reasoning that the associate dean's letter could not create a contract because, by statute, only the board of regents had authority to appoint faculty members. The intermediate appellate court reversed, reasoning that the associate dean could have created a contract because he could have been acting under the authority subdelegated to him by the board. The Supreme Court of Colorado then reversed the intermediate court and reinstated the trial court decision, holding that hiring authority is not delegable unless "expressly authorized by the legislature."

In *People* v. *Ware*, 368 N.Y.S.2d 797 (App. Div. 1975), however, an appellate court upheld a delegation of power from a system-wide board of trustees to the president of an individual institution and thence to campus police officers employed by that institution. The trial court had dismissed a prosecution against an illegal trespasser at the State University of New York (SUNY) at Buffalo because the officer making the arrest did not have authority to do so. This court reasoned that the New York Education Law, sec. 355(2)(m), required that the SUNY board of trustees appoint peace officers, whereas the arresting officer had been appointed by the president of the university. In reversing, the appellate court reasoned that the board had authority under the Education Law to promulgate rules and regulations, and the rules and regulations promulgated by the board provided for the delegation of power to SUNY's executive and administrative officers. By resolution passed under these rules and regulations the board had authorized administrative officers of each state institution to appoint peace officers for their campuses. Since the SUNY president had properly appointed the arresting officer pursuant to this resolution, the officer had authority to make the arrest.

Even when an institutional officer or administrator acts beyond the scope of her delegated power, so that the act is unauthorized, the board of trustees may subsequently "ratify" the act if that act was within the scope of the board's own authority. "Ratification" converts the initially unauthorized act into an authorized act. In the *Silverman* case discussed previously in this section, for instance, the intermediate appellate court held that even if the associate dean did not have authority to reappoint the plaintiff-professor, the plaintiff was entitled to prove that the offer of reappointment had been ratified by the board of regents (541 P.2d 93, 96 (1975)). Similarly, in *In Re Tuskegee Institute* v. *May Refrigeration Company*, 344 So.2d 156 (Ala. 1977), two employees of a special program operated by Tuskegee had ordered an air conditioning unit from the May Company. May delivered and installed the unit but was not paid the agreed-upon price. An intermediate appellate court reversed a damages award for May on the theory that the Tuskegee employees who ordered the unit had no authority to do so. The highest state court then reversed the intermediate court. It reasoned that, even though the employees had no actual or apparent authority, Tuskegee had kept and used the unit which the employees ordered and therefore could have ratified their unauthorized acts.

Even when an officer or administrator acts without authority and a higher officer or administrator or the board of trustees has not ratified the act, a court will occasionally estop the institution from denying the validity of the act. Under this doctrine of estoppel, courts may treat an unauthorized act as if it had been authorized where necessary to prevent injustice to persons who had justifiably relied on the unauthorized act. In the *Silverman* case, the plaintiff-professor argued that various officials of the school had "advised her that her position was secure for the coming academic year" and that she "reasonably relied on these representations to her detriment in that she did not seek other employment." The intermediate appellate court ruled that, if plaintiff's allegations regarding the assurances, the reasonableness of her reliance, and the detriment were true, then "the doctrine of estoppel may be invoked if necessary to prevent manifest injustice." The Colorado Supreme Court reversed, recognizing the estoppel doctrine but holding that the facts did not justify its application in this case. The court reasoned that, since the professor had received adequate notice of nonrenewal, there was no "manifest injustice" necessitating estoppel and that, since the Faculty Handbook clearly stated that the Board of Regents makes all faculty appointments, the professor's "reliance on statements made by university officials was misplaced."

Another illustration of estoppel is provided by *Blank* v. *Board of Higher Education of the City of New York*, 51 Misc.2d 724, 273 N.Y.S.2d 796 (1966). The plaintiff-student sought to compel the defendant board to award him a bachelor of arts degree. The question about the student's degree developed after he was advised that he could take advantage of a Professional Option Plan which allowed him to complete a certain minimum amount of course work without attending any classes. This arrangement enabled him to begin law school in Syracuse before he had finished all of his course work at Brooklyn College. The student had been advised by faculty members, the head of the department of psychology, and a member of the counseling and guidance staff, and the arrangement had been approved by the professors of the psychology courses involved, each of whom gave him the necessary assignments. At the time of his expected graduation, however, the student was denied his degree because he had not completed the courses "in attendance."

In defending its refusal to grant the degree, the college argued that only the dean of the faculty had the authority to determine a student's eligibility for the Professional Option Plan and that the dean had not exercised such authority regarding the plaintiff. The college further argued that the dean had devised regulations concerning the Professional Option Plan and that these regulations contained residence requirements which the student had not met. While the court did not dispute these facts, it emphasized, as a contrary consideration, that the plaintiff had "acted in obvious reliance upon the counsel and advice of members of the staff of the college administration to whom he was referred and who were authorized to give him such counsel and advice." Moreover:

> "The authority of an agent is not only that conferred upon him by his commission, but also as to third persons that which he is held out as possessing. The principal is often bound by the act of his agent in excess or abuse of his authority, but this is only true between the principal

and third persons, who believing and having a right to believe that the agent was acting within and not exceeding
his authority, would sustain loss if the act was not considered that of the principal" (*Walsh* v. *Hartford Fire Insurance Co.*, 73 N.Y. 5, 10).

The Dean of Faculty may not escape the binding
effect of the acts of his agents performed within the scope
of their apparent authority, and the consequences that must
equitably follow therefrom. Having given permission to
take the subject courses in the manner prescribed, through
his agents . . . , he cannot, in the circumstances, later assert
that the courses should have been taken in another manner
[273 N.Y.S.2d at 802–03].

Thus "all of the elements of an estoppel exist" and the "doctrine
should be invoked" against the college. The court ordered the
college to award the plaintiff the A.B. degree.

2.2.3. Campus organizations. Authority in postsecondary
institutions may be delegated not only to individual officers or
administrators but also to various campus organizations which are
accorded some role in governance. Common examples include
academic senates, faculty assemblies, departmental faculties, and
student or university judicial systems. (See Section 4.13.3 for a
discussion of the last-named organization.)

Searle v. *The Regents of the University of California*, 23 Cal.
App.2d 448, 100 Cal. Rptr. 194 (1972), is a leading case. By a
standing order of the regents, the academic senate was given
authority to "authorize and supervise all courses and curricula."
Pursuant to this authority, the senate approved a course in which
fifty percent of the lectures would be taught by a nonfaculty
member (Eldridge Cleaver). Subsequent to the Senate's approval of
the course, the regents adopted two pertinent resolutions. One
resolution provided that a person without an appropriate faculty
appointment could not lecture more than once during a university
quarter in a course offering university credit; the other provided
that if the course to be taught by Cleaver could not be restructured,
it could not be offered for credit.

The course was taught as originally planned. When the
regents resolved that the course not be given academic credit,
sixteen students who took the course and six faculty members sued

to compel the regents to grant the credit and to rescind its first two resolutions. The plaintiffs argued that the standing order granting the academic senate authority over courses and curricula deprived the regents of power to act. The court, however, found that the regents had specifically retained the power to appoint faculty members and concluded that the situation in this case involved an appointment to the faculty rather than just the supervisory power over courses provided by the standing order: "To designate a lecturer for a university course is to name the person to conduct the course, at least to the extent of the lectures to be given by him. When the designation is of one to conduct a full half of the course, it appears to be a matter of appointment to the faculty, which is clearly reserved to the regents." Moreover, the court indicated that the authority of the academic senate was subject to further diminishment by the regents:

> In any event, the power granted to the senate is neither exclusive nor irrevocable. The bylaws specifically provide that neither they nor the standing orders "shall be construed, operate as, or have the effect of an abridgment or limitation of any rights, powers, or privileges of The Regents." This limitation not only is authorized, but seems required, by the overriding constitutional mandate which vests the regents with "full powers of organization and government" of the university, and grants to them as a corporation "all the powers necessary or convenient for the effective administration of its trust." (Cal. Const. Art. IX, sec. 9.) To accept appellants' argument would be to hold that a delegation of authority, even though specifically limited, amounts to a surrender of authority [100 Cal. Rptr. at 195–96].

The court therefore determined that the regents, and not the senate, had authority over the structuring of the course in question.

Sec. 2.3. Institutional Liability for Acts of Trustees, Administrators, and Other Agents

2.3.1. Institutional tort liability. A tort is broadly defined as a civil wrong, other than a breach of contract, for which the courts will allow a damage remedy. While any act fitting this definition may be considered a tort, there are certain classic torts for which the essential elements of the plaintiff's prima facie case and the defendant's acceptable defenses are already established. The two classic torts which most frequently arise in the setting of postsecondary education are negligence[1] and defamation.

Public institutions can sometimes escape tort liability by asserting sovereign or governmental immunity. The availability of this defense varies greatly from state to state. While the sovereign immunity doctrine was generally recognized in early American common law, the doctrine has been abrogated or modified in many states by judicial decisions, state legislation, or a combination of the two.[2] In *Brown* v. *Wichita State University*, 219 Kan. 2, 547

[1]The relevant cases and authorities are collected in an extensive series of annotations: Annot., "Tort Liability of Public Schools and Institutions of Higher Learning for Accidents Due to Condition of Buildings or Equipment," 34. A.L.R.3d 1166 (1970); Annot., "Tort Liability of Public Schools and Institutions of Higher Learning for Accidents Associated with the Transportation of Students," 34 A.L.R.3d 1210 (1970); Annot., "Tort Liability of Public Schools and Institutions of Higher Learning for Accidents Occurring During School Athletic Events," 35 A.L.R.3d 725 (1970); Annot., "Tort Liability of Public Schools and Institutions of Higher Learning for Accidents Associated with Chemistry Experiments, Shopwork, and Manual or Vocational Training," 35 A.L.R.3d 758 (1970); Annot., "Tort Liability of Private Schools and Institutions of Higher Learning for Accidents Due to Condition of Buildings, Equipment, or Outside Premises," 35 A.L.R.3d 975 (1970); Annot., "Tort Liability of Public Schools and Institutions of Higher Learning for Injuries Caused by Acts of Fellow Students," 36 A.L.R.3d 330 (1970); Annot., "Tort Liability of Public Schools and Institutions of Higher Learning for Accidents Occurring in Physical Education Classes," 36 A.L.R.3d 361 (1970); Annot., "Tort Liability of Public Schools and Institutions of Higher Learning for Accidents Occurring During Use of Premises and Equipment for Other Than School Purposes," 37 A.L.R.3d 712 (1971); Annot., "Tort Liability of Public Schools and Institutions of Higher Learning for Injuries Due to Condition of Grounds, Walks, and Playgrounds," 37 A.L.R.3d 738 (1971); Annot., "Tort Liability of Public Schools and Institutions of Higher Learning for Injuries Resulting from Lack or Insufficiency of Supervision," 38 A.L.R.3d 830 (1971); Annot., "Tort Liability of Private Schools and Institutions of Higher Learning for Negligence of, or Lack of Supervision by, Teachers and Other Employees or Agents," 38 A.L.R.3d 908 (1971). All annotations are supplemented periodically with recent cases.

[2]The cases and authorities are collected in Annot., "Modern Status of Doctrine of Sovereign Immunity As Applied to Public Schools and Institutions of Higher Learning," 33 A.L.R.3d 703 (1970 and periodic supp.).

P.2d 1015 (1976), the university faced both tort and contract claims for damages arising from the crash of an airplane carrying the university's football team. In Kansas, the university's home state, the common law doctrine of immunity had been partly abrogated by judicial decision in 1969, the court holding that the state and its agencies could be liable for negligence in the conduct of "proprietary" (as opposed to "governmental") activities. But in 1970, the Kansas legislature had passed a statute reinstituting the immunity abrogated by the court. The university in *Brown* relied on this statute to assert sovereign immunity to the tort claim. The court rejected plaintiffs' arguments that the statute was unconstitutional and allowed the university to assert the immunity defense.

Although private institutions can make no claim to sovereign immunity, nonprofit schools may sometimes be able to assert a limited "charitable" immunity defense to certain tort actions.[3] The availability of this defense also varies considerably from state to state. Overall, the charitable immunity defense appears to be more limited and less recognized than sovereign immunity. In a leading precedent, *President and Directors of Georgetown College* v. *Hughes,* 76 App. D.C. 123, 130 F.2d 810 (1942), the court struck a common note by heavily criticizing charitable immunity and refusing to apply it to a tort suit brought by a special nurse injured on the premises of the college's hospital.

When the postsecondary institution is not immune from negligence suits under either sovereign or charitable immunity, legal liability depends initially on whether the institution owed a duty to the injured party to exercise care to avoid injury. The existence of a legal duty may depend on a variety of factors, among the most important being the status of and relationship between the injured party and the institution. In *Lumbard* v. *Fireman's Fund Insurance Company,* 302 So.2d 394 (Ct. App. La. 1974), the duty was found to depend on the plaintiff's status while on the institution's property. The plaintiff was a student going to a class held on the second floor of a Southern University building. When

---

[3]The cases and authorities are collected in Annot., "Immunity of Private Schools and Institutions of Higher Learning from Liability in Tort," 38 A.L.R.3d 480 (1971 and periodic supp.). *See generally* Note, "The Doctrine of Charitable Immunity: The Persistent Vigil of Outdated Law," 4 *U. Baltimore L. Rev.* 125 (1975).

the student reached the second floor, she noticed it was slippery but continued to walk the fifteen feet to her classroom. The student slipped and fell, injuring her back. The slipperiness was caused by an excess amount of oil which janitors had placed on the floors. In holding the university liable, the court determined that the plaintiff was an "invitee" on the university's property, as opposed to a trespasser, and applied the general tort law principle "that the owner of property owes to invitees . . . the duty of exercising reasonable care to keep the premises in a safe condition, or of warning invitees of hidden or concealed perils of which he knows or should have known in the exercise of reasonable care."

Once a legal duty is found to exist, the next question is what standard of care the defendant will be held to under the circumstances. This issue was considered in *Mortiboys* v. *St. Michael's College,* 478 F.2d 196 (2d Cir. 1973). A student sued the institution for injuries sustained while skating on an outdoor ice rink maintained by the college for student pleasure skating. The student had fallen when his skate hit a one-inch-high lump of ice. The court refused to hold the college liable and articulated the standard of care owed by the college as "reasonable care under all the circumstances." For the college to be held liable, the dangerous condition would either have to be "known . . . or have existed for such a time that it was [the college's] duty to know it." The court concluded that it was "a matter of speculation what caused the lump to be formed and whether it had been there for any substantial length of time." Expensive maintenance equipment which would be used for indoor intercollegiate hockey rinks "cannot reasonably be required of a college providing an outdoor rink for the kind of use contemplated and to which this rink was actually being put at the time of the accident."

Before the postsecondary institution will be found negligent, the plaintiff must be able to prove that the institution's breach of duty was the proximate cause of the injury. In *Mintz* v. *State,* 362 N.Y.S.2d 619 (App. Div. 1975), the State University at New Paltz was found not liable for the deaths of two students who drowned on a canoe trip sponsored by an outing club. The court held that "it was the terrible, severe, and unforeseen weather conditions on the lake, and not any negligence on the part of the University, which were the proximate cause of the deaths herein."

Even when the plaintiff establishes all of the elements for a prima facie case of negligence, the postsecondary institution may avoid liability by asserting and proving the defense of "contributory negligence" by the plaintiff or of the "assumption of the risk" of injury by the plaintiff.

While failing to find the plaintiff contributorily negligent, the court in the *Lumbard* case, discussed earlier in this section, acknowledged the acceptability of such a defense. The court said that it is "generally accepted that the invitee in a slip and fall case is under a duty to see dangers which are obvious and can be detected and avoided by the degree of care exercised by a reasonably prudent person." Under the facts presented, however, "it was not unreasonable for plaintiff to traverse the slippery floor after she discovered its slippery condition for only a few feet."

Liability will not be imposed where the plaintiff is found to have assumed the risk of the injury which occurred. This "assumption of risk" doctrine was applied in *Rubtchinsky* v. *State University of New York*, 260 N.Y.S.2d 256 (Ct. Claims, 1965), where a student was injured in a pushball game between freshmen and sophomores conducted by the student association as part of an orientation program. The court found that the student voluntarily assumed the risks of the game, since the student, who was offered various orientation activities, chose to play pushball.

The second typical tort asserted against a postsecondary institution, defamation, is committed by the oral or written publication of matter that tends to injure a person's reputation. The matter must have been published to some third person and must have been capable of defamatory meaning and understood as referring to the plaintiff in a defamatory sense. (See Sections 4.9.4 and 4.9.5 for a further discussion of defamation.)

One of the most important defenses against a defamation action is the conditional privilege of fair comment and criticism. An application of this privilege occurred in *Greenya* v. *George Washington University*, 512 F.2d 556 (D.C. Cir. 1975). A part-time off-campus instructor with George Washington University brought suit against the university alleging a common law claim of defamation. The alleged defamatory statement was a comment written on an index card in the office of academic staffing stating, "Do not staff." The plaintiff claimed that "the phrase carries an innuendo of either incompetence or dishonesty." The court applied general tort law and found the following:

> It is well accepted that officers and faculty members of educational organizations enjoy a qualified privilege to discuss the qualifications and character of fellow officers and faculty members if the matter communicated is pertinent to the functioning of the educational institution. . . . Concomitantly we believe the privilege extends to internal records in which such matters are discussed or recorded. For a plaintiff to overcome the privilege he must prove the publication occurred outside normal channels or that the normal manner of handling such information resulted in an unreasonable degree of publication in light of the purposes of the privilege or that publication was made with malicious intent.

Another conditional privilege that is important for administrators in state institutions is the privilege afforded to executive and administrative officers of government. In *Shearer* v. *Lambert*, 547 P.2d 98 (Ore. 1976), an assistant professor at Oregon State University brought a libel action against the head of her department. While admitting that the statement was defamatory, the defendant argued that the privilege of government officers should be extended to lesser executive or administrative officers such as the head of a department. The court agreed, reasoning that, since "the privilege is designed to free public officials from intimidation in the discharge of their duties, we are unable to explain why this policy would not apply equally to inferior as well as to high-ranking officers." This qualified privilege is available, however, only where the defendant "publishes the defamatory matter in the performance of his official duties."

There is also a constitutional privilege based on the First Amendment which is sometimes assertable as a defense in a defamation action (Section 4.9.4). Under this privilege, certain defamations of "public figures" are considered to be protected speech under the First Amendment. While it appears that the personnel of postsecondary institutions could sometimes attain the status of "public figures" such that an institution could assert the constitutional privilege against them, this issue is still unsettled in the law.

Thus, a postsecondary institution is not subject to liability for every tortious act of its trustees, administrators, or other agents. But the institution will generally be liable, lacking immunity, for tortious acts which are committed within the scope of the actor's employment or which are otherwise authorized by the institution or subject to its control. In the *Lumbard* case discussed in this section, for instance, the institution was liable for the acts of its janitors committed in the course of their building maintenance duties. And in *Butler* v. *Louisiana State Board of Education*, 331 So.2d 192 (La. 1976), after finding that a professor had been negligent in allowing a biology experiment to be conducted without appropriate safeguards, the court asserted that the professor's "negligence must be attributed to the defendant university and to the State Board of Education."

In some circumstances a postsecondary institution may also be liable for the acts of its student organizations. In *Wallace* v. *Weiss*, 372 N.Y.S.2d 416 (Sup. Ct. 1975), a libel action based on material printed in a student publication, the University of Rochester moved for judgment in its favor on the ground that it was not responsible for the acts of a student organization. The court denied the motion because "the question of the University's responsibility should not be determined until all the facts are presented at the trial." According to this court:

> [A university] may be in a position to take precautions against the publication of libelous matter in its student publications. . . .
> The university, by furnishing and providing to the organization money, space and in lending its name, may well be responsible for the acts of the organization at least insofar as the University has the power to exercise control. By assisting the organization in its activities, it cannot avoid responsibility by refusing to exercise control or by delegating that control to another student organization [372 N.Y.S.2d at 422].

Various techniques are available to postsecondary institutions for managing the risks of tort liability, as discussed in Section 2.5.

2.3.2. Institutional contract liability. The institution may be characterized as a "principal" and its trustees, administrators, and other employees as "agents" for purposes of discussing the potential liability of each on contracts which an agent transacts for, or on behalf of, the institution. The fact that an agent acts with the principal in mind does not necessarily excuse the agent from personal liability (see Section 2.4.2), nor does it automatically make the principal liable. The key to the institution's liability is authorization, that is, that the institution either authorized the agent's action before it occurred or subsequently ratified it. However, even when an agent's acts were properly authorized, an institution may be able to escape liability by raising a legally recognized defense, such as sovereign immunity.

Although the principles of agency law generally apply to both public and private institutions, for one purpose it is important to distinguish the two. A public institution may have more defenses against liability than a private institution in the same state. The primary example is the sovereign immunity defense. As with tort liability (see Section 2.3.1), the existence and scope of sovereign immunity from contract liability varies from state to state. In *Charles E. Brohawn & Bros., Inc.* v. *Board of Trustees of Chesapeake College*, 304 A.2d 819 (Md. 1973), the court recognized a very broad immunity defense. The plaintiffs had sued the board to compel them to pay the agreed upon price for work and materials provided under the contract, including the construction of buildings for the college. In considering the college's defense the court reasoned:

> The doctrine of sovereign immunity exists under the common law of Maryland. By this doctrine, a litigant is precluded from asserting an otherwise meritorious cause of action against this sovereign State or one of its agencies which has inherited its sovereign attributes, unless expressly waived by statute or by a necessary inference from such a legislative enactment. . . . The doctrine of sovereign immunity or, as it is often alternatively referred to, governmental immunity was before this Court in *University of Maryland* v. *Maas*, 173 Md. 554, 197 A. 123 (1938), where our predecessors reversed a judgment recovered against the University for breach of contract in connection with the construction of a dormitory at College Park. That opinion, after extensively reviewing the prior decisions of this Court,

succinctly summed up their holdings by stating: "So it is established' that neither in contract nor tort can a suit be maintained against a governmental agency, first, where specific legislative authority has not been given, second, even though such authority is given, if there are no funds available for the satisfaction of the judgment, or no power reposed in the agency for the raising of funds necessary to satisfy a recovery against it." *Id.* at 559, 197 A. at 125 [304 A.2d at 820 (notes and citations omitted)].

Finding that the cloak of the sovereign's immunity was inherited by the community college and had not been waived, the court rejected the plaintiff's contract claim.

Regarding contract liability, there is little distinction to be made among trustees, administrators, employees, and other agents of the institution. Whether the actor is a member of the board of trustees or its equivalent, the president, the athletic director, the dean of arts and sciences, or some other functionary, the critical question is whether his action was authorized by the institution.

The issue of authorization can become very complex. In *Brown* v. *Wichita State University*, 217 Kan. 279, 540 P.2d 66 (1975),[4] the court discussed the issue at length:

To determine whether the record establishes an agency by agreement, it must be examined to ascertain if the party sought to be charged as principal had delegated authority to the alleged agent by words which expressly authorize the agent to do the delegated act. If there is evidence of that character, the authority of the agent is express. If no express authorization is found, then the evidence must be considered to determine whether the alleged agent possesses implied powers. The test utilized by this court to determine if the alleged agent possesses implied powers is whether, from the facts and circumstances of the particular case, it appears there was an implied intention to create an agency, in which event the relation may be held to exist, notwithstanding either a

[4]This decision reverses and remands a summary judgment in favor of the university by the lower court. Similar action taken with regard to a summary judgment for the Physical Education Corporation is reported at 538 P.2d 713 (1975). See also 547 P.2d 1015 (1976). The tort liability aspects of the case are discussed in Section 2.3.1.

denial by the alleged principal, or whether the parties understood it to be an agency.

"On the question of implied agency, it is the manifestation of the alleged principal and agent as between themselves that is decisive, and not the appearance to a third party or what the third party should have known. An agency will not be inferred because a third person assumed that it existed, or because the alleged agent assumed to act as such, or because the conditions and circumstances were such as to make such an agency seem natural and probable and to the advantage of the supposed principal, or from facts which show that the alleged agent was a mere instrumentality" [quoting *Corpus Juris Secundum,* a leading legal encyclopedia]. . . .

The doctrine of apparent or ostensible authority is predicated upon the theory of estoppel. An ostensible or apparent agent is one whom the principal has intentionally or by want of ordinary care induced and permitted third persons to believe to be his agent even though no authority, either express or implied, has been conferred upon him.

Ratification is the adoption or confirmation by a principal of an act performed on his behalf by an agent which act was performed without authority. The doctrine of ratification is based upon the assumption there has been no prior authority, and ratification by the principal of the agent's unauthorized act is equivalent to an original grant of authority. Upon acquiring knowledge of his agent's unauthorized act, the principal should promptly repudiate the act, otherwise it will be presumed he has ratified and affirmed the act. Knowledge of the unauthorized act is essential for the principal to ratify the act, and must be shown or facts proved that its existence is a necessary inference therefrom [540 P.2d at 74–75].

As mentioned in Section 2.3.1, the *Brown* case arose after the crash of a plane carrying the Wichita State football team. The survivors and personal representatives of the deceased passengers sued Wichita State University (W.S.U.) and the Physical Education Corporation (P.E.C.) at the school for breaching their Aviation Service Agreement by failing to provide passenger liability insurance for the football team and other passengers. The plaintiffs claimed they were third-party beneficiaries of the Service Agreement entered into by W.S.U., the P.E.C., and the aviation company. The Service Agreement was signed by the athletic director of W.S.U. and by an agent of the Aviation Company. The university asserted that it did not have the authority to enter the agreement without the board of regents' approval, which it did not have; that it did not grant the athletic director the authority to enter the agreement on its behalf; that the athletic director only had authority to act as the agent of the P.E.C.; that W.S.U. could not ratify the agreement because it lacked authority to enter it initially; and that as a state agency, it could not be estopped from denying the validity of the agreement.

The court held that the P.E.C. was the agent of the university and that the athletic director, "as an officer of the corporate agent [P.E.C.], had the implied power and authority to bind the principal—Wichita State University." The court further held that failure to obtain the board of regents' approval did not invalidate the contract:

> The Legislature has delegated to the Board of Regents the authority to control, operate, manage, and supervise the universities and colleges of this state. For such control, operation, management, or supervision, the Board of Regents may make contracts and adopt orders, policies, or rules and regulations and do or perform such other acts as are authorized by law or are appropriate for such purposes. (K.S.A. 1974 Supp. 76-712.) . . . However, no policy, rule, or regulation of the Board of Regents has been cited or furnished to this court regarding contract matters, and none can be found in the Kansas Administrative Regulations. . . . [A]bsent any such rules or regulations, Wichita State cannot use the statute to deny the validity of the Aviation Service Agreement following execution and partial performance. Common honesty forbids repudiation now.[5]

The fact that the agreement had been partly performed was particularly persuasive to the court:

[5]Not all courts will be so willing to find institutional authority in cases concerning public institutions. Other courts in other circumstances may assert that a person who deals with a public institution "does so at his peril," as in *First Equity Corp.* v. *Utah State University*, 544 P.2d 887 (Utah 1975), where the court upheld the university's refusal to pay for stocks ordered by one of its employees.

Today, the use of separate corporate entities in collegiate athletics appears to be common, perhaps wide-
spread, but indeed shadowy as to involvement and responsibility. Whether such arrangements should continue is not a
question for this court. But when the involvement is such as
presented in the instant case, then it begs logic to hold no
agency relations exist, and that the principles thereof do not
apply. Performance under the contract had begun and payments made; this constituted tacit, effective approval of the
Aviation Agreement Contract.

Besides asserting that the purported agent lacked authority
or that the institution lacked authority in its own right, an
institution sued on a contract can raise defenses arising from the
contract itself or from some circumstance unique to the institution.
Defenses that arise from the contract include the other party's
fraud, the other party's breach of the contract, and the absence of
one of the requisite elements (offer, acceptance, consideration) in
the formation of a contract (see J. Calamari and J. Perillo, *The
Law of Contracts* (West, 1970)). Defenses unique to the institution
may include a counterclaim against the other party, the other
party's previous collection of damages from the agent, or, for
public institutions, the sovereign immunity defense discussed
earlier. Even if one of these defenses is successfully asserted, as
where the agent or institution lacked authority or a contract
element was absent, a private institution may be held liable for
any benefit which it received as a result of the other party's
performance. But public institutions may sometimes not even be
required to pay for benefits received under such circumstances.

The variety of contract and agency law principles that may
bear on contract liability makes the area a complex one, calling for
frequent involvement of legal counsel. The postsecondary institution's main concern in managing liability should be the delineation of the contracting authority of each of its agents. By carefully
defining such authority, and by repudiating any unauthorized
contracts of which they become aware, postsecondary administrators can protect the institution from unwanted liability. While
protection may also be found in other defenses to contract actions,
such as sovereign immunity, advance planning of authority is the

surest way to limit contract liability and the fairest to the parties with whom the institution's agents may deal.

2.3.3. Institutional federal civil rights liability. The tort and contract liabilities of postsecondary institutions (see Sections 2.3.1 and 2.3.2) are based in state law and, for the most part, are relatively well settled. The institution's potential civil rights liability, in contrast, is primarily a matter of federal law, which is undergoing a complex and uncertain evolutionary development.[6] The key statute is 42 U.S.C. sec. 1983, commonly known as "Section 1983":

> Every person who, under color of any statute, ordinance, regulation, custom, or usage, of any State or Territory, subjects, or causes to be subjected, any citizen of the United States or other persons within the jurisdiction thereof to the deprivation of any rights, privileges, or immunities secured by the Constitution and laws, shall be liable to the person injured in an action at law, suit in equity, or other proper proceedings for redress.

Section 1983's coverage is limited in two major ways. First, it imposes liability only for actions carried out "under color of" state law, custom, or usage. Under this language, the statute applies only to actions attributable to the state in much the same way that, under the state action doctrine (see Section 1.4.2), the U.S. Constitution applies only to actions attributable to the state. While public institutions clearly meet this statutory test, private postsecondary institutions cannot be subjected to Section 1983 liability unless the action complained of was so connected with the state that it can be said to have been done under color of state law, custom, or usage.

Second, Section 1983 imposes liability only on a "person"— a term not defined in the statute. Thus Section 1983's application to postsecondary institutions also depends on whether the particular institution being sued is considered to be a person, as the courts

[6]Legal analyses of the various federal civil rights laws and extensive citations to important cases can be found in C. Antieau, *Federal Civil Right Acts* (Lawyers' Cooperative, 1971 and periodic supp.).

construe that term. Although private institutions would usually meet this test because they are corporations, which are considered to be legal persons under state law, most private institutions would be excluded from Section 1983 anyway under the color-of-law test. Thus the crucial coverage question under Section 1983 is one that primarily concerns administrators of public institutions: Is a public postsecondary institution a person for purposes of Section 1983 and thus subject to civil rights liability under that statute?

To date the courts have not provided a clear answer to this question. While the U.S. Supreme Court has held that certain "political subdivisions" of the state (such as a county in *Moor* v. *County of Alameda*, 411 U.S. 693 (1973)) are not Section 1983 persons, it has not yet addressed how these precedents apply to public postsecondary institutions. In the absence of Supreme Court guidance, lower federal courts have developed a variety of analytical approaches to the question. In effect, the characterization of a public postsecondary institution as a Section 1983 person has depended on its characterization under state law; and the courts differ markedly in the terminology and concepts they use in making the state-law characterization.

In *Samuel* v. *University of Pittsburgh*, 375 F. Supp. 1119 (W.D. Pa. 1974), the court reasoned that "state instrumentalities" could not be persons under Section 1983, but then found that Pitt, Temple, and Penn State were all Section 1983 persons because they were not sufficiently under the control of the state to be considered state instrumentalities. In *Roseman* v. *Hassler*, 382 F. Supp. 1328 (W.D. Pa. 1974), reversed on other grounds, 520 F.2d 1364 (3rd Cir. 1975), the court found that Indiana University of Pennsylvania was not a Section 1983 person because it was a subdivision of the state department of education rather than a separately chartered corporation. In *Marin* v. *University of Puerto Rico*, 377 F. Supp. 613 (D.P.R. 1973), the court reasoned that a "political subdivision" of the state was not a Section 1983 person, but then held that the defendant university was a person because it was not a political subdivision but rather "a public corporation of the Commonwealth of Puerto Rico with statewide impact, under the control and budget of the Commonwealth of Puerto Rico." In *Stebbins* v. *Weaver*, 396 F. Supp. 104 (W.D. Wisc. 1975) affirmed, 537 F.2d 939

(7th Cir. 1976), the court identified the university's board of regents as a "state agency," as distinguished from a "political subdivision," and held that the board was thus a Section 1983 person. In *Anthony* v. *Cleveland*, 355 F. Supp. 789 (D.Hawaii 1973), the court also found the university to be a state agency, but then held that it was *not* a Section 1983 person because agencies of the state should be treated the same as political subdivisions of the state, which are not persons.[7]

To add to the confusion, state institutions are sometimes immune from suit in federal courts under Article III and the Eleventh Amendment of the federal Constitution. Thus, even if a state postsecondary institution is determined to be a person for Section 1983 purposes, it will still not be suable in federal court in certain kinds of cases. When the lawsuit is one requesting damages or other monetary relief, and the money would come from funds of the state if a judgment were entered against the institution, the institution will be immune from federal court suit unless the state has expressly or implicitly consented to such suit. Many courts focus on the university's charter or other legislative authority establishing the university to determine whether the state has consented. In *Soni* v. *Board of Trustees of University of Tennessee*, 513 F.2d 347 (6th Cir. 1975), the court held that a clause in the university's charter authorizing it to sue and be sued "in any court of law or equity" constituted consent to suit in federal court and was thus a waiver of constitutional immunity. But in *Martin* v. *University of Louisville*, 541 F.2d 1171 (6th Cir. 1976), the court held that a charter provision authorizing the institution to sue and be sued "in its corporate name" was not an implied waiver of constitutional immunity. Whether a particular institution is immune from suit may also depend on the strength of its ties to the state. Thus, in *Gerdenstein* v. *University of Delaware* 381, F. Supp. 718 (D. Del. 1974), the court held that whether the university is so closely related to the state that it shares its immunity depends on

[7]A U.S. Supreme Court case (decided after this book went to press) substantially affects the analysis in these cases. *Monell* v. *Dept. of Social Services*, 98 S. Ct. 2018 (1978), overrules the decisions that political subdivisions are not Section 1983 persons (see page 68) and holds that local school boards and other local governments *are* Section 1983 persons.

the extent to which a judgment against it would burden the state treasury.

Special immunity problems may exist when a community college is sued. Community colleges may be established under the authority of local political subdivisions of the state, such as a county, city, or community college district. The Eleventh Amendment does not apply to such political subdivisions of the state. The community colleges which establish these subdivisions therefore would not share the state's constitutional immunity from federal court suit. (See *Hander* v. *San Joaquin Junior College*, 519 F.2d 273 (5th Cir. 1975).) Under Section 1983, however, creation by a political subdivision has the opposite effect on a community college's suability. Since political subdivisions are not "persons" for Section 1983 purposes, community colleges created by such subdivisions are beyond Section 1983's reach.[8]

Although there is much confusion in the law regarding the Section 1983 liability of public institutions, and although the Constitution protects public institutions from some federal court suits under Section 1983 and other civil rights laws, administrators should not read these circumstances as justification for assigning lower priority to civil rights matters on campus. Even if the courts ultimately determine that they are not Section 1983 persons, public institutions are still suable under some other civil rights laws (see, for example, Section 3.3.2) and may be suable directly under the U.S. Constitution, without the aid of Section 1983, on constitutional claims (such as equal protection) that would fall within Section 1983 if public institutions were persons. See generally Bodensteiner, "Federal Court Jurisdiction of Suits Against 'Nonpersons' for Deprivation of Constitutional Right," 8 *Valparaiso L. Rev.* 215 (1974). Moreover, trustees and administrators of public institutions are sometimes suable in their individual capacities under Section 1983 even where the institution could not be sued. (See Section 2.4.3.) The constitutional immunity under Article III and the Eleventh Amendment will not protect institutions from

[8]See note 7 above. Under *Monell*, community colleges established by political subdivisions apparently would be Section 1983 persons.

such suits in federal courts where the plaintiffs seek injunctive relief or other relief which would not require a monetary award from state funds.

Even if such risks of civil rights liability did not exist for public institutions, social and humanitarian considerations likely would prompt administrators to continue to give a high priority to the protection of civil rights on campus. Much the same point can be made regarding private institutions, which, though largely immune from civil rights liability because they do not meet state action or color-of-law tests, probably will still want to emphasize such protection of civil rights.

Sec. 2.4. Personal Liability of Trustees, Administrators and Other Agents

2.4.1. Personal tort liability. A trustee, administrator, or other agent of a postsecondary institution may be liable for his torts even if they are committed while conducting the institution's affairs. The individual must actually have committed the tortious act, directed it, or otherwise participated in its commission, however, before personal liability will attach. He will not be personally liable for torts of other institutional agents merely because he represents the institution for whom the other agents were acting. The elements of a tort and the defenses against a tort claim (see Section 2.3.1) in suits against the individual personally are generally the same as those in suits against the institution. An individual sued in his personal capacity, however, is usually not shielded by the sovereign immunity and charitable immunity defenses which sometimes protect the institution (Section 2.3.1).

If a trustee, administrator, or other institutional agent commits a tort while acting on behalf of the institution and within the scope of the authority delegated to him, both he and the institution may be liable for the harm caused by the tort (Section 2.3.1). But the institution's potential liability does not relieve the individual of any measure of liability; the injured party could choose to collect a judgment solely from the individual, and the individual would have no claim against the institution for any part of the judgment which he was required to pay. However, where individual and institution are both potentially liable, the individual may receive practical relief from liability if the injured party squeezes the entire judgment from the institution or the institution chooses to pay the entire amount.

If a trustee, administrator, or other institutional agent commits a tort while acting outside the scope of authority delegated to her, she may be personally liable but the institution would not be liable (Section 2.3.1). Thus the injured party could obtain a judgment only against the individual, and only the individual would be responsible for satisfying the judgment. The institution, however, may affirm the individual's unauthorized action ("affirmance" is similar to the "ratification" discussed in connection with contract liability in Section 2.3.2), in which case the individual will be deemed to have acted within her authority, and both institution and individual will be potentially liable.

Officers and employees of public institutions can sometimes escape tort liability by proving the defense of "official immunity." For this defense to apply, the individual's act must have been within the scope of his authority and must have been a discretionary act involving policy judgment. Because it involves this element of discretion and policy judgment, official immunity is more likely to apply to a particular individual the higher in the authority hierarchy he is.

In *Tarasoff* v. *The Regents of the University of California,* 551 P.2d 334 (Cal. 1976), the parents of a girl murdered by a psychiatric patient at the university hospital sued the university regents, four psychotherapists employed by the hospital, and the campus police. The patient had confided his intention to kill the daughter to a staff psychotherapist. Though the patient was briefly detained by the campus police at the psychotherapist's request, no further action was taken to protect the daughter. The parents alleged that this constituted a tortious failure to confine a dangerous patient and a tortious failure to warn them or their daughter of a dangerous patient. The psychotherapists and campus police claimed official immunity under a California statute freeing "public employee(s)" from liability for acts or omissions which result from "the exercise of discretion vested in [them]" (Calif.

Gov't Code sec. 820.2). The court accepted the official immunity defense in relation to the failure to confine, because that failure involved a "basic policy decision" sufficient to constitute discretion under the statute. But regarding the failure to warn, the court refused to accept the psychotherapists' official immunity claim because the decision whether to warn was not a basic policy decision. The campus police needed no official immunity from their failure to warn, because the court held that they had no legal duty (see Section 2.3.1) to warn in light of the facts in the complaint.

The official immunity defense is not available to officers and employees of private institutions. But it appears that at least the trustees of private nonprofit institutions will be leniently treated by some courts out of deference to the trustees' special discretionary functions. (See Porth, "Personal Liability of Trustees of Higher Educational Institutions," 2 *J. of College and University Law* 143 (1975).) As a result, the personal liability of such trustees may be limited in a way somewhat akin to the official immunity limitation available to officers and employees of public institutions.

Institutions should consider whether or not they wish to protect their personnel from the financial consequences of personal tort liability. Insurance coverage and indemnity agreements, discussed in Section 2.5.2, may be utilized for this purpose.

2.4.2. Personal contract liability. A trustee, administrator, or other agent who signs a contract on behalf of an institution may be personally liable for its performance if the institution breaches. The extent of personal liability depends on whether his participation on behalf of the institution was authorized—either by a grant of express authority, an implied authority, an apparent authority, or a subsequent ratification by the institution. (See the discussion of authority in Section 2.3.2.) If the individual's participation was properly authorized, and if he signed the contract only in the capacity of an institutional agent, he will not be personally liable for performance of the contract. If, however, the individual's participation was not properly authorized, or if he signed in an individual capacity rather than as an institutional agent, he may be personally liable.

In some cases, the other contracting party may be able to sue both the institution and the agent or to choose between them. This option is presented when the contracting party did not know at the time of contracting that the individual participated in an agency capacity, but later learns that was the case. The option is also presented when the contracting party knows that the individual is acting as an institutional agent, but the individual also gives a personal promise that the contract will be performed. In such situations, if the contracting party obtains a judgment against both the institution and the agent, the judgment may be satisfied against either or against both, but the contracting party may receive no more than the total amount of the judgment. Where the contracting party satisfies the judgment against only one of the two liable parties, the paying party may have a claim against the nonpayor for part of the judgment amount.

If the agent is a party to the contract in his personal capacity and thus potentially liable on it, he can assert the same defenses that are available to any contracting party. These defenses may arise from the contract—such as the absence of some formality necessary to complete the contract or fraud or inadequate performance by the other party—or may be personal to the agent, such as a particular counterclaim against the other party.

2.4.3. Personal federal civil rights liability. The federal civil rights liability of trustees, administrators, and other employees of postsecondary institutions is determined under the same body of law that determines the liability of the institutions themselves, and presents many of the same legal issues (see Section 2.3.3). As with institutional liability, an individual's action must usually be done "under color of" state law, or must be characterizable as "state action," before federal civil rights liability will attach. Like tort and contract liability, the civil rights liability of individual trustees, administrators, and other employees is not coterminous with the institution's liability. Defenses that may be available to the institution (such as the constitutional immunity defense) may not be available to individuals sued in their individual capacities; but conversely, defenses that may be available to individuals (such as the qualified immunity discussed later in this section) may not be available to the institution.

The federal statute referred to as Section 1983, quoted in

Section 2.3.3 of this chapter, is again the key civil rights statute. While the institution's status under that statute has not yet been resolved, an individual trustee, administrator, or employee is clearly a "person" under Section 1983 and thus subject to its provisions whenever one has acted under color of state law. But courts have long recognized a qualified immunity from Section 1983 liability for certain public officers and employees. In 1974 and again in 1975, the U.S. Supreme Court attempted to explain the scope of this immunity as it applies to school officials.

In *Scheuer* v. *Rhodes*, 416 U.S. 232 (1974), the Court considered a suit for damages brought on behalf of three students killed in the May 1970 disturbances at Kent State University. The Court rejected the contention that the president of Kent State and other state officials had an absolute "official immunity" protecting them from personal liability. The Court instead accorded the president and officials a "qualified immunity" under Section 1983:

> [I]n varying scope, a qualified immunity is available to officers of the executive branch of Government, the variation being dependent upon the scope of discretion and responsibilities of the office and all the circumstances as they reasonably appeared at the time of the action on which liability is sought to be based. It is the existence of reasonable grounds for the belief formed at the time and in light of all the circumstances, coupled with good-faith belief, that affords a basis for qualified immunity of executive officers for acts performed in the course of official conduct [416 U.S. at 247–48].

Because the availability of this immunity depended on facts not yet in the record, the Supreme Court remanded the case to the trial court for further proceedings.

In *Wood* v. *Strickland*, 420 U.S. 308 (1975), the Supreme Court extended, and added enigma to, its discussion of Section 1983 immunity in the institutional context. After the school board in this case had expelled some students from high school for violating a school disciplinary regulation, several of them sued the members of the school board. In a controversial decision with strong dissents, the Court held that school board members, as public school officials, are entitled to a qualified immunity from such suits:

Liability for damages for every action which is found subsequently to have been violative of a student's constitutional rights and to have caused compensable injury would unfairly impose upon the school decision-maker the burden of mistakes made in good faith in the course of exercising his discretion within the scope of his official duties. . . . The imposition of monetary costs for mistakes which were not unreasonable in the light of all the circumstances would undoubtedly deter even the most conscientious school decisionmaker from exercising his judgment independently, forcefully, and in a manner best serving the long-range interest of the school and the students. . . .

But at the same time, the judgment implicit in this common-law development is that absolute immunity would not be justified since it would not sufficiently increase the ability of school officials to exercise their discretion in a forthright manner to warrant the absence of a remedy for students subjected to intentional or otherwise inexcusable deprivations. . . .

We think there must be a degree of immunity if the work of the schools is to go forward; and, however worded, the immunity must be such that public school officials understand that action taken in the good-faith fulfillment of their responsibilities and within the bounds of reason under all the circumstances will not be punished and that they need not exercise their discretion with undue timidity. . . .

The official must himself be acting sincerely and with a belief that he is doing right, but an act violating a student's constitutional rights can be no more justified by *ignorance or disregard of settled, indisputable law* on the part of one entrusted with supervision of students' daily lives than by the presence of actual malice. To be entitled to a special exemption from the categorical remedial language of §1983 in a case in which his action violated a student's constitutional rights, a school board member, who has voluntarily undertaken the task of supervising the operation of the school and the activities of the students, must be held to a standard of conduct based not only on permissible intentions, but also on *knowledge of the basic, unquestioned constitutional rights* of his charges. Such a standard neither imposes an unfair burden upon a person assuming a responsible public office requiring a high degree of intelligence and judgment for the proper fulfillment of its duties, nor an unwarranted burden in light of the value which civil rights have in our legal system. Any lesser standard would deny much of the promise of §1983. Therefore, in the specific context of school discipline, we hold that a school board member *is not immune from liability for damages under §1983 if he knew or reasonably should have known that the action he took within his sphere of official responsibility would violate the constitutional rights of the student affected, or if he took the action with the malicious intention to cause a deprivation of constitutional rights or other injury to the student.* That is not to say that school board members are "charged with predicting the future course of constitutional law." *Pierson v. Ray,* 386 U.S. at 557. A compensatory award will be appropriate only if the school board member has acted with such an impermissible motivation or with such disregard of the student's clearly established constitutional rights that his action cannot reasonably be characterized as being in good faith [420 U.S. at 319-22 (emphasis added)].

The Court's reliance on the *Scheuer* case at several points in its *Wood* opinion suggests that the *Wood* liability standard will apply to public officials in postsecondary education as well. Clearly the qualified immunity would be available to trustees and executive heads of public postsecondary institutions. The immunity of lower-level administrators and faculty members is less clear, for as the Court noted in *Scheuer* and reaffirmed in *Wood,* the immunity's existence and application would depend in each case on the "scope of discretion and responsibilities of the office."

The availability of the immunity also depends—for administrators and faculty members as well as trustees and executive officers—on the good faith and reasonableness of the individual's action under all the particular circumstances of the case. A key consideration under *Wood* is whether the action violated "settled, indisputable law" or "basic, unquestioned constitutional rights" of which the individual was or should have been aware. In effect, the individual is charged with the responsibility for knowing such law or rights, and disregarding them is considered to be a bad-faith or unreasonable act outside the immunity's scope. Since it is debatable what law and rights are sufficiently settled to come within the Court's description, and since at any rate the immunity's availability depends on the facts of each case, administrators will find it difficult at best to predict what actions will fall under the immunity umbrella. The best bet for maximizing the immunity's availability to institutional personnel is to assure that they have sufficient access to legal counsel and enough information on elementary constitutional law to be generally knowledgeable of settled legal principles.[9]

Not only do institutional personnel have only limited immunity under Section 1983, but they also generally are not protected by the constitutional immunity that sometimes protects public institutions from suits in federal courts (see Section 2.3.3). In the *Scheuer* case (discussed earlier in this section), the Court also held that the president of Kent State was not immune from suit under the Constitution:

> [T]he Eleventh Amendment provides no shield for a state official confronted by a claim that he had deprived another of a federal right under the color of state law. . . . [W]hen a state officer acts under a state law in a manner violative of the Federal Constitution, he "comes into conflict with the superior authority of that Constitution, and he is in that case stripped of his official or representative character and is subjected *in his person* to the consequences of his individual conduct" [quoting *Ex Parte Young*, 209 U.S. 123, 159 (1908)] [416 U.S. at 237].

If a state university president has no immunity under the Constitution, it follows that trustees, lower-level administrators,

---

[9]When their actions cannot be brought within the scope of Section 1983 immunity, individuals may be liable for both compensatory and punitive damages under the statute. To collect compensatory damages, a plaintiff must normally prove "actual injury," tangible or intangible; the court normally will not presume that damage occurred from a violation of civil rights and will award compensatory damages only to the extent of injury proved. *Carey* v. *Piphus*, 98 S. Ct. 1042 (1978). To collect punitive damages, a plaintiff must prove that the defendant's action "' manifests a reckless indifference to the property rights of others, ill-will, a desire to injure, or malice'" (*Endress* v. *Brookdale Community College*, 364 A.2d 1080 (*N.J.* Super. 1976) (see Section 1.1), quoting *Silver* v. *Cormier*, 529 F.2d 161, 163 (10th Cir. 1976)).

and faculty members would have no immunity either. The *Scheuer* case notes one circumstance, however, under which such persons would enjoy the constitutional immunity: when they are sued only as titular parties in a suit that is actually seeking money damages from the state treasury. Only in this case would the suit be considered to be against the state itself and thus barred by the Eleventh Amendment.

The state of the law under Section 1983 and the Eleventh Amendment, taken together, gives administrators of public postsecondary institutions no cause to feel confident that either they or other institutional officers or employees are insulated from personal civil rights liability. To minimize the liability potential in this critical area of law and social responsibility, administrators should make legal counsel available to institutional personnel for consultation on civil rights matters, encourage review by counsel of institutional policies that may affect civil rights, and provide personnel with information or training on basic civil rights law. To absolve personnel of the financial drain of any liability that does occur, administrators may wish to consider the purchase of special insurance coverage or the development of indemnity plans. As discussed in Section 2.5.2, public policy in some states may limit the use of these techniques in the civil rights area.

Sec. 2.5. Institutional Management of Liability Risks[10]

The risk of financial liability for injury to another party has increased dramatically since the early sixties for postsecondary institutions as well as their governing board members and personnel. This section examines some methods for purposefully controlling the risks of such exposure to liability and thus minimizing the detrimental effect of liability on the institution and its personnel. Such risk management may be advisable not only because it helps stabilize the institution's financial condition over time but also because it can improve the morale and performance

---

[10]This section relies heavily on the 1976 monograph *Legal Liabilities in Higher Education: Their Scope and Management,* which is noted in the Selected Annotated Bibliography at the end of this chapter and cited occasionally in the text of this section.

of institutional personnel by alleviating their concerns about potential personal liability. In addition, risk management can implement the institution's humanistic concern for minimizing and compensating any potential injuries which its operations may cause to innocent third parties.

The major methods of risk management may be called risk avoidance, risk control, risk transfer, and risk retention.

2.5.1. Risk avoidance and risk control. The most certain method for managing a known exposure to liability is risk avoidance, that is, the elimination of the behavior, condition, or program which is the source of the risk. This method is often not realistic, however, since it could require institutions to forgo activities important to their educational missions. It might also require greater knowledge of the details of myriad campus activities than administrators typically can acquire and greater certainty regarding the legal principles of liability (see Section 2.3) than the law typically affords.

Risk control is less drastic than risk avoidance. The goal is to reduce, rather than eliminate entirely, the frequency or severity of potential exposures to liability. Risk control is generally accomplished by either improving the physical environment or modifying hazardous behavior or activities in ways that reduce the recognized risks. Although this method may have less impact on an institution's educational mission than risk avoidance, it may similarly require considerable detailed knowledge of campus facilities and functions and of legal liability principles.

2.5.2. Risk transfer. By purchasing commercial insurance or entering a "hold harmless" or "indemnification" agreement, an institution can transfer its own liability risks to another or transfer to itself the liability risks of its officers and other personnel. A commercial insurance policy shifts potential future financial losses (up to a maximum amount) to the insurance company in exchange for payment of a specified premium. The institution can insure against liability for its own acts, as well as liability assessed against it as the result of a "hold harmless" agreement which it makes with its personnel. With the advice of insurance experts, the institution can determine the kinds and amounts of liability protection it needs and provide for the necessary premium expenditures in its budgeting process.

Generally, liability insurance policies cover bodily injury and property damage which have been accidentally caused. Intentionally or maliciously caused damage and damage caused by acts which violate penal laws are usually excluded from coverage as being against public policy (see Section 2.5.4). Financial liability arising from the violation of an individual's constitutional or civil rights is also commonly excluded from standard insurance coverage—an exclusion which can pose considerable problems for administrators and institutions whose exposure to such liability has been greatly increasing in recent years. To effectively cover such risks, the institution may find it necessary to combine a standard policy with one or more specialty endorsements or companion policies. When even this arrangement does not provide coverage meeting the institution's needs, the institution may request a "manuscript" policy tailored to its specific needs. Such policies, however, are expensive.

A second method of risk transfer is a hold harmless or indemnification agreement. In a broad sense the term *indemnification* refers to any compensation for loss or damage. Insurance is thus one method of indemnifying someone. But in the narrow sense used here, an indemnification agreement refers to an arrangement whereby one party, for example the institution, agrees to "hold" another party, for example an individual officer or employee, "harmless" from financial liability for certain acts or omissions of that party which cause damage to another:

> In brief synopsis, the mechanism of a typical indemnification will shift to the institution the responsibility for defense and discharge of claims asserted against institutional personnel individually by reason of their acts or omissions on behalf of the institution, if the individual believed in good faith that his actions were lawful and within his institutional authority and responsibility. That standard of conduct is, of course, very broadly stated; and the question of whether or not it is satisfied must be determined on a case-by-case basis [R. Aiken, *Legal Liabilities in Higher Education: Their Scope and Manage-*

ment, Pt. I, p. 193 (Association of American Colleges, 1976)].

Although with respect to its own personnel the institution would typically be the "indemnitor," that is, the party with ultimate financial liability, the institution can sometimes also be an "indemnitee," the party protected from liability loss. The institution could negotiate for "hold harmless" protection for itself, for instance, in contracts it enters with outside contractors.

Like an insurance policy, an indemnification agreement often does not cover liability resulting from intentional or malicious action or from action violating the state's penal laws, because such actions are considered contrary to public policy. Just as public policy may limit the types of acts or omissions that may be insured against, it may also limit those for which indemnification may be received.

Both public and private institutions may enter indemnification agreements. A public institution, however, may need specific authorizing legislation (see, for example, Md. Ann. Code art. 77, sec. 10A), whereas private institutions usually can rely on the general laws of their states for sufficient authority. Some states provide for indemnification of all state employees for injuries caused by their acts or omissions on behalf of the state (see Wis. Stat. sec. 270.58).

2.5.3. Risk retention. The most practical option for the institution in some circumstances may be to retain the risk of financial liability. Adams and Hall note eight situations under which risk retention may be appropriate, including situations where commercial insurance is unavailable or too costly, the expected losses are so small that they can be considered normal operating expenses, or the probability of loss is so remote that it does not justify any insurance expense (J. F. Adams, J. W. Hall, *Legal Liabilities in Higher Education: Their Scope and Management,* Pt. II, pp. 241–242 (Association of American Colleges, 1976)). Both insurance policy deductibles and methods of self-insurance are examples of risk retention. The deductible amounts in an insurance policy allocate the first dollar coverage of liability, up to the amount of the deductible, to the institution. The institution becomes a self-insurer by maintaining a separate bank account to pay appropriate claims. The institution's risk managers must determine the amount to be available in the account and the frequency and amount of regular payments to the account. This approach is distinguished from simple noninsurance by the planning and actuarial calculations that it involves.

2.5.4. *Legal considerations.* An institution's ability to transfer risk is limited by the law to situations which do not contravene "public policy." When financial liability is incurred as a result of willful wrongdoing, it is generally considered contrary to public policy to protect the institution or individual from responsibility for such behavior through insurance or indemnity. Wrongdoing which is malicious, fraudulent, immoral, or criminal will often fall within this category; thus insurance companies may decline to cover such action, or provisions in insurance policies or indemnification agreements which do cover it may be void and unenforceable under state law. Common actions to which this public policy may apply include assault and battery, abuse of process, defamation, invasion of privacy, and deprivation of constitutional or civil rights. Institutions may have to manage the risk of such acts by avoiding or controlling it or through self-insurance. Similarly, institutions may be unable to transfer the risk of loss from punitive damages awards (awards designed to punish or deter the responsible party rather than to compensate the victim) because such awards are based on a type of willful wrongdoing for which the wrongdoer should remain personally responsible.

A different kind of legal problem may exist for postsecondary institutions that enjoy some degree of sovereign or charitable immunity from financial liability. (See Section 2.3.1.) For public institutions there may be some question whether they have the authority to purchase liability insurance covering acts within the scope of their immunity. Where such authority exists, and the institution does purchase insurance, the question is whether such circumstances affect the institution's sovereign or charitable immunity. Sometimes a statute authorizing insurance coverage may itself waive sovereign immunity to the extent of coverage. In *Shriver* v. *Athletic Council of Kansas State University,* 222 Kan. 216, 564 P.2d 456 (1977), for example, the court held that the defendant had authority to purchase liability insurance and that, under a Kansas statute, such purchase waived the defendant's sovereign immunity to the extent of policy coverage. When such a waiver is lacking, in most states the purchase of insurance appears not to affect immunity, and the insurance protection is operable only for acts found to be outside the scope of immunity. In some states, however, the law appears to treat the authorized purchase of insurance as a waiver or narrowing of the institution's immunity, to the extent of the insurance coverage.[11]

Selected Annotated Bibliography

Sec. 2.1 (The Question of Authority)

1. Hornby, D. B., "Delegating Authority to the Community of Scholars," 1975 *Duke L. J.* 279, provides excellent legal and policy analysis regarding delegations of authority within public systems of postsecondary education; considers constitutional and statutory delegations to both statewide governing boards and individual boards of trustees, and subdelegations of that authority to officials, employees, and other bodies within individual institutions; contains many useful citations to both legal and policy materials.
2. Seavey, W. A., *Agency* (West, 1964), provides a thorough explanation of the principles of agency law, with copious citations to cases; includes discussion of kinds of authority, estoppel, ratification, and tort and contract liabilities among principals, agents, and third parties.

Sec. 2.2 (Sources and Scope of Authority)

1. Berry, C. R., and Buchwald, G. J., "Enforcement of College Trustees' Fiduciary Duties: Students and the Problem of Standing," 9 *University of San Francisco L. Rev.* 1 (1974),

[11]Relevant cases are collected in Annot., "Liability or Indemnity Insurance Carried by Governmental Unit as Affecting Immunity from Tort Liability," 68 A.L.R.2d 1438 (1959 and periodic supp.); and Annot., "Immunity of Private Schools and Institutions of Higher Learning from Liability in Tort," 38 A.L.R.3d 480, 501–02 (1971 and periodic supp.).

discusses the history, present status and effectiveness, and future direction of the law regarding trustee responsibilities and potential liability, particularly with respect to university finances; emphasis on the question of who, besides the state attorney general, can sue to enforce fiduciary responsibilities.

2. Porth, W. C., "Personal Liability of Trustees of Educational Institutions," 1 *J. of College and University Law* 84 (1973) and 2 *J. of College and University Law* 143 (1974), collects and discusses the small number of cases on trustee liability and suggests approaches future courts may take to the problem; emphasis is on the *Sibley Hospital* case.

3. Weiler, J. J., "Fiduciary Provisions of the Employee Retirement Income Security Act of 1974," 36 *Louisiana L. Rev.* 897 (1976), discusses ERISA (see Sec. 7.2.3) provisions on fiduciary responsibilities, prohibited transactions, fiduciary liability, and delegation of investment responsibility.

4. Zwingle, J. L., and Mayville, W. V., *College Trustees: A Question of Legitimacy* (ERIC Clearinghouse on Higher Education, Research Rpt. No. 10, 1974), provides a policy-oriented discussion and a review of the literature on the structure, role, and functions of trustee boards; includes discussions of authority, delegation of authority, academic tenure, and collective bargaining.

Sec. 2.3 (Institutional Liability for Acts of Trustees, Administrators, and Other Agents)

1. Aiken, R., Adams, J., and Hall, J., *Legal Liabilities in Higher Education: Their Scope and Management* (Association of American Colleges, 1976), printed simultaneously in 3 *J. of College and University Law* 127 (1976), provides an in-depth examination of legal and policy issues of institutional liability and the problems of protecting institutions and their personnel against liability by insurance and risk management.

2. Clague, M. W., "Suing the University 'Black Box' Under the Civil Rights Act of 1871," 62 *Iowa L. Rev.* 337 (1976), considers the applicability of 42 U.S.C. sec. 1983 to postsecon-

dary institutions; focuses on the use of Section 1983 in suits against institutions or their governing boards, the impact of Eleventh Amendment immunity on such suits, and the possibilities for bringing such suits directly under the federal Constitution when Section 1983 is not applicable.
3. Prosser, W. L., *Handbook on the Law of Torts*, 4th ed. (West, 1971), is a comprehensive survey of tort doctrines and concepts, with discussion of leading cases and relevant statutes; includes discussion of sovereign and charitable immunity, defamation, negligence, and the contributory negligence and assumption of risk defenses.
4. See entry no. 2 for Section 2.1.

Sec. 2.4 (Personal Liability of Trustees, Administrators, and Other Agents)

1. Crandall, D., *The Personal Liability of Community College Officials* (ERIC Clearinghouse for Junior Colleges, Topical Paper No. 61, 1977), is a guide for administrators that "illustrates the kinds of actions taking place in the courts and provides useful background information on personal liability"; though written for community college administrators, useable by other postsecondary administrators as well.
2. See entry no. 2 for Section 2.2.
3. See entry no. 2 for Section 2.1.

Sec. 2.5 (Institutional Management of Liability Risks)

1. See entry no. 1 for Section 2.3.

Chapter III

⚜⚜⚜⚜⚜⚜⚜⚜⚜⚜⚜⚜

The College
and the Faculty

The legal relationship between a postsecondary educational institution and its faculty is defined by an increasingly complex web of principles and authorities. The core of the relationship is contract law (see especially Section 3.1), but that core is encircled by expanding layers of labor relations law (Section 3.2), employment discrimination law (Section 3.3), and, in public institutions, constitutional law (see especially Sections 3.5 and 3.6) and public employment statutes and regulations.

Sec. 3.1. The Contract of Employment

3.1.1. What constitutes the contract? It is not uncommon for faculty members and administrators to be unsure of the full scope of the faculty-institution contract. Depending on the institution, the contract may range from a brief notice of appointment, with the appropriate blanks filled in on a form, to a lengthy collective bargaining agreement negotiated under federal or state labor laws. Even in the latter situation, the formal writing does not necessarily encompass all the terms of the contract. Other terms from other documents may be included in the contract through "incorporation by reference," that is, by referring to other documents in a way which suggests that all or some of their terms are incorporated in the contract. Still other terms may be implied in the contract by reference to past custom and usage at the institution. Administrators should continually be sensitive to the question of what institutional documents or practices are, or should be, part of the faculty contract. Where ambiguity exists, administrators should determine whether there is some good policy reason for maintaining the ambiguity. If not, the contracts should be clarified.

A contract's meaning is ascertained primarily by reference to the express terms of the contract itself. Where the contract language is unambiguous, it will govern any factual situation to which it clearly applies. *Billmyre* v. *Sacred Heart Hospital of Sisters of Charity,* 331 A.2d 313 (Md. Ct. App. 1975) illustrates this principle of contract interpretation. A nurse was employed as a coordinator-instructor at the hospital's nursing school under a contract which specified that either the employer or the employee could terminate the contract "at the end of the school year by giving notice in writing to the other not later than May 1 of such school year." On May 18 the nurse received a letter terminating her employment as a teacher. The court held that the hospital had breached the contract since the contract language unambiguously provided for teacher notification before May 1 to effectuate a termination of the contract.

In some cases the contract language clearly refers to some other writing as being incorporated in the terms of employment. For a postsecondary institution, such typical documents as the faculty handbook, institutional bylaws, or guidelines of the American Association of University Professors (AAUP) may be referred to in the contract. The extent to which the terms of such outside writings become part of the faculty employment contract is discussed in *Brady* v. *Board of Trustees of Nebraska State Colleges,*

242 N.W.2d 616 (Neb. 1976), where a tenured professor at Wayne State College was employed under a contract which incorporated "the college bylaws, policies, and practices relating to academic tenure, and faculty dismissal procedures." When the institution dismissed the professor using procedures which violated a section of the bylaws, the court held that the termination was ineffective: "There can be no serious question but that the bylaws of the governing body with respect to termination and conditions of the employment became a part of the employment contract between the college and [the professor]. At the time of the offer and acceptance of initial appointment . . . [the professor] was advised in writing that the offer and acceptance . . . constituted a contract honoring the policies and practices set forth in the faculty handbook, which was furnished to him at that time."

Even where such outside documents are not specifically referred to in the contract language, the court, as in *Greene* v. *Howard University*, 412 F.2d 1128 (D.C. Cir. 1969), may look to outside writings to determine the customs and usual practices of the institution and interpret the contract in light of such custom and usage. The plaintiffs in *Greene* were five nontenured professors who had been fired after a university investigation purported to find that they had been involved in disorders on campus. When the university terminated the professors as of the close of the academic year, the professors asserted that the university had breached a contractual obligation to give appropriate advance notice of nonrenewal or to provide a hearing prior to nonrenewal. The court concluded that "The contractual relationships existing here, when viewed against the regulations provided for, and the practices customarily followed in, their administration, required the university in the special circumstances here involved to afford the teachers an opportunity to be heard."

The court derived the institution's customary practices from the faculty handbook, buttressed by testimony in court, even though the handbook was not specifically incorporated by reference and even though it stated that the university did not have a contractual obligation to follow the notice of nonreappointment procedures. The professors were found to be relying "not only on personal assurances from University officials and on their recognition of the common practice of the University, but also on the written statements of University policy contained in the Faculty Handbook under whose terms they were employed." The court reasoned:

> Contracts are written, and are to be read, by reference to the norms of conduct and expectations founded upon them. This is especially true of contracts in and among a community of scholars, which is what a university is. The readings of the market place are not invariably apt in this noncommercial context. . . .
>
> The employment contracts of [the professors] here comprehend as essential parts of themselves the hiring policies and practices of the University as embodied in its employment regulations and customs [412 F.2d at 1135].

Although academic custom and usage can fill in gaps in the employment contract, it cannot be used to contradict the contract's express terms. In *Lewis* v. *Salem Academy and College*, 208 S.E.2d 404 (N. Car. 1974), a professor had been employed from 1950 to 1973 under a series of successive one-year contracts. The college had renewed the contract the last two years even though the professor had reached age sixty-five, but did not renew the contract for the 1973–74 academic year. The professor argued that he had a right to continue teaching until seventy because that was a usual and customary practice of the college and an implied benefit used to attract and retain faculty. The college's faculty guide, however, which was incorporated in all faculty contracts, had an explicit retirement policy providing for continued service beyond sixty-five to age seventy on a year-to-year basis at the discretion of the board of trustees. The court held that custom and usage could not modify this clear contract provision:

> Here . . . plaintiff had his own individual written contracts of employment, and the Faculty Guide, which was expressly incorporated into each of these contracts, specifically covered in clear and unambiguous language the conditions under which his employment after age 65 might be continued. "A custom or usage may be proved in explanation and qualification of the terms of a contract

which otherwise would be ambiguous, or to show that the words in which the contract is expressed are used in a particular sense different from that which they usually impart, and, in some cases, to annex incidents to the contract in matters upon which it is silent; but evidence of a usage or custom is never admitted to make a new contract or to add a new element to one previously made." 55 Am. Jur., Usages and Customs sec. 31, 292 [208 S.E.2d at 408].

3.1.2. Amendment of the contract. The terms of the original employment contract need not remain static through the entire life of the contract. Courts have accepted the proposition that employment contracts may be amended. In *Rehor* v. *Case Western Reserve University*, 331 N.E.2d 416 (Ohio 1975), the court found amendments to be valid either where the right to amend was reserved in the original contract or where there was mutual consent of the parties to amend and good consideration was given in return for the changed terms. The plaintiff in *Rehor* was a tenured professor employed under contract at Western Reserve University from 1942 to 1967. Throughout this period the retirement age was always seventy. After Case Institute of Technology joined with Western Reserve to form Case Western Reserve University, Case Western, which took over the faculty contracts, adopted a resolution requiring faculty members over sixty-eight to petition to be reappointed. The university bylaws provided that "the board of trustees shall from time to time adopt such rules and regulations governing the appointment and tenure of the members of the faculty as the board of trustees deems necessary." The court held that this bylaw language "includes a reservation of the right to change the retirement age of the faculty" and thus defeats the plaintiff's claim that the university was in breach of contract. Since the retirement policy is part of tenure, "the reserved right to change rules of tenure includes the right to change the retirement policy." The court also approved of the university's assertion that "an employment contract between a university and a tenured faculty member may be amended by the parties in writing when supported by adequate consideration." These considerations were satisfied in *Rehor* by the professor's execution of reappointment forms and acceptance of an increased salary after the new retirement policy was put into effect. (For a criticism of the case, see M. Finkin, "Contract, Tenure, and Retirement: A Comment on *Rehor* v. *Case Western Reserve University*," 4 *Human Rights* 343 (1975).)

Occasionally contracts may also be amended unilaterally by subsequent state legislation. But the state's power to legislatively modify its own contracts or to regulate contracts between private parties is circumscribed by Article I, Section 10 (1), of the U.S. Constitution, known as the contract clause, which states that

> No state shall . . . pass any . . . law impairing the obligation of contracts.

In *Indiana ex rel. Anderson* v. *Brand*, 303 U.S. 95 (1938) (discussed in Section 3.1.4), for instance, the U.S. Supreme Court held that an Indiana law which had the effect of cancelling the tenure rights of certain public school teachers was an unconstitutional impairment of their employment contracts. Under this and subsequent contract clause precedents, a state may not impair either its own or private contracts unless such impairment is both "reasonable and necessary to serve an important public purpose," with "necessary" meaning that the impairment is essential and no viable alternative for serving the state's purpose exists. (*United States Trust Company of New York* v. *New Jersey*, 97 S. Ct. 1505 (1977).)

3.1.3. Waiver of contract rights. Once a contract has been formed, the parties may sometimes waive their contract rights either intentionally by a written agreement or unintentionally by their actions. *Chung* v. *Park*, 514 F.2d 382 (3d Cir. 1975), concerned a professor who after teaching at Mansfield State College for five years was notified that his contract would not be renewed. Through his counsel, the professor negotiated with the state attorney general and agreed to submit the issue of the termination's validity to an arbitration panel. When the panel upheld the termination, the professor brought suit, alleging that the college did not follow the termination procedures set out in the tenure regulations and was therefore in breach of contract. The court, after pointing out that under the state law contract rights may be waived by subsequent agreement between the parties, upheld the district court's finding "that the parties had reached such a subsequent agreement when, after extensive negotiations, they specifically stipulated to the hearing procedures actually employed."

Public policy considerations may, however, preclude the waiver of certain contract terms. In *McLachlan* v. *Tacoma Community College District No. 22*, 541 P.2d 1010 (Wash. 1975), the court addressed this issue, but found the rights in question to be properly waivable. The two plaintiffs were employed by the college district under contracts which specifically stated that "the employee waives all rights normally provided by the tenure laws of the state of Washington." The plaintiffs, who were aware that they were employed to replace people on year sabbaticals, contended that the contracts should not be enforced for reasons of public policy. While avoiding the broad issue of whether a blanket waiver of tenure rights contravenes public policy, the court said that "we envision no serious public policy considerations which would prohibit a teacher from waiving the statutory nonrenewal notice provisions in advance of the notice date, provided he knows the purpose of his employment is to replace the regular occupant of that position who is on a one-year sabbatical leave."

3.1.4. Special contract problems in public institutions. A public institution's legal relationship with faculty members may be defined by statute and administrative regulation as well as by written employment contract. Tenure rights, for instance, may be created by a state tenure statute rather than by the terms of the employment contract; or pay scales may be established by board of regents or Civil Service Commission rules rather than the employment contract. The distinction between statutory rights and contract rights can be critical. A right created by statute or by administrative rule can be revoked or modified by a subsequent statute or rule, with the result that the public institution has no further obligation to recognize that right. A contract right, however, usually cannot be revoked or modified by subsequent statute or rule unless the parties have made provision for such changes in the contract itself.

The case of *Busbee* v. *Georgia Conference, AAUP*, 221 S.E.2d 437 (Ga. 1975), arose after the Georgia legislature had passed an appropriations act on the basis of which faculty members in the university system of Georgia had received contracts with salary increases. The legislature subsequently reduced the appropriations, and the regents revoked the salary increases. When the faculty members sued to enforce their contracts, the regents argued that (1) the various state budgeting and fiscal laws were part of the faculty contract, and that the pattern of such laws, taken together, permitted the salary revocation; and (2) even if the revocation breached the faculty contracts, the state had the power to so impair contracts if it acted out of economic necessity. The court found that (1) although the law existing when the contract is signed may be made part of the contract, the state budgetary and fiscal laws could not be read to permit the salary revocation; and (2) the state had no power to impair the faculty contracts in this case because no economic necessity for such action existed. The court therefore held that the increased salary contracts were valid and binding on the regents and that failure to pay faculty members the increased salary would be an illegal breach of contract.

Even if particular rights emanate from statute or regulation, they may become embodied in contracts and thus be enforceable as contract rights. The contract may provide that certain statutory rights become part of the contract. Or the statute or regulation may itself be so written or interpreted that the rights it creates become enforceable as contract rights. This latter approach has twice been dealt with by the U.S. Supreme Court in cases concerning statutory tenure laws. *Phelps* v. *Board of Education of West New York*, 300 U.S. 319 (1937), concerned a New Jersey act of 1909, which provided that teachers employed by local school boards could only be dismissed or subject to reduced salary for cause. By an act of 1933, the state enabled the school boards to fix and determine salaries. When one board invoked this authority to reduce salaries without cause, teachers claimed that this action impaired their contracts in violation of the U.S. Constitution's contract clause (see Section 3.1.2). The Supreme Court held that there was no constitutional impairment, since the act of 1909 did not create a contract between the state and the teachers. The Court followed the New Jersey court's interpretation of the statute as establishing "a legislative status for teachers" but failing to establish "a contractual one that the legislature may not modify." Thus, "although the act of 1909 prohibited the board, a creature of the state, from reducing the teacher's salary or discharging him without cause, . . . this was but a regulation of the conduct of the board and not a continuing contract of indefinite duration with the individual teacher."

A year after *Phelps,* the Supreme Court came to a contrary conclusion in a similar impairment case. *Indiana ex rel. Anderson* v. *Brand,* 303 U.S. 95 (1938), dealt with Indiana's Teachers Tenure Act adopted in 1927, which provided that, once a teacher had tenure, his contract "shall be deemed to be in effect for an indefinite period." Sometime after the act was amended in 1933 to omit township school corporations, the job of the plaintiff, a tenured teacher, was terminated. The Court found the act of 1927 created a contract with the teacher because the title of the act was "couched in terms of contract," the "tenor of the Act indicates that the word 'contract' was not used inadvertently or in other than its usual legal meaning," and the state courts had previously viewed the act of 1927 as creating a contract. The Court then held that the 1933 amendment unconstitutionally impaired the contracts created by the act of 1927.

Given the fundamental distinction between contract and statutory rights, and the sometimes subtle interrelationships between them, administrators of public institutions should pay particular attention to the source of faculty members' legal rights and should consult counsel whenever attempting to define or change a faculty member's legal status.

Sec. 3.2. *Collective Bargaining*

The emergence of collective bargaining on campus has been extensively discussed and analyzed in both popular and professional media.[1] By the end of 1975, roughly 95,000 of approximately

---

[1]The major issues concerning postsecondary education bargaining have been discussed more in articles, books, and speeches than in court and labor board cases. This section will therefore cite the literature extensively to compensate for the absence of case law and provide a broad range of sources for pursuing the many complexities in this area. Other sources are also included in the Selected Annotated Bibliography at the end of this chapter.

600,000 higher education faculty members were employed at unionized institutions. Faculties at almost three hundred institutions, most in the public sector, had chosen collective bargaining agents. And the trend continues. In fact, collective bargaining promises to be a major focus of controversy in postsecondary education for the foreseeable future.

Collective bargaining presents administrators with a complex mixture of the familiar and the foreign. Many faculty demands, such as for lighter teaching loads, smaller class sizes, and larger salaries, may be familiar on many campuses; but other demands, such as for standardized pay scales rather than individualized "merit" salary determinations, may present new situations. If a shift in emphasis from "academic" to "economic" issues occurs, it may prompt a reorganization of institutional budgetary priorities and governance procedures. Legal, policy, and political issues may arise concerning the extent to which collective bargaining and the bargained agreement ("the contract"; see 3.1 above) preempt or circumscribe not merely traditional administrative elbow room, but also the customary forms of faculty and student self-government. How or whether traditional collective bargaining features such as seniority can be reconciled with academic standbys such as tenure is similarly an open question. And potential tension for academia clearly exists in the participation in campus affairs of the "outsiders" involved in bargaining agent certification elections, negotiation of agreements, fact finding, mediation, conciliation, arbitration, and ultimate resolution of internal disputes through state or federal administrative agencies and courts.

The mix of factors involved, the importance of the policy questions, and the complexity of the law make collective bargaining a most difficult area for administrators. Heavy involvement of legal counsel is clearly called for. Use of professional negotiators, or of administrators experienced in the art of negotiation, is also usually appropriate—particularly when the faculty has such professional expertise on its side of the bargaining table.

3.2.1. The public-private dichotomy in collective bargaining. Theoretically, the legal aspects of collective bargaining divide into two distinct categories: public and private. However, these categories are not necessarily defined in the same way as they are for constitutional state action purposes in Section 1.4.2. In relation to collective bargaining, "public" and "private" are defined by the collective bargaining legislation and interpretive precedents. Privately chartered institutions (see Section 6.3) are likely to be considered private for collective bargaining purposes even if they receive substantial government support. In *University of Vermont and State Agricultural College,* 223 NLRB No. 46 (1976), for instance, the National Labor Relations Board (NLRB) asserted jurisdiction over an institution receiving 25 percent of its support directly from the state, because the institution was chartered as private and nonprofit and was not a political subdivision of the state.

Private sector bargaining is governed by the federal Labor Management Relations Act (the Taft-Hartley Act), 29 U.S.C. secs. 141 *et seq.* (See Section 7.2.2.) The NLRB first asserted jurisdiction over private nonprofit postsecondary institutions in *Cornell University,* 183 NLRB 329 (1970), and made clear that its jurisdiction extended to faculty members in *C. W. Post Center of Long Island University,* 189 NLRB 904 (1971). The board's jurisdiction was judicially confirmed in *NLRB* v. *Wentworth Institute,* 515 F.2d 550 (1st Cir. 1975), where the court enforced an NLRB order finding that Wentworth had engaged in an unfair labor practice in refusing to bargain with the certified faculty bargaining representative. Now, all private postsecondary institutions, at least all those large enough to have a significant effect on interstate commerce, are included within the federal sphere. Disputes arising from the collective bargaining process in private institutions are thus subject to the limited body of statutory authority and the vast body of administrative and judicial precedent regarding the Taft-Hartley Act.

Legal authority and precedent provide few easy answers, however, for collective bargaining issues in postsecondary education. The uniqueness of academic institutions, procedures, and customs poses new problems not previously encountered in the NLRB's administration of the national labor law in other employment contexts. There are, moreover, many ambiguities and unsettled areas in the national labor law even in nonacademic contexts. They derive in part from the intentionally broad language of the federal legislation and in part from the NLRB's historic insistence on proceeding case by case rather than under a policy of systematic rule making (see K. Kahn, "The NLRB and Higher Education: The Failure of Policy Making Through Adjudication," 21 *U.C.L.A. L. Rev.* 63 (1973); and A. P. Menard and N. DiGiovanni, Jr., "NLRB Jurisdiction over Colleges and Universities: a Plea for Rulemaking," 16 *Wm. and Mary L. Rev.* 599 (1975)). Administrators will find working with the NLRB's body of piecemeal precedential authority to be a very different experience from working with the detailed regulations of other agencies such as HEW.

Public postsecondary education, on the other hand, is exempt from NLRB jurisdiction (see 29 U.S.C. sec. 152-2) and subject only to state authority. By the end of 1975, almost half the states had passed some type of legislation permitting at least some form of collective bargaining in public postsecondary education (see Academic Collective Bargaining Information Service, *Analysis of Legislation in Twenty-Four States Enabling Faculty Collective Bargaining in Postsecondary Education* (Spec. Rept. No. 17, Update May 1976)). Such legislation is often limited in coverage or in the extent to which it authorizes or mandates the full panoply of collective bargaining rights and services. A statute may grant employees rights as narrow as the right to "meet and confer" with administration representatives. In *Lipon* v. *Regents of University of California,* 54 Cal.App.3d 215, 126 Cal. Reptr. 515 (1976), for instance, the defendant had only the obligation to "meet and confer" with the organization representing the University of California faculty regarding revisions in the defendant's administrative manual—an obligation which the court held was met. The permissibility of strikes is also a major variable among state statutes.

Frequently, state legislation is designed to cover public employees generally and makes little, if any, special provision for the unique circumstances of postsecondary education. (For analyses of what a state statute should contain, see Comment, "The Legislation Necessary to Effectively Govern Collective Bargaining in Public Higher Education," 1971 *Wisconsin L. Rev.* 275; and R. Sensenbrenner, "Collective Bargaining Legislation for Public

Higher Education from the Management Side of the Table," 4 *J. of College and University Law* 27 (1977)). State labor law may be just as unsettled as the federal labor law, providing few easy answers for postsecondary education, and may also have a much smaller body of administrative and judicial precedents. State agencies and courts often fill in the gaps by relying on federal labor law precedents.

Even where state collective bargaining legislation does not cover public postsecondary institutions, some "extralegal" bargaining may still take place. A public institution's faculty members, like other public employees, have a constitutional right, under First Amendment freedom of speech and association, "to organize collectively and select representatives to engage in collective bargaining" (*University of New Hampshire Chapter AAUP* v. *Haselton*, 397 F. Supp. 107 (D.N.H. 1975)). But faculty members do not have a constitutional right to require the public institution "to respond to . . . [faculty] demands or to enter into a contract with them." The right to require the employer to bargain in good faith must be created by statute. Even if the public institution desires to bargain with faculty representatives, it may not have the authority to do so under state law. The employment powers of public institutions may be vested by law in the sole discretion of institutional governing boards, and thus sharing such powers with collective bargaining representatives or arbitrators appointed under collective bargaining agreements may be construed as an improper delegation of authority. In *Board of Trustees of Junior College District No. 508* v. *Cook County College Teachers Union*, 62 Ill.2d 470, 343 N.E.2d 473 (1976), the court held that the board's powers to decide which faculty members to employ and promote were "nondelegable" and thus not subject to binding arbitration under the collective bargaining agreement. (See generally G. M. Alley and V. J. Facciolo, "Concerted Public Employee Activity in the Absence of State Authorization," 2 *J. Law and Educ.* 401 (1973); E. Green, "Concerted Public Employer Collective Bargaining in the Absence of Explicit Legislative Authorization," 2 *J. Law and Educ.* 419 (1973).)

3.2.2. *Organization, recognition, and certification.* Once a faculty or some substantial portion of it has concluded that it would like to bargain collectively with the institution, its spokespersons can ask the administration to recognize them for collective bargaining purposes. A private institution has two choices at this point. It can voluntarily recognize the faculty representatives and commence negotiations, or it can withhold recognition and insist that the faculty representatives seeking recognition petition the NLRB for a certification election. (See *Linden Lumber Div. v. NLRB*, 419 U.S. 817 (1974).) Public institutions that have authority to bargain under state law usually have the same two choices, although elections and certification would be handled by the state labor board.

Administrators should consider two related legal implications of choosing the first alternative. First, it is a violation of the Taft-Hartley Act (and most state acts) for an employer to voluntarily recognize a minority union, that is, a union supported by less than 50 percent of the faculty in the bargaining unit. (See 29 U.S.C. sec. 158(a)(1) and (2), and *International Ladies Garment Workers Union v. NLRB*, 366 U.S. 731 (1961).) Second, it is also a violation of Taft-Hartley (and most state acts) to recognize any union (even one with apparent majority support) when a rival union makes a "substantial claim of support," which the NLRB interprets to mean a claim "not . . . clearly unsupportable and lacking in substance" (*American Can Co.*, 218 NLRB 102, 103 (1975)). Thus, unless a union seeking recognition can prove the clear support of the majority of the members of the proposed bargaining unit (usually through "authentication cards" or a secret ballot poll), and the administration has no reason to believe that a rival union with a "substantial claim of support" is also seeking recognition, it is usually not wise to recognize any union without a certification election.

In the interim between the beginning of organizational activity and the actual certification of a union, the institution is in a delicate position. In the private sector, the Taft-Hartley Act prohibits the employer from doing anything that would appear to favor any of the contenders for recognition (29 U.S.C. sec. 158(a)(2)) or that would "interfere with, restrain, or coerce employees in the exercise of their rights" to self-organize, form or join a union, or bargain collectively (29 U.S.C. sec. 158(a)(1)). This would include promises of benefits, threats of reprisals, coercive interrogation, or surveillance. Furthermore, the institution may not take any action that could be construed as a discrimination against union organizers or supporters because of their exercise of rights under the Act (29 U.S.C. sec. 158(a)(3)). In the public sector, state laws generally contain comparable prohibitions on certain kinds of employer activities.

Another crucial aspect of the organizational phase is the definition of the "bargaining unit," that is, the portion of the institution's employees that will be represented by the particular bargaining agent seeking certification. Again, most state laws parallel the federal law. Generally, the NLRB or its state equivalent has considerable discretion to determine the appropriate unit (see 29 U.S.C. sec. 159(b)). The traditional rule has been that there must be a basic "community of interest" among the individuals included in the unit, so that the union will represent the interests of everyone in the unit when it negotiates with the employer. Moreover, under the Taft-Hartley Act (see 29 U.S.C. sec. 152(3) and (11)) and most state laws, supervisory personnel are excluded from any bargaining unit. Individual determinations must be made, in light of the applicable statutory definition, of whether particular personnel are excluded from the unit as supervisors.

Generally, several factors have traditionally been used to determine a "community of interest," including the history of past bargaining (if any), the extent of organization, the skills and duties of the employees, and common supervision. But these factors are difficult to apply in postsecondary education's complex world of collegially shared decision making. To define the proposed unit as "all faculty members" does not resolve the issue. For example, does the unit include all faculty of the institution, or only the faculty of a particular school, such as the law school? Part-time as well as full-time faculty members? Researchers and librarians as well as teachers? Graduate teaching assistants? Chairpersons of small departments whose administrative duties are incidental to their primary teaching and research functions? The problems are compounded in multicampus institutions, especially if the programs offered by the individual campuses vary significantly from one another. (See, for example, E. Moore, "The Determination of Bargaining Units for College Faculties," 37 *U. of Pittsburgh L. Rev.* 43 (1975); M. W. Finkin, "The NLRB in Higher Education," 5 *U. of Toledo L. Rev.* 608, 612–645 (1974); Comment, "The Bargaining Unit Status of Academic Department Chairmen," 40 *U. of Chicago L. Rev.* 442 (1973).)

Once the bargaining unit is defined and the union recognized or certified, the union becomes the exclusive bargaining agent of all employees in the unit, whether or not they become union members and whether or not they are willing to be represented. (See *J. I. Case Co. v. NLRB,* 321 U.S. 332 (1944).)

3.2.3. Bargainable subjects. Once the unit has been defined and the agent certified, the parties must proceed to negotiations. In the private sector, under Taft-Hartley, the parties may negotiate on any subject they wish, although other laws (such as federal employment discrimination laws) may make some subjects illegal. In the public sector, the parties may negotiate on any subject which is not specifically excluded from the state's collective bargaining statute or preempted by other state law, such as a tenure statute. Those terms that may be raised by either party and that are negotiable with the consent of the other are referred to as "permissive" subjects for negotiation. Academic collective bargaining can range, and has ranged, over a wide variety of such permissive subjects. (See M. Moskow, "The Scope of Collective Bargaining in Higher Education," *Wisconsin L. Rev.* 33 (1971).) It is not an unfair labor practice to refuse to negotiate a permissive subject of bargaining; on the contrary, it may be an unfair labor practice to insist that a permissive subject be covered by the bargaining agreement.

The heart of the collective bargaining process, however, is found in those terms over which the parties *must* negotiate. These "mandatory" subjects of bargaining are defined in the Taft-Hartley Act as "wages, hours, and other terms and conditions of employment" (29 U.S.C. sec. 158(d)). Most state acts use similar or identical language, but often exclude particular subjects from the scope of that language or add particular subjects to it. (See Academic Collective Bargaining Information Service, *Scope of Public Sector Bargaining in Fourteen Selected States* (Spec. Rpt. No. 25, Nov. 1975).) The parties must bargain in good faith over mandatory subjects of bargaining; failure to do so is an unfair labor practice under the Taft-Hartley Act (see 29 U.S.C. secs. 158(a)(5) and 158(b)(3)) and most state statutes.

The statutory language regarding the mandatory subjects is often vague (for example, "terms and conditions of employment") and subject to broad construction by labor boards and courts. Thus, the distinction between mandatory and permissive subjects is difficult to draw, particularly in postsecondary education, where faculties have traditionally participated in shaping their jobs to a much greater degree than have employees in industry. Internal governance and policy issues which may never arise in industrial bargaining may thus be critical in postsecondary education. There are few court or labor board precedents in either federal or state law to help administrators determine whether educational governance and educational policy issues are mandatorily or permissibly bargainable. Nor in the states, where some subjects may be impermissible, are there many precedents to help administrators determine when particular subjects fall into that category. One court case, *Association of New Jersey State College Faculties* v. *Dungan,* 64 N.J. 338, 316 A.2d 425 (1974), concerned a state statute that gave public employees the right to bargain over the "terms and conditions of employment" and "working conditions." The court held that rules for granting tenure are not "mandatorily negotiable" under the statute because such rules "represent major educational policy pronouncements entrusted by the Legislature [under the state Education Law] to the Board . . . [of Higher Education's] educational expertise and objective judgment." Under such reasoning, tenure rules could also be beyond the scope of permissible bargaining, as a nondelegable function of the board (see the *Cook County College Teachers Union* case in Section 3.2.1) or a function preempted by other state laws. Other courts or agencies, however, particularly when dealing with private institutions under the Taft-Hartley Act, may reason that tenure is a mandatory, or at least permissible, bargaining subject because it concerns job security (see A. Menard, "May Tenure Rights of Faculty Be Bargained Away?" 2 *J. of College and University Law* 256 (1975)).

When the parties are unable to reach agreement on an item

subject to mandatory bargaining (called *impasse*), a number of resolution techniques may be available to them. It is critical to distinguish between bargaining impasse in the private sector and in the public sector. In the private sector, the Taft-Hartley Act specifically recognizes that employees have the right to strike under certain circumstances. (See 29 U.S.C. sec. 163.) The basic premise of the Act is that, given the free play of economic forces, employer and union can and will bargain collectively and reach agreement, and the ultimate economic force available to a union is the strike. In the public sector, however, it is almost unanimously regarded as unlawful, either by state statute or state judicial decision, for a public employee to strike. The rationale is that states have a vital interest in assuring that government services remain available to the public without interruption that would be created by a strike. (The statutes and cases are collected in Annot., "Labor Law: Right of Public Employees to Strike or Engage in Work Stoppage," 37 A.L.R.3rd 1147 (1971 and periodic supp.).)

Consequently, almost all state statutes prescribe impasse resolution techniques to take the place of strikes. Depending on the statute, these include mediation, fact-finding, and interest arbitration. Mediation—the appointment of a mediator who may make recommendations to the parties but does not dictate any terms of settlement—is the most commonly prescribed impasse procedure. Fact-finding is sometimes mandatory if the parties fail to reach agreement within a specified time period; at other times, a fact-finder is appointed by order of a labor board or agreement of the parties. (See J. Stern, "The Wisconsin Public Employee Fact-Finding Procedure," 20 *Industrial and Labor Rel. Rev.* 3 (1966).) Interest arbitration can be either compulsory, in which case the statute requires the submission of unresolved issues to an arbitrator who makes a final decision, or voluntary, in which case the parties decide for themselves whether to resort to binding arbitration.

The same techniques used to resolve an impasse in bargaining may also be used in the public sector to resolve disputes concerning the application or interpretation of the bargaining agreement after it has gone into force. The most common technique for resolving such disputes is grievance arbitration. (See W. Edmonson and A. Simon, "Arbitration in Higher Education," 29 *Arbitration J.* 217 (1974); M. Finkin, "The Arbitration of

Faculty Status Disputes in Higher Education," 30 *Southwestern Law J.* 389 (1976); B. Mintz and A. Golden, "In Defense of Academic Judgment: Settling Faculty Collective Bargaining Agreement Grievances Through Arbitration," 22 *Buffalo L. Rev.* 523 (1973).)

In the private sector, there are only two techniques for resolving an impasse in negotiating an agreement—mediation and interest arbitration—and the latter is rarely used. Mediation is available through the Federal Mediation and Conciliation Service, which may "proffer its services in any labor dispute . . . either upon its own motion or upon the request of one or more of the parties" (29 U.S.C. sec. 173(b)). Interest arbitration may be used when the parties already have a collective bargaining agreement in effect, due to expire, in which they have agreed to submit to arbitration terms they cannot agree upon when negotiating their new agreement. Interest arbitration has no statutory basis and is entirely the creature of an existing agreement between the parties. Negotiated agreements in the private sector usually provide for grievance arbitration to resolve disputes concerning the application or interpretation of the agreement.

3.2.4. Coexistence of collective bargaining and traditional academic practices. Collective bargaining contracts traditionally come in two kinds, those with a "zipper" clause and those with a "past practices" clause. A zipper clause usually states that the union agrees to forgo its rights to bargain about any employment term or condition not contained in the contract; prior relationships between the parties thus become irrelevant. A past practices clause incorporates previous customary relationships between the parties in the agreement, at least insofar as they are not already inconsistent with its specific terms. Administrators faced with collective bargaining should carefully weigh the relative merits of each clause. The interpretation of a contract without either clause will likely be consistent with past practice in order to fill in gaps or ambiguities in the contract terms. (See Sections 1.3.8 and 3.1.)

The availability of the past practices clause, however, by no means assures that such traditional academic practices as tenure and faculty participation will endure under collective bargaining. Many commentators argue that such academic practices will steadily and inevitably disappear in the new climate. (For example, see D. Fellers, "General Theory of the Collective Bargaining Agreement," 61 *California L. Rev.* 663, 718–856 (1973).) The theory is that collective bargaining will bring with it the economic warfare of the industrial bargaining model, forcing the two parties into much more clearly defined employee and management roles and eliminating the collegiality which has been characteristic of postsecondary education. The opposing view is that collective bargaining can be domesticated in the postsecondary environment with minimal disruption of academic practices (see M. Finkin, "Collective Bargaining and University Government," 1971 *Wisconsin L. Rev.* 125; and M. Finkin, "Faculty Collective Bargaining in Higher Education: An Independent Perspective," 3 *J. of Law and Education* 439 (1974)). Thus a critical issue for administrators is the extent to which faculty involvement in institutional governance should and can be maintained by incorporating such arrangements in the bargaining agreement, through either a past practices clause or a more detailed description of forms and functions. (See F. R. Kemerer and J. V. Baldridge, *Unions on Campus: A National Study of the Consequences of Faculty Bargaining* (Jossey-Bass, 1975).)

3.2.5. *Students and collective bargaining.* Students have become increasingly concerned with collective bargaining's potential impact on their interests. The questions are basically whether faculty and student interests are potentially, or necessarily, inconsistent and whether collective bargaining will reduce student power by reducing the policy issues in which students participate or the internal remedies which they can utilize. If either of these effects flows from collective bargaining, another question then arises: Should students have a formal role in bargaining, and if so, what kind? As of the end of 1976, three state legislatures had provided such a role for students in public institutions. Oregon passed a law in 1975 providing an independent observer-participant role for students (Ore. Rev. Stat. secs. 243.650–243.782, ch. 679(1)). Montana passed a law in 1975 allowing students to be part of the administration bargaining team (Rev. Code Mont., ch. 16, sec. 1602(1)). And Maine passed a law in 1976 giving students the formal opportunity to consult with both administrators and faculty members before bargaining begins and with administrators at reasonable intervals during negotiations. In states without such statutes, some formal student participation has been provided by institutional or state governing board regulations or by agreement of the bargaining parties. Such action, however, may raise legal questions concerning institutional authority, particularly if students are authorized to postpone or veto the resolution of issues by the faculty and administration bargaining teams.

3.2.6. *Collective bargaining and antidiscrimination laws.* A body of case law is developing on the applicability of federal and state laws prohibiting discrimination in employment (see Section 3.3) to the collective bargaining process. Courts have interpreted federal labor relations law (Section 3.2.1) to impose on unions a duty to fairly represent each employee without arbitrariness, discrimination, or bad faith. (See *Vaca* v. *Sipes*, 386 U.S. 171 (1967).) In addition, some antidiscrimination statutes, such as Title VII and the Age Discrimination in Employment Act, apply directly to unions as well as employers. But these laws have left open several questions concerning the relationships between collective bargaining and antidiscrimination statutes. For instance, when employment discrimination problems are covered in the bargaining contract, can such coverage be construed to preclude faculty members from seeking other remedies under antidiscrimination statutes? If a faculty member resorts to a negotiated grievance procedure to resolve a discrimination dispute, can that faculty member then be precluded from using remedies provided under antidiscrimination statutes?

Most cases presenting such issues have arisen under Title VII of the Civil Rights Act of 1964. (See Section 3.3.2.1.) The leading case is *Alexander* v. *Gardner-Denver Co.*, 415 U.S. 36 (1974). A discharged black employee had contested his discharge in a grievance proceeding provided under a collective bargaining contract. He claimed that his discharge was a result of racial discrimination. Having lost before an arbitrator in the grievance proceeding, and having had a complaint to the federal Equal Employment Opportunity Commission dismissed, the employee filed a Title VII action in federal district court. After the district court had held that the employee was bound by the arbitration decision and thus had no right to sue under Title VII, the U.S. Supreme Court reversed. The Court held that the employee could still sue under Title VII, which creates statutory rights "distinctly separate" from the contractual right to arbitration under the collective bargaining agreement. Such independent rights "are not waived either by inclusion of discrimination disputes within the collective bargaining agreement or by submitting the nondiscrimination claim to arbitration."

Thus collective bargaining does not provide an occasion for postsecondary administrators to lessen their attention to the institution's Title VII responsibilities, nor, presumably, to its responsibilities under most other antidiscrimination laws. Faculty members can avail themselves of rights and remedies both under the bargaining agreement and under antidiscrimination statutes. There is one exception, however, noted by the Court in the *Gardner-Denver* case: It may be possible to waive a Title VII cause of action (and presumably actions under other statutes) "as part of a voluntary settlement" of a discrimination claim. The employee's consent to such a settlement would have to be "voluntary and knowing," however, and "mere resort to the arbitral forum to enforce contractual rights" could not constitute such a waiver. (See 415 U.S. at 52.)

Sec. 3.3. Nondiscrimination in Employment

3.3.1. The statutory, regulatory, and constitutional thicket. The problem of employment discrimination is probably more heavily blanketed with overlapping statutory and regulatory requirements than any other area of postsecondary education law.[2] The federal government has no less than eight major employment discrimination statutes and one major executive order applicable to postsecondary education, each with its own comprehensive set of administrative regulations or guidelines (see Sections 3.3.2 and 3.3.4). Many states also have fair employment practices statutes,

[2]Although this section deals directly with discrimination issues concerning faculty members, the laws and legal principles discussed also apply generally to discrimination problems involving nonfaculty employees of postsecondary institutions.

some of which may exclude educational institutions (such as Md. Ann. Code art. 49B, sec. 20), and others of which may apply to educational institutions and overlap federal statutes. New York has a statute, for instance, which was the basis of extended proceedings culminating in *State Division of Human Rights* v. *Columbia University*, 39 N.Y.2d 612, 350 N.E.2d 396 (1976). In that case a rejected faculty applicant filed a sex discrimination complaint, as provided by the statute, with the State Division of Human Rights. The division held an investigation and hearing and found no discrimination; the Human Rights Appeal Board reversed and held the applicant had been discriminated against; and the New York Court of Appeals reversed the appeal board, holding that the applicant had been rejected for legitimate staffing and financial reasons rather than on grounds of sex.

Because of their national scope and comprehensive coverage of problems and remedies, and because they take precedence over any conflicting state law, the federal antidiscrimination statutes have assumed greater importance than the state statutes. The federal statutes, moreover, supplemented by those of the states, have outstripped the importance of the federal Constitution (see Sections 3.3.3 and 3.3.4) as a remedy for employment discrimination. The statutes cover almost all major categories of discrimination and tend to impose more affirmative and stringent requirements on employers than does the Constitution.

Race discrimination in employment is covered by Title VII of the Civil Rights Act of 1964, as amended; by 42 U.S.C. sec. 1981; and by Executive Order 11246 as amended. Sex discrimination is covered by Title VII, by Title IX of the Education Amendments of 1972, by the Equal Pay Act, and by Executive Order 11246. Age discrimination is covered, in part, by the Age Discrimination in Employment Act. Discrimination against the handicapped is covered by the Rehabilitation Act of 1973. Discrimination on the basis of religion is covered by Title VII and Executive Order 11246. Discrimination on the basis of national origin is covered by Title VII and by Executive Order 11246. Discrimination against aliens is covered indirectly under Title VII (see note 4 in Section 3.3.2.1) and directly by 42 U.S.C. sec. 1981. Discrimination against veterans is covered in part by 38 U.S.C. sec. 2012.

The nondiscrimination aspects of the statutes and Executive Order 11246 are discussed in Section 3.3.2. The affirmative action aspects of the statutes and Executive Order 11246 are discussed in Section 3.3.4. And the interstitial importance of the federal Constitution is discussed in Sections 3.3.3 and 3.3.4.

3.3.2. Nondiscrimination under federal statutes and executive orders. The major federal employment discrimination statutes vary in scope, in the character of the requirements they impose on postsecondary institutions, and in the methods by which their statutory requirements are enforced. While the deeper complexities of these statutes are beyond this book's scope, the following discussion provides a basic road map.

3.3.2.1. Title VII. Title VII of the Civil Rights Act of 1964, 42 U.S.C. secs. 2000e *et seq.*, is the most comprehensive and most litigated of the federal employment discrimination laws. It was extended in 1972 to cover educational institutions both public and private. According to the statute's basic prohibition, 42 U.S.C. sec. 2000e–2:

> (a) It shall be an unlawful employment practice for an employer—
> (1) to fail or refuse to hire or to discharge any individual, or otherwise to discriminate against any individual with respect to his compensation, terms, conditions, or privileges of employment, because of such individual's race, color, religion[3], sex, or national origin[4]; or

[3](Author's footnote.) A subsequent provision of Title VII, 42 U.S.C. sec. 2000e(j), defines religion to include "all aspects of religious observance and practice, as well as belief." This provision requires an employer to "reasonably accommodate to" an employee's religion unless the employer can demonstrate an inability to do so "without undue hardship." This provision has been narrowly construed. See *Trans World Airlines* v. *Hardison,* 97 S. Ct. 2272 (1977) (requiring employer to bear more than de minimus costs in accommodating employees' religious beliefs is undue hardship).

[4](Author's footnote.) The U.S. Supreme Court has ruled that the term "national origin" in Title VII does not, as such, cover discrimination on the basis of citizenship, that is, discrimination against aliens (*Espinoza* v. *Farah Manufacturing Co.,* 414 U.S. 86 (1973)). The Court cautioned, however, that citizenship requirements may sometimes be part of a scheme of, or a pretext for, national origin discrimination and that "Title VII

(2) to limit, segregate, or classify his employees or applicants for employment in any way which would deprive or tend to deprive any individual of employment opportunities or otherwise adversely affect his status as an employee, because of such individual's race, color, religion, sex, or national origin.

The major exception to this general prohibition is the "BFOQ" exception, which permits hiring and employing based on "religion, sex, or national origin" when such a characteristic is a "bona fide occupational qualification necessary to the normal operation of that particular business or enterprise" (42 U.S.C. sec. 2000e-2(e)(1)). A related exception, applicable specifically to educational institutions, permits the hiring and employing of persons "of a particular religion" if the institution is "owned, supported, controlled, or managed" by a particular religion or if the institution's curriculum "is directed toward the propagation of a particular religion" (42 U.S.C. sec. 2000e-2(e)(2)).

Though Title VII broadly prohibits employment discrimination, it does not hamstring postsecondary institutions in hiring faculty members on the basis of job-related qualifications and ability. Nor does it prevent postsecondary institutions from distinguishing among faculty members on the basis of seniority or merit in their pay, promotion, and tenure policies, so long as such distinctions "are not the result of an intention to discriminate because of race, color, religion, sex, or national origin" (42 U.S.C. sec. 2000e-2(h)). The institution's discretion in hiring, promoting, and rewarding faculty members can be limited, however, to the extent it is ordered to take affirmative action to remedy the effects of past discrimination. (See Section 3.3.4.) The institution could, for instance, be required to retroactively award seniority in rank to compensate for any period of time during which a faculty member or prospective member was denied a rank due to discrimination.

---

prohibits discrimination on the basis of citizenship [alienage] whenever it has the purpose or effect of discriminating on the basis of national origin." The Court also made clear that aliens, as individuals, are covered by Title VII if they have been discriminated against on the basis of race, color, religion, or sex, as well as national origin.

(See *Franks* v. *Bowman Transportation Co.*, 424 U.S. 747 (1976).)

As explained by the U.S. Supreme Court in *Griggs* v. *Duke Power Co.*, 401 U.S. 424 (1971), the objective of Title VII is to

> remove barriers that have operated in the past to favor an identifiable group of white employees over other employees. Under the Act, practices, procedures, or tests neutral on their face, and even neutral in terms of intent, cannot be maintained if they operate to "freeze" the status quo of prior discriminatory employment practices.
>
> . . . Congress did not intend by Title VII, however, to guarantee a job to every person regardless of qualifications. In short, the Act does not command that any person be hired simply because he was formerly the subject of discrimination, or because he is a member of a minority group. Discriminatory preference for any group, minority or majority, is precisely and only what Congress has proscribed. What is required by Congress is the removal of artificial, arbitrary, and unnecessary barriers to employment when the barriers operate invidiously to discriminate on the basis of racial or other impermissible classification.
>
> Congress has now provided that tests or criteria for employment or promotion may not provide equality of opportunity merely in the sense of the fabled offer of milk to the stork and the fox. On the contrary, Congress has now required that the posture and condition of the job seeker be taken into account. It has—to resort again to the fable—provided that the vessel in which the milk is proffered be one all seekers can use. The Act proscribes not only overt discrimination but also practices that are fair in form, but discriminatory in operation. The touchstone is business necessity. If an employment practice which operates to exclude Negroes cannot be shown to be related to job performance, the practice is prohibited [401 U.S. at 429=431].

Subsequent to *Griggs*, in *McDonald* v. *Sante Fe Trail Transportation Co.*, 427 U.S. 273 (1976), the U.S. Supreme Court made clear that Title VII's prohibition on racial discrimination protects white persons, as well as minorities, against discrimination.

The *Griggs* case is still the leading precedent construing Title VII. In a unanimous opinion, the Court expansively interpreted Title VII to prohibit employment practices which (1) operate to exclude or otherwise discriminate against employees or prospective employees on grounds of race, color, religion, sex, or national origin, and (2) are unrelated to job performance. Both requirements must be met before Title VII is violated. Under the first requirement, it need not be shown that the employer intended to discriminate; it is the *effect* of the employment practice, not the *intent* behind it, that controls. Under the second requirement, the employer, not the employee, has the burden of showing the job-relatedness of the employment practice in question.

Once a Title VII violation has been shown, courts have broad powers to remedy the violation by "making persons whole for injuries suffered through past discrimination" (*Albermarle Paper Co.* v. *Moody*, 422 U.S. 405 (1975)). Remedies may include back pay awards *(Albermarle)* and awards of retroactive seniority *(Franks)*.

Title VII is administered by the Equal Employment Opportunity Commission (EEOC), which has implemented the statute with a series of regulations and guidelines published at 29 C.F.R. Parts 1600 through 1610. The EEOC may receive, investigate, and conciliate complaints of unlawful employment discrimination and may sue violators in court or issue right-to-sue letters to complainants (29 C.F.R. Part 1601).

3.3.2.2. Executive Orders 11246 and 11375. Executive Order 11246, 30 Fed. Reg. 12319, as amended by Executive Order 11375, 32 Fed. Reg. 14303 (adding sex to the list of prohibited discriminations), prohibits discrimination "because of race, color, religion, sex, or national origin," thus paralleling Title VII (Section 3.3.2.1). Unlike Title VII, the Executive Orders apply only to contractors and subcontractors under federal government contracts and federally assisted construction contracts. Contracts with each such contractor must include an equal opportunity clause (41 C.F.R. sec. 60-1.4) and contractors must file post-award compliance reports and annual compliance reports thereafter (41 C.F.R. sec. 60-1.7(a)) with the federal contracting agency.

The executive orders are administered by the U.S. Department of Labor, which has issued a lengthy series of implementing regulations compiled in 41 C.F.R. ch. 60, as amended in 1977 by 42 Fed. Reg. 3454. The regulations contain exemptions for various contracts and contractors (41 C.F.R. sec. 60-1.5), including an exemption for church-related educational institutions which is the same as Title VII's (41 C.F.R. sec. 60-1.5(a)(5)). While the regulations contain a partial exemption for state and local government contractors, "educational institutions and medical facilities" are specifically excluded from this exemption (41 C.F.R. sec. 60-1.5(a)(4)). The federal agency issuing the contract, or awarding the federal funds used for construction contracts, is primarily responsible for obtaining compliance with the regulations (41 C.F.R. sec. 60-1.6). The responsible agency or the Department of Labor may hold compliance reviews (41 C.F.R. sec. 60-1.20), receive and investigate complaints from employees and applicants (41 C.F.R. secs. 60-1.21 to 60-1.24), and hold hearings on alleged violations of equal opportunity (41 C.F.R. sec. 60-1.24(c); 60-1.26). When a contractor is found to be out of compliance, its contracts may be cancelled, terminated, or suspended, and the contractor may be debarred from further contracts and subcontracts (41 C.F.R. sec. 60-1.24(c)(3); 60-1.26(b)(2)).

In addition to their equal opportunity provisions, the executive orders and regulations place heavy emphasis on affirmative action by federal contractors, as discussed in Section 3.3.4.

3.3.2.3. Title IX. Title IX of the Education Amendments of 1972, 20 U.S.C. sec. 1681 *et seq.*, prohibits sex discrimination by public and private educational institutions receiving federal funds. (See Section 7.4.3.) The statute is administered by the Office for Civil Rights (OCR) of the U.S. Department of Health, Education and Welfare. The HEW regulations contain provisions on employment (45 C.F.R. secs. 86.51 through 86.61) which are similar in many respects to EEOC's sex discrimination guidelines under Title VII. Like Title VII, the Title IX regulations contain a provision permitting sex-based distinctions in employment where sex is a "bona fide occupational qualification" (45 C.F.R. sec. 86.61). Also like Title VII, Title IX contains an exemption applicable to some religious institutions. Title IX's is differently worded, however, to exempt "an educational institution which is controlled by a religious organization" if Title IX's requirements "would not be consistent with the religious tenets of such organization" (20 U.S.C. sec. 1681(a)(3); 45 C.F.R. sec. 86.12).

    3.3.2.4. Equal Pay Act. The Equal Pay Act of 1963, as amended, 29 U.S.C. secs. 206 *et seq.,* covers only sex discrimination in the context of wage rates. The basic prohibition in 29 U.S.C. sec. 206(d)(1), applicable to both public and private institutions, provides that

> [n]o employer having employees subject to any provisions of this section shall discriminate, within any establishment in which such employees are employed, between employees on the basis of sex by paying wages to employees in such establishment at a rate less than the rate at which he pays wages to employees of the opposite sex in such establishment for equal work on jobs the performance of which requires equal skill, effort, and responsibility, and which are performed under similar working conditions, except where such payment is made pursuant to (i) a seniority system; (ii) a merit system; (iii) a system which measures earnings by quantity or quality of production; or (iv) a differential based on any other factor other than sex: *Provided,* That an employer who is paying a wage rate differential in violation of this subsection shall not, in order to comply with the provisions of this subsection, reduce the wage of any employee.

The principle behind this provision is simple and straightforward: "'equal work will be rewarded by equal wages'" as between the sexes (*Corning Glass Workers* v. *Brennan,* 417 U.S. 188 (1974)).

    The Equal Pay Act is administered by the Department of Labor. The department has issued regulations in 29 C.F.R. Part 800 that, in particular, define which employees are covered by the act and define the act's concept of equal skill, effort, and responsibility. The Secretary of Labor may enforce the act by suing alleged violators. The secretary has the burden of proving that the employer pays workers of one sex more than workers of the other sex for equal work. Once the secretary carries this burden, "the burden shifts to the employer to show that the differential is justified under one of the . . . four exceptions [set out in sec. 206(d)(1)]" (*Corning Glass Workers*).

The Equal Pay Act has been applied to discrimination against men as well as against women. In *Board of Regents of University of Nebraska* v. *Dawes*, 522 F.2d 380 (8th Cir. 1975), the university had, under pressure of a threatened federal fund cut-off, developed a complicated numerical formula for computing the average salary of male faculty members. The university used this average as the minimum salary for female faculty members. In a declaratory judgment action by the university, the court held that the practice violated the Equal Pay Act because ninety-two male faculty members received less than the female minimum even though they had substantially equal qualifications.

3.3.2.5. Age Discrimination in Employment Act (ADEA). This act, 29 U.S.C. secs. 621 *et seq.*, prohibits age discrimination only with respect to persons who are at least forty years of age. Prior to the Act's amendment in 1978, the upper age limit was sixty-five (29 U.S.C. sec. 631). The 1978 amendments raised that limit to seventy, effective January 1, 1979. There are a few exceptions, one of which applies to tenured faculty members of postsecondary institutions. Until July 1, 1982, postsecondary institutions may continue to require mandatory retirement of tenured faculty members at age sixty-five. For all purposes other than retirement, however, the upper limit for tenured faculty members also is seventy as of January 1, 1979.

Within these age limits, the Act's basic provision, applicable to both public and private institutions, makes it unlawful for an employer

> (1) to fail or refuse to hire or to discharge any individual with respect to his compensation, terms, conditions, or privileges of employment, because of such individual's age;
> (2) to limit, segregate, or classify his employees in any way which would deprive or tend to deprive any individual of employment opportunities or otherwise adversely affect his status as an employee, because of such individual's age; or
> (3) to reduce the wage rate of any employee in order to comply with this chapter.[5]

[5]Relevant authorities construing the act are collected in Annot.,

The act contains a BFOQ exception which permits employers to make age distinctions "where age is a bona fide occupational qualification reasonably necessary to the normal operation of the particular business" (29 U.S.C. sec. 623(f)(1); 29 C.F.R. sec. 860.102).

ADEA and its 1978 amendments have engendered considerable debate on employers' policies concerning involuntary retirement of their employees. Where age is the reason for involuntary retirement, the Act prohibits employers from requiring retirement prior to the prescribed upper age limits. Thus, under ADEA, postsecondary institutions may not require retirement before seventy, except that for tenured faculty members institutions may continue to require retirement at sixty-five until July 1, 1982. The 1978 amendments make clear that employers may not rely on seniority systems or pension plans as justifications for involuntarily retiring an employee prior to the Act's prescribed upper age limit.

ADEA is administered by the U.S. Department of Labor. The department may investigate and conciliate violations of the act (29 U.S.C. secs. 626(a) and 626(b)), and both the department and the injured employees may sue in court to enforce the act (29 U.S.C. secs. 626(c) and 626(d)). As under other statutes, the burden of proof has been an issue in court litigation. Generally, the plaintiff must make a prima facie showing of age discrimination, at which point the burden shifts to the employer to show that distinctions among employees or applicants were "based on reasonable factors other than age" (29 U.S.C. sec. 623(f)(1)); that age is a bona fide occupational qualification for the particular position at issue (29 U.S.C. sec. 623(f)(1)); or that, in the case of discipline or discharge, the action was taken "for a good cause" (29 U.S.C. sec. 623(f)(3)). See *Laugeson* v. *Anaconda Co.*, 510 F.2d 307 (6th Cir. 1975), and *Hodgson* v. *First Federal S&L*, 455 F.2d 818 (5th Cir. 1972).

3.3.2.6. *Rehabilitation Act of 1973, as amended by the Rehabilitation Act Amendments of 1974* (handicapped). Section 504 of the Rehabilitation Act, 29 U.S.C. sec. 794 (also discussed in

"Construction and Application of Age Discrimination in Employment Act of 1967," 24 A.L.R. Fed. 808 (1975 and periodic supp.).

Section 7.4.4), is patterned after the Title VII and Title IX
provisions that prohibit, respectively, race and sex discrimination
in federally funded programs and activities. HEW's Office for Civil
Rights administers the statute using a fund-termination process
similar to Title VI and IX's as the primary enforcement
mechanism.

Regarding employment, the HEW regulations implementing Section 504 have the following provisions:

> (a) *General.* (1) No qualified handicapped person
> shall, on the basis of handicap, be subjected to discrimina-
> tion in employment under any program or activity. . . .
> (2) A recipient that receives assistance under the
> Education of the Handicapped Act shall take positive steps
> to employ and advance in employment qualified handi-
> capped persons in programs assisted under that Act.
> (3) A recipient shall make all decisions concerning
> employment under any program or activity to which this
> part applies in a manner which ensures that discrimination
> on the basis of handicap does not occur and may not limit,
> segregate, or classify applicants or employees in any way
> that adversely affects their opportunities or status because of
> handicap.
> (4) A recipient may not participate in a contractual
> or other relationship that has the effect of subjecting
> qualified handicapped applicants or employees to discrimi-
> nation prohibited by this subpart. The relationships
> referred to in this subparagraph include relationships with
> employment and referral agencies, with labor unions, with
> organizations providing or administering fringe benefits to
> employees of the recipient, and with organizations provid-
> ing training and apprenticeship programs.
> (b) *Specific activities.* The provisions of this subpart
> apply to:
> (1) Recruitment, advertising, and the processing of
> applications for employment;
> (2) Hiring, upgrading, promotion, award of tenure,
> demotion, transfer, lay-off, termination, right of return
> from lay-off, and rehiring;
> (3) Rates of pay or any other form of compensation
> and changes in compensation;
> (4) Job assignments, job classifications, organiza-

tional structure, position descriptions, lines of progression, and seniority lists;

(5) Leaves of absence, sick leave, or any other leave;

(6) Fringe benefits available by virtue of employment, whether or not administered by the recipient;

(7) Selection and financial support for training, including apprenticeship, professional meetings, conferences, and other related activities, and selection for leaves of absence to pursue training;

(8) Employer sponsored activities, including social or recreational programs; and

(9) Any other term, condition, or privilege of employment.

(c) A recipient's obligation to comply with this subpart is not affected by any inconsistent term of any collective bargaining agreement to which it is a party [45 C.F.R. sec. 84.11].

For purposes of this section, a qualified handicapped person is defined as one who "with reasonable accommodation can perform the essential functions" of the job in question (45 C.F.R. sec. 84.3(k)(1)). The regulations impose an affirmative obligation on the recipient to make "reasonable accommodation to the known physical or mental limitations of an otherwise qualified handicapped applicant or employee unless the recipient can demonstrate that the accommodation would impose an undue hardship on the operation of its program" (45 C.F.R. sec. 84.12(a)). Reasonable accommodations can take the form of modification of the job site, of equipment, or of a position itself. What hardship would relieve a recipient of the obligation to make reasonable accommodation depends on the facts of each case. As a related affirmative requirement, the recipient must adapt its employment tests to accommodate an applicant's sensory, manual, or speaking handicap unless the tests are intended to measure those types of skills (45 C.F.R. sec. 84.13(b)).

The regulations include explicit prohibitions regarding employee selection procedures and preemployment questioning. As a general rule, the fund recipient cannot make any preemployment inquiry or require a preemployment medical examination to determine whether an applicant is handicapped or to determine the nature or severity of a handicap (45 C.F.R. sec. 84.14(a)). Nor can a recipient use any employment criterion, such as a test, which has the effect of eliminating qualified handicapped applicants, unless the criterion is job-related and there is no alternative job-related criterion which does not have the same effect (45 C.F.R. sec. 84.13(a)).

3.3.2.7. Section 1981 (Race and Alienage). A post–Civil War civil rights statute, 42 U.S.C. sec. 1981, commonly known as "Section 1981" ("equal rights under the law"), states:

> All persons within the jurisdiction of the United States shall have the same right in every State and Territory to make and enforce contracts, to sue, be parties, give evidence, and to the full and equal benefit of all laws and proceedings for the security of persons and property as is enjoyed by white citizens, and shall be subject to like punishment, pains, penalties, taxes, licenses, and exactions of every kind, and to no other.

Section 1981 is enforced through court litigation by persons denied the equality which the statute guarantees.

Section 1981 covers racially based employment discrimination against white persons as well as racial minorities (*McDonald v. Sante Fe Trail Transportation Co.,* 427 U.S. 273 (1976)). It also has been held to apply to employment discrimination against aliens (*Guerra* v. *Manchester Terminal Corp.,* 498 F.2d 641 (5th Cir. 1974)). Section 1981 prohibits discrimination in both public and private employment, as the U.S. Supreme Court affirmed in *Johnson* v. *Railway Express Agency,* 421 U.S. 454 (1975).

While Section 1981 overlaps Title VII (see Section 3.3.2.1) in its coverage of racial discrimination in employment, a back-pay award is not restricted to two years of back pay under Section 1981 as it is under Title VII (see *Johnson* v. *Railway Express Agency*). Moreover, Section 1981 directly covers discrimination against aliens, which Title VII does not (see Section 3.3.2.1, note 4); and Title VII covers religious, sex, and national-origin discrimination, whereas Section 1981 does not.

3.3.3. Constitutional prohibitions against employment discrimination. While the 14th Amendment's equal protection clause applies to employment discrimination by public institutions (see Section 1.4.2), the constitutional standards for justifying discrimination are generally more lenient than the various federal statutory standards. (See the discussions of constitutional equal protection standards in Sections 4.2.4 and 4.2.5.) Even where constitutional standards are very strong, as for race and alienage discrimination, the courts usually strike down only discrimination found to be intentional; the federal statutes, on the other hand, generally do not require a showing of discriminatory intent. In *Washington* v. *Davis*, 426 U.S. 229 (1976), for instance, the U.S. Supreme Court distinguished between Title VII (see Section 3.3.2.1) and the equal protection clause, noting that equal protection cases "have not embraced the proposition that a law or other official act, without regard to whether it reflects a racially discriminatory purpose, is unconstitutional solely because it has a racially disproportionate impact." Under Title VII, in contrast, "discriminatory purpose need not be proved." Title VII thus "involves a more probing judicial review of, and less deference to, the seemingly reasonable acts of administrators and executives than is appropriate under the Constitution where special racial impact, without discriminatory purpose, is claimed."

Besides its less vigorous standards, the equal protection clause also lacks the administrative implementation and enforcement mechanisms that exist for most federal statutes. On the one hand, this means postsecondary administrators will have more guidance, via regulations and interpretive bulletins, in understanding and complying with the statutes than the Constitution. On the other hand, this means administrators will be subject to more detailed and technical rules, and to a broader range of remedies for assuring compliance, under the statutes than under the Constitution.

In employment discrimination, the Constitution assumes its greatest importance in areas not covered by any federal statute. Age discrimination against persons seventy or more years old or less than forty years old is one such area, since the Age Discrimination in Employment Act does not cover those ages (see Section 3.3.2.5). Another important uncovered area is discrimination on the basis of sexual preference (such as discrimination against homosexuals).[6] (See G. Siniscalso, "Homosexual Discrimination in Employment," 16 *Santa Clara L. Rev.* 495 (1976).) Discrimination on the basis of residence is a third important example.[7] In such areas public institutions are subject to some restraints even if no applicable federal or state statute exists. But the restraints may be relatively lax. In an age discrimination case, *Weiss* v. *Walsh*, 324 F. Supp. 75 (S.D. N.Y. 1971), for instance, the plaintiff was denied the Schweitzer Chair at Fordham University allegedly because of his age, which at that time was seventy. The court broadly rejected the plaintiff's equal protection argument:

> I am constrained to hold that Professor Weiss is not the victim of an invidious and impermissible discrimination. Notwithstanding great advances in gerontology, the era when advanced age ceases to bear some reasonable statistical relationship to diminished capacity or longevity is still future. It cannot be said, therefore, that age ceilings upon eligibility for employment are inherently suspect, although their application will inevitably fall injustly in the individual case. If the precision of the law is impugnable by the stricture of general applicability, vindication of the exceptional individual may have to attend the wise discretion of the administrator. On its face, therefore, the denial of a teaching position to a man approaching seventy years of age is not constitutionally infirm [324 F. Supp. at 77 affirmed, 461 F.2d 846 (2d. Cir. 1972)].

[6]Such discrimination is often challenged on freedom of speech or association grounds rather than equal protection. See *Aumiller* v. *University of Delaware*, 434 F. Supp. 1273 (D. Del. 1977), where the court ordered reinstatement and $15 thousand damages for a lecturer whose freedom of speech was violated when the university refused to renew his contract because of statements he had made on homosexuality. For an equal protection case, see *McConnell* v. *Anderson*, 451 F.2d 193 (8th Cir. 1971), rejecting a discrimination claim of a homosexual applicant for a university library position.

[7]See, for example, *McCarthy* v. *Philadelphia Civil Service Commission*, 424 U.S. 645 (1976) (upholding continuing residency requirement for city employees); and *Cook County College Teachers Union* v. *Taylor*, 432 F. Supp. 270 (N.D. Ill. 1977) (upholding similar requirement for college faculty members). Compare the student residency cases, Section 4.3.4.

3.3.4. Affirmative action in employment. Affirmative action is an intensely controversial concept in many areas of American life. It has perhaps generated more controversy in education than in any other area. While the debate on affirmative action in student admissions (Section 4.2.5) parallels the affirmative action debate on faculty employment in its intensity, the latter has been even more controversial because it is more crowded with federal regulations and requirements. In many ways the future character and mission of postsecondary education depends on the outcome of the debates.

Affirmative action has become a major issue because the federal government's initiatives regarding discrimination have a dual aim: the goal is not only to "bar like discrimination in the future" but also to "eliminate the discriminatory effects of the past" (*Albermarle Paper Co.* v. *Moody,* 422 U.S. 405 (1975)). Addressing this latter objective under Title VII, courts may "order such affirmative action as may be appropriate" (*Franks* v. *Bowman Transportation Co.,* 424 U.S. 747 (1976), quoting *Albermarle).* Affirmative action can be appropriate under *Franks* even though it may adversely affect other employees, since "a sharing of the burden of the past discrimination is presumptively necessary." Under statutes other than Title VII, and under Executive Orders 11246 and 11375, courts or administrative agencies may similarly require employers, including public and private postsecondary institutions, to engage in affirmative action to eliminate the effects of past discrimination.

Executive Orders 11246 and 11375 (see Section 3.3.2.2) have been the major focus of federal affirmative action initiatives. Aside from their basic prohibition of race, color, religion, sex, and national origin discrimination, these executive orders require federal nonconstruction contractors and subcontractors with specified amounts of contracts and numbers of employees to develop affirmative action plans. Under section 60-2.10 of the Department of Labor's implementing order, known as "Revised Order No. 4" (41 C.F.R. Part 60-2, as amended in 1977 by 42 Fed. Reg. 3454),

[a]n acceptable affirmative action program must include an analysis of areas within which the contractor is

deficient in the utilization of minority groups and women,
and further goals and timetables to which the contractor's
good-faith efforts must be directed to correct the deficiencies, and thus to achieve prompt and full utilization of
minorities and women, at all levels and in all segments of
his work force where deficiencies exist.

Section 60-2.12 of the implementing order requires that a
contractor's affirmative action program include affirmative action
goals and timetables. There has been considerable confusion and
controversy over the concept of goals. While the order states "that
[g]oals should be specific for planned results, with timetables for
completion" (sec. 60-2.12(d)), it also states that "[g]oals may not be
rigid and inflexible quotas which must be met, but must be targets
reasonably attainable by means of applying every good-faith effort
to make all aspects of the entire affirmative action program work"
(sec. 60-2.12(e)).

Since the obligation which this requirement places on
postsecondary institutions has been somewhat unclear, administrators should be prepared to push for clarification and support from
each agency with which their institution has federal contracts. The
order does make clear, however, that an institution cannot achieve
compliance by having a disproportionately high number of
minorities or women in one or a few schools or departments.
Section 60-2.13 provides for the establishment of goals and
timetables by "organizational units and job groups."

Postsecondary institutions contracting with the federal
government are also subject to federal affirmative action requirements regarding handicapped persons, disabled veterans, and
Vietnam veterans. Handicapped persons are covered by section 503
of the Rehabilitation Act of 1973, 29 U.S.C. sec. 793, which
provides that

(a) [a]ny contract in excess of $2,500 entered into by
any Federal department or agency for the procurement of
personal property and nonpersonal services (including
construction) for the United States shall contain a provision
requiring that, in employing persons to carry out such
contract, the party contracting with the United States shall

take affirmative action to employ and advance in employment qualified handicapped individuals.

Section 402 of the Vietnam Era Veterans' Readjustment Assistance
Act of 1974, 38 U.S.C. sec. 2012, contains similar language covering
disabled veterans as well as Vietnam veterans whether or not
disabled. Section 402, however, applies to contracts "of $10,000 or
more" rather than the lower figure specified in section 503. Section
402, moreover, deletes the language in section 503 which requires
affirmative action only "in employing persons to carry out such
contract," thus suggesting that section 402 has a broader scope
than section 503.[8]
     The Department of Labor has issued regulations to
implement both section 503 (41 C.F.R. Part 60-741) and section 402
(41 C.F.R. Part 60-250). Both sets of regulations provide that any
job qualification which tends to screen out members of the covered
groups must be job-related and consistent with business necessity
(41 C.F.R. 60-741.6(c)(1); 41 C.F.R. 60-250.6). The regulations also
require contractors to accommodate the physical and mental
limitations of handicapped persons and disabled veterans "unless
the contractor can demonstrate that such an accommodation would
impose an undue hardship on the conduct of the contractor's
business" (41 C.F.R. 60-741.6(d); 41 C.F.R. 60-250.6(d)).
     Under the various affirmative action provisions in federal
law, the most sensitive nerves are hit when affirmative action

[8]This language distinction between section 402 (veterans) and
section 503 (handicapped) does not appear to be reflected in the
Department of Labor regulations implementing the two statutes. Both sets
of regulations, as well as the regulations under E.O. 11246 and 11375,
contemplate affirmative action for a wider group of employees than those
working directly on the contract. All three sets of regulations, however,
permit contractors to request waivers of affirmative action requirements
concerning facilities not connected with the contract. Under 41 C.F.R. 60-
1.5(b)(2), 60-250.3(a)(5), and 60-741.3(a)(5), the Department of Labor may
grant waivers "with respect to any of a prime contractor's or subcontractor's facilities which he or she finds to be in all respects separate and
distinct from activities of the prime contractor or subcontractor related to
the performance of the contract or subcontract, provided that . . . [it] also
finds that such a waiver will not interfere with or impede the effectuation
of the Act."

creates "reverse discrimination," that is, when the employer eradicates the effects of past discrimination by granting employment preferences to members of the class subject to past discrimination, thus discriminating "in reverse" against other employees or applicants.[9] Besides creating policy issues of the highest order, such affirmative action measures create two sets of complex legal issues: (1) To what extent does the applicable statute, executive order, or implementing regulation require or permit the employer to utilize such employment preferences? (2) What limitations does the U.S. Constitution place on the federal government's authority to require or permit, or the employer's authority to utilize, such employment preferences?

The response to the first question depends on a close analysis of the particular legal authority involved. The answer is not necessarily the same under each authority. In general, however, federal law is more likely to require or permit hiring preferences when necessary to overcome the effects of the employer's own past discrimination than it is when no such past discrimination is shown or when preferences are not necessary to eliminate its effects. Section 703(j) of Title VII, for instance, relieves employers of any obligation to give "preferential treatment" to an individual or group merely because of an "imbalance" in the number or percentage of employed persons from that group compared with the number or percentage of persons from that group in the "community, state, section, or other area" (42 U.S.C. sec. 2000e-2(j)). But where an imbalance does not arise innocently but rather arises because of the employer's discriminatory practices, courts in Title VII suits have sometimes required the use of hiring preferences or goals to remedy the effects of such discrimination. (See, for example, *United States* v. *International Union of Elevator Constructors,* 538 F.2d 1012 (3d Cir. 1976).)

Constitutional limitations on the use of employment preferences stem from the Fourteenth Amendment's equal protection clause. (See the discussion of equal protection's application to

[9]The relevant authorities are collected in Annot., "What Constitutes Reverse or Majority Discrimination on Basis of Sex or Race Violative of Federal Constitution or Statutes," 26 A.L.R. Fed. 13 (1976 and periodic supp.).

admissions preferences in Section 4.2.5.) Even if the applicable statute, executive order, or regulation is construed to require or permit employment preferences, such preferences may still be invalid under the federal Constitution. Courts have usually held hiring preferences to be constitutional where necessary to eradicate the effects of the employer's past discrimination, as in *Carter* v. *Gallagher*, 452 F.2d 315 (8th Cir. 1971). Where there is no such showing of past discrimination, the constitutionality of employment preferences is more in doubt. The law on this controversial issue is still in its formative stages, with the student admissions cases leading the way.

The reverse discrimination conundrum arose in the postsecondary context in *Cramer* v. *Virginia Commonwealth University*, 415 F. Supp. 673 (E.D. Va. 1976). The plaintiff was a male teaching applicant who had been rejected by the defendant university on account of his sex. The university admitted that only females were considered for the two vacancies and claimed that its female-only hiring policy was the result of its attempted compliance with Executive Orders 11246 and 11375. The university stipulated that it had discriminated on the basis of sex and that the plaintiff's qualifications were as good as or better than those of the two females who were hired. The plaintiff argued that the hiring preference for females violated both the equal protection clause of the federal Constitution and section 703(j) of Title VII. The court agreed. Even if the university had discriminated against females in the past and the effects of such discrimination remained, according to the court, the university could not consider sex in hiring its instructors. The court also held that Executive Orders 11246 and 11375 could not be applied so as to override Title VII's limitation on the use of hiring preferences.

The *Cramer* opinion may be inconsistent with some earlier cases approving hiring preferences when necessary to overcome the effects of the employer's past discrimination. It is also questionable whether the court should have relied on section 703(j) of Title VII, which limits only the scope of Title VII, to limit the scope of executive orders to which 703(j) was not intended to apply. It thus remains to be seen how much of *Cramer* will be accepted in later case developments.

3.3.5. Coping with the equal employment thicket. There is no magic machete which postsecondary administrators can use to cut through the equal employment thicket. Though they embody critical social goals, the complex tangle of statutes, executive orders, regulations, and court cases create a formidable administrative challenge under the best of circumstances. The challenge is not one for amateurs. Postsecondary institutions need equal employment officers and other administrators who are qualified specialists on the subject. Postsecondary institutions also need legal counsel in the formation of equal employment policies and should encourage a smooth working relationship between equal opportunity officers and legal advisors.

The various laws provide many channels for challenging alleged discrimination in an institution's employment decisions. Administrators should be attentive to the increased possibilities for such challenges from faculty members, applicants, or government agencies. In order to avoid or overcome charges of employment discrimination, administrators should attempt to assure not merely that some nondiscriminatory reason can be given for each employment decision but that discrimination played no part in any decision. As the court noted in an age discrimination case, *Laugeson* v. *Anaconda Co.*, 510 F.2d 307, 317 (6th Cir. 1975): "There could be more than one factor in the decision to discharge . . . [the employee] and . . . he was nevertheless entitled to recover if one such factor was his age and if in fact it made a difference in determining whether he was to be retained or discharged." See also the discussion of the *Mt. Healthy* case in Section 3.6.5.

Sec. 3.4. Standards and Criteria for Faculty Personnel Decisions

Postsecondary institutions commonly have written and published standards or criteria to guide decision making regarding faculty appointments, contract renewals, promotions, and tenure. Since they will often constitute part of the contract between the institution and the faculty member (see Section 3.1) and thus be binding on the institution, such evaluative standards and criteria should receive the careful attention of administrators and faculty members alike. If particular standards are not intended to be legally binding or are not intended to apply to certain kinds of personnel decisions, those limitations should be made clear in the standards themselves.

While courts will enforce standards or criteria found to be part of the faculty contract, the law accords postsecondary institutions wide discretion in determining the content and specificity of those standards and criteria. Courts are less likely to become involved in disputes concerning the *substance* of standards and criteria than in disputes over *procedures* for enforcing standards and criteria. (Courts draw the same distinction in cases concerning students; see the discussion in Sections 4.4 through 4.6.) In rejecting the claims of a nontenured professor, for example, the court in *Stebbins* v. *Weaver*, 537 F.2d 939 (7th Cir. 1976), emphasized that it would not review the merits or wisdom of denying tenure or refusing to rehire. And the court in *Brouillette* v. *Board of Directors of Merged Area IX*, 519 F.2d 126 (8th Cir. 1975), rejecting the claims of a community college faculty member, quoted an earlier case to note that "such matters as the competence of teachers and the standards of its measurement are not, without more, matters of constitutional dimensions. They are peculiarly appropriate to state and local administration."

Despite a generally deferential judicial attitude, there are several bases on which an institution's evaluative standards and criteria may be legally scrutinized. When standards or criteria are part of the faculty contract, both public and private institutions' disputes over interpretation may wind up in court or in the institution's internal grievance process. The "financial exigency" disputes discussed in Section 3.7.1 are a recent example. For public institutions, standards or criteria may also be embodied in state statutes or administrative regulations subject to interpretation by courts, state administrative agencies (such as boards of regents or civil service commissions), or the institution's internal grievance process. Cases on attaining tenure and dismissal from tenured positions for "just cause" are prominent examples.[10] And under the

[10]The cases and authorities for both statutes and contract clauses are collected in Annot., "Construction and Effect of Tenure Provisions of Contract or Statute Governing Employment of College or University Faculty Member," 66 A.L.R. 3d 1018 (1975 plus periodic supp.).

various federal nondiscrimination statutes discussed in Section 3.3, public and private institutions' standards and criteria may be scrutinized for their discriminatory impact by courts or federal administrative agencies or in an internal grievance process when one is required by federal regulations.

In public institutions, standards and criteria may also be subjected to constitutional scrutiny under the First and Fourteenth Amendments. Under the First Amendment, a standard or criterion can be challenged as "overbroad" if it is so broadly worded that it can be used to penalize a faculty member for having exercised constitutionally protected rights of free expression. Under the Fourteenth Amendment a standard or criterion can be challenged as "vague" if it is so unclear that institutional personnel cannot understand its meaning. In *Adamian* v. *Jacobson*, 523 F.2d 929 (9th Cir. 1975), for instance, a tenured professor who had led an allegedly disruptive demonstration was dismissed under a standard requiring faculty members "to exercise appropriate restraint [and] to show respect for the opinions of others." The professor challenged the standard as overbroad and vague. After the lower court found for the professor (359 F. Supp. 825 (D.Nev. 1973)), the appellate court reversed. It held that the regulation would violate the First Amendment if interpreted broadly but could be constitutional if narrowly interpreted, as prescribed in AAUP guidelines, so as not to refer to the content of a professor's remarks. The case went back to the lower court for a determination of which interpretation the university used. (The overbreadth and vagueness doctrines are discussed further in Sections 4.4.1 and 4.7.2.)

The leading U.S. Supreme Court case on public employment standards is *Arnett* v. *Kennedy*, 416 U.S. 134 (1974), in which a federal civil servant was dismissed under a statute authorizing dismissal "for such cause as will promote the efficiency of the service." A majority of the Court held that this standard, as applied to the federal service, was neither overbroad nor vague. While the result suggests that the overbreadth and vagueness doctrines do not substantially restrict the standard-setting process, that does not necessarily mean public postsecondary institutions could use the standard approved in *Arnett*. Employment standards should be adapted to the characteristics and functions of the group to which the standards apply. A standard acceptable for a large heterogeneous group such as the federal civil service may not be acceptable for a smaller, more homogeneous group such as a college faculty. (See, for example, *Bence* v. *Breier,* 501 F.2d 1185 (7th Cir. 1974), which held that the discharge standard of a local police force must be more stringently scrutinized under the overbreadth and vagueness doctrines than was the federal discharge standard in *Arnett.*) Courts may thus require somewhat more of a postsecondary institution's standards than of those of the federal government. This is particularly so for the overbreadth doctrine, which, in connection with the academic freedom principles discussed in Section 3.6, is likely to remain an important limit on institutional discretion in devising employment standards.

Sec. 3.5. Procedures for Faculty Personnel Decisions

3.5.1. General principles. Postsecondary educational institutions have established varying procedural requirements for making and internally reviewing faculty personnel decisions. These requirements are the first place administrators should look in attempting to resolve procedural issues concerning appointment, retention, promotion, and tenure. Whenever such requirements can reasonably be construed as part of the faculty member's contract with the institution (see Section 3.1), the law will usually require both public and private institutions to comply with their own procedures. In *Skehan* v. *Board of Trustees of Bloomsburg State College,* 501 F.2d 31 (3d Cir. 1976), for instance, a nonrenewed professor alleged that the institution had not complied with a college policy statement providing for hearings in academic freedom cases. The appellate court held that the college would have to follow the policy statement if, on remand, the lower court found that the statement granted a contractual right under state law and that the professor's case involved academic freedom within the meaning of the statement. The lower court then held that the professor did possess a contractual right to the procedures specified in the statement (431 F. Supp. 1379 (M.D. Pa. 1977)).

Public institutions will also often be subject to state statutes or administrative regulations which establish procedures applicable to faculty personnel decisions. In *Brouillette* v. *Board of Directors of Merged Area IX*, 519 F.2d 126 (8th Cir. 1975), for example, the court applied a public hearing statute for terminated teachers to a community college faculty member, concluding that the institution had complied with the statute. In a "turnabout" case, *Rutcosky* v. *Board of Trustees of Community College District No. 18*, 14 Wash. App. 786, 545 P.2d 567 (1976), the court found that the plaintiff faculty member had not complied with a state procedural requirement applicable to termination-of-employment hearings and therefore refused to grant him any relief.

The procedures used by a state institution or other institution whose personnel decision is considered state action (see Section 1.4.2) are also subject to constitutional requirements of procedural due process. These requirements are discussed in Section 3.5.2.

3.5.2. The public faculty member's right to constitutional due process. In two landmark cases, *Board of Regents* v. *Roth*, 408 U.S. 564 (1972), and *Perry* v. *Sindermann*, 408 U.S. 593 (1972), the U.S. Supreme Court established that faculty members have a right to a fair hearing whenever a personnel decision deprives them of a "property interest" or a "liberty interest" under the Fourteenth Amendment's due process clause. The "property" and "liberty" terminology is derived from the wording of the Fourteenth Amendment itself, which provides that states shall not "deprive any person of life, liberty, or property, without due process of law." (The identification of property and liberty interests is also important to many procedural due process questions concerning students; see Sections 4.3.1, 4.3.6.2, 4.6.2, 4.6.3, and 4.11.1.)

In identifying these property and liberty interests, one must make the critical distinction between faculty members who are under continuing contracts and those whose contracts have expired. It is clear, as *Roth* notes, that "a public college professor dismissed from an office held under tenure provisions . . . and college professors and staff members dismissed during the terms of their contracts . . . have interests in continued employment that are safeguarded by due process." But the situation is not clear with respect to faculty members whose contracts are expiring and are up for renewal.

Roth and *Perry* are the leading cases on the nonrenewal of faculty contracts. The respondent in *Roth* had been hired as an assistant professor at Wisconsin State University for a fixed term of one year. A state statute provided that all state university teachers would be employed for one-year terms and would be eligible for tenure only after four years of continuous service. The professor was notified before February 1 that he would not be rehired. No reason for the decision was given nor was there an opportunity for a hearing or an appeal.

The issue addressed by the Supreme Court was "whether the [professor] had a constitutional right to a statement of reasons and a hearing on the University's decision not to rehire him for another year." The Court ruled that he had no such right because he had neither a "liberty" nor a "property" interest under the Fourteenth Amendment that had been violated by the nonrenewal. Concerning liberty interests, the Court reasoned:

> The State, in declining to rehire the respondent, did not make any charge against him that might seriously damage his standing and associations in his community. It did not base the nonrenewal of his contract on a charge, for example, that he had been guilty of dishonesty, or immorality. Had it done so, this would be a different case. For "[w]here a person's good name, reputation, honor, or integrity is at stake because of what the government is doing to him, notice and an opportunity to be heard is essential" [citation omitted]. In such a case, due process would accord an opportunity to refute the charge before University officials. In the present case, however, there is no suggestion whatever that the respondent's "good name, reputation, honor, or integrity" is at stake.
>
> Similarly, there is no suggestion that the State, in declining to reemploy the respondent, imposed on him a stigma or other disability that foreclosed his freedom to take advantage of other employment opportunities. The State, for example, did not invoke any regulations to bar the respondent from all other public employment in state universities. Had it done so, this, again, would be a different case. . . .
>
> Hence, on the record before us, all that clearly appears is that the respondent was not rehired for one year at one university. It stretches the concept too far to suggest

that a person is deprived of "liberty" when he simply is not
rehired in one job but remains as free as before to seek
another [408 U.S. at 573–74, 575].

The Court also held that the respondent had not been
deprived of any property interest in future employment:

> The Fourteenth Amendment's procedural protection
> of property is a safeguard of the security of interests that a
> person has already acquired in specific benefits. . . . To have
> a property interest in a benefit, a person clearly must have
> more than an abstract need or desire for it. He must have
> more than a unilateral expectation of it. He must, instead,
> have a legitimate claim of entitlement to it. . . .
>   Property interests, of course, are not created by the
> Constitution. Rather they are created and their dimensions
> are defined by existing rules or understandings that stem
> from an independent source such as state law—rules or
> understandings that secure certain benefits and that support
> claims of entitlement to those benefits. . . . [R]espondent's
> "property" interest in employment at Wisconsin State
> University–Oshkosh was created and defined by the terms of
> his appointment [which] specifically provided that the
> respondent's employment was to terminate on June 30.
> They did not provide for contract renewal absent "sufficient
> cause." Indeed, they made no provision for renewal
> whatsoever.
>   . . . In these circumstances, the respondent surely
> had an abstract concern in being rehired, but he did not
> have a *property* interest sufficient to require the University
> authorities to give him a hearing when they declined to
> renew his contract of employment [408 U.S. at 578].

Since the professor had no protected liberty or property
interest, his Fourteenth Amendment rights had not been violated
and the university was not required to provide a reason for its
nonrenewal of the contract or to afford the professor a hearing on
the nonrenewal.

In the *Perry* case, the respondent had been employed as a
professor by the Texas state college system for ten consecutive
years. While employed, he was actively involved in public
disagreements with the board of regents. He was employed on a

series of one-year contracts, and at the end of his tenth year the board elected not to rehire him. The professor was given neither an official reason nor the opportunity for a hearing. Like Roth, Perry argued that the board's action violated his Fourteenth Amendment right to procedural due process.

But in the *Perry* case, unlike the *Roth* case, the Supreme Court ruled that the professor had raised a genuine claim to "de facto" tenure which would create a constitutionally protected property interest in continued employment. The professor relied on tenure guidelines promulgated by the Coordinating Board of the Texas College and University System and on an official faculty guide which stated that "Odessa College has no tenure system. The Administration of the College wishes the faculty member to feel that he has permanent tenure as long as his teaching services are satisfactory and as long as he displays a cooperative attitude toward his co-workers and his superiors, and as long as he is happy in his work."

According to the Court,

> the respondent [professor] offered to prove that a teacher with his long period of service at this particular State College had no less a "property" interest in continued employment than a formally tenured teacher at other colleges, and had no less a procedural due process right to a statement of reasons and a hearing before college officials upon their decision not to retain him.
>
> We have made clear in *Roth* . . . that "property" interests subject to procedural due process protection are not limited by a few rigid technical forms. Rather, "property" denotes a broad range of interests that are secured by "existing rules or understandings." A person's interest in a benefit is a "property" interest for due process purposes if there are such rules or mutually explicit understandings that support his claim of entitlement to the benefit and that he may invoke at a hearing.
>
> A written contract with an explicit tenure provision clearly is evidence of a formal understanding that supports a teacher's claim of entitlement to continued employment unless sufficient "cause" is shown. Yet absence of such an explicit contractual provision may not always foreclose the possibility that a teacher has a "property" interest in reemployment. . . .

> In this case, the respondent has alleged the existence of rules and understandings, promulgated and fostered by state officials, that may justify his legitimate claim of entitlement to continued employment absent "sufficient cause." We disagree with the Court of Appeals insofar as it held that a mere subjective "expectancy" is protected by procedural due process, but we agree that the respondent must be given an opportunity to prove the legitimacy of his claim of such entitlement in light of "the policies and practices of the institution" [citation omitted]. Proof of such a property interest would not, of course, entitle him to reinstatement. But such proof would obligate officials to grant a hearing at his request, where he could be informed of the grounds for his nonretention and challenge their sufficiency [408 U.S. at 603].

One other, more recent Supreme Court case should be read together with *Roth* and *Perry* for a fuller understanding of the Court's due process analysis. *Bishop* v. *Wood*, 426 U.S. 341 (1976), concerned a policeman who had been discharged, allegedly on the basis of incorrect information, and orally informed of the reasons in a private conference. With four judges strongly dissenting, the Court held that the discharge infringed neither property nor liberty interests of the policeman. Regarding property, the Court, adopting a stilted lower court interpretation of the ordinance governing employment of policemen, held that it gave the plaintiff no expectation of continued employment but only conditioned dismissal on compliance with certain procedures that had been provided in this case. Regarding liberty, the Court held that the charges against an employee cannot form the basis for a deprivation-of-liberty claim if they are privately communicated to the employee and not made public. The Court also held that the truth or falsity of the charges is irrelevant to the question of whether a liberty interest has been infringed.

Under *Roth*, *Perry*, and *Bishop*, there are three basic situations in which courts will require that a nonrenewal decision be accompanied by appropriate procedural safeguards:

(1) when the existing rules, policies, or practices of the institution, or "mutually explicit understandings" between the faculty member and the institution, support the faculty member's

claim of entitlement to continued employment. Such circumstances would create a property interest. In *Soni* v. *Board of Trustees of University of Tennessee*, 513 F.2d 347 (6th Cir. 1975), for example, the court held that a nonrenewed, nontenured mathematics professor had such a property interest based on the voting and retirement plan privileges extended to him and the representations made to him concerning his status.

(2) when the institution, in the course of nonrenewal, makes charges against the faculty member that could seriously damage his or her reputation, standing, or associations in the community. Such circumstances would create a liberty interest.[11] *Roth,* for instance, suggests that charges of dishonesty or immorality accompanying nonrenewal could infringe a faculty member's liberty interest. And in *Wellner* v. *Minnesota State Junior College Board,* 487 F.2d 153 (8th Cir. 1973), the court held that charges of racism deprived the faculty member of a liberty interest.

The *Bishop* case makes clear that such charges must in some way be made public before they can form the basis of a liberty claim. Although *Bishop* did not involve faculty members, a pre-*Bishop* case, *Ortwein* v. *Mackey,* 511 F.2d 696 (5th Cir. 1975), applies essentially the same principle in the university setting. Under *Ortwein* the institution must have made, or be likely to make, the stigmatizing charges "public 'in any official or intentional manner, other than in connection with the defense of [related legal] action.'" Thus, there are still questions to be resolved concerning when a charge has become sufficiently "public" to fall within *Ortwein* and *Bishop.*

(3) when the nonrenewal imposes a "stigma or other disability" on the faculty member that "foreclose[s] his freedom to take advantage of other employment opportunities." Such circumstances would create a liberty interest. *Roth,* for instance, suggests

---

[11]In *Paul* v. *Davis,* 424 U.S. 693 (1976), the U.S. Supreme Court held that "defamation, standing alone," does not infringe a liberty interest. But defamation can still create a liberty infringement when combined with some "alteration of legal status" under state law, and termination or nonrenewal of public employment is such a change in status. Defamation "in the course of declining to rehire" would therefore infringe a faculty member's liberty interest even under *Paul* v. *Davis.*

that a nonrenewal which bars the faculty member from other employment in the state higher education system would infringe a liberty interest. Presumably charges impugning the faculty member's professional competence or integrity could also infringe a liberty interest if the institution keeps records of the charges whose contents had been or would be divulged to potential future employers of the faculty member.

And there is possibly a fourth situation in which a liberty or property interest would be infringed: when the nonrenewal is based on, and thus would penalize, the faculty member's exercise of freedom of expression. The Supreme Court dealt with this issue briefly in a footnote in the *Roth* case (408 U.S. at 575 n. 14), appearing to suggest that a hearing may be required in some circumstances where the nonrenewal "would directly impinge upon interests in free speech or free press." Whenever a nonrenewed faculty member has a basis for making such a claim (see Section 3.6), administrators should consider providing a hearing. Properly conducted (see Section 3.5.3), a hearing may not only vitiate any subsequent procedural due process litigation by the faculty member but may also resolve or defuse First Amendment claims that otherwise might be taken to court.

Clearly, then, whenever the institution's personnel decision infringes a property or liberty interest, constitutional due process requires that the institution afford the faculty member procedural safeguards. Decisions to terminate tenured faculty members or faculty members in mid-contract must always be accompanied by such safeguards, since such decisions always infringe property interests. Nonrenewal decisions may or may not require procedural safeguards, depending on whether they fall within the property and liberty guidelines above.

The crux of the required safeguards is giving notice and an opportunity for a hearing. The institution, in other words, must notify the faculty member of the reasons for the decision and provide a fair opportunity to challenge the reasons in a hearing before an impartial body. Though courts have not spelled out all the specific attributes of such a hearing, the constitutionally required procedures would apparently be much the same as those in the student suspension cases, such as *Dixon* v. *Alabama State*

Board, discussed in Section 4.6.2. It is clear that a full-scale hearing need not be provided before the personnel decision is tentatively made. Some courts, however, require a hearing before the decision is actually implemented by terminating the faculty member's pay or other substantial employment benefits. *Skehan* v. *Board of Trustees of Bloomsburg State College,* 501 F.2d 31 (3d Cir. 1974), for instance, involved a faculty member who had been relieved of his duties, dismissed, and removed from the payroll for almost three months before he was afforded a hearing. The court held that the hearing, because of its timing, did not meet due process requirements. In *Peacock* v. *Board of Regents of University and State Colleges of Arizona,* 510 F.2d 1324 (9th Cir. 1975), however, the court upheld a posttermination hearing where the faculty member had been removed only from a nonpaying position as department head; and in *Chung* v. *Park,* 514 F.2d 382 (3d Cir. 1975), the court upheld a hearing which had been provided after the decision to terminate was made but before job benefits were actually terminated.[12]

3.5.3. Implementing procedural requirements. An institution's procedures for making and internally reviewing the various kinds of faculty personnel decisions should be in writing and made generally available. Public institutions (see Section 1.4.2) must, at a minimum, comply with the constitutional due process requirements in Section 3.5.2 and may choose to provide additional procedures beyond those which the Constitution would require. Private institutions are not required to comply with constitutional requirements but may wish to use these requirements as a guide in establishing their own procedures.

Though personnel procedures can be administratively burdensome, that is not the whole story. They can also help the institution avoid or rectify mistaken assessments, protect the academic freedom of the faculty, foster faculty confidence in the institution, and encourage the resolution of nonrenewal and

---

[12]The closest Supreme Court case is *Arnett* v. *Kennedy,* 416 U.S. 134 (1974), involving the discharge of a federal civil service employee; while the Court held that a full scale pretermination hearing was not required under the particular facts of that case, a majority of the justices could not agree on the reasoning for reaching that result.

termination disputes in-house rather than in the courts. When effective personnel procedures do exist, courts may require, under the "exhaustion of remedies" doctrine, that the faculty member "exhaust" those procedures before filing suit. In *Rieder* v. *State University of New York*, 47 App. Div. 2d 865, 366 N.Y.S.2d 37 (1975), affirmed 39 N.Y.2d 845, 351 N.E.2d 747 (1976), for instance, employees at a state institution were covered by a collective bargaining agreement containing a four-step grievance procedure. When some employees filed suit while awaiting a determination at step two, the appellate courts ordered the suit dismissed for failure to exhaust administrative remedies. Similarly, in *Beck* v. *Bd. of Trustees of State Colleges*, 32 Conn. Sup. 153, 344 A.2d 273 (1975), faculty members sought to enjoin the board of trustees of the state colleges from implementing proposed new personnel policies which allegedly threatened the rights of tenured faculty. The court dismissed the suit under the exhaustion doctrine because the state administrative procedure act "provides a comprehensive, potentially inexpensive, and completely adequate method of resolving the issues raised in the present . . . [suit]."[13]

In cases such as *Rieder* and *Beck*, where public institutions are involved, it is the administrative law of the state which provides the source of the exhaustion doctrine. Such administrative law principles do not apply to private institutions, since they are not agencies of the state. Private institutions may be subject to a comparable exhaustion doctrine, however, which stems from the common law of "private associations." (See Section 4.11.4, note 13 and accompanying text.) For an overview of this common law exhaustion doctrine, see "Developments in the Law—Judicial Control of Actions of Private Associations," 76 *Harvard L. Rev.* 983, 1069–80 (1963).

In devising or reviewing procedures, administrators should carefully consider the question of timing, that is, what procedural safeguards are to be provided before making the personnel decision

[13]Exhaustion presents special problems when the plaintiff brings the suit under the federal Civil Rights Acts. (See Section 2.3.3.) Courts are divided over whether such civil rights plaintiffs must exhaust state administrative remedies. See *Burrell* v. *McCray*, 516 F.2d 357 (4th Cir. 1975), writ dismissed as improvidently granted, 426 U.S. 471 (1976).

or before suspending or terminating job benefits, as opposed to after. The question of when and in what detail statements of reasons for personnel decisions are to be given must also be carefully considered. The question of who shall preside over hearings is likewise important, with impartiality being the key consideration. Other critical issues are the confidentiality of the statements of reasons—and of any proceedings in which the faculty member challenges these reasons—and the question of what permanent records should be kept of adverse personnel decisions and who should have access to them. While the legal principles in Sections 3.5.1 and 3.5.2 create some limits on administrative discretion in these areas, considerable flexibility remains for administrators to make wise policy choices.

Sec. 3.6. Faculty Academic Freedom

3.6.1. Background and general principles. The concept of academic freedom eludes precise definition. It is a concept which draws meaning from both the world of education and the world of law. Courts have increasingly used academic freedom as the catch-all term to describe the legal rights and responsibilities of the teaching profession. This judicial conception of academic freedom is essentially an attempt to reconcile basic legal principles with the court's notions of academic freedom's social and intellectual role in American education.

Though courts usually discuss academic freedom in cases concerning the constitutional rights of faculty members, the legal boundaries of academic freedom are initially defined by contract law. Faculty members possess whatever academic freedom is guaranteed them under the faculty contract (see Section 3.1). The AAUP's *1940 Statement of Principles on Academic Freedom and Tenure* and the *1970 Interpretive Comments* (60 *AAUP Bulletin* 269 (1974)), and the AAUP's *1976 Recommended Institutional Regulations on Academic Freedom and Tenure* (62 *AAUP Bulletin* 184 (1976)) are often looked to as the prevailing policy statements on academic freedom, and it is crucial for administrators to determine whether either document has been—or should be—incorporated in the faculty contract. Courts will interpret and enforce the terms of the AAUP documents by reference to contract law principles to the extent those terms have become a part of the faculty contract. Even when the documents have not been incorporated in the contract, they may be an important source of academic "custom and usage" which courts will consider in interpreting unclear contract terms. (See Sections 1.3.8 and 3.1.)

In private institutions, the faculty contract may be the only legal restriction on the administrator's authority to regulate academic freedom. But in public institutions (see Section 1.4.2), administrators are also limited by state statutes or administrative regulations and by constitutional concepts of academic freedom. (The same constitutional concepts would limit legislatures and other government officials whose regulatory actions affected academic freedom whether in public or private institutions.) Whereas contract and statutory provisions may distinguish between tenured and nontenured faculty (see note 9, Section 3.4), tenure and job status are immaterial to most constitutionally based academic freedom claims. In *Perry* v. *Sindermann*, 408 U.S. 593 (1972), discussed in Section 3.5.2, the U.S. Supreme Court held that a nonrenewed faculty member's "lack of a contractual or tenure right to reemployment . . . is immaterial to his free speech claim" and that "regardless of the . . . [teacher's] contractual or other claim to a job," government cannot "deny a benefit to a person because of his constitutionally protected speech or associations."[14]

In a series of leading cases in the 1950s and 1960s the U.S. Supreme Court gave academic freedom constitutional status under the First Amendment freedoms of speech and association, the Fifth Amendment protection against self-incrimination, and the Fourteenth Amendment guarantee of due process. The opinions in these cases include several ringing declarations on the importance of academic freedom. In *Sweezy* v. *New Hampshire*, 354 U.S. 234 (1957), for example, the Court reversed a contempt judgment

---

[14]The *Perry* Court also held, in contrast, that the professor's job status, "though irrelevant to his free speech claim, is highly relevant to his procedural due process claim." The Fourteenth Amendment due process clause is the one constitutional basis for an academic freedom claim which distinguishes among faculty members on the basis of job status (see Section 3.5.2).

against a professor who had refused to answer questions concerning a lecture delivered at the state university. The plurality opinion of four justices (with two concurring justices expressing similar thoughts) declared that

> [t]he essentiality of freedom in the community of American universities is almost self-evident. No one should underestimate the vital role in a democracy that is played by those who guide and train our youth. To impose any strait jacket upon the intellectual leaders in our colleges and universities would imperil the future of our Nation. No field of education is so thoroughly comprehended by man that new discoveries cannot yet be made. Particularly is that true in the social sciences, where few, if any, principles are accepted as absolutes. Scholarship cannot flourish in an atmosphere of suspicion and distrust. Teachers and students must always remain free to inquire, to study and to evaluate, to gain new maturity and understanding; otherwise our civilization will stagnate and die [354 U.S. at 250].

In *Shelton* v. *Tucker*, 364 U.S. 479 (1960), in invalidating a state statute which compelled public school and college teachers to reveal all organizational affiliations or contributions for the previous five years, the Court remarked:

> The vigilant protection of constitutional freedoms is nowhere more vital than in the community of American schools. "By limiting the power of the States to interfere with freedom of speech and freedom of inquiry and freedom of association, the Fourteenth Amendment protects all persons, no matter what their calling. But, in view of the nature of the teacher's relation to the effective exercise of the rights which are safeguarded by the Bill of Rights and by the Fourteenth Amendment, inhibition of freedom of thought, and of action upon thought, in the case of teachers brings the safeguards of those amendments vividly into operation. Such unwarranted inhibition upon the free spirit of teachers . . . has an unmistakable tendency to chill that free play of the spirit which all teachers ought especially to cultivate and practice; it makes for caution and timidity in their associations by potential teachers." *Wieman* v. *Updegraff*, 344 U.S. 183, 195, 73 S. Ct. 215, 221, 97 L. Ed. 216 (concurring opinion) [364 U.S. at 487].

And in *Keyishian* v. *Board of Regents,* 385 U.S. 589 (1967), discussed below, the Court quoted both *Sweezy* and *Shelton,* and added:

> Our Nation is deeply committed to safeguarding academic freedom, which is of transcendent value to all of us and not merely to the teachers concerned. That freedom is therefore a special concern of the First Amendment, which does not tolerate laws that cast a pall of orthodoxy over the classroom. . . . The classroom is peculiarly the "marketplace of ideas." The Nation's future depends upon leaders trained through wide exposure to that robust exchange of ideas which discovers truth "out of a multitude of tongues, [rather] than through any kind of authoritative selection." *United States* v. *Associated Press,* 52 F. Supp. 362, 372 [385 U.S. at 603].

However, the legal principles which emerge from cases such as these are not as broad as the Court's academic freedom pronouncements might suggest. The faculty's constitutional rights evolving from the cases of the 1950s and 1960s are succinctly summarized in W. Van Alstyne, "The Constitutional Rights of Teachers and Professors, 1969 *Duke L. J.* 841 847–48 (1970):

> 1. Membership per se in political organizations, not excluding the Communist Party, or economic organizations such as labor unions is not a permissible ground for terminating teachers or disqualifying applicants to the profession. Arguably, moreover, not even active and knowing membership including some degree of personal sympathy for the illegal objections of the group may be sufficient, short of some concrete act in furtherance of an illegal objective inconsistent with one's lawful obligations as a teacher.
>
> 2. Correspondingly, disclaimer oaths requiring that one forswear activities or associations he is otherwise constitutionally privileged to pursue as a private citizen are beyond the constitutional pale. In all likelihood, the state may go no further than to require that one be willing to affirm a general commitment to uphold the Constitution and faithfully to perform the duties of the position he holds.[15]

[15](Author's footnote.) In *Cole* v. *Richardson,* 405 U.S. 676 (1972),

The College and the Faculty145

　　　　While neither the First Amendment nor the Fifth
Amendment entitles a teacher to withhold information
when his employer has questioned his competence or
professional integrity on the basis of reasonably specific and
creditable allegations "of impropriety related to his job,"
information elicited under such circumstances by a public
employer may not be utilized for purposes of criminal
prosecution, and vague or general fishing expeditions on
mere suspicion are not permissible.

The centerpiece of these constitutional developments is the
Supreme Court's 1967 decision in the *Keyishian* case, quoted above.
The appellants were State University of New York faculty members
who refused to sign a certificate (the "Feinberg Certificate") stating
they were not and never had been Communists. This certificate was
required under a set of laws and regulations designed to prevent
"subversives" from obtaining employment in the state education
system. The faculty members lost their jobs and sued the state on
the grounds that the dismissal violated their First Amendment
rights. They challenged the certificate requirement and the
underlying law barring employment to members of subversive
organizations, as well as other provisions authorizing dismissal for
the "utterance of any treasonable or seditious word or words or the
doing of any treasonable or seditious act" and for "by word of
mouth or writing wilfully and deliberately advocating, advising, or
teaching the doctrine of forceful overthrow of the government."

The Court held that the faculty members' First Amendment
freedom of association had been violated by the existence and
application of a series of laws and rules that were both vague and
overbroad. (See Section 3.4 above regarding the vagueness and overbreadth doctrines.) The word "seditious" was held to be unconstitutionally vague, even when defined as advocacy of criminal
anarchy:

---

the U.S. Supreme Court later upheld an oath which included not only a
general commitment to "uphold and defend" the Constitution but also a
commitment to "oppose the overthrow of the government . . . by force,
violence, or by any illegal or unconstitutional method." To maintain the
second commitment's constitutionality, the Court read it very narrowly as
merely "a commitment not to use illegal and constitutionally unprotected
force to change the constitutional system," which "does not expand the
obligation of the first [commitment]."

[T]he possible scope of "seditious utterances or acts" has virtually no limit. For under Penal Law sec. 161, one commits the felony of advocating criminal anarchy if he "publicly displays any book . . . containing or advocating, advising or teaching the doctrine that organized government should be overthrown by force, violence, or other unlawful means." Does the teacher who carries a copy of the Communist Manifesto on a public street thereby advocate criminal anarchy? . . . The teacher cannot know the extent, if any, to which a "seditious" utterance must transcend mere statement about abstract doctrine, the extent to which it must be intended to and tend to indoctrinate or incite to action in furtherance of the defined doctrine. The crucial consideration is that no teacher can know just where the line is drawn between "seditious" and nonseditious utterances and acts [385 U.S. at 598–99].

The Court also found that the state's entire system of "intricate administrative machinery" was "a highly efficient *in terrorem* mechanism. . . . It would be a bold teacher who would not stay as far as possible from utterances or acts which might jeopardize his living by enmeshing him in this intricate machinery. . . . The result may be to stifle 'that free play of the spirit which all teachers ought especially to cultivate and practice.'"

The Court rejected the older case of *Adler* v. *Board of Education,* 342 U.S. 485 (1951), which permitted New York to bar employment to teachers who were members of listed subversive organizations. Noting that "the stifling effect on the academic mind from curtailing freedom of association in such a manner is manifest," the Court applied a new rule:

Mere knowing membership without a specific intent to further the unlawful aims of an organization is not a constitutionally adequate basis for exclusion from such positions as those held by appellants. . . . [L]egislation which sanctions membership unaccompanied by specific intent to further the unlawful goals of the organization or which is not active membership violates constitutional limitations [385 U.S. at 606, 608].

One year after *Keyishian,* the Supreme Court stepped

gingerly into a new type of academic freedom controversy. *Pickering* v. *Board of Education,* 391 U.S. 563 (1968), concerned a public high school teacher who had been dismissed for writing a letter to the local newspaper which was highly critical of the board of education's financial plans for the high schools. Pickering brought suit alleging that the dismissal violated his First Amendment freedom of speech. The school board argued that the dismissal was justified because the letter "damaged the professional reputations of . . . [the school board] members and of the school administrators, would be disruptive of faculty discipline, and would tend to foment 'controversy, conflict, and dissension' among teachers, administrators, the Board of Education, and the residents of the district."

In balancing the teacher's freedom of speech against the state's interest in maintaining an efficient education system, the Court identified and considered the following factors: (1) Is there a close working relationship between the teacher and those he criticized? (2) Is the substance of the letter a matter of legitimate public concern? (3) Did the letter have a detrimental impact on the administration of the educational system? (4) Was the teacher's performance of his daily duties impeded? (5) Was the teacher writing in his professional capacity or as a private citizen? The Court found that Pickering had no working relationship with the board, that the letter dealt with a matter of public concern, that Pickering's letter was greeted with public apathy and therefore had no detrimental effect on the schools, that Pickering's performance as a teacher was not hindered by the letter, and that he wrote as a citizen, not a teacher. The Court concluded that under all these facts the interest of the school administration in limiting teachers' opportunities to contribute to public debate is not significantly greater than its interest in limiting a similar contribution by any member of the general public [and that] "in a case such as this, absent proof of false statements knowingly or recklessly made by him, a teacher's exercise of his right to speak on issues of public importance may not furnish the basis for his dismissal from public employment."

Many questions concerning academic freedom are still unanswered. Lower courts have often looked to the specific facts of

Pickering to limit the protections it originally appeared to have provided. The lower court cases fall into three major areas where teachers and administrators may clash over academic freedom: (1) in the classroom, (2) in institutional affairs, and (3) in private life.

3.6.2. Academic freedom in the classroom. Courts are generally most reticent to become involved in academic freedom disputes concerning course content, teaching methods, or classroom behavior. Courts view these as matters best left to the competence of the administrators and educators who have primary responsibility over academic affairs. The following two cases illustrate this judicial attitude.

Hetrick v. *Martin*, 480 F.2d 705 (6th Cir. 1973), concerned the refusal of a state university to renew a nontenured faculty member's contract because the university disapproved of her "pedagogical attitude." Her troubles with the school administration apparently began when unnamed students and the parents of one student complained about certain of her in-class activities. Specifically, to illustrate the "irony" and "connotative qualities" of the English language, the faculty member once told her freshman students, "I am an unwed mother." At that time, she was a divorced mother of two, but she did not reveal that fact to her class. On occasion she also apparently discussed the war in Vietnam and the military draft with one of her freshman classes.

The faculty member sued the university alleging that her First Amendment rights had been infringed. The court ruled that the nonrenewal was not based on any statements the faculty member might have made but on her "pedagogical attitude." The faculty member believed her students should be free to organize assignments in terms of their own interests, while the university expected her to "go by the book." Viewing the case as a dispute over teaching methods, the court refused to equate the teaching methods of professors with constitutionally protected speech:

> We do not accept plaintiff's assertion that the school administration abridged her First Amendment rights when it refused to rehire her because it considered her teaching philosophy to be incompatible with the pedagogical aims of the University. Whatever may be the ultimate scope of the amorphous "academic freedom" guaranteed to our

Nation's teachers and students . . . , it does not encompass
the right of a nontenured teacher to have her teaching style
insulated from review by her superiors when they determine
whether she has merited tenured status just because her
methods and philosophy are considered acceptable some-
where in the teaching profession [480 F.2d at 709].

Clark v. *Holmes,* 474 F.2d 928 (7th Cir. 1972), also involved
a teacher's methods and behavior. Clark was a nontenured,
temporary substitute teacher at Northern Illinois University, a state
institution. Clark had been told he would be rehired if he was
willing to remedy certain deficiencies, namely that he "counseled
an excessive number of students instead of referring them to
NIU's professional counselors; he overemphasized sex in his
health survey course; he counseled students with his office door
closed; and he belittled other staff members in discussions with
students." After discussions with his superiors, in which he
defended his conduct, Clark was rehired; but in the middle of the
year he was told he would not teach in the spring semester because
of these same problems.

Clark brought suit claiming that, under *Pickering,* the
university had violated his First Amendment rights by not rehiring
him because of his speech activities. The court, disagreeing, refused
to apply *Pickering* to this situation: (1) Clark's disputes with his
colleagues about course content were not matters of public
concern, as were the matters raised in Pickering's letter; and (2)
Clark's disputes involved him as a teacher, not as a private citizen,
whereas Pickering's situation was just the opposite. The court then
held that the institution's interest as employer overcame any free
speech interest the teacher may have had:

But we do not conceive academic freedom to be a
license for uncontrolled expression at variance with established curricular contents and internally destructive of the
proper functioning of the institution. First Amendment
rights must be applied in light of the special characteristics
of the environment in the particular case. *Tinker* v. *Des
Moines Indep. Community School Dist.,* 393 U.S. 503, 506,
89 S. Ct. 733, 21 L.Ed.2d 731 (1969); *Healy* v. *James,* 408
U.S. 169 (1972). The plaintiff here irresponsibly made

captious remarks to a captive audience, one, moreover, that
was composed of students who were dependent upon him
for grades and recommendations. . . .

Furthermore, *Pickering* suggests that certain legitimate interests of the State may limit a teacher's right to say
what he pleases: for example, (1) the need to maintain
discipline or harmony among co-workers; (2) the need for
confidentiality; (3) the need to curtail conduct which
impedes the teacher's proper and competent performance of
his daily duties; and (4) the need to encourage a close and
personal relationship between the employee and his superiors, where that relationship calls for loyalty and confidence
[474 F.2d at 931].

3.6.3. Academic freedom in institutional affairs. Just as a
faculty member's duties extend beyond the classroom, so do the
possibilities for academic freedom disputes involving faculty
members. Faculty members may claim academic freedom protections for opinions and behavior involving other official or
unofficial job responsibilities or other campus activities. In these
situations the interests that both the institution and the faculty
member seek to protect are different from those relating to
expression or behavior in the classroom. The state may be less
concerned with the effect such speech has on students. The state's
main interests may be protecting the educational institution from
losing public confidence and maintaining a harmonious relationship between the faculty and the institution. The faculty member is
not as interested in maintaining an atmosphere of free debate
within the classroom as in protecting the right to express his or her
views or personality on campus without fear of reprisal.

In cases involving institutional affairs, faculty members
have fared better with the courts than in the classroom cases. The
following cases are illustrative.

Smith v. *Losee,* 485 F.2d 334 (10th Cir. 1973), concerned a
nontenured associate professor of history at Dixie College, who had
addressed a meeting of the faculty association in his capacity as the
association's president. His speech criticized the college administration. Consequently Smith was dismissed from his faculty position,
and he brought suit asserting his First Amendment right to free
speech. The court stated that even though he was speaking in his

capacity as president of the faculty association, Smith was entitled to criticize the administration in such a manner without fear of being dismissed:

> The plaintiff having proved that his dismissal was grounded upon the exercise of his First Amendment rights, the burden of proof thereby shifted to the defendants to show by clear and convincing evidence that the plaintiff's activities and speech "materially and substantially interfere with the requirements of appropriate discipline in the operation" of the college. *Tinker* v. *Des Moines Indep. Community School Dist.*, 393 U.S. at 509 [485 F.2d at 339–40].

Finding that the college could not make such a showing, the court concluded that Smith's interest in free speech "far outweighed the interests of the defendants in promoting the efficiency and harmony of Dixie College."

Rampey v. *Allen*, 501 F.2d 1090 (10th Cir. 1974), arose after a college president had characterized eleven professors and three staff members as "divisive" and had caused them not to be rehired. By "divisive," the court later found, the president meant that the professors refused to parrot his views or would talk to students and other faculty members about problems the school was having. The fourteen plaintiffs sued, alleging that the nonrenewal of their contracts was in retaliation for their exercise of First Amendment rights. The court agreed:

> While a college president is entitled to respect and authority within his sphere, this does not extend to the exercise of absolute control over the associations and expressions of the faculty members. Whether they demonstrate loyalty to him personally, whether they relate to him personally, and whether they have a similar philosophy is not, as we view it, a requisite and he cannot demand such attitudes at the expense of the individual rights of the faculty members and there can be little question but that such demands infringe the rights of the faculty members to express legitimate views in the course of formulating ideas in an academic atmosphere. There is not the slightest suggestion in the evidence that the plaintiffs in exercising

their rights constituted any threat to the valid authority of
President Carter in the conduct of his duties. Nor does it
appear that these plaintiffs were in a relationship with Dr.
Carter which required personal loyalty or devotion [501
F.2d at 1098].

In *Starsky* v. *Williams,* 353 F. Supp. 900 (D.Ariz. 1972),
affirmed in pertinent part, 512 F.2d 109 (9th Cir. 1975), the
plaintiff was a philosophy professor who had been dismissed on a
series of eight charges, some involving on-campus activity and
others involving off-campus activity. (The charges in the latter
category are discussed in Section 3.6.4.) Professor Starsky was
tenured and had taught at Arizona State University for six years.
After several incidents, generally involving activity aimed at
disseminating knowledge about socialism, the board of regents
directed the president to institute proceedings against Professor
Starsky. After carefully considering the evidence, the disciplinary
committee found that the charges did not support a recommendation for dismissal. The board nevertheless terminated Starsky's
employment, and the professor sought redress in the courts.

The district court held that the termination violated
Starsky's constitutional right to free speech, and the court of
appeals affirmed. The district court discussed the eight charges at
length, dismissing some as not being supported by the evidence.
One charge found to be true was that Professor Starsky had
deliberately cut a class in order to participate in a rally on campus.
The court ruled that Starsky had broken no specific regulation by
cancelling the class and that the incident was a minor one usually
handled informally within the department. The court chastised the
board for selectively enforcing its general attendance policy and
dismissed the charge. Another more serious charge concerned the
peaceful distribution of a leaflet to other faculty members. The
leaflet was a philosophical and political discussion of activity
taking place at Columbia University and quoted a Columbia
student who advocated socialism. The university charged that
"Professor Starsky has failed to exercise appropriate restraint or to
exercise critical self-discipline and judgment in using, extending,
and transmitting knowledge." The evidence stated that the
university found his activity to be not in keeping with "the austere

surroundings of a faculty meeting" and to have exhibited "complete disrespect for authority." The court, quoting the academic freedom declaration from the *Keyishian* case, stated:

> There is a serious constitutional question as to whether speech can be stifled because the ideas or wording expressed upset the "austere" faculty atmosphere; certainly the Board has no legitimate interest in keeping a university in some kind of intellectual austerity by an absence of shocking ideas. Insofar as the plaintiff's words upset the Legislature or faculty because of the contents of his views, and particularly the depth of his social criticism, this is not the kind of detriment for which plaintiff can constitutionally be penalized [353 F. Supp. at 920].

While these cases create substantial academic freedom protections, faculty members by no means always win cases regarding institutional affairs.

Roseman v. *Indiana University of Pennsylvania*, 520 F.2d 1364 (3d Cir. 1975), is a case which is not easily reconcilable with the *Smith* v. *Losee* case above. An associate professor alleged that her nonrenewal was in retaliation for having complained to the dean and to the faculty at a department meeting, concerning the department head's alleged impropriety in the selection process for a new department chairman. The professor claimed that this complaint was First Amendment protected speech. The court, finding that *Pickering*, above, did not apply, rejected the professor's claim because (1) her comments "were essentially private communications in which only members . . . [of the department and the dean] had any interest," whereas Pickering's letter was a public communication on a matter of public interest; and (2) her comments had a "potentially disruptive impact on the functioning of the Department" because they "called into question the integrity of . . . [the department head]," whereas Pickering's letter had no such impact.

The plaintiff–faculty member in *Duke* v. *North Texas State University*, 469 F.2d 829 (5th Cir. 1973), had been fired after she used profane language while addressing an unauthorized meeting of students before freshman orientation. She was specifically fired on this charge: "The actions and statements of . . . [the faculty member] demonstrate a lack of academic responsibility required by Sec. II of the Statement on Academic Freedom at North Texas State University in that: (a) her actions and statements before a group of students and her participation in meetings which violate the rules and regulations of the University impair her efficiency as a teacher and her judgment as a scholar, and (b) by her actions and statements upon the occasions in question, . . . [the faculty member] failed to recognize and appreciate that the public will judge No.T.S.U. and its teaching faculty by such statements and actions, thereby demonstrating the lack of professional integrity required of the teaching faculty at North Texas State University." The court found that "the interests the University sought to protect were to maintain a competent faculty and to perpetuate public confidence in the educational institution." Weighing these interests against the faculty member's interest in free speech, the court held for the university:

> As a past and prospective instructor, Mrs. Duke owed the University a minimal duty of loyalty and civility to refrain from extremely disrespectful and grossly offensive remarks aimed at the administrators of the University. By her breach of this duty, the interests of the University outweighed her claim for protection [469 F.2d at 840].

3.6.4. Academic freedom in private life. Faculty members' activities would seem most insulated from state or institutional interference in their private lives. Indeed, the faculty member can be seen as an ordinary citizen who happens to teach in a postsecondary institution. But the faculty member's private activities are not completely immune from interference by the state or the institution, however, because such activities may have an impact on teaching responsibilities or other legitimate interests of the institution.

A professor's private life may involve activities which are not traditionally thought of as First Amendment rights. *Hander* v. *San Jacinto Junior College*, 519 F.2d 273 (5th Cir. 1975), concerned a state college's authority to enforce faculty grooming regulations. A professor was dismissed when he refused to shave his beard. In holding for the professor on due process and equal protection grounds, the court first distinguished university faculty from other government employees: "Teachers even at public institutions such as San Jacinto Junior College simply do not have the exposure or community-wide impact of policemen and other employees who deal directly with the public. Nor is the need for discipline as acute in the educational environment as in other types of public service." The court then enunciated this role for teachers:

> School authorities may regulate teachers' appearance and activities only when the regulation has some relevance to legitimate administrative or educational functions. . . .
>
> The mere subjective belief in a particular idea by public employers is, however, an undeniably insufficient justification for the infringement of a constitutionally guaranteed right. . . . [I]t is illogical to conclude that a teacher's bearded appearance would jeopardize his reputation or pedagogical effectiveness with college students [519 F.2d at 277].

Another aspect of faculty freedom in private life is illustrated by *Trister* v. *University of Mississippi*, 420 F.2d 499 (5th Cir. 1969), where the court ruled it was unconstitutional for a state law school to prohibit some part-time faculty members from working part time at outside legal jobs while allowing other faculty members to do so. Certain part-time faculty members had continued working at a legal services office of the Office of Economic Opportunity (OEO) despite a warning from the administration that they would lose their jobs at the university if they continued. There was no evidence that the OEO jobs consumed any more time than the part-time jobs of other faculty members. In upholding the plaintiffs' right to work at the OEO office, the court based its decision not on the First Amendment but on the Fourteenth Amendment equal protection clause:

> We are not willing to take the position that plaintiffs have a constitutional right to participate in the Legal Services Program of the OEO, or in any other program. Nor do they have a constitutional right to engage in part-time employment while teaching part time at the

> Law School. No such right exists in isolation. Plaintiffs,
> however, do have the constitutional right to be treated by a
> state agency in no significantly different manner from
> others who are members of the same class, that is, members
> of the faculty of the University of Mississippi School of
> Law [420 F.2d at 502].

Other courts may be more willing to find a limited constitutional
right to outside employment, under the First Amendment or
Fourteenth Amendment due process, where such employment does
not interfere with any substantial interest of the institution.

Starsky v. *Williams*, 353 F. Supp. 900 (D. Ariz. 1972),
affirmed, 512 F.2d 109 (9th Cir. 1975), discussed in Section 3.6.3,
illustrates yet another aspect of faculty freedom in private life. The
plaintiff filed suit seeking reinstatement as a member of the faculty
at Arizona State University. He had made a television speech which
criticized the board of regents and had called them hypocrites. He
had also issued a press release which criticized the board. The
court, finding for Professor Starsky, stated:

> In each of these communications, plaintiff spoke or
> wrote as a private citizen on a public issue, and in a place
> and context apart from his role as faculty member. In none
> of these public utterances did he appear as a spokesman for
> the University, or claim any kind of expertise related to his
> profession. He spoke as any citizen might speak and the
> Board was, therefore, subject to its own avowed standard
> that when a faculty member "speaks or writes as a citizen,
> he should be free from institutional censorship or disci-
> pline" [353 F. Supp. at 920].

*3.6.5. Administrators' authority over faculty academic free-
dom.* The foregoing discussions have made clear that academic
freedom is an area in which the law provides no firm guidelines for
administrators. This is particularly true for private institutions,
since the decided cases are almost all constitutional decisions
applicable only to public schools. Even the constitutional cases are
sometimes incompletely reasoned or difficult to reconcile with one
another. The fact that decisions often depend heavily on a vague
balancing of faculty and institutional interests in light of the

peculiar facts of the case makes it difficult to generalize from one case to another. Thus with respect to academic freedom, more than to most administrative concerns, it is crucial for institutions to develop their own guidelines and to have internal systems for protecting academic freedom in accordance with institutional policy. Often the AAUP guidelines (see Section 3.6.1) can be of considerable assistance in this endeavor.

The constitutional court decisions do provide some guidance, however, and they do restrict public-institution administrators' authority to limit faculty academic freedom. The classroom (Section 3.6.2) is clearly the arena where administrative authority is greatest and courts are most hesitant to enter. Beyond the classroom faculty members have considerable freedom to express themselves on public issues and, as private citizens, to associate with whom they please and engage in outside activities of their choice. In general, whether in the classroom or out, administrative authority over teacher behavior or activities increases as the job-relatedness of the behavior or activities increases and as the adverseness of their impact on teaching performance or other institutional functions increases.

When establishing or reviewing institutional regulations on academic freedom, administrators of public institutions should assure that such regulations avoid the constitutional dangers of "overbreadth" and "vagueness." (See Section 3.4.) Administrators should also assure that such regulations avoid interference with the content (or substance) of faculty members' speech, particularly outside the classroom; courts permit narrow regulation of the time, place, or manner of speech but seldom of its content as such (see Section 4.7.2). In addition, administrators should assure that institutional academic freedom regulations follow procedural due process requirements in situations where their application would deprive a faculty member of a "liberty" or "property" interest (see Section 3.5.2). While these requirements bind only public institutions, they may provide useful guidance for private institutions as well.

When deciding whether to hire, renew, promote, tenure, or dismiss a particular faculty member, administrators should carefully avoid decisions based on actions of that faculty member that are protected by academic freedom. Sticky problems can arise when the faculty member has engaged in possibly protected action but has also engaged in other, unprotected, action that might justify an adverse personnel decision. Suppose, for instance, that a faculty member up for renewal had made public statements critical of the school administration (probably protected) and also had often failed to meet his classes (unprotected). What must an administrator do to avoid later judicial overruling of a decision not to renew?

The U.S. Supreme Court addressed this problem in *Mt. Healthy City School District Board of Education* v. *Doyle*, 97 S. Ct. 568 (1977). The plaintiff school teacher had made statements regarding school policy to a radio broadcaster who promptly broadcast the information as a news item. A month later the school board informed the teacher that he would not be rehired and gave the radio broadcast as one reason. It also gave several other reasons, however, including an incident in which the teacher made an obscene gesture to two students in the school cafeteria. The Supreme Court stated that although the radio communication was protected by the first amendment and played a substantial part in the nonrenewal decision, the nonrenewal was still valid if the school board could prove it would not have rehired the teacher even had the radio incident never occurred:

> Initially, in this case, the burden was properly placed upon . . . [the teacher] to show that his conduct was constitutionally protected, and that this conduct was a "substantial factor"—or to put it in other words, that it was a "motivating factor" in the Board's decision not to rehire him. [The teacher] having carried that burden, however, the District Court should have gone on to determine whether the Board had shown by preponderance of the evidence that it would have reached the same decision as to . . . [the teacher's] reemployment even in the absence of the protected conduct [97 S. Ct. at 576].

Mt. Healthy was applied to postsecondary education in *Franklin* v. *Atkins*, 562 F.2d 1188 (10th Cir. 1977). Challenging the Board of Regents' refusal to appoint him to a faculty position at the University of Colorado, professor Bruce Franklin argued that the board had relied on constitutionally protected conduct he had engaged in while on the faculty at Stanford University. The court rejected Franklin's claim, holding that (1) he failed to prove that his conduct described in a report from a Stanford hearing board was constitutionally protected and (2) even if his conduct was protected, he failed to prove that it "was a 'substantial' or 'motivating factor' in the Regents' decision."

By placing substantial burdens on faculty members asserting violations of academic freedom, the *Mt. Healthy* and *Franklin* cases give administrators breathing space in making personnel decisions where faculty members may have engaged in protected activity. The goal for administrators still should be a decision untainted by any considerations of protected conduct. But in the real world this goal is not always attainable—either because it is difficult under current legal standards to determine whether particular conduct is protected, or because events involving academic freedom are too widely known to completely isolate decision makers from such information. In these cases, administrators can still avoid judicial invalidation if they assure that strong and dispositive grounds, independent of any grounds impinging academic freedom, exist for every adverse decision, and that such independent grounds are considered in making the decision and are documented in the institution's records.

While *Mt. Healthy* and *Franklin,* as First Amendment cases, also bind only public institutions, they can help private institutions to establish review standards for their own internal hearings on personnel disputes, and they may, by analogy, assist courts in reviewing academic freedom claims based on a contract theory. (See Section 3.6.1.)

Sec. 3.7. Staff Reduction Due to Financial Exigency

The financial difficulties that began for postsecondary education in the late sixties have created a new and particularly sensitive faculty personnel issue.[16] In an era of inflation and

[16]This section is limited to financial exigency problems concerning faculty. But financial exigency also affects students, and an institution's response to financial exigency may occasionally give students a basis on which to sue. See *Eden* v. *State University of New York,* 49 App.Div.2d 686

shrinking resources, what are the legal responsibilities of an institution which must terminate an academic program or otherwise initiate a reduction in force? On this question, likely to be stalking postsecondary education for the foreseeable future, the law is just beginning to develop. But enough judicial ink has been spilled to give administrators a fair idea of how to prepare for the unwelcome necessity of terminating faculty jobs in a financial crunch.

3.7.1. Contractual considerations. The faculty contract (Section 3.1) is the starting point for determining both a public and a private institution's financial exigency responsibilities. Administrators should consider several questions concerning the faculty contract. Does it, and should it, provide for termination due to financial exigency? Does it, and should it, define financial exigency or stipulate how the existence of such a condition is to be determined? Does it, and should it, set forth criteria for determining which faculty members will be released in case of financial exigency? Does it, and should it, require that other alternatives be explored (such as transfer to another department) before termination becomes permissible? Does it, and should it, provide a hearing or other recourse for a faculty member chosen for dismissal because of financial exigency? Does it, and should it, provide the released faculty member with any priority right to be rehired when other openings arise or the financial situation eases?

Whenever the faculty contract has any provision on financial exigency, the institution should follow it; failure to do so will likely be a breach of contract. Whether such contractual provisions exist may depend on whether the AAUP guidelines[17] on

---

(1975), discussed in Section 4.2.3; and see generally Section 4.1.3, concerning an institution's contractual obligation to students.

[17]See *1976 Recommended Institutional Regulations on Academic Freedom and Tenure*, Regulation 4, published at 62 *AAUP Bulletin* 184, 185 (1976), and *On Institutional Problems Resulting from Financial Exigency: Some Operating Guidelines*, 60 *AAUP Bulletin* 267 (1974). The 1968 version of the AAUP guidelines, specifically the 1968 version of Regulation 4(c), were interpreted in the *Browzin* case, discussed in the text in this section. The court concluded that the defendant-university had not

financial exigency have been incorporated into the faculty contract. In *Browzin* v. *Catholic University of America*, 527 F.2d 843 (D.C. Cir. 1975), for instance, the parties stipulated that the AAUP guidelines had been adopted as part of the faculty contract, and the court noted that such adoption was "entirely consistent with the Statutes of the University and the University's previous responses to AAUP actions." As in *Browzin*, it is important for administrators to understand the legal status of AAUP guidelines within their institutions; any doubt should be resolved by consulting counsel.

The contract provisions for tenured and nontenured faculty members may differ, and administrators should note any differences. Nontenured faculty members generally pose far fewer legal problems during financial exigency, since administrators may simply not renew their contracts at the end of the contract term. (See Section 3.5.2.) If the faculty contract is silent regarding financial exigency, in relation to either tenured or nontenured faculty members, that does not necessarily mean the institution has no power to terminate. Under the common law doctrine of "impossibility," the institution may be able to extricate itself from contractual obligations to the extent that unforeseen events have made it impossible to perform those obligations. The doctrine of impossibility has been stated as follows:

> When an unforeseen event which makes impossible the performance of a contractual duty occurs subsequent to the formation of the contract and prior to the time when the duty to perform becomes absolute, it is often held that the promisor is excused from performing. Such holdings are exceptions to the general rule that when a contractual promise is made, the promisor must perform or pay damages for his failure to perform no matter how burdensome performance has become as a result of unforeseen circumstances [J. D. Calamari and J. M. Perillo, *Contracts*, sec. 186, at 296 (West, 1970); and see generally Calamari and Perillo, Ch. 11].

---

violated the requirement that it "make every effort" to place terminated faculty members "in other suitable positions."

The leading contract case on financial exigency is *AAUP* v. *Bloomfield College*, 129 N.J. Super. 249, 322 A.2d 846 (1974), affirmed, 136 N.J. Super. 249, 346 A.2d 615 (1975). On June 29, 1973, Bloomfield College, a private school, notified thirteen tenured faculty members that their services would not be needed as of June 30, 1973. The college gave financial exigency as the reason for this action. The college also notified the remaining faculty members, tenured and nontenured, that they would be put on one-year terminal contracts for 1973–74, after which they would have to negotiate new contracts with the school.

The thirteen fired faculty members brought suit based on their contracts of employment. Paragraph C(3) of the "policies" which were part of the contract provided that "a teacher will have tenure and his services may be terminated only for adequate cause, except in case of retirement for age, or under extraordinary circumstances because of financial exigency of the institution." Paragraph C(6) provided that "[t]ermination of continuous appointment because of financial exigency of the institution must be demonstrably bona fide. A situation which makes drastic retrenchment of this sort necessary precludes expansion of the staff at other points at the same time, except in extraordinary circumstances."

The faculty members alleged that no bona fide financial exigency existed and that the hiring of twelve new staff members three months after the plaintiffs were dismissed violated the requirement that during a financial exigency new staff persons would be hired only "in extraordinary circumstances." Thus, the issues were whether there was a "demonstrably bona fide" financial exigency and whether there were such extraordinary circumstances as would justify the hiring of new faculty members.

The trial court analyzed the college's finances and determined that no bona fide financial exigency existed because the college owned a large piece of valuable property that it could have sold to meet its needs. The appellate court, however, disagreed:

> In our opinion, the mere fact that this financial strain existed for some period of time does not negate the reality that a "financial exigency" was a fact of life for the

college administration within the meaning of the underlying contract. The interpretation of "exigency" as attributed by the trial court is too narrow a concept of the term in relation to the subject matter involved. A more reasonable construction might be encompassed within the phrase "state of urgency." In this context, the evidence was plentiful as to the proof of the existence of the criterion of the financial exigency required by the contract.

In this vein it was improper for the judge to rest his conclusion in whole or in part upon the failure of the college to sell the knoll property which had been acquired several years before in anticipation of the creation of a new campus at a different locale. . . . Whether such a plan of action to secure financial stability on a short-term basis is preferable to the long-term planning of the college administration is a policy decision of the institution. Its choice of alternative is beyond the scope of judicial oversight in the context of this litigation [346 A.2d at 617].

Though the appellate court thus held that the college was in a state of financial exigency, it was unwilling to find that the faculty members were fired because of the college's financial condition. The trial court had determined that the reason for the terminations was the college's desire to abolish tenure, and the appellate court found ample evidence to support this finding.

On the issue of whether extraordinary circumstances existed sufficient to justify the hiring of twelve new faculty members, the trial court also held in favor of the plaintiffs. The college had argued that its actions were justified because it was developing a new type of curriculum, but the court noted that the evidence put forth by the college was vague and did not suggest that any financial benefit would result from the new curriculum. The appellate court did not disturb this part of the trial court's decision, nor did it even discuss the issue.

A major overarching issue of the case concerned the burden of proof. Did the college have the burden of proving that it had fulfilled the contract conditions justifying termination? Or did the faculty members have the burden of proving that the contractual conditions had *not* been met? The issue has critical practical importance; because the evidentiary problems can be so difficult, the outcome of financial exigency litigation may often depend on who has the burden of proof. The trial court assigned the burden to the college, and the appellate court agreed:

> It is manifest that under the controlling agreement among the parties the affected members of the faculty had attained the protection of tenure after completing a seven-year probationary service. This was their vested right which could be legally divested only if the defined conditions occurred. The proof of existence of those conditions as a justifiable reason for terminating the status of the plaintiffs plainly was the burden of the defendants [346 A.2d at 616].

Since the college had not proven that it had met the contract conditions justifying termination, the courts ordered the reinstatement of the terminated faculty members.

   3.7.2. Constitutional considerations. Public institutions (see Section 1.4.2) must be concerned not only with contract considerations relating to financial exigency but also with constitutional considerations under the First and Fourteenth Amendments. Even if a termination (or other personnel decision) does not violate the faculty contract or any applicable state statutes or administrative regulations,[18] it will be subject to invalidation by the courts if it infringes the faculty member's constitutional rights.

   Under the First Amendment, a faculty member may argue that financial exigency was only a pretext for termination and that termination was actually a retaliation for the faculty member's exercise of First Amendment rights. (See Note, "Economically Necessitated Faculty Dismissal as a Limit on Academic Freedom," 52 *Denver L. J.* 911 (1975); and see generally Section 3.6.) The burden of proof on this issue is primarily on the faculty member (see the *Mt. Healthy* case discussed in Section 3.6.5). *Mabey* v. *Reagan*, 537 F.2d 1036 (9th Cir. 1976), is illustrative. The college-

---

   [18]A public institution's legal responsibilities during financial exigency may be defined not only by contract as such but also by state statutes or administrative regulations. See, for example, *Mabey* v. *Reagan*, discussed below in this section, which considers, in part, the applicability of a California statute governing lay-offs for "lack of work or lack of funds"; and *Johnson* v. *Board of Regents*, also discussed below in this section, which considers a Wisconsin statute governing employment terminations.

defendant had not renewed the appointment of a nontenured philosophy instructor. The instructor argued that the nonrenewal was due to an argument he had had with other faculty members in an academic senate meeting and that his argument was a protected First Amendment activity. The college argued that this activity was not protected under the First Amendment and that, at any rate, the nonrenewal was also due to overstaffing in the philosophy department. In remanding the case to the trial court for further fact findings, the appellate court noted:

> [W]e emphasize that the trier [of fact] must be alert to retaliatory terminations. . . . Whenever the state terminates employment to quell legitimate dissent or punishes protected expressive behavior, the termination is unlawful. . . .
> We stress that this holding does not shield those who are legitimately not reappointed. Where the complainant . . . does not meet his burden of proof that the state acted to suppress free expression, . . . the termination will stand.

Under the Fourteenth Amendment, a faculty member whose job is terminated by a public institution may argue that the termination violated the due process clause. To proceed with this argument, the faculty member must show that the termination infringed a "property" or "liberty" interest, as discussed in Section 3.5.2. If such a showing can be made, the questions then are (1) what procedural protections is the faculty member entitled to, and (2) what kinds of arguments can the faculty member raise in his or her "defense"? A case which addresses both issues is *Johnson v. Board of Regents of University of Wisconsin System*, 377 F. Supp. 227 (W.D. Wis. 1974), affirmed without opinion, 510 F.2d 975 (7th Cir. 1975). The Wisconsin legislature had mandated budget reductions for the university system. To accommodate this reduction, as well as a further reduction caused by lower enrollments on several campuses, the university officials devised a program for "laying off" tenured faculty. The chancellor of each campus determined who would be laid off, after which each affected faculty member could petition a faculty committee for "reconsideration" of the proposed lay-off. The faculty committee could consider only two questions: whether the lay-off decision was supported by sufficient evidence, and whether the chancellor had followed the procedures established for identifying the campus's fiscal and programmatic needs and determining who should be laid off. Thirty-eight tenured professors selected for lay-off sued the university system.

The court determined that the due process clause required the following minimum procedures in a financial exigency lay-off: "furnishing each plaintiff with a reasonably adequate written statement of the basis for the initial decision to lay off; furnishing each plaintiff with a reasonably adequate description of the manner in which the initial decision had been arrived at; making a reasonably adequate disclosure to each plaintiff of the information and data upon which the decision makers had relied; and providing each plaintiff the opportunity to respond" (377 F. Supp. at 240). Measuring the procedures actually used against these requirements, the court held the university system had not violated procedural due process. The most difficult issue was the adequacy of information disclosure (the third requirement above), about which the court said:

> Plaintiffs have shown in this court that the information disclosed to them was bulky and some of it amorphous. They have shown that it was not presented to the reconsideration committees in a manner resembling the presentation of evidence in court. They have shown that in some situations . . . they encountered difficulty in obtaining a coherent explanation of the basis for the initial lay-off decisions, and that, as explained in some situations, the basis included judgments about personalities. But as I have observed, the Fourteenth Amendment does not forbid judgments about personalities in this situation, nor does it require adversary proceedings. The information disclosed was reasonably adequate to provide each plaintiff the opportunity to make a showing that reduced student enrollments and fiscal exigency were not in fact the precipitating causes for the decisions to lay off tenured teachers in this department and that; and it was also reasonably adequate to provide each plaintiff the opportunity to make a showing that the ultimate decision to lay off

each of them, as compared with another tenured member of their respective departments, was arbitrary and unreasonable. I emphasize the latter point. On this record, plaintiffs' allegations about the inadequacy and imprecision of the disclosure related principally to those stages of the decision making which preceded the ultimate stage at which the specific teachers, department by department, were selected.

Had the disclosure as it was made not been "reasonably adequate," it is possible that it could have been made adequate by permitting plaintiffs some opportunity to confront and even to cross-examine some of the decision makers. But I hold that the opportunity to confront or to cross-examine these decision makers is not constitutionally required when the disclosure is reasonably adequate, as it was here [377 F. Supp. at 242].

The court also determined that the university system could limit the issues which the faculty members could address in challenging a termination under the above procedures:

I am not persuaded that after the initial decisions had been made, the Fourteenth Amendment required that plaintiffs be provided an opportunity to persuade the decision makers that departments within their respective colleges, other than theirs, should have borne a heavier fiscal sacrifice; that noncredit-producing, nonacademic areas within their respective campus structures should have borne a heavier fiscal sacrifice; that campuses, other than their respective campuses, should have borne a heavier fiscal sacrifice; or that more funds should have been appropriated to the university system. However, I believe that *each plaintiff was constitutionally entitled to a fair opportunity to show: (1) that the true reason for his or her lay-off was a constitutionally impermissible reason; or (2) that, given the chain of decisions which preceded the ultimate decision designating him or her by name for lay-off, that ultimate decision was nevertheless wholly arbitrary and unreasonable.* I believe that each plaintiff was constitutionally entitled to a fair opportunity to make such a showing in a proceeding within the institution, in order to permit prompt reconsideration and correction in a proper case. Also, if necessary, each plaintiff was and is constitutionally entitled to a fair opportunity to make such a showing thereafter in a court [377 F. Supp. at 239–40; emphasis added].

Although the Constitution requires that institutions avoid terminations for a "constitutionally impermissible reason" and "wholly arbitrary" terminations, the court made clear that the Constitution does not prescribe any particular bases for selection of the faculty members to be terminated:

> [The Constitution does not require] that the selection be made on one specific basis or another: in inverse order of seniority within the department, for example; or in order of seniority; or in terms of record performance or potential for performance; or in inverse order of seniority, but with exceptions for the necessity to retain teachers in the department with specific skills or funds of knowledge. I believe that the federal Constitution is silent on these questions, and that the identity of the decision maker and the choice of a basis for selection lie within the discretion of the state government [377 F. Supp. at 238].

3.7.3. Preparing for financial exigency terminations. Everyone agrees that institutions, both public and private, should plan ahead to avoid the legal difficulties that can arise should financial pressures necessitate staff reductions. Much can be done to plan ahead. Faculty contracts should be reviewed in light of the questions raised in Section 3.7.1. Where the contract does not clearly reflect the institution's desired position concerning financial exigency, its provisions should be revised to the extent possible without breaching existing contracts. Where the institution has authority for financial exigency staff reductions, it should have a policy and standards for determining when a financial exigency exists. It should also have a policy and standards for identifying which faculty members' positions will be terminated and procedures by which the faculty member can challenge the propriety of his or her selection for termination. If administrators make a termination decision, they should assure that (1) a financial exigency does actually exist under the institution's policy, and (2) financial exigency is in fact the reason for each termination decision that is made. In making the latter assurance, they would be wise to ascertain whether the terminations will have the effect of alleviating the exigency, as well as whether any other nonfinancial motivation for a particular termination may exist. After dismissing faculty members, administrators should be extremely careful in hiring new ones, to avoid the impression, as in the *Bloomfield* case above, that the financial exigency was a pretext for abolishing tenure or otherwise replacing old faculty members with new.

Finally, administrators should remember that, in this sensitive area, some of their decisions may wind up in court despite careful planning. Administrators should thus keep complete records and documentation of their financial exigency policies, decisions, and internal review processes for possible use in court and should work closely with counsel both in planning ahead and in making the actual termination decisions.

Selected Annotated Bibliography

General

1. American Association of University Professors, *Policy Documents and Reports* (AAUP, 1977), collects the AAUP's major policy statements concerning academic freedom and tenure, collective bargaining, institutional governance, and other topics.
2. Belcher, L., "Dispute Settlements—Grievance and Arbitration Procedures," in D. H. Blumer (ed.), *Legal Issues for Postsecondary Education: Briefing Papers II* 61–78 (American Association of Community and Junior Colleges, 1976), outlines the major considerations pertaining to the development and use of internal systems for resolving disputes between institution and faculty; includes description of formal grievance procedures and suggestions and forms for implementing them.
3. Bickel, D., and Brechner, J., *The College Administrator and the Courts* (College Administration, 1977 plus periodic supplements), provides, in chap. 5, briefs and supporting comments on court cases concerning the employment relationship between institution and faculty; includes appendix containing text of relevant federal regulations; addition of new cases by quarterly supplements.
4. AAUP/AAC Commission on Academic Tenure, *Faculty Tenure:*

A Report and Recommendations (Jossey-Bass, 1973), is an
evaluation by a commission cosponsored by the Association
of American Colleges and the American Association of University Professors; includes special essays on "Legal Dimensions of Tenure" by V. Rosenblum and "Faculty Unionism
and Tenure" by W. McHugh.

Sec. 3.2 (Collective Bargaining)

1. Angell, G. W., Kelly, E. P., Jr., and Associates, *Handbook of
   Faculty Bargaining* (Jossey-Bass, 1977), serves as a comprehensive guide to collective bargaining for administrators;
   provides information and recommendations on preparing
   for collective bargaining, negotiating contracts, administering contracts, and exerting institutional leadership in the
   bargaining context; special chapter on statewide bargaining
   in state postsecondary systems.
2. Bartosic, F., and Hartley, R. C., *Labor Relations Law in the Private Sector* (American Law Institute, 1977), is a restatement
   and analysis of the federal law of union organization and
   collective bargaining. Primarily for legal counsel who are
   not labor law specialists; also useable by specialists as a
   ready-reference manual and by administrators as a readable
   explanatory text; can also help in dealing with public sector
   labor law in states with law patterned after the federal law.
3. Finkin, M., "The NLRB in Higher Education," 5 *University of
   Toledo L. Rev.* 608 (1974), probes the whole gamut of
   NLRB authority and activity in postsecondary education;
   discusses and criticizes NLRB decisions dealing with jurisdiction over private institutions, faculty status as managers,
   supervisors, or employees, appropriate bargaining units,
   and employers' unfair labor practices.
4. Research Project on Students and Collective Bargaining, *Final
   Report* (National Student Education Fund, 1976), studies
   student participation in faculty collective bargaining; surveys current state of the law and practice regarding student
   participation; analyzes bargaining's impact on students; and
   discusses various bargaining contract provisions.

5. Vladeck, J., and Vladeck, S. (eds.), *Collective Bargaining in Higher Education: The Developing Law* (Practising Law Institute, 1975), is a multiauthored text covering all the major aspects of bargaining between faculty and institution.

Sec. 3.3 (Nondiscrimination in Employment)

1. Brooks, R. L., "Use of the Civil Rights Acts of 1886 and 1871 to Redress Employment Discrimination," 62 *Cornell L. Rev.* 258 (1977), analyzes the role that 42 U.S.C. sec. 1981 can play in employment discrimination suits; also discusses 42 U.S.C. secs. 1983 and 1985(3); includes consideration of rights and remedies available under these statutes that may not be available under other employment discrimination statutes, and the procedural and jurisdictional issues that may arise in litigation under these statutes.
2. Bureau of National Affairs, *Affirmative Action Compliance Manual* (BNA, published and updated periodically), is a comprehensive guide for federal contractors that provides detailed and continually updated information on the federal government's affirmative action program and the compliance responsibilities and procedures of the Departments of Labor, HEW, Defense, and other federal agencies.
3. Carnegie Council on Policy Studies in Higher Education, *Making Affirmative Action Work in Higher Education: An Analysis of Institutional and Federal Policies with Recommendations* (Josscy-Bass, 1975), critically examines federal policies and programs of affirmative action that affect post-secondary institutions; discusses the academic job market, salary differentials, impact of federal statutes on internal personnel decisions, goals, and timetables, and grievance and enforcement procedures; makes recommendations on the direction federal policies should take.
4. Haslam, C. L., "Age Discrimination in Campus Employment," 4 *Human Rights* 321 (1975), reprinted in 2 *J. of College and University Law* 326 (1975), discusses the application of the

Age Discrimination in Employment Act to postsecondary education personnel decisions.

5. Johnson, J. A., "Equal Pay Act of 1963: A Practical Analysis," 24 *Drake L. Rev.* 570 (1975), discusses the background and scope of the Equal Pay Act, the power of the Secretary of Labor in its enforcement, and the case law that has developed.

6. National Association of College and University Business Officers (NACUBO), *Federal Regulations and the Employment Practices of Colleges and Universities* (1974 and periodic supp.) is a looseleaf service, which provides information and guidance on applying federal regulations affecting personnel administration in postsecondary institutions.

7. Symposium, "The First Decade of Title VII of the Civil Rights Act: Past Developments and Future Trends," 20 *St. Louis University L. Rev.* 219 (1976), is a collection of articles on various aspects of Title VII; discusses the role of the Equal Employment Opportunity Commission as well as private enforcement by individual plaintiffs or by class actions; also explores the implications of the *Gardner-Denver* case discussed in the text in Section 3.2.6.

Sec. 3.5 (Procedures for Faculty Personnel Decisions)

1. Baird, J., and McArthur, M. R., "Constitutional Due Process and the Negotiation of Grievance Procedures in Public Employment," 5 *J. of Law and Education* 209 (1976), compares and contrasts grievance procedures in the public and private sectors; imports due process considerations into the collective bargaining process and suggests ways public employers can deal with due process requirements in devising grievance procedures.

Sec. 3.6 (Faculty Academic Freedom)

1. "Developments in the Law—Academic Freedom," 81 *Harvard L. Rev.* 1045 (1968), is a comprehensive analysis of academic freedom by the staff of the *Harvard Law Review;* Part Two

discusses "Academic Freedom of Teachers"; though outdated on case law, the discussion of concepts, principles, and
problems is still very valuable.

Sec. 3.7 (Staff Reduction Due to Financial Exigency)

1. Tucker, J. C., "Financial Exigency—Rights, Responsibilities,
   and Recent Decisions," 2 *J. College and University Law* 103
   (1975), though somewhat outdated on case law, provides a
   perceptive discussion of the major legal themes and practical
   considerations regarding financial exigency. To pick up
   later case law, this article can be read together with J.
   Wilson, "Financial Exigency: Examination of Recent Cases
   Involving Layoff of Tenured Faculty," 4 *J. of College and
   University Law* 187 (1978).

Chapter IV

꙳꙳꙳꙳꙳꙳꙳꙳꙳꙳꙳꙳

The College
and the Students

Sec. 4.1. The Legal Status of Students

4.1.1. The evolutionary process. The legal status of students in postsecondary institutions changed dramatically in the 1960s and is still evolving. For most purposes students are no longer second-class citizens under the law. They are recognized under the federal Constitution as "persons" with 'their own enforceable constitutional rights. They are recognized as adults, with the rights and responsibilities of adults, under many state laws. And they are accorded their own legal rights under various federal statutes. The background of this evolution is traced in Section 1.2, while the new legal status that emerges from these developments, and its impact on postsecondary administration, is explored throughout this chapter.

Perhaps the key case in forging the new student status was *Dixon* v. *Alabama State Board of Education,* discussed in Section 4.6.2. Not only did the case reject the notion that education in state schools is a "privilege" to be dispensed on whatever conditions the state in its sole discretion deemed advisable; the case also implicitly rejected the in loco parentis concept under which the law had bestowed on schools all the powers over students that parents had over minor children. The *Dixon* approach became a part of U.S. Supreme Court jurisprudence in cases such as *Tinker* v. *Des Moines School District* (see Section 4.7.1), *Healy* v. *James* (Sections 4.7.1 and 4.8.1), and *Goss* v. *Lopez* (Section 4.6). The impact of these public institution cases spilled over onto private institutions, as courts increasingly viewed students as contracting parties having rights under express and implied contractual relationships with the institution. Congress gave both public and private school students new rights under various civil rights acts and, in the Buckley Amendment (Section 4.12.1), gave postsecondary students certain rights which were expressly independent of and in lieu of parental rights. New state statutes lowering the age of majority also enhanced the independence of students from their parents and brought the bulk of postsecondary students, even undergraduates, into the category of adults.

4.1.2. The new age of majority. The age of majority is established by state law in all states. There may be a general statute prescribing an age of majority for all or most business and personal dealings in the state, or there may be specific statutes or regulations specifying varying ages of majority for specific purposes. Until the 1970s, twenty-one was typically the age of majority in most states. But since the 1971 ratification of the Twenty-Sixth Amendment lowering the voting age to eighteen, most states have lowered the age of majority to eighteen or nineteen for many other purposes as well. The Michigan statute (Mich. Stat. Ann. sec. 25, 244 (51), M.C.L.A. sec. 722.51) illustrates the comprehensive approach adopted by some states:

> Notwithstanding any other provision of law to the contrary, a person who is eighteen years of age but less than twenty-one years of age when this act takes effect, and a

person who attains eighteen years of age thereafter, is
deemed to be an adult of legal age for all purposes
whatsoever and shall have the same duties, liabilities,
responsibilities, rights and legal capacity as persons hereto-
fore acquired at twenty-one years of age.

Other states have adopted more limited or more piecemeal
legislation, sometimes using different minimum ages for different
purposes. Given the lack of uniformity, administrators and counsel
should carefully check state law in their own states.

The new age of majority laws can affect many postsecondary
regulations and policies. The effect of the laws may be to permit
students at age eighteen to enter binding contracts without the
need for a co-signer, to give consent to medical treatment, to
declare financial independence, to establish a legal residence apart
from the parents', and to consume alcoholic beverages. This new
legal capacity enables institutions to deal with students as adults at
age eighteen, but it does not necessarily require that institutions
do so. Particularly in private institutions, administrators may still
be able as a policy matter to require a co-signer on contracts with
students, for instance, or to have higher drinking ages (or no
drinking) in campus buildings. Similarly, institutions may still be
able to consider the resources of parents in awarding financial aid,
even though the parents have no legal obligation to support the
student. An institution's legal capacity to adopt such policy
positions depends on the interpretation of the applicable age of
majority law and the possible existence of special state law
provisions for postsecondary institutions, such as a dependency or
residency provision in a state loan program, or special authority
for public institutions to regulate alcoholic beverages on campus.
Administrators will thus confront two questions: What do the new
age of majority laws require that I do in particular areas? And
should I, where I am under no legal obligation, establish age
requirements higher than the legal age in particular areas, or
should I instead pattern institutional policies on the general legal
standard?

4.1.3. The contractual rights of students.[1] Both public and

[1] The contract theory is by far the primary theory for according

private institutions often have express contractual relationships with students. Under the new age of majority laws such contractual relationships are likely to increase in number and importance. The most common examples are probably the housing contract or lease (Section 4.10), the food service contract, and the loan agreement (Section 4.3). When problems arise in these areas, the written contract, including institutional regulations incorporated by reference in the contract, is usually the first source of legal guidance.

The contractual relationship between student and institution, however, extends beyond the terms of express contracts. There also exists the more amorphous contractual relationship recognized in *Carr* v. *St. Johns University* (Sections 4.4.2 and 4.6.4), the modern root of the contract theory of student status. In reviewing the institution's dismissal of students for having participated in a civil marriage ceremony, the court based its reasoning on the principle that "when a student is duly admitted by a private university, secular or religious, there is an implied contract between the student and the university that, if he complies with the terms prescribed by the university, he will obtain the degree which he sought." Construing a harsh and vague regulation in the university's favor, the court upheld the dismissal because the students had failed to comply with the university's prescribed terms.

A subsequent New York case, *Healy* v. *Larsson*, 323 N.Y.S.2d 625, affirmed, 35 N.Y.2d 653, 318 N.E.2d 608 (1971), indicated that "there is no reason why . . . the *Carr* principle should not apply to a public university or community college." Other courts have increasingly utilized the contract theory for both public and private institutions, as well as for both academic and

---

legal status to students beyond that derived from the Constitution and state and federal statutes. Other theories have occasionally been suggested by commentators, but they are seldom reflected in court opinions. See, for example, A. L. Goldman, "The University and the Liberty of Its Students—A Fiduciary Theory," 54 *Kentucky L. J.* 643 (1966); Note, "Judicial Review of the University-Student Relationship: Expulsion and Governance," 26 *Stanford L. Rev.* 95 (1973) (common law of private associations).

disciplinary disputes. The theory, however, does not necessarily apply identically to all such situations. A public institution may have more defenses against a contract action. *Eden* v. *Board of Trustees of State University*, 49 App. Div. 277, 374 N.Y.S.2d 686 (1975), for instance, recognizes both an *ultra vires* defense and the state's power to terminate a contract when necessary in the public interest. And courts may accord both public and private institutions more flexibility in drafting and interpreting contract terms involving academics than they do contract terms involving discipline. *Mahavongsanan* v. *Hall*, 529 F.2d 448 (5th Cir. 1976), for example, recognizes broad flexibility in holding that Georgia State University had not breached its contract with a student when it withheld a master's degree for refusal to meet academic degree requirements.

Use of the contract theory does not always favor the institution. In *Healy* v. *Larsson*, for instance, the plaintiff student had transferred to the Schenectady County Community College and had taken all courses his guidance counselors specified but was denied a degree. The court held that he was contractually entitled to the degree because he had "satisfactorily completed a course of study at . . . [the] community college as prescribed to him by authorized representatives of the college." Nevertheless, the cases tend to be more like *Carr* than like *Healy* in construing the student-institution contract in favor of the institution. Courts have recognized "implied" or "inherent" institutional powers beyond those set out in writing, such as the power to maintain order on campus. (See Section 2.1.) Institutions have been given wide latitude in interpreting their regulations and have been permitted to change the regulations to which students are subjected as they progress through the institution. The *Mahavongsanan* case, for instance, rejected the plaintiff-student's contract claim both "because of the wide latitude and discretion afforded by the courts to educational institutions in framing their academic requirements" and because an institution "clearly is entitled to modify [its regulations] so as to properly exercise its educational responsibility." Nor have institutions been subjected to the rigors of contract law as it applies in the commercial world. The plaintiff-student in *Slaughter* v. *Brigham Young University* (Sections 4.4.2 and 4.6.4) had been awarded $88,283 in damages in the trial court in a suit alleging erroneous dismissal from school. The appellate court reversed:

> The trial court's rigid application of commercial contract doctrine advanced by plaintiff was in error, and the submission on that theory alone was error. . . .
> It is apparent that some elements of the law of contracts are used and should be used in the analysis of the relationship between plaintiff and the University to provide some framework into which to put the problem of expulsion for disciplinary reasons. This does not mean that "contract law" must be rigidly applied in all its aspects, nor is it so applied even when the contract analogy is extensively adopted. . . . The student-university relationship is unique, and it should not be and cannot be stuffed into one doctrinal category [514 F.2d at 676].

There are indications, however, that the contract theory is becoming a stronger source of rights for students. The *Healy* case above is a major example of the theory's potential in that direction. Two other major examples are the *Steinberg* and *Eden* cases, discussed in Section 4.2.3, where students won victories in admissions cases. Other evidence comes from *Paynter* v. *New York University*, 319 N.Y.S.2d 893 (App. Div. 1971), and *Zumbrun* v. *University of Southern California*, 25 Cal. App. 3d 1, 101 Cal Rptr. 499 (1972), both suits seeking tuition refunds after classes had been cancelled for part of a semester during antiwar protests. Although *Paynter* held in favor of the university and *Zumbrun* remanded the case to the trial court for further proceedings, both opinions recognized that the courses to be taken by a student and the services to be rendered in the courses are part of the student-institution contract. Moreover, the opinions indicate that the institution may make only "minor" or "minimal" changes in the schedule of classes and the course of study which a student has undertaken for a particular semester; more substantial deviations could constitute a breach of contract.

Much development is yet to take place in the contract theory. The means for identifying the terms and conditions of the student-institution contract, the extent to which the school catalogue constitutes part of the contract, and the extent to which the institution retains implied or inherent authority not expressed in any written regulation or policy are all still questionable.

Also still unclear is the extent to which courts will rely on certain contract law concepts such as "unconscionable" contracts and "contracts of adhesion." An unconscionable contract is one which is so harsh and unfair to one of the parties that a reasonable person would not freely and knowingly agree to it. Unconscionable contracts are not enforceable in the courts. In *Albert Merrill School* v. *Godoy*, 357 N.Y.S.2d 378 (Civ. Ct., N.Y. City, 1974), for example, the school sought to recover money due on a contract to provide data processing training. Finding that the student did not speak English well and that the bargaining power of the parties was uneven, the court held the contract unconscionable and refused to enforce it. A contract of adhesion is one offered by one party (usually the party in the stronger bargaining position) to the other party on a "take-it-or-leave-it" basis, with no opportunity to negotiate the terms. Although courts will often construe adhesion contracts in favor of the weaker party where there is ambiguity, such contracts are enforceable unless determined by the court to be unconscionable. In *K. D.* v. *Educational Testing Service*, 386 N.Y.S.2d 747 (Sup. Ct. 1976), the court viewed the plaintiff's agreement with ETS to take the Law School Admissions Test (LSAT) as a contract of adhesion but held it valid, explaining that "[w]here the court finds that an agreement is a contract of adhesion, effort will frequently be made to protect the weaker party from the agreement's harsher terms by a variety of pretexts, while still keeping the elementary rules of the law of contracts intact." Since unconscionability principles depend partly on the weak position of one of the parties, courts are unlikely to apply these principles against institutions that deal fairly with their students, for instance, by following a good practice code, operating grievance mechanisms for student complaints (see 4.13.1 through 4.13.3), or affording students significant opportunity to participate in institutional governance.

As further developments unfold, postsecondary administrators should be sensitive to the language used in all institutional rules and policies affecting students. Language suggestive of a commitment (or promise) to students should be used only when the institution is prepared to live up to the commitment. Limitations on the institution's commitments should be clearly noted where possible. Administrators should consider the adoption of an official policy, perhaps even a "code of good practice," on fair dealing with students. (See E. H. El-Khawas, *New Expectations for Fair Practice: Suggestions for Institutional Review* (American Council on Education, 1976).)

Sec. 4.2. Admissions

4.2.1. Basic legal requirements. Postsecondary institutions have traditionally been accorded wide discretion in formulating admissions standards. The law's deference to administrators' autonomy stems from the notion that tampering with admissions criteria is tampering with the expertise of educators. In recent years, however, the wall of deference has been crumbling, as dissatisfied applicants have successfully pressed the courts for relief and legislatures and administrative agencies have sought to regulate certain aspects of the admissions process.

Administrators are subject to three general constraints in formulating admissions policies: (1) the selection process must not be arbitrary or capricious; (2) the institution may be bound, under a contract theory, to adhere to its published admissions standards and to honor its admissions decisions; and (3) the institution may not have admissions policies which unjustifiably discriminate on the basis of race, sex, age, handicap, or citizenship.

Although administrators are also constrained in the admissions process by the "Buckley" regulations on school records (Section 4.12.1), the regulations have only limited applicability to admissions records. The regulations do not apply to the records of persons who are not or have not been *students* at the institution; thus admissions records are not covered until such time as the applicant has been accepted and is in attendance at the institution (45 C.F.R. 99.1(d), 99.3 ("student")). Admissions records may be destroyed before the applicant attends the institution if the institution so desires (45 C.F.R. 99.13). The institution may also maintain the confidentiality of letters of recommendation if the student has waived the right of access; such a waiver may be sought during the application process (45 C.F.R. 99.7). Moreover, when a student from one component unit of an institution applies for admission to another unit of the same institution, the student is treated as an *applicant* rather than a *student* with respect to the second unit's admissions records; those records are therefore not subject to Buckley until the student is in attendance in the second unit (45 C.F.R. 99.3 ("student")).

4.2.2. Arbitrariness. The "arbitrariness" standard of review is the one most protective of the institution's prerogatives. The cases reflect a judicial hands-off attitude toward any admission decision arguably based on academic qualifications. *Lesser* v. *Bd. of Education of New York,* 18 App.Div.2d 388, 239 N.Y.S.2d 776 (1963), provides a classic example. Lesser sued Brooklyn College after being rejected because his grade average was below the cut-off. He argued that the college acted arbitrarily and unreasonably in not considering that he had been enrolled in a demanding high school honors program. The court declined to overturn the judgment of the college, reasoning that

> [c]ourts may not interfere with the administrative discretion exercised by agencies which are vested with the administration and control of educational institutions, unless the circumstances disclosed by the record leave no scope for the use of that discretion in the matter under scrutiny. . . .
>
> More particularly, a court should refrain from interjecting its views within those delicate areas of school administration which relate to the eligibility of applicants and the determination of marking standards, unless a clear abuse of statutory authority or gross error has been shown [239 N.Y.S.2d at 779].

The court in *Arizona Bd. of Regents* v. *Wilson,* 24 Ariz. App. 469, 539 P.2d 943 (1975), expressed similar sentiment. In that case a woman was rejected from the graduate school of art at the University of Arizona because the faculty did not consider her art work to be of sufficiently high quality. She challenged the admissions process on the basis that it was a rolling admissions system with no written guidelines. The court entered judgment in favor of the university:

> This case represents a prime example of when a court should not interfere in the academic program of a university. It was incumbent upon appellee to show that her rejection was in bad faith, or arbitrary, capricious or unreasonable. The court may not substitute its own opinions as to the merits of appellee's work for that of the members of the faculty committee who were selected to make a determination as to the quality of her work [539 P.2d at 946].

The review standards in these cases establish a formidable barrier for disappointed applicants to cross. But occasionally someone succeeds. *State ex rel. Bartlett* v. *Pantzer*, 158 Mont. 126, 489 P.2d 375 (1971), arose after the admissions committee of the University of Montana School of Law had advised an applicant that he would be accepted if he completed a course in financial accounting. He took such a course and received a "D." The law school refused to admit him and claimed that although a "D" was an "acceptable" grade it was not a "satisfactory" grade. The student argued that it was unreasonable for the law school to inject a requirement of receiving a "satisfactory grade" after he had completed the course. The court agreed:

> Thus, we look to the matter of judgment or "discretion" in the legal sense. To cause a young man, who is otherwise qualified and whose entry into Law School would not interfere with the educational process in any discernible fashion, to lose a year and an opportunity for education on the technical, unpublished distinction between the words "satisfactory" and "acceptable" as applied to a credit-earning grade from a recognized institution is, in our view, an abuse of discretion [489 P.2d at 379].

All these cases involve public institutions, and whether their principles would apply to private institutions is unclear. The "arbitrary and capricious" standard apparently arises from concepts of due process and administrative law that are applicable only to public institutions. Courts may be even less receptive to arbitrariness arguments lodged against private schools, although common law may provide some relief even here. In *In Re Press*, 45 U.S. L.W. 2238 (N.Y. Sup. Ct., Oct. 27, 1976), for instance, the court held that an arbitrariness claim was a valid basis upon which New York University, a private institution, could be sued. And in *Levine* v. *George Washington University* (Section 4.2.6), common law contract principles protected a student at a private institution against the institution's arbitrary interpretation of a contractual relationship between student and school.

4.2.3. The contract theory. The plaintiffs in *Eden* v. *State University of New York*, 49 App.Div.2d 277, 374 N.Y.S.2d 686 (1975), had been accepted for admission to a new school of podiatry being established at SUNY Stony Brook. Shortly before the scheduled opening, the state suspended its plans for the school, citing fiscal pressures in state government. The students argued that they had a contract with SUNY entitling them to instruction in the podiatry school. The court agreed that SUNY's "acceptance of the petitioners' applications satisfies the classic requirements of a contract." Though the state could legally abrogate its contracts when necessary in the public interest to alleviate a fiscal crisis, and though "the judicial branch . . . must exercise restraint in questioning executive prerogative," the court nevertheless ordered the state to enroll the students for the ensuing academic year. The court found that a large federal grant as well as tuition money would be lost if the school did not open, that the school's personnel were already under contract and would have to be paid anyway, and that postponement of the opening therefore would not save money. Since the fiscal crisis would not be alleviated, the state's decision was "deemed arbitrary and capricious" and a breach of contract.

The *Eden* case establishes that a prospective student has a contract with the school once the school accepts his or her admission application. A subsequent case takes the contract analysis one step further, applying it to applicants not yet accepted. In *Steinberg* v. *University of Health Sciences/Chicago Medical School*, 41 Ill. App. 3d 804, 354 N.E.2d 586 (1976), an intermediate appellate court held that a rejected applicant could sue for breach of contract on the theory that the medical school had deviated from the admissions criteria in its catalogue. The applicant alleged that the school had used unstated criteria, such as the existence of alumni in the applicant's family and the ability to pledge large sums of money to the school. Although conceding that it had no authority to interfere with the substance of a private school's admissions requirements, the court asserted that the school has a contractual duty to its applicants to judge their qualifications only by its published standards unless it has specifically reserved the right to reject any applicant for whatever reason it desires.

The court reasoned that the school's catalogue was an invitation to make an offer; the applicant's application in response to that invitation was an offer; and the medical school's retention of the application fee was the acceptance of the offer.

> We believe that he [Steinberg] and the school entered into an enforceable contract; that the school's obligation under the contract was stated in the school's bulletin in a definitive manner and that by accepting his application fee—a valuable consideration—the school bound itself to fulfill its promises. Steinberg accepted the school's promises in good faith, and he was entitled to have his application judged according to the school's stated criteria [354 N.E.2d at 591].

The court thus ordered a trial on the applicant's allegations. The Illinois Supreme Court affirmed the order; 69 Ill.2d 320, 371 N.E.2d 634 (1977).

Thus, the contract theory clearly applies to both public and private schools, although, as *Eden* suggests, public institutions may have defenses not available to private schools. While the contract theory does not require administrators to adopt or to forgo any particular admissions standard, it does require that administrators honor their acceptance decisions once made and honor their published policies in deciding whom to accept and to reject. Administrators should thus carefully review their published admissions policies and any new policies to be published. The institution may wish to omit standards and criteria from its policies in order to avoid being pinned down under the contract theory. Conversely, the institution may decide that full disclosure is the best policy. In either case administrators should assure that published admissions policies state only what the institution is willing to abide by. If the institution needs to reserve the right to depart from or supplement its published policies, such reservation should clearly be inserted, with counsel's assistance, into all such policies.

4.2.4. The principle of nondiscrimination. Postsecondary institutions are prohibited in varying degrees and by varying legal authorities from discriminating in their admissions process on the basis of race, sex, handicap, age, residence, and alien status. The first four are discussed in this section. The other two types—discrimination against nonresidents (residents of other states) and discrimination against aliens (citizens of other countries who are residing in the United States)—are discussed in Sections 4.3.4 and 4.3.5 because the leading cases concern financial aid rather than admissions. The legal principles in these sections also apply generally to admissions. Under these principles, generally speaking, admissions preferences for state residents (see, for example, Calif. Educ. Code sec. 22522) may be permissible (see *Rosenstock* v. *Board of Governors of University of North Carolina*, 423 F. Supp. 1321, 1326-27 (M.D.N.C. 1976)), but among state residents, a preference for those who are U.S. citizens is probably impermissible.

4.2.4.1. Race. It is clear under the Fourteenth Amendment's equal protection clause that in the absence of a "compelling state interest" (see Section 4.2.5), no public institution may discriminate in admissions due to race. The leading case, of course, is *Brown* v. *Board of Education*, 347 U.S. 483 (1954). Though *Brown* concerned elementary and secondary schools, the precedent clearly applies to postsecondary education as well, as the Supreme Court affirmed in *Florida ex rel. Hawkins* v. *Board of Control*, 350 U.S. 413 (1956). Cases involving postsecondary education have generally considered racial segregation within a state postsecondary system rather than within a single institution. One leading case, *Alabama State Teachers Association* v. *Alabama Public School and College Authority*, 289 F. Supp. 784 (D. Ala. 1968), affirmed without majority opinion, 393 U.S. 400 (1969), concerned the state's establishment of a branch of a predominantly white institution in a city already served by a predominantly black institution. The court rejected the plaintiff's argument that this action unconstitutionally perpetuated segregation in the state system, holding that states do not have an affirmative duty to dismantle segregated higher education (as opposed to elementary and secondary education). But in *Norris* v. *State Council of Higher Education*, 327 F. Supp. 1368 (E.D. Va. 1971), affirmed without opinion, 404 U.S. 907 (1971), where the state planned to expand a predominantly white two-year institution into a four-year institution in an area where a predominantly black four-year institution already existed, the court overturned the action because it impeded desegregation in the state system. As the seeming discordance between these cases and the scarcity of other precedents suggest, Fourteenth Amendment law on the desegregation of postsecondary education is still in the early stages of development.

Nevertheless, the forces against racial discrimination are increasing. Title VI of the Civil Rights Act of 1964, 42 U.S.C. 2000d (discussed in Section 7.4.2), prohibits such discrimination by any school, public or private, which receives federal money (see 45 C.F.R. 80.3(b)(1)(v), 80.4(d), and 80.5(c)). In addition, the Internal Revenue Service's Revenue Procedure 75-50, Cum. Bull. 1975-2, 40 Fed. Reg. 53, 409, requires private schools which desire tax exempt status to demonstrate that they do not discriminate on the basis of race. And recent U.S. Supreme Court decisions have recognized yet another prohibition against racial discrimination by private schools. In *Fairfax-Brewster* v. *Gonzales*, 427 U.S. 160 (1976), the Court held that 42 U.S.C. section 1981, a post–Civil War statute guaranteeing freedom of contract to blacks, prohibits private white elementary schools from discriminating against blacks in their admissions policies. This statute would apply in the same way to private postsecondary institutions. And in *McDonald* v. *Sante Fe Transportation Co.*, 427 U.S. 273 (1976), the Court ruled that 42 U.S.C. section 1981 applies to discrimination against white persons as well as blacks. These two cases make clear that private schools, regardless of whether they receive federal funds or hold a federal tax exemption, may no longer discriminate against any person on the basis of race. Thus federal statutory law and constitutional law have combined to comprehensively outlaw (with a possible

exception for affirmative action policies, discussed in Section 4.2.5)
race discrimination in admission to postsecondary education.

    4.2.4.2. Sex. The law relating to sex discrimination
remains in a state of flux. Under a leading 1971 U.S. Supreme
Court decision, sex-based classifications are permissible if "reasonable, not arbitrary, and . . . rest[ing] upon some ground of
difference having a fair and substantial relationship to the object of
[the law which includes the classification] so that all persons
similarly circumstanced shall be treated alike" (*Reed* v. *Reed*, 404
U.S. 71 (1971)). And according to a later case, sex-based
classifications "must serve important governmental objectives and
must be substantially related to achievement of those objectives"
(*Craig* v. *Boren*, 429 U.S. 190 (1976)). The impact of this confusing
constitutional verbiage on a public institution's admissions policy
has not been settled, though the precedents to date, discussed
below, do permit sex-segregated institutions in some instances.

    Amid the uncertainty, Title IX of the Education Amend-
ments of 1972, 20 U.S.C. 1681 *et seq.* (see Section 7.4.3), has
partially filled the void. While Title IX and its implementing
regulations, 45 C.F.R. Part 86, apply to all institutions receiving
federal funds, there are special exemptions concerning admissions.
For the purposes of applying these admissions exemptions, each
"administratively separate unit" of an institution is considered a
separate institution (45 C.F.R. 86.15(b)). An "administratively
separate unit" is "a school, department or college . . . admission to
which is independent of admission to any other component of such
institution" (45 C.F.R. 86.2(o)). *Private undergraduate institutions
are not prohibited from discriminating in admissions on the basis
of sex* (20 U.S.C. 1681(a)(1); 45 C.F.R. 86.15(d)). Nor are *public
undergraduate institutions which have always been single-sex
institutions* (20 U.S.C. 1681(a)(5); 45 C.F.R. 86.15(e)). The
remaining institutions, which are prohibited from discriminating
in admissions, are (1) graduate schools; (2) professional schools,
unless part of an undergraduate institution exempted from Title
IX's admissions requirements (see 45 C.F.R. 86.2(m)); (3) vocational schools, unless part of an undergraduate institution
exempted from Title IX's admissions requirements (see 45 C.F.R.
86.2(n)); and (4) public undergraduate institutions which are not,

or have not always been, single-sex schools.[2] Any of these four types of institutions which were single-sex schools must become coeducational if they wish to continue to receive federal funds, although they may have a transition period, extending no later than June 23, 1979, in which to complete the process if they have had a transition plan approved by the U.S. Commissioner of Education (45 C.F.R. 86.16–.17).

Besides this basic "integration" requirement, institutions subject to Title IX admissions requirements are prohibited from treating persons differently on the basis of sex in any phase of admissions and recruitment (45 C.F.R. 86.21–.23). Specifically, section 86.21(b) of the regulations provides that a covered institution, in its admissions process, shall not

> (i) Give preference to one person over another on the basis of sex, by ranking applicants separately on such basis, or otherwise;
> (ii) Apply numerical limitations upon the number or proportion of persons of either sex who may be admitted; or
> (iii) Otherwise treat one individual differently from another on the basis of sex.

Section 86.21(c) prohibits covered institutions from treating the sexes differently in regard to "actual or potential parental, family, or marital status"; from discriminating against applicants because of pregnancy or conditions relating to childbirth; and from making preadmission inquiries concerning marital status. Sections 86.22 and 86.23(b) prohibit institutions from having admissions preference or recruitment emphases favoring single-sex or predominantly

[2]It is possible that the admissions exemption for private undergraduate institutions in the regulations is broader than that authorized by the Title IX statute. For an argument that "administratively separate" professional and vocational components of private undergraduate institutions should not be exempt and that private undergraduate schools which are primarily professional and vocational in character should not be exempt, see W. Kaplin and M. McGillicuddy, "Scope of Exemption for Private Undergraduate Institutions from Admissions Requirements of Title IX," memorandum printed in the *Congressional Record*, Jan. 23, 1975 (daily ed.), S779–80.

single-sex schools, if such preference or emphasis has "the effect of discriminating on the basis of sex."

Furthermore, institutions exempt from Title IX admissions requirements are not necessarily free to discriminate at will on the basis of sex. Some will be caught in the net of other statutes or of constitutional equal protection principles. A federal law prohibiting discrimination in admissions to medical, nursing, and health training schools, for instance, may catch some undergraduate programs exempted from Title IX (42 U.S.C. 295h-9, 298b-2). A state statute such as the Massachusetts statute prohibiting sex discrimination in vocational training institutions may catch some other exempted undergraduate programs (Mass. Gen. Laws Ann. ch. 151, sec. 2A(a)). More important, the Fourteenth Amendment's equal protection clause places some restrictions on public undergraduate schools even if they are single-sex schools exempt from Title IX. *Kirstein* v. *University of Virginia*, 309 F. Supp. 184 (E.D. Va. 1970), concerned several female applicants who had been denied admission to the university's undergraduate school because it enrolled only males. The court ordered the university to accept the applications from the female plaintiffs, since no educational opportunity comparable to that offered by the University of Virginia was available to them elsewhere in the state system. Thus, under the Constitution, a state institution can be sex-segregated only if the state system provides other educational opportunities for the excluded sex equal to those provided in the institution(s) from which they are excluded.[3]

4.2.4.3. Handicap. The country's conscience is awakening to the problem of discrimination against handicapped persons. The landmark event thus far is the passage of Section 504 of the Rehabilitation Act of 1973, 29 U.S.C. sec. 794, as amended by Section 111(a) of the Rehabilitation Act Amendments of 1974. (See

[3]This general approach has also been used to justify separate public high schools for males and females where the schools were found to be equal; see *Vorcheimer* v. *School Dist. of Philadelphia*, 532 F.2d 880 (3rd Cir. 1976), affirmed by an equally divided court, 430 U.S. 703 (1971) (per curiam). See also *Williams* v. *McNair*, 316 F. Supp. 134 (D. S.Car. 1970), affirmed without opinion, 401 U.S. 951 (1971), where the court refused to invalidate South Carolina's women-only policy for Winthrop College.

Section 7.4.4.) Before that act there were a few scattered federal provisions concerning discrimination against the handicapped, such as 20 U.S.C. sec. 1684, which prohibits discrimination against blind persons by institutions receiving federal funds; and there had been a few constitutional equal protection cases on discrimination against handicapped students by public elementary and secondary schools, such as *PARC* v. *Pennsylvania*, 334 F. Supp. 1257 (E.D. Pa. 1971). But none of these developments has nearly the potential impact on postsecondary admissions that Section 504 has.

As applied to postsecondary education, Section 504 generally prohibits discrimination on the basis of handicap by any institution receiving federal funds. Section 84.42 of the implementing regulations, 45 C.F.R. Part 84, prohibits discrimination on the basis of handicap in admissions and recruitment. This section contains several specific provisions similar to those prohibiting sex discrimination in admissions under Title IX. (See Section 4.2.4.2.) With regard to admissions, a fund recipient may not (1) apply limitations on "the number or proportion of handicapped persons who may be admitted" (sec. 84.42(b)(1)); (2) make use of any admissions criterion "that has a disproportionately adverse effect" on the handicapped, unless the criterion, as used, is shown to predict success validly and no alternative, nondiscriminatory criterion is available (sec. 84.42(b)(2)); or (3) make a preadmission inquiry about whether the applicant is handicapped, unless the recipient needs the information in order to correct the results of past discrimination and to overcome past conditions which resulted in limited participation by the handicapped (secs. 84.42(b)(4); 84.42(c)).

These prohibitions apply to discrimination directed against "qualified handicapped" persons. A handicapped person is qualified, with respect to postsecondary and vocational services, if he or she "meets the academic and technical standards requisite to admission or participation in the recipient's education program or activity" (sec. 84.3(k)(3)). Thus, while the regulations do not prohibit an institution from denying admission to a handicapped person who does not meet the institution's "academic and technical" admissions standards, they do prohibit an institution from denying admission on the basis of the handicap as such.

Davis v. *Southeastern Community College*, 574 F.2d 1158 (4th Cir. 1978) concerned a nursing school applicant who was denied admission because she was deaf. The appellate court held that the denial violated the Section 504 regulations because the institution had specifically considered the applicant's handicap rather than considering only the academic and technical standards appropriate to other applicants.

After a student is admitted, however, the institution may make confidential inquiry concerning his handicaps (45 C.F.R. sec. 84.42(b)(4)). In this way the institution may obtain advance information concerning handicaps that may require accommodation.

In addition to these prohibitions, the institution has an affirmative duty to ascertain that its admissions tests are structured to accommodate applicants with handicaps that impair sensory, manual, or speaking skills, unless the test is intended to measure these skills. Such adapted tests must be offered as often and in as timely a way as other admissions tests and must be "administered in facilities that, on the whole, are accessible" to the handicapped (sec. 84.42(b)(3)).

4.2.4.4. Age. In *Massachusetts Board of Retirement* v. *Murgia*, 427 U.S. 367 (1976), the U.S. Supreme Court held that age discrimination is not subject to the high standard of justification that the Constitution requires, for instance, for race discrimination. Rather, age classifications are permissible if they "rationally further" some legitimate governmental objective. Although the Court in *Murgia* called this a "relatively relaxed standard" of review, it will not necessarily serve to uphold all public institution admissions policies which discriminate by age. In *Miller* v. *Sonoma Co. Junior College Dist.*, No. C-74-0222 (N.D. Cal. 1974) (unpublished opinion decided before *Murgia*), for example, two sixteen-year-old students won the right to attend a California junior college. The court held that the college's minimum age requirement of eighteen was an arbitrary and irrational basis for exclusion because not related to the state's interest in providing education to qualified students.

Both public and private institutions which receive federal funds are subject to the federal Age Discrimination Act of 1973, 42

U.S.C. secs. 6101 *et seq.* Section 6101 of the act, with certain exceptions listed in sections 6103(b) and 6103(c), prohibits "unreasonable discrimination on the basis of age in programs or activities receiving Federal financial assistance." Unlike the statutes prohibiting race, sex, and handicap discrimination, this act prohibits only "unreasonable" forms of discrimination. How this unreasonableness concept applies to postsecondary education, and particularly to admissions policies, will depend on the content of the regulations to be promulgated under the act. (As this book went to press, draft regulations were being worked on by HEW and by the United States Civil Rights Commission.)

State law also occasionally prohibits age discrimination against students. In its Fair Educational Practices statute, for example, Massachusetts prohibits age discrimination in admissions to graduate programs and vocational training institutions (Mass. Gen. Laws Ann. chap. 151, secs. 2(d), 2A(a)).

Although the Constitution, the incipient federal law, and occasional state laws all have some application to age discrimination against students, none of these sources appear to prohibit all consideration of age in admissions. That, of course, does not mean that age requirements are desirable. Maximum age policies, explicit or not, may provide an increasing problem as greater numbers of older persons seek to return to school; minimum age policies may create barriers for precocious students or graduates of innovative programs of expedited study. Administrators considering an age policy for admissions will want to carefully balance the policy interests whether or not the law requires they do so.

4.2.5. Affirmative action programs. A particularly sensitive area of concern for postsecondary administrators is affirmative action programs. Designed to increase the number of minority persons admitted to educational programs, affirmative action programs pose delicate social and legal questions that have yet to be definitively resolved. Educators have agonized over the extent to which the social goal of greater minority representation justifies the admission of less or differently qualified applicants into educational programs, particularly in the professions, while courts have grappled with the complaints of qualified but rejected nonminority applicants who claim to be victims of "reverse discrimination" because minority applicants were admitted in preference to them. Though two cases have reached the U.S. Supreme Court, *DeFunis* and *Bakke* (both discussed later), neither case established comprehensive requirements regarding affirmative action. But the varied opinions of the justices in the June 1978 *Bakke* decision (46 U.S. Law Week 4896) contain valuable insight and guidance concerning the legal and social issues of affirmative action. Read together with Justice Douglas' opinion in *DeFunis* and with other lower court cases, *Bakke* forms a baseline against which all affirmative action programs should be measured.

The legal issues can be cast in both constitutional and statutory terms and apply to both public and private institutions. The constitutional issues, pertaining only to public institutions, arise under the Fourteenth Amendment's equal protection clause. The statutory issues arise under Title VI of the Civil Rights Act of 1964 and Title IX of the Education Amendments of 1972, which prohibit race and sex discrimination by public and private institutions receiving federal funds (see Sections 4.2.4.1 and 4.2.4.2) and under 42 U.S.C. Sec. 1981, which has been construed to prohibit race discrimination in admissions by private schools whether or not they receive federal money (see Section 4.2.4.1). In the *Bakke* case, a majority of the justices agree that Title VI uses constitutional standards for determining the validity of affirmative action programs (see 46 U.S. Law Week at 4900–01, 4912–15, 4935). Standards comparable to the Constitution's would presumably also be used under 42 U.S.C. sec. 1981 and under Title IX. Thus, a core of uniform legal parameters for affirmative action, applicable to public and private institutions alike, may develop from the groundwork of *Bakke*.

Prior to *Bakke*, regulations and a statutory amendment under Titles VI and IX had dealt briefly with affirmative action. When an institution has discriminated in the past, the regulations require it to implement affirmative action programs to overcome the effects of that discrimination (45 C.F.R. secs. 80.3(b)(6)(i) and 80.5(i); 45 C.F.R. sec. 86.3(a)). The institution cannot be required to use admission quotas as part of an affirmative action plan, however, because section 408 of the Education Amendments of 1976, 90 Stat. 2081 at 2233, 20 U.S.C. sec. 1232i(c), provides that:

> It shall be unlawful for the Secretary [of HEW] to defer or limit any federal financial assistance on the basis of any failure to comply with the imposition of quotas (or any other numerical requirements which have the effect of imposing quotas) on the student admission practices of an institution of higher education or community college receiving federal financial assistance.

When the institution has not discriminated, the regulations nevertheless permit affirmative action to overcome the effects of societal discrimination (45 C.F.R. secs. 80.3(b)(6)(ii) and 80.5(j); 45 C.F.R. sec. 86.3(b)). Courts have seldom addressed the possible incongruity between flatly banning discrimination on the one hand and authorizing affirmative action on the other (see *Flanagan* v. *President and Directors of Georgetown College,* 417 F. Supp. 377 (D.D.C. 1976), discussed in Section 4.3.3), but the *Bakke* opinions do discuss this issue with a majority of the justices looking to constitutional principles for its resolution.

The first case to confront the constitutionality of affirmative action admissions programs in postsecondary education was *DeFunis* v. *Odegaard,* 507 P.2d 1169 (1973), dismissed as moot, 416 U.S. 312 (1973), on remand, 529 P.2d 438 (1974). After DeFunis, a white male, was denied admission to the University of Washington Law School, he filed suit alleging that less qualified minority applicants had been accepted and that, but for the affirmative action program, he would have been admitted. He claimed that the university discriminated against him on the basis of his race in violation of the equal protection clause.

The law school admissions committee had calculated each applicant's Predicted First-Year Average (PFYA) through a formula that considered the applicant's Law School Admissions Test (LSAT) scores and junior-senior undergraduate average. The committee had attached less importance to a minority applicant's PFYA and had considered minority applications separately from other applications. Although the committee accepted minority applicants whose PFYA's were lower than those of other applicants, in no case did it accept any person whose record indicated that he or she would not be able to successfully complete the program. The committee established no quotas; rather, its goal was the inclusion of a reasonable representation of minority groups. DeFunis' PFYA was higher than those of all but one of the minority applicants admitted in the year he was rejected.

The state trial court ordered that DeFunis be admitted, and he entered the law school. The Washington State Supreme Court reversed the lower court and upheld the law school's affirmative action program as a constitutionally acceptable admissions tool. According to this court, the consideration of race in admissions is justified by several compelling state interests:

> We believe the state has an overriding interest in promoting integration in public education. In light of the serious underrepresentation of minority groups in the law schools, and considering that minority groups participate on an equal basis in the tax support of the law school, we find the state interest in eliminating racial imbalance within public legal education to be compelling. . . .
>
> The state also has an overriding interest in providing *all* law students with a legal education that will adequately prepare them to deal with the societal problems which will confront them upon graduation. As the Supreme Court has observed, this cannot be done through books alone. . . .
>
> The legal profession plays a critical role in the policy-making sector of our society, whether decisions be public or private, state or local. That lawyers, in making and influencing these decisions, should be cognizant of the views, needs, and demands of all segments of society is a principle beyond dispute. The educational interest of the state in producing a racially balanced student body at the law school is compelling.
>
> Finally, the shortage of minority attorneys—and, consequently, minority prosecutors, judges and public officials—constitutes an undeniably compelling state interest [507 P.2d at 1182-84].

When DeFunis sought review in the U.S. Supreme Court, he was permitted to remain in school pending the Court's final disposition of the case. Subsequently, in a *per curiam* opinion with four justices dissenting, the Court declared the case moot because, by then, DeFunis was in his final quarter of law school, and the university had asserted that his registration would remain effective regardless of the case's final outcome. The Court vacated the Washington State Supreme Court's judgment and remanded the case to that court for appropriate disposition. Though the *per curiam* opinion does not discuss the merits of the case, Justice Douglas' dissent presents a thought-provoking analysis of affirmative action in admissions:

> The Equal Protection Clause did not enact a requirement that law schools employ as the sole criterion for admissions a formula based upon the LSAT and undergraduate grades, nor does it prohibit law schools from evaluating an applicant's prior achievements in light of the barriers that he had to overcome. A black applicant who pulled himself out of the ghetto into a junior college may thereby demonstrate a level of motivation, perseverance and ability that would lead a fairminded admissions committee to conclude that he shows more promise for law study than the son of a rich alumnus who achieved better grades at Harvard. That applicant would be offered admission not because he is black, but because as an individual he has shown he has the potential, while the Harvard man may have taken less advantage of the vastly superior opportunities offered him. Because of the weight of the prior handicaps, that black applicant may not realize his full potential in the first year of law school, or even in the full three years, but in the long pull of a legal career his achievements may far outstrip those of his classmates whose earlier records appeared superior by conventional criteria. There is currently no test available to the admissions committee that can predict such possibilities with assurance, but the committee may nevertheless seek to gauge it as best it can and weigh this factor in its decisions. Such a policy would not be limited to blacks, or Chicanos or Filipinos, or American Indians, although undoubtedly groups such as these may in practice be the principal beneficiaries of it. But a poor Appalachian white, or a second generation Chinese in San Francisco, or some other American whose lineage is so diverse as to defy ethnic labels, may demonstrate similar potential and thus be accorded favorable consideration by the committee.
>
> The difference between such a policy and the one presented by this case is that the committee would be making decisions on the basis of individual attributes, rather than according a preference solely on the basis of

race. To be sure, the racial preference here was not absolute—the committee did not admit all applicants from the four favored groups. But it did accord all such applicants a preference by applying, to an extent not precisely ascertainable from the record, different standards by which to judge their applications, with the result that the committee admitted minority applicants who, in the school's own judgment, were less promising than other applicants who were rejected. Furthermore, it is apparent that because the admissions committee compared minority applicants only with one another, it was necessary to reserve some proportion of the class for them, even if at the outset a precise number of places were not set aside. That proportion, apparently 15 to 20 percent, was chosen, because the school determined it to be "reasonable," although no explanation is provided as to how that number rather than some other was found appropriate. Without becoming embroiled in a semantic debate over whether this practice constitutes a "quota," it is clear that given the limitation on the total number of applicants who could be accepted, this policy did reduce the total number of places for which DeFunis could compete—solely on account of his race [416 U.S. at 331-33].

Justice Douglas did not conclude that the university's policy was therefore unconstitutional but rather that it would be unconstitutional unless, after a new trial, the court found that it took account of "cultural standards of a diverse rather than a homogeneous society" in a "racially neutral" way.

The next major case was *Alevy* v. *Downstate Medical Center,* 39 N.Y.2d 326, 384 N.Y.S.2d 82, 348 N.E.2d 537 (1976). The petitioner was a white male who had been rejected from medical school. The admissions committee had begun its selection process by assigning a "screening code" to each applicant. This code was computed on the basis of the applicant's grades and Medical College Admissions Test (MCAT) scores. Applicants with screening codes above a particular number were automatically interviewed. Other applicants were reviewed by the committee, and those whose code numbers were too low were rejected. However, minority applicants were automatically reviewed regardless of their screening code.

Unlike the *DeFunis* court, the New York Court of Appeals

believed the compelling state interest test was too stringent to use in determining the validity of affirmative action because "[i]t would indeed be ironic and, of course, would cut against the very grain of the amendment, were the equal protection clause used to strike down measures designed to achieve real equality for persons it was intended to aid." The court also added that there was little of the stigma normally associated with racial discrimination when the majority takes steps to rectify past discrimination. In place of the compelling state interest test, the court substituted a "substantial interest" test coupled with a "less objectionable alternative" test:

> In determining whether a substantial state interest underlies a preferential treatment policy, courts should inquire whether the policy has a substantial basis in actuality and is not merely conjectural. At a minimum, the state sponsored scheme must further some legitimate, articulated governmental purpose. However, the interest need not be urgent, paramount, or compelling. Thus, to satisfy the substantial interest requirement, it need be found that, on the balance, the gain to be derived from the preferential policy outweighs its possible detrimental effects.
>
> If it be found that the substantial interest requirement is met, a further inquiry must be made as to whether the objectives being advanced by the policy could not be achieved by a less objectionable alternative; for example, by reducing the size of the preference, or by limiting the time span of the practice. Additionally, where preference policies are indulged, the indulgent must be prepared to defend them. Courts ought not to be required to divine the diverse motives of legislators, administrators, or, as here, educators.
>
> In sum, in proper circumstances, reverse discrimination is constitutional. However, to be so, it must be shown that a substantial interest underlies the policy and practice and, further, that no nonracial, or less objectionable racial, classifications will serve the same purpose [348 N.E.2d at 545–46].

The court found that the medical center had practiced reverse discrimination but that such discrimination satisfied the substantial interest test. The court did not require the medical center to show that less objectionable alternatives were available because the petitioner had failed to show that he would have been admitted if no affirmative action program had been in existence.[4]

While *DeFunis* and *Alevy* upheld affirmative action programs, the court in *Hupart* v. *Board of Higher Education of City of New York*, 420 F. Supp. 1087 (S.D.N.Y. 1976), ruled that the Center for Biomedical Education's admissions process violated the Fourteenth Amendment's equal protection and due process clauses. The medical school had been created to increase the number of primary care physicians in urban areas. The program, affiliated with the City College of the City University of New York, was under community pressure to increase the number of minority students. Without the approval of the university or medical school, the admissions committee set a quota of approximately 50 percent minority students.

The court based its decision on the fact that the committee's use of race as a factor deviated from the policy of the university:

> Whatever standard of scrutiny is ultimately fashioned in "reverse discrimination" cases, it is clear that the state cannot justify making distinctions on the basis of race without having first made a deliberate choice to do so. . . .
> While perhaps not every classification by race is "odious," every distinction made on a racial basis is at least suspect and must be justified. . . . It cannot be accomplished thoughtlessly or covertly, then justified after the fact. The defendants cannot sustain their burden of justification by coming to court with an array of hypothetical and *post-facto* justifications for discrimination that has occurred either without their approval or without their conscious and formal choice to discriminate as a matter of official policy. It is not for the court to supply a rational or

[4]A similar problem was encountered by the petitioner, a white female denied admission to the University of Arkansas School of Law, in *Henson* v. *University of Arkansas*, 519 F.2d 576 (8th Cir. 1975). The Court of Appeals affirmed the dismissal of the complaint on the basis that the petitioner had failed to show that she would have been admitted had no minority admissions program been in effect. In the *Bakke* case, the California Supreme Court presumed that the plaintiff would have been admitted unless the defendant school could affirmatively show otherwise, 18 Cal.3d at 63–64, 553 P.2d at 1172. The U.S. Supreme Court did not pass on the issue, 46 U.S. Law Week 4899 n. 13, 4934.

compelling basis (or something in between) to sustain the
questioned state action. That task must be done by
appropriate state officials *before* they take any action. As the
record now stands, the state, as represented by these
defendants, rejects race as a proper admission criterion, even
in a program with objectives that might arguably justify its
use. There is, then, no basis for the distinctions that were
made by the state's agents on the basis of race [420 F. Supp.
at 1106].

Shortly after *Hupart,* the California Supreme Court, over a
strong dissent, issued its decision in *Bakke* v. *The Regents of the
University of California,* 18 Cal.3d 342, 553 P.2d 1152 (1976), the
case which became the subject of the June 1978 U.S. Supreme
Court decision. The plaintiff, a white male twice rejected from the
Medical School of the University of California at Davis, challenged
the affirmative action program that the school used to select a
portion of its entering class each year that he had been rejected.
The particular facts concerning this program's operation were
critical to its legality and were subject to dispute in the court
proceedings. They are best taken from a portion of Justice Powell's
opinion in the U.S. Supreme Court, to which a majority of the
justices agreed:

The faculty devised a special admissions program to
increase the representation of "disadvantaged" students in
each medical school class. The special program consisted of
a separate admissions system operating in coordination
with the regular admissions process. . . .
The special admissions program operated with a
separate committee, a majority of whom were members of
minority groups. On the 1973 application form, candidates
were asked to indicate whether they wished to be considered
as "economically and/or educationally disadvantaged"
applicants; on the 1974 form the question was whether they
wished to be considered as members of a "minority group,"
which the medical school apparently viewed as "blacks,"
"Chicanos," "Asians," and "American Indians." If these
questions were answered affirmatively, the application was
forwarded to the special admissions committee. No formal
definition of "disadvantaged" was ever produced, but the
chairman of the special committee screened each applica-

tion to see whether it reflected economic or educational deprivation. Having passed this initial hurdle, the applications then were rated by the special committee in a fashion similar to that used by the general admissions committee, except that special candidates did not have to meet the 2.5 grade point average cut-off applied to regular applicants. About one fifth of the total number of special applicants were invited for interviews in 1973 and 1974. Following each interview, the special committee assigned each special applicant a benchmark score. The special committee then presented its top choices to the general admissions committee. The latter did not rate or compare the special candidates against the general applicants but could reject recommended special candidates for failure to meet course requirements or other specific deficiencies. The special committee continued to recommend special applicants until a number prescribed by faculty vote were admitted. While the overall class size was still fifty, the prescribed number was eight; in 1973 and 1974, when the class size had doubled to 100, the prescribed number of special admissions also doubled, to sixteen.

From the year of the increase in class size—1971— through 1974, the special program resulted in the admission of twenty-one black students, thirty Mexican-Americans, and twelve Asians, for a total of sixty-three minority students. Over the same period, the regular admissions program produced one black, six Mexican-Americans, and thirty-seven Asians, for a total of forty-four minority students. Although disadvantaged whites applied to the special program in large numbers, none received an offer of admission through that process. Indeed, in 1974, at least, the special committee explicitly considered only "disadvantaged" special applicants who were members of one of the designated minority groups [46 U.S. Law Week at 4897–98].

The university sought to justify its program by citing the great need for doctors to work in underserved minority communities, the need to compensate for the effects of societal discrimination against minorities, the need to reduce the historical deficit of minorities in the medical profession, and the need to diversify the student body. In analyzing these justifications, the California Supreme Court applied a compelling state interest test such as that used in *DeFunis* along with a less objectionable alternative test such as used in *Alevy*. Although it assumed that the university's interests were compelling, this court held the affirmative action program unconstitutional because the university had not demonstrated that the program was the least burdensome alternative available for achieving its goals. The court suggested these alternatives:

> The University is entitled to consider, as it does with respect to applicants in the special program, that low grades and test scores may not accurately reflect the abilities of some disadvantaged students, and it may reasonably conclude that although their academic scores are lower, their potential for success in the school and the profession is equal to or greater than that of an applicant with higher grades who has not been similarly handicapped.
>
> In addition, the University may properly, as it in fact does, consider other factors in evaluating an applicant, such as the personal interview, recommendations, character, and matters relating to the needs of the profession and society, such as an applicant's professional goals. . . .
>
> In addition to flexible admission standards, the University might increase minority enrollment by instituting aggressive programs to identify, recruit, and provide remedial schooling for disadvantaged students of all races who are interested in pursuing a medical career and have an evident talent for doing so.
>
> Another ameliorative measure which may be considered is to increase the number of places available in the medical schools, either by allowing additional students to enroll in existing schools or by expanding the schools. . . .
>
> None of the foregoing measures can be related to race, but they will provide for consideration and assistance to individual applicants who have suffered previous disabilities, regardless of their surname or color. So far as the record discloses, the University has not considered the adoption of these or other nonracial alternatives to the special admission program.
>
> [T]here are [also] more precise and reliable ways to identify applicants who are genuinely interested in racial problems of minorities than by race. An applicant of whatever race who has demonstrated his concern for disadvantaged minorities in the past and who declares that practice in such a community is his primary professional

goal would be more likely to contribute to alleviation of the medical shortage than one who is chosen entirely on the basis of race and disadvantage. In short, there is no empirical data to demonstrate that any one race is more selflessly socially oriented or by contrast that another is more selfishly acquisitive.

Moreover, while it may be true that the influence exerted by minorities upon the student body and the profession will persuade some nonminority doctors to assist in meeting these community medical needs, it is at best a circuitous and uncertain means to accomplish the University's objective. It would appear that more directly effective methods can be devised, such as academic and clinical courses directed to the medical needs of minorities and emphasis upon the training of general practitioners to serve the basic needs of the poor [553 P.2d at 1166–67].

Thus concluding that the university's program did not satisfy applicable constitutional tests, the California court held that the program operated to exclude Bakke on account of his race and ordered that Bakke be admitted to medical school. It further held that the Constitution prohibited the university from giving *any* consideration to race in its admissions process and enjoined the university from doing so.

The U.S. Supreme Court affirmed this decision in part and reversed it in part (46 U.S. Law Week 4896 (1978)). The justices wrote six opinions, none of which commanded a majority of the court. But a bare majority of the justices, four relying on Title VI and one relying on the Constitution, did agree that the University of California at Davis program unlawfully discriminated against Bakke, thus affirming the first part of the California court's judgment. And a different majority of five justices (Justice Powell being the common member) agreed that "the state has a substantial interest that legitimately may be served by a properly devised admissions program involving the competitive consideration of race and ethnic origin" (46 U.S. Law Week at 4910, Part V(C)), thus reversing the second part of the California court's judgment. The various opinions debated the issues of what equal protection tests should apply, how Title VI should be interpreted in this context, what the appropriate justifications for affirmative action programs are, and the extent to which such programs can be race conscious. No majority agreed on any of these issues, however, except that Title VI embodies constitutional principles of equal protection (see previous discussion).

The divisions within the U.S. Supreme Court in *Bakke* and the varying results of the preceding lower court cases strikingly demonstrate the complexity of the affirmative action issue. Besides posing legal questions for which no firm precedents exist, the affirmative action cases involve volatile social questions of balancing the competing interests of different ethnic and racial groups as well as the interests of educational institutions and professions. Since a consensus of judicial opinion has yet to develop, administrators who deal with this issue in concrete terms should involve legal counsel in every phase of considering any affirmative action admissions policy.

The following guidelines will assist administrators charting a course through the murky affirmative action waters:

1. The institution should be particularly sensitive to situations in which it may itself have discriminated in admissions against minorities. If it or the educational system of which it is a part has discriminated, the law will permit and may require the institution to use affirmative action to the extent necessary to overcome the present effects of the past discrimination. In the absence of such past discrimination, the law may still permit but does not require institutions to have affirmative action programs for admissions. (See the Title VI and IX discussion earlier and 46 U.S. Law Week at 4904–05, 4916, 4921.)

2. In considering whether to employ an affirmative action program, the institution should carefully determine its purposes and objectives and make its decisions in the context of these purposes and objectives. The institution may choose one or a combination of three basic approaches to affirmative action which are reflected in the cases: the *uniform* system, the *differential* system, and the *preferential* system. While all three systems can be implemented lawfully, the potential for legal challenge increases as the institution proceeds down the list. The potential for substantially increasing minority enrollments also increases, however, so

that an institution which is deterred by the possibility of legal action may also be forsaking part of the means to achieve its educational and societal goals.

3. A uniform system of affirmative action consists of changing the institution's general admission standards or procedures to more sensitively attune them to the qualifications and potential contributions of disadvantaged and minority individuals. These changes are then applied uniformly to all applicants. For example, all applicants might be given credit for work experience, demonstrated commitment to working in a particular geographical area, or overcoming handicaps or disadvantages. Such a system would thus allow all candidates, regardless of race, ethnicity, or sex to demonstrate particular qualities that may not be reflected in grades or test scores. It would not preclude the use of numerical cutoffs where administrators believe that applicants with grades or test scores above or below a certain number should be automatically accepted or rejected. In *DeFunis*, Justice Douglas discusses aspects of such a system (416 U.S. at 331–32), as does the California Supreme Court in *Bakke* (553 P.2d at 1165–66).

4. A differential system of admissions is based on the concept that equal treatment of differently situated individuals may itself create inequality; different standards for such individuals become appropriate when use of uniform standards would in effect discriminate against them. If, for instance, the institution determined that a standardized admissions test that it used was culturally biased as applied to its disadvantaged or minority applicants, it might use a different standard for assessing their performance on the test or employ some other criterion in lieu of the test.

In *Bakke*, Justice Powell referred to a differential system by noting: "Racial classifications in admissions conceivably could serve a . . . purpose . . . which petitioner does not articulate: fair appraisal of each individual's academic promise in the light of some bias in grading or testing procedures. To the extent that race and ethnic background were considered only to the extent of curing established inaccuracies in predicting academic performance, it might be argued that there is no 'preference' at all" (46 U.S. Law Week at 4906 n. 43). Justice Douglas' *DeFunis* opinion also refers extensively to differential standards and procedures:

> [P]rofessional persons, particularly lawyers, are not selected for life in a computerized society. The Indian who walks to the beat of Chief Seattle of the Muckleshoot tribe in Washington has a different culture than examiners at law schools. . . .
>
> [T]he admissions committee acted properly in my view in setting minority applications apart for separate processing. These minorities have cultural backgrounds that are vastly different from the dominant Caucasian. Many Eskimos, American Indians, Filipinos, Chicanos, Asian Indians, Burmese, and Africans come from such disparate backgrounds that a test sensitively tuned for most applicants would be wide of the mark for many minorities. . . .
>
> I think a separate classification of these applicants is warranted, lest race be a subtle force in eliminating minority members because of cultural differences. . . .
>
> The reason for the separate treatment of minorities as a class is to make more certain that racial factors do not militate *against an applicant or on his behalf.* . . .
>
> The key to the problem is consideration of such applications *in a racially neutral way* [416 U.S. at 334-36, 340].

To remain true to the theory of a differential system, standards or procedures can be modified only to the extent necessary to counteract the discriminatory effect of applying uniform standards, and the substituted standards or procedures must be designed to select only candidates whose qualifications and potential contributions are comparable to those of candidates selected under the general standards.

5. A preferential system of affirmative action is explicitly "race conscious" and allows some form of preference for minority applicants. The admissions programs at issue in the cases discussed here can be viewed, for the most part, as preferential systems. It is the preference available only to minorities that creates the reverse discrimination claim. Depending on the institution's objectives, some form of racial preference may indeed be necessary. Four justices agreed in *Bakke* that:

> [T]here are no practical means by which . . . [the university] could achieve its ends in the foreseeable future without the use of race conscious measures. With respect to any factor (such as poverty or family educational background) that may be used as a substitute for race as an indicator of past discrimination, whites greatly outnumber racial minorities simply because whites make up a far larger percentage of the total population and therefore far outnumber minorities in absolute terms at every socioeconomic level. . . . Moreover, while race is positively correlated with differences in . . . [grades and standardized test] scores, economic disadvantage is not. Thus, it appears that economically disadvantaged whites do not score less well than economically advantaged whites while economically advantaged blacks score less well than do disadvantaged whites. These statistics graphically illustrate that the University's purpose to integrate its classes by compensating for past discrimination could not be achieved by a general preference for the economically disadvantaged or the children of parents of limited education unless such groups were to make up the entire class [46 U.S. Law Week at 4924–25].

Unlike differential systems, preferential systems are not limited to curing inaccuracies and unfairness in evaluating qualifications; they may be designed to fulfill other, broader, objectives. As *Bakke* demonstrates, debate continues concerning what objectives are sufficiently important to justify a preference. The leading candidates for that category are apparently the objectives of attaining a diverse student body and of remedying the institution's own past discrimination. It is particularly important in a preferential system that the institution exercise care in determining its objectives and relating its system to them. Administrators should rely demonstrably on the institution's educational expertise and involve policy makers at the highest levels of authority over the institution.

The permissible types and scope of preference are also subject to continuing debate. Under *Bakke*, a preferential system that employs explicit racial or ethnic quotas is, by a 5–4 vote, reverse discrimination and thus prohibited. But some other forms of preference are permissible. Until the U.S. Supreme Court speaks again, the best guideline is Justice Powell's opinion in *Bakke*. Four justices approve of explicit, specific preferences; a fifth vote is needed to form a majority; and of the remaining justices only Powell acknowledges support for any form of preferential admissions system.[5] Justice Powell's opinion thus sets a boundary which administrators should stay within to have reasonable expectation of legality.

For Powell, and thus currently for administrators, the key to a lawful preference system is "a policy of individual comparisons" that "assures a measure of competition among all applicants" and does not result in any "systematic exclusion of certain groups" on grounds of race or ethnicity from competition for a portion of the places in a class (see 46 U.S. Law Week at 4909 n. 53). In implementing such a system, "race or ethnic background may be deemed a 'plus' in a particular applicant's file" so long as it is only "one element—to be weighed fairly against other elements—in the selection process. . . . [A] Court would not assume that a university, professing to employ [such] a racially nondiscriminatory admissions policy, would operate it as a cover for the functional equivalent of a quota system" (46 U.S. Law Week at 4909). (Powell's model of a constitutional preference policy is the "Harvard Plan," set out in an appendix to his opinion and referred to favorably by four other justices (46 U.S. Law Week at 4908–09, 4910–11, 4925).)

With the law still in flux after *Bakke,* it remains difficult, at best, to define the full extent of institutional flexibility to implement affirmative action in admissions. But there is considerable room in which the institution can operate with some reasonable expectation of legality. By pursuing the five suggested

[5]The position of the other four justices is not entirely clear. Justice Stevens' opinion expressing their views can be read both broadly and narrowly. It states that under Title VI, "race cannot be the basis of excluding anyone from participation in a federally funded program," suggesting that all racial preferences may be unlawful. But it also states that "the question whether race can ever be used as a factor in an admissions decision is not an issue in this case, and . . . discussion of that issue is inappropriate." If this issue is indeed left open, possibly one or more of these four justices could in the future permit some form of racial consideration in admissions.

steps with the active involvement of legal counsel, an institution can maximize the likelihood that its particular admissions plan will clear constitutional and statutory hurdles.

4.2.6. Readmission. The readmission of previously excluded students can pose additional legal problems for postsecondary institutions. Although the legal principles in Section 4.2 apply generally to readmissions, the contract theory (Section 4.2.3) may assume added prominence because the student-institution contract (see Section 4.1.3) may include provisions concerning exclusion and readmission. The principles in Sections 4.4 through 4.6 may also apply generally to readmissions where the student challenges the validity of the original exclusion.

Institutions should have an explicit policy on readmission, even if that policy is simply "excluded students will never be considered for readmission." An explicit readmission policy can give students advance notice of their rights, or lack of rights, concerning readmission and, where readmission is permitted, can provide standards and procedures to promote fair and evenhanded decision-making. If the institution has an explicit admissions policy, administrators should take pains to follow it, especially since its violation could be considered a breach of contract. Similarly, if administrators make an agreement with a student concerning readmission, they should firmly adhere to it. *Levine* v. *George Washington University,* C.A. 8230–76 (D.C. Super. Ct. 1976), for instance, concerned a medical student who had done poorly in his first year but, by agreement with the school, was allowed to repeat the year subject to being excluded for a "repeated performance of marginal quality." On the second try, he passed all his courses but ranked low in each. The school excluded him. The court used contract principles to overturn the exclusion, finding that the school's subjective and arbitrary interpretation of "marginal quality," without prior notice to the student, breached the agreement between student and school. In contrast, the court in *Giles* v. *Howard University,* 428 F. Supp. 603 (D.D.C. 1977), held that the university's refusal to readmit a former medical student was not a breach of contract because the refusal was consistent with the "reasonable expectations" of the parties.

Sec. 4.3. Financial Aid

4.3.1. General principles. The legal principles affecting financial aid have a wide variety of sources. Some principles apply generally to all financial aid whether awarded as scholarships, assistantships, loans, fellowships, preferential tuition rates, or in some other form. Other principles depend on the particular source of funds being used and thus may vary with the aid program or the type of award. Sections 4.3.2 through 4.3.6 discuss the principles, and specific legal requirements resulting from them, that present the most difficult problems for financial aid administrators. This section discusses other more general principles affecting financial aid.

The principles of contract law may apply to financial aid awards, since an award once made may create a contract between the institution and the aid recipient. Typically the institution's obligation is to provide a particular type of aid at certain times and in certain amounts. The student-recipient's obligation depends on the type of aid. With loans the typical obligation is to repay the principal and a prescribed rate of interest at certain times and in certain amounts. With other aid the obligation may be only to spend the funds for specified academic expenses or to achieve a specified level of academic performance in order to maintain aid eligibility. Sometimes, however, the student-recipient may have more extensive obligations, such as performance of instructional or laboratory duties, participation on a varsity athletic team, or provision of particular services after graduation. The defendant-student in *State of New York* v. *Coury*, 359 N.Y.S.2d 486 (Sup. Ct. 1974), for instance, had accepted a scholarship and agreed, as a condition of the award, to perform internship duties in a welfare agency for one year after graduation. When the student did not perform the duties, the state sought a refund of the scholarship money. The court held for the state because the student had "agreed to accept the terms of the contract" and had not performed as the contract required.[6]

[6]Illustrative cases are collected in Annot., "Construction and Application of Agreement by Medical or Social Work Student to Work in Particular Position or at Particular Location in Exchange for Financial

The law regarding gifts, grants, wills, and trusts may also apply to financial aid awards. These legal principles would generally require aid administrators to adhere to any conditions that the donor, grantor, testator, or settlor placed on use of the funds. Funds provided by government agencies or private foundations, for instance, must be used in accordance with conditions in the program regulations, grant instrument, or other legal document formalizing the transaction. Section 4.3.2 illustrates such conditions in the context of federal aid programs.

Similarly, funds made available to the institution under wills or trusts must be used in accordance with conditions in the will or trust instrument. Conditions in testamentary or *inter vivos* trusts can sometimes be modified by a court under the *cy pres* doctrine, however, as in *Howard Savings Institution* v. *Peep*, 34 N.J. 494, 170 A.2d 39 (1961). Amherst College had been unable to accept a trust establishing a scholarship loan fund because one of its provisions violated the college's charter. The provision, stipulating that recipients of the funds had to be "Protestant" and "Gentile," was deleted by the court. Similarly, in *Wilbur* v. *University of Vermont*, 129 Vt. 33, 270 A.2d 889 (1970), the court deleted a provision in a financial aid trust that had placed numerical restrictions on the size of the student body at the university's College of Arts and Sciences. In each case, the court found that the dominant purpose of the person establishing the trust could still be achieved with the restriction removed. As the court in the *Peep* case explained, "The doctrine of *cy pres* is a judicial mechanism for the preservation of a charitable trust when accomplishment of the particular purpose of the trust becomes

---

Aid in Meeting Costs of Education," 83 A.L.R.3d 1273 (1978 plus periodic supp.). Supplementing general contract principles, state law regarding the age of majority (see Section 4.1.2) and parents' obligation to support their children affect questions of with whom the institution should contract in awarding financial aid and how the institution should compute the amount of aid. Administrative and policy problems in determining dependency and possible constitutional challenges to the dependency determinations of public institutions are discussed in D. J. Hanson, *The Lowered Age of Majority: Its Impact on Higher Education*, 11–17, 36–37 (Association of American Colleges, 1975).

impossible, impracticable or illegal. In such a situation if the settlor manifested an intent to devote the trust to a charitable purpose more general than the frustrated purpose, a court, instead of allowing the trust to fail, will apply the trust funds to a charitable purpose as nearly as possible to the particular purpose of the settlor" (170 A.2d at 42).[7]

A third relevant body of legal principles is that of constitutional due process. These principles apply generally to public institutions and apply to private institutions when they make awards from public funds. (See Section 1.4.2.) Since termination of aid may affect both "property" and "liberty" interests (see Section 3.5.2) of the student-recipients, courts may sometimes require that termination be accompanied by some form of procedural safeguards. *Corr* v. *Mattheis*, 407 F. Supp. 847 (D.R.I. 1976), for instance, involved students who had had their federal aid terminated in midyear under a federal student unrest statute, after they had participated in a campus protest against the Vietnam War. The court found that the students had been denied a property interest in continued receipt of funds awarded to them, as well as a liberty interest in being free from stigmas foreclosing further educational or employment opportunities. Termination thus had to be preceded by notice and a meaningful opportunity to contest the decision. In other cases, where the harm or stigma to students is less or aid is terminated for academic rather than disciplinary reasons, the required procedural safeguards will be less stringent. In the latter case, procedural safeguards may be almost nonexistent, with courts following the distinction between academic deficiency problems and misconduct problems drawn in Section 4.6.3.

4.3.2. Federal programs. The federal government provides or guarantees many millions of dollars per year in student aid for postsecondary education. To protect its investment and assure the fulfillment of national priorities and goals, the federal government imposes many requirements on the way institutions manage and

---

[7]As to trusts generally, see G. C. Bogert and G. T. Bogert, *Handbook of the Law of Trusts* (West, 5th ed., 1973). As to wills, see T. E. Atkinson, *Law of Wills* (West, 2nd ed., 1953). As to grants, see A. Willcox, "The Function and Nature of Grants," 22 *Administrative Law Review* 125, 128–31 (1970).

spend funds under federal programs. Some are general requirements applicable to student aid and all other federal assistance
programs. Others are specific programmatic requirements applicable to one, or a related group, of student aid programs. These
requirements constitute the most prominent—and critics would
add, most prolific and burdensome—source of specific restrictions
on an institution's administration of financial aid.

The most prominent general requirements are the nondiscrimination requirements discussed in Section 4.3.3, which apply
to all financial aid whether or not it is provided under federal
programs. In addition, the federal Buckley Amendment (discussed
in Section 4.12.1) imposes various requirements on the institution's
record-keeping practices regarding all financial aid. The Buckley
regulations, however, do partially exempt financial aid records
from nondisclosure requirements. They provide that an institution
may disclose personally identifiable information from a student's
records, without the student's consent, to the extent "necessary for
such purposes as" determining the student's eligibility for financial
aid, determining the amount of aid and the conditions that will be
imposed regarding it, or enforcing the terms or conditions of the
aid (45 C.F.R. sec. 99.31(a)(4)).

The specific programmatic restrictions on federal student aid
depend on the particular program. Under some programs, the
federal government provides funds to institutions to establish
revolving loan funds, as in the National Direct Student Loan
program (NDSL), 20 U.S.C. secs. 1087aa *et seq.*, 45 C.F.R. Pt. 144.
Under other programs the government grants funds to institutions,
which in turn grant them to students, as in the Supplemental
Educational Opportunity Grant program (SEOG), 20 U.S.C. secs.
1070b *et seq.*, 45 C.F.R. Pt. 176, and the College Work Study
Program (CWSP), 42 U.S.C. sec. 2751, 45 C.F.R. Pt. 175.
Sometimes the institution merely participates in government-
sponsored programs by performing certain functions for students
who receive funds from the government, as in the G.I. Bill
program, 38 U.S.C. sec. 1651, 38 C.F.R. 21.1020, and the Basic
Educational Opportunity Grant program (BEOG), 20 U.S.C. sec.
1070a, 45 C.F.R. Part 190, or from third-party lenders, as in the
Guaranteed Student Loan Program (GSLP), 20 U.S.C. secs. 1071 *et*

seq., 45 C.F.R. Pt. 177. Each such program has its own regulations placing various requirements on the institution.

In addition, the Education Amendments of 1976 have created an overlay of requirements applicable to the major student aid programs administered by the U.S. Commissioner of Education. Under section 131 of the amendments, "Student Consumer Information," a postsecondary institution receiving administrative cost allowances under the NDSL, GSL, CWS, SEOG, or BEOG program must, on request, provide prospective and enrolled students with a long list of information. This includes information accurately describing its financial aid programs, its review standards for making financial aid awards, attendance costs, the refund policy, and data concerning student retention (20 U.S.C. sec. 1088b-1(a)). Each institution must designate personnel to assist students seeking such information (20 U.S.C. sec. 1088b-1(b)). Regulations implementing section 131 are published in 45 C.F.R. Part 178. Under section 133 of the amendments, "Fiscal Responsibility," the institution must meet certain standards of financial responsibility and institutional capability regarding its administration of federal aid programs and must avoid "misrepresentation of the nature of its educational program, its financial charges, or the employability of its graduates" (20 U.S.C. sec. 1088f-1(a) and sec. 1088f-1(c)). The Commissioner of Education can enforce both provisions and their implementing regulations, as well as other regulations under Office of Education student aid programs, by limiting, suspending, or terminating the institution's eligibility to participate in federal student aid programs (20 U.S.C. sec. 1088f-1(a)(4)). Regulations implementing this authority are published in 45 C.F.R. Part 168, Subpart H.

Requirements similar to sections 131 and 133 were also added to the G.I. Bill program by the Veterans Education and Employment Assistance Act of 1976. To obtain approval of courses so that enrolled veterans may receive Veterans' Administration (VA) benefits, an institution now must submit "its catalog or bulletin which must be certified as true and correct in content and policy" to the State Approval Agency (38 U.S.C. sec. 1775). The catalogue must include twelve specific types of information regarding the institution, including standards of progress for graduation, policy and regulations on student conduct, policy on refunds of tuition and fees, and specific course descriptions for all courses to be approved (38 U.S.C. sec. 1776(b)). These VA requirements, taken together with the requirements in Sections 131 and 133, carve out an extensive federal supervisory role over postsecondary institutions participating in federal student aid programs which will long be studied and debated. Institutions seeking to improve their information systems, either to comply with these federal requirements or for their own administrative policy reasons, may be helped by these two companion volumes: E. H. El-Khawas, *Better Information for Student Choice: Report of a National Task Force*, and J. S. Stark, *Inside Information: A Handbook for Institutions Interested in Better Information*, both published in 1978 by the American Association for Higher Education. Administrators will also be helped through the regulatory maze of the various federal student aid programs by information available from the U.S. Commissioner of Education. The Education Amendments of 1976 add another new section, 493A(c), to the Higher Education Act, 20 U.S.C. sec. 1088b-1(c), which requires the commissioner to prepare "descriptions of Federal student assistance programs including the rights and responsibilities of student and institutional participants." (For a discussion of federal aid programs in general, see Section 7.3.)

4.3.3. Nondiscrimination. The legal principles of nondiscrimination apply to the financial aid process in much the same way they apply to the admissions process. (See Sections 4.2.4 and 4.2.5.) The same constitutional principles of equal protection apply to financial aid. The relevant statutes and regulations on nondiscrimination—Title VI, Title IX, and Section 504—all apply to financial aid, although Title IX's and Section 504's coverage and specific requirements for financial aid are different from those for admissions. And the affirmative action problem poses difficulties for financial aid programs similar to those it poses for admissions programs. In addition, the Age Discrimination Act of 1973, 42 U.S.C. secs. 6101 *et seq.* (see Section 4.2.4.4), apparently will affect financial aid once the act is implemented by regulations.

Of the federal statutes, Title IX has the most substantial impact on the financial aid programs and policies of postsecondary institutions. Section 86.37 of the regulations (45 C.F.R. 86.37), with four important exceptions, prohibits the use of sex-restricted scholarships and virtually every other sex-based distinction in the financial aid program. Section 86.37(a)(1) prohibits the institution from providing "different amounts or types" of aid, "limiting eligibility" for "any particular type or source" of aid, "applying different criteria," or otherwise discriminating "on the basis of sex" in awarding financial aid. Section 86.37(a)(2) prohibits giving any assistance, "through solicitation, listing, approval, provision of facilities or other services," to any "foundation, trust, agency, organization, or person" which discriminates on the basis of sex in providing financial aid to the institution's students. Section 86.37(a)(3) also prohibits aid eligibility rules which treat the sexes differently "with regard to marital or parental status."

The four exceptions to this broad nondiscrimination policy permit sex-restricted financial aid under certain circumstances. Section 86.37(b) permits an institution to "administer or assist in the administration of" sex-restricted financial assistance which is "established pursuant to domestic or foreign wills, trusts, bequests, or similar legal instruments or by acts of a foreign government." Institutions must administer such awards, however, so that their "overall effect" is "nondiscriminatory" according to standards set out in section 86.37(b)(2). Section 86.31(c) creates the same kind of exception for sex-restricted foreign study scholarships awarded to the institution's students or graduates. Such awards must be established through the same legal channels specified for the first exception, and the institution must make available "reasonable opportunities for similar [foreign] studies for members of the other sex." The third exception, for athletic scholarships, is discussed in Section 4.11.2. A fourth exception was added by an amendment to Title IX included in the Education Amendments of 1976. Section 412(a)(4) of the amendments (20 U.S.C. sec. 1681(a)(9)) permits institutions to award financial assistance to winners of pageants based on "personal appearance, poise, and talent," even though the pageant is restricted to members of one sex.

Section 504 of the Rehabilitation Act of 1973 (see Section 7.4.4), as implemented by the HEW regulations, restricts postsecondary institutions' financial aid processes as they relate to handicapped persons. Section 84.46(a) of the regulations (45 C.F.R. Part 84) prohibits the institution from providing "less assistance" to qualified handicapped students, from placing a "limit [on] eligibility for assistance," and from otherwise discriminating or assisting any other entity to discriminate on the basis of handicap in providing financial aid. The major exception to this nondiscrimination requirement is that the institution may still administer financial assistance provided under a particular discriminatory will or trust as long as "the overall effect of the award of scholarships, fellowships, and other forms of financial assistance is not discriminatory on the basis of handicap" (45 C.F.R. sec. 84.46(a)(2)).

The affirmative action/reverse discrimination dilemma hit the financial aid area in *Flanagan* v. *President and Directors of Georgetown College*, 417 F. Supp. 377 (D.D.C. 1976). The law school at Georgetown had allocated 60 percent of its financial aid for the first-year class to minority students, who constituted 11 percent of the class. The remaining 40 percent of the aid was reserved for nonminorities, the other 89 percent of the class. Within each category, funds were allocated on the basis of need, but because of Georgetown's allocation policy, the plaintiff, a white law student, received less financial aid than some minority students even though his financial need was greater. The school's threshold argument was that this program *did not discriminate by race* because disadvantaged white students were also included within the definition of minority. The court quickly rejected this argument:

> Certain ethnic and racial groups are automatically accorded "minority" status, while whites or Caucasians must make a particular showing in order to qualify. . . . Access to the "favored" category is made more difficult for one racial group than another. This in itself is discrimination as prohibited by Title VI as well as the Constitution [417 F. Supp. at 382].

The school then defended its policy as part of an affirmative action program to increase minority enrollment. The student argued that the policy discriminated against nonminorities in violation of Title VI of the Civil Rights Act. (See Section 7.4.2.) The court sided with the student:

> Where an administrative procedure is permeated with social and cultural factors (as in a law school's admission process), separate treatment for "minorities" may be justified in order to insure that all persons are judged in a racially neutral fashion.
>
> But in the instant case, we are concerned with the question of financial need, which, in the final analysis, cuts across racial, cultural, and social lines. There is no justification for saying that a "minority" student with a demonstrated financial need of $2,000 requires more scholarship aid than a "nonminority" student with a demonstrated financial need of $3,000. To take such a position, which the defendants have, is reverse discrimination on the basis of race which cannot be justified by a claim of affirmative action [417 F. Supp. at 384].

Although *Flanagan* broadly concludes that allotment of financial aid on an explicit racial basis is impermissible, the subsequent *Bakke* decision (see Section 4.2.5) may preserve some room for racial considerations in financial aid programs. To fit within *Bakke*, however, the institution would have to demonstrate that its use of race was necessary to diversify the student body, rectify its own past discrimination, or achieve some comparably important goal. Moreover, to fit within Justice Powell's requirements in *Bakke*, the institution would apparently have to award aid on an individual competitive basis, using race as one of a mix of evaluative criteria, and not systematically exclude any group from competition for any portion of the aid.

4.3.4. Discrimination against nonresidents. State institutions have often imposed significantly higher tuition fees on out-of-state students. Courts have generally permitted such discrimination in favor of the state's own residents. The U.S. Supreme Court, in the context of a related issue, said, "We fully recognize that a state has a legitimate interest in protecting and preserving the quality of its colleges and universities and the right of its own bona fide residents to attend such institutions on a preferential tuition basis (*Vlandis*

v. *Kline*, 412 U.S. 441, 452–53 (1973)). Not all preferential tuition systems, however, are beyond constitutional challenge.

In a variety of cases students have questioned the constitutionality of the particular criteria which states use to determine who is a resident for purposes of the lower tuition rate. In *Starns* v. *Malkerson*, 326 F. Supp. 234 (D. Minn. 1970), students challenged this regulation: "No student is eligible for resident classification in the University, in any college thereof, unless he has been a bona fide domiciliary of the state for at least a year immediately prior thereto." The students argued, as have the plaintiffs in some similar cases, that discrimination against nonresidents affects "fundamental" rights to travel interstate and to obtain an education and that such discrimination is permissible under the equal protection clause only if necessary to the accomplishment of some "compelling state interest." The court dismissed the students' argument, concluding that "the one-year waiting period does not deter any appreciable number of persons from moving into the state. There is no basis in the record to conclude, therefore, that the one-year waiting period has an unconstitutional 'chilling effect' on the assertion of the constitutional right to travel." The U.S. Supreme Court affirmed the decision without opinion, 401 U.S. 985 (1971).

Other cases are consistent with *Starns* in upholding durational residency requirements of up to one year for public institutions. Courts have agreed that equal protection law requires a high standard of justification when discrimination infringes fundamental rights. But as in *Starns*, courts have not agreed that the fundamental right to travel is infringed by durational residency requirements. Since they have also rejected the notion that access to postsecondary education is a fundamental right (see *San Antonio Indep. School Dist.* v. *Rodriguez*, 411 U.S. 1 (1973)), courts have not applied the compelling interest test to durational residency requirements of a year or less. In *Sturgis* v. *Washington*, 414 U.S. 1057 (1973), affirming 368 F. Supp. 38 (W.D. Wash. 1973), the Supreme Court again recognized these precedents by affirming, without opinion, the lower court's approval of Washington's one-year durational residency statute.

However, the Supreme Court held another kind of residency requirement to be unconstitutional in *Vlandis* v. *Kline*, discussed earlier in this section. A Connecticut statute provided that a student's residency at the time of application for admission would remain her residency for the entire time she was a student. The Supreme Court noted that, under such a statute, a person who had been a lifelong state resident, except for a brief period in another state just prior to admission, could not reestablish Connecticut residency as long as she remained a student. But a lifelong out-of-state resident who moved to Connecticut before applying could receive in-state tuition benefits even if she had lived in the state for only one day. Because such unreasonable results could flow from Connecticut's "permanent irrebuttable presumption" of residency, the Court held that the statute violated due process. At the same time the Court reaffirmed the state's broad discretion to use more flexible and individualized criteria for determining residency, such as "year-round residence, voter registration, place of filing tax returns, property ownership, driver's license, car registration, marital status, vacation employment," and so on. In subsequent cases, the Court has explained *Vlandis* as applying only to "those situations in which a state 'purports to be concerned with [domicile, but] at the same time den[ies] to one seeking to meet its test of [domicile] the opportunity to show factors clearly bearing on that issue.'" *Elkins* v. *Moreno*, 98 S. Ct. 1338 (1978), quoting *Weinberger* v. *Salfi*, 422 U.S. 749, 771 (1975).

Other rulings on different residency criteria include *Kelm* v. *Carlson*, 473 F.2d 1267 (6th Cir. 1973), where the court of appeals invalidated a University of Toledo requirement that a law student show proof of employment in Ohio before being granted resident status. In a later decision the same court rejected a student's claim that voter registration alone showed state residency for lower state tuition purposes. (*Hayes* v. *Board of Regents of Kentucky State University*, 495 F.2d 1326 (6th Cir. 1974).) And in *Samuel* v. *University of Pittsburgh*, 375 F. Supp. 1119 (W.D. Pa. 1974), a class action brought by female married students, the court invalidated a residency determination rule which made a wife's residency status dependent on her husband's residency. While the state defended the rule by arguing the factual validity of the common law presumption that a woman has the domicile of her husband, the court found the rule to discriminate on the basis of sex and thus to violate equal protection principles.

4.3.5. Discrimination against aliens. In the 1977 case of *Nyquist* v. *Jean-Marie Mauclet,* 432 U.S. 1 (1977), the U.S. Supreme Court set forth constitutional principles applicable to discrimination against aliens in student financial aid programs. The case involved a New York state statute that barred resident aliens from eligibility for Regents' college scholarships, tuition assistance awards, and state-guaranteed student loans. Resident aliens denied financial aid argued that the New York law unconstitutionally discriminated against them in violation of the equal protection clause of the Fourteenth Amendment. The Supreme Court agreed.

The Supreme Court's opinion makes clear that alienage, somewhat like race, is a "suspect classification." Discrimination against aliens in awarding financial aid can thus be justified only if the discrimination is necessary in order to achieve some legitimate and substantial governmental interest. The *Nyquist* opinion indicates that offering an incentive for aliens to become naturalized, or enhancing the educational level of the electorate, are not state governmental interests sufficient to justify discrimination against resident aliens with regard to financial aid.

Since the case was brought against the state rather than against individual postsecondary institutions, *Nyquist*'s most direct effect is to prohibit states from discriminating against resident aliens in state financial aid programs. It does not matter whether the state programs are for students in public institutions, in private institutions, or both, since in any case the state has created the discrimination. In addition, the case clearly would prohibit public institutions from discriminating against resident aliens in operating their own separate financial aid programs. Private institutions are affected by these constitutional principles only to the extent that they are participating in government-sponsored financial aid programs or are otherwise engaging in "state action" (see Section 1.4.2) in their aid programs.

Administrators whose institutions are subject to the *Nyquist* principles can comply by assuring that U.S. citizenship, applying for U.S. citizenship, or filing a statement of intent to do so is not used as an eligibility requirement for financial aid administered by the institution. This does not mean that *all* aliens must be eligible for aid. While *Nyquist* indicates that resident aliens as a class do not differ sufficiently from U.S. citizens to permit different treatment, courts may not reach the same conclusion regarding temporary nonresident aliens. Institutions may deem temporary nonresident aliens ineligible, at least if the aliens have no demonstrable present intention to become permanent residents. (See the similar eligibility standard for the federal Guaranteed Student Loan Program, 45 C.F.R. sec. 177.1(a).)

Moreover, since *Nyquist* does not affect state residency requirements, aliens who are not state residents may still be deemed ineligible when the principles in Section 4.3.3 permit it—not because they are aliens but because they are nonresidents of the state. Although state residency for aliens may be determined in part by their particular status under federal immigration law (see especially 8 U.S.C. sec. 1101(a)(15)), it is well to be cautious in relying on federal law. In *Elkins* v. *Moreno,* 98 S. Ct. 1338 (1978), the University of Maryland had denied "in-state" status, for purposes of tuition and fees, to aliens holding G-4 nonimmigrant visas (for employees of international treaty organizations and their immediate families) under federal law. The university argued that their federal status precluded such aliens from demonstrating an intent to become permanent Maryland residents. The U.S. Supreme Court rejected this argument, holding that G-4 aliens (unlike some other categories of nonimmigrant aliens) are not incapable under federal law of becoming permanent residents and thus are not precluded from forming an intent to reside permanently in Maryland. The Court then certified to the Maryland state court the question whether the plaintiff aliens qualified for "in-state" status under the state's common law.

In sum, while neither public institutions nor private institutions using public funds may blanketly exclude all aliens from federal aid programs, it is apparently permissible to exclude aliens who are not and do not intend to become permanent U.S. residents or who are not residents of the state.

4.3.6. Collection of student debts. When an institution extends financial aid to students in the form of loans, it has the additional problem of assuring that students repay their loans according to the schedule and conditions in the loan agreement. Enforcing payment of loans can involve the institution in a legal quagmire, several aspects of which are discussed in this section.

4.3.6.1. Federal Bankruptcy Law. Numerous student borrowers of aid funds have sought to extinguish their loan obligations by filing for bankruptcy under the federal Bankruptcy Act, 11 U.S.C. secs. 1 *et seq.* Federal bankruptcy law supersedes all state law inconsistent with the act's provisions or purpose (to allow the honest bankrupt a fresh start free from the burden of indebtedness). Students may initiate bankruptcy proceedings by petitioning the appropriate federal court for discharge of all provable debts. Following receipt of a bankruptcy petition, the court issues an order fixing times for the filing and hearing of objections to the petition before a referee in bankruptcy. Notice of this order is given to all potential creditors, usually by means of newspaper publication. Under the act, 11 U.S.C. sec. 32, a debt is dischargeable when it is provable and when any timely objections to its dischargeability are refuted by the bankrupt. A discharge in bankruptcy releases the bankrupt from all obligations to repay provable debts, demands, or claims.

While the Bankruptcy Act would apply generally to student loans, whether under federal programs, state programs, or institutions' own programs, there is one major exception. The act's debt dischargeability provisions do not apply to loans under the federal Guaranteed Student Loan Program (GSLP) (see Section 4.3.2) until five years (exclusive of any applicable suspension of the repayment period) after the commencement of the loan repayment period, 20 U.S.C. sec. 1087-3. Prior to expiration of this five-year period, a debt arising from a federally guaranteed (or insured) student loan may be released by a discharge in bankruptcy only if the court determines that later payment of the debt would impose undue hardship on the debtor or his dependents in terms of future income or other wealth. This limitation on dischargeability was created by Congress in 1976 to apply to all bankruptcy proceedings begun after September 30, 1977, in order to prevent student bankruptcies from undermining the purposes of the Guaranteed Student Loan Program. A similar provision, but lacking the hardship exception, was added to the Health Professions Insured Loan Program, 42 U.S.C. secs. 294 *et seq.*, at sec. 294f(g).

The question of what debts are provable in bankruptcy depends on the facts adduced in the bankruptcy proceeding. The contingency of repayment of a loan does not preclude provability unless the contingent repayment obligation is incapable of reasonable valuation. The case of *State* v. *Wilkes,* 41 N.Y.2d 655, 394 N.Y.S.2d 849, 363 N.E.2d 555 (1977), illustrates the problem of dischargeability of contingent debts. New York State sought to recover on notes signed by a student as evidence of his repayment obligations under the National Direct Student Loan (NDSL) program. The student asserted a previous discharge in bankruptcy as a complete defense. The loans in issue, however, were not yet due at the time of the bankruptcy proceedings, so the State had filed no objections or claims for payment. The State requested the court to determine the effect of the prior discharge on the student loans now due. The court emphasized that the loans were repayable over an extended period of more than ten years, and that the debt would be terminated if the student died or became disabled and reduced if the student taught in certain schools during the repayment period. Finding that these contingencies made "the ultimate amount of liability impossible to ascertain or even to approximate," the court held that the debts were not provable at the time of the bankruptcy proceeding and therefore were not dischargeable.

As the *Wilkes* case demonstrates, discharge of a student debtor in bankruptcy does not necessarily eliminate all collection possibilities. The postsecondary institution may, as in *Wilkes,* argue that particular student loans were not dischargeable, and the Bankruptcy Act (11 U.S.C. sec. 35(c)) authorizes state courts to determine the effect of a bankruptcy discharge on particular debts. The institution may also apply to federal court for revocation of a student's discharge on grounds that the student used fraud in obtaining the discharge (11 U.S.C. sec. 33). Third, the institution may pursue any co-signer of the student's loan notes, since the act provides that discharge of a bankrupt does not alter the liability of any co-debtor, guarantor, or surety of the debtor (11 U.S.C. sec. 34).

4.3.6.2. *Withholding certified transcripts.* Aside from the instances listed at the end of Section 4.3.6.1, the Bankruptcy Act would prohibit postsecondary institutions from resorting to courts or other legal process to collect debts discharged in bankruptcy (11 U.S.C. sec. 32(f)(2)). There is some question, however, whether the Act would prohibit more informal internal means of collection such as withholding certified transcripts of grades from a bankrupt. The answer may depend on whether the institution is public or private. In *Girardier* v. *Webster College,* 563 F.2d 1267 (8th Cir. 1977), the court held that the Bankruptcy Act did not prohibit a private institution from withholding certified transcripts. The court reasoned that the act precluded resort to state laws or legal actions or processes to induce payment of discharged debts but did not preclude resort to private rules or nonlegal actions or processes. The decision probably has no application to state institutions. A regulation or policy of a state institution authorizing withholding would likely be considered to be state law inconsistent with the Bankruptcy Act's purpose (see *Handsome* v. *Rutgers Univ.,* 445 F. Supp. 1362 (D.N.J. 1978)), or to involve legal actions or processes for collection which are prohibited by the act (11 U.S.C. sec. 32(f)(2)).

The situation is different if, as in the majority of situations, the student debtor has not been adjudicated a bankrupt. Nothing in the federal Bankruptcy Act would prohibit either public or private institutions from withholding certified transcripts from student debtors. Nor does the federal Buckley Amendment on student records (Section 4.12.1) prohibit such withholding. If an institution enters grades in a student's records, the Buckley Amendment would give the student a right to see and copy the grade records. But the Buckley Amendment would not give the student any right to a *certified* transcript of grades, nor would it obligate the institution to issue a certified transcript or other record of grades to third parties. See *Girardier* v. *Webster College,* 421 F. Supp. 45, 48 (D.Mo. 1976).

The most likely legal difficulty would arise under the federal Constitution's due process clause, whose requirements limit only public institutions (see Section 1.4.2). The basic issue is whether withholding a certified transcript deprives the student of a "liberty" or "property" interest protected by the due process clause (see generally Section 3.5.2). If so, the student would have the right to be notified of the withholding and the reason for it, and to be afforded some kind of hearing on the sufficiency of the grounds for withholding. Courts have not yet defined liberty or property interests in this context. But under precedents in other areas, if the institution has regulations or policies entitling students to certified transcripts, these regulations or policies could create a property interest that would be infringed by withholding without notice or hearing. And withholding certified transcripts from a student applying to professional or graduate school, or for professional employment, may so foreclose the student's freedom to pursue education or employment opportunities as to be a deprivation of liberty. Thus, despite the lack of cases in point, public institution administrators should consult counsel before implementing a policy of withholding transcripts for failure to pay loans, or for any other reason.

4.3.6.3. *Federal student loan program requirements on debt collection.*[8] The National Direct Student Loan program statute and regulations contain several provisions affecting the institution's debt collection practices. The statute provides, in 20 U.S.C. sec. 1087cc(5), that where a note or written agreement evidencing an NDSL loan has been in default for at least two years despite the institution's due diligence in attempting to collect the debt, the institution may assign its rights under the note or agreement to the United States without recompense. If the debt is thereafter collected by the United States, the sums are deposited in the general Treasury fund. The NDSL regulations provide, at 45 C.F.R. sec. 144.41, that each institution that establishes a loan fund

[8]Besides these student loan requirements, there is a growing body of state and federal statutes and court decisions on debt collection practices. See generally *Model UCCC Statute,* sec. 5.108(5) (Commissioners on Uniform State Laws, 1974); S. Rester, "Regulating Debt Collection Practices: The Social and Economic Needs and a Congressional Response," 11 *Clearing-House Review* 547 (1977); M. Greenfield, "Coercive Collection Tactics—An Analysis of the Interests and the Remedies," 1972 *Washington Univ. L. Q.* 117 (1972).

shall accept responsibility for and use due diligence in effecting collection of all amounts due and payable to the fund in connection with loan transactions. Due diligence includes: (1) providing borrowers with full disclosures of their rights and obligations when or before they sign the promissory notes; (2) conducting exit interviews and providing borrowers with copies of repayment schedules indicating the total amount of the loans and the dates and amounts of installments as they become due; (3) maintaining a written record of interviews and retaining signed copies of borrowers' repayment schedules; (4) staying in contact with the borrowers in order to facilitate billing and keep them informed of changes in the program that may affect the rights and obligations of the parties. This regulation also requires that the institution use the collection practices that are set forth in section 144.43 including a statement of notice and demand for payment for accounts which are more than fifteen days overdue. If the billing procedures set forth in section 144.43 are unsuccessful, the university shall utilize the services of a collection agency to obtain payment.

The Guaranteed Student Loan Program includes fewer provisions related to debt collection, since institutions are not usually the lenders under that program. The statute contains the provision (discussed in Section 4.3.6.1) limiting dischargeability of GSLP loans in bankruptcy. The regulations require, at 45 C.F.R. sec. 177.62(a), that participating institutions establish and maintain such administrative and fiscal procedures and records as may be necessary to protect the United States from unreasonable risk of loss due to defaults.

Sec. 4.4. Disciplinary Rules and Regulations

Postsecondary institutions customarily have rules of conduct or behavior which students are expected to follow. It has become increasingly common to commit these rules to writing and embody them in codes of conduct binding on all students. Although the trend toward written codes is a sound one, legally speaking, because it gives students fairer notice of what is expected from them and often results in a better thought-out and administered system, written rules also provide a specific target to aim at in a lawsuit. Thus in many recent cases students subjected to disciplinary action have contested the validity of the rule under which they were reprimanded.

4.4.1. Public institutions. In public institutions, students frequently contend that the rule violates some specific guarantee of the Bill of Rights as made applicable to state institutions by the Fourteenth Amendment. (See Section 1.4.2.) These situations, the most numerous of which implicate the free speech and press clauses of the First Amendment, are discussed in various sections of this chapter. In other situations the contention is a more general one—that the rule is so vague that its enforcement violates due process, that is, the rule is unconstitutionally "vague" or "void for vagueness."

Soglin v. *Kauffman,* 418 F.2d 163 (7th Cir. 1969), is illustrative. The University of Wisconsin had expelled students for engaging in protest activity attempting to block access to an off-campus recruiter. The university had charged the students under a rule prohibiting "misconduct" and argued in court that it had inherent power to discipline which need not be exercised through specific rules. Both the U.S. district court and the U.S. court of appeals held the misconduct policy to be unconstitutionally vague. The appellate court reasoned:

> No one disputes the power of the University to protect itself by means of disciplinary action against disruptive students. Power to punish and the rules defining the exercise of that power are not, however, identical. Power alone does not supply the standards needed to determine its application to types of behavior or specific instances of "misconduct." As Professor Fuller has observed: "The first desideratum of a system for subjecting human conduct to the governance of rules is an obvious one: there must be rules." L. Fuller, *The Morality of Law,* p. 46 ([Yale University Press,] rev. ed. 1969). The proposition that government officers, including school administrators, must act in accord with rules in meting out discipline is so fundamental that its validity tends to be assumed by courts engaged in assessing the propriety of specific regulations. . . . The [doctrine] of vagueness . . . , already applied in academic contexts, [presupposes] the existence of rules whose coherence and boundaries may be questioned. . . . These same

considerations also dictate that the rules embodying standards of discipline be contained in properly promulgated regulations. University administrators are not immune from these requirements of due process in imposing sanctions. Consequently, in the present case, the disciplinary proceedings must fail to the extent that the defendant officials of the University of Wisconsin did not base those proceedings on the students' disregard of university standards of conduct expressed in reasonably clear and narrow rules.

. . . The use of "misconduct" as a standard in imposing the penalties threatened here must therefore fall for vagueness. The inadequacy of the rule is apparent on its face. It contains no clues which could assist a student, an administrator, or a reviewing judge in determining whether conduct not transgressing statutes is susceptible to punishment by the University as "misconduct."

Pursuant to appropriate rule or regulation, the University has the power to maintain order by suspension or expulsion of disruptive students. Requiring that such sanctions be administered in accord with preexisting rules does not place an unwarranted burden upon university administration. We do not require university codes of conduct to satisfy the same rigorous standards as criminal statutes. We only hold that expulsion and prolonged suspension may not be imposed on students by a university simply on the basis of allegations of "misconduct" without reference to any preexisting rule which supplies an adequate guide [418 F.2d at 167–68].

While similar language about vagueness is often found in other court opinions, the actual result in *Soglin* (the invalidation of the rule) is unusual. Most university rules subjected to judicial tests of vagueness have survived, sometimes because the rule at issue is less egregious than the "misconduct" rule in *Soglin*, sometimes because a court accepts the "inherent power to discipline" argument raised by the *Soglin* defendants and declines to undertake any real vagueness analysis, and sometimes because the student conduct at issue was so contrary to the judges' own standards of decency that they tended to ignore the defects in the rules in light of the obvious "defect" in behavior. The case most often cited in opposition to *Soglin*, *Esteban* v. *Central Missouri State College*, 415 F.2d 1077 (8th Cir. 1969), reveals all three of these distinctions. There students contested their suspension under a regulation prohibiting "participation in mass gatherings which might be considered as unruly or unlawful." In upholding the suspension the court emphasized the need for "flexibility and reasonable breadth, rather than meticulous specificity, in college regulations relating to conduct" and recognized the institution's "latitude and discretion in its formulation of rules and regulations." The approach has often been followed in later cases, as for instance in *Jenkins* v. *Louisiana State Board of Education*, 506 F.2d 992 (5th Cir. 1975), where the court upheld a series of regulations dealing with disorderly assembly and disturbing the peace on campus.

Although the judicial trend suggests that most rules and regulations will be upheld, administrators should not thus assume they have a free hand in promulgating codes of conduct. *Soglin* signals the institution's vulnerability where it has no written rules at all or where the rule provides no standard to guide conduct. And even *Esteban* warns that "we do not hold that any college regulation, however loosely framed, is necessarily valid." To avoid such pitfalls, disciplinary rules should provide standards sufficient to guide both the students in their conduct and the disciplinarians in their decision making. A rule will likely pass judicial scrutiny if the standard "conveys sufficiently definite warning as to the proscribed conduct when measured by common understanding and practices" (*Sword* y. *Fox*, 446 F.2d 1091 (4th Cir. 1971), upholding a regulation that "demonstrations are forbidden in any areas of the Health Center, inside any buildings and congregating in the locations of fire hydrants"). Regulations need not be drafted by a lawyer—in fact, heavy student involvement in drafting may be valuable to ensure an expression of their "common understanding" —but it would usually be wise to have a lawyer play a general advisory role in the process.

4.4.2. Private institutions. Private institutions, not being subject to federal constitutional constraints (see Section 1.4.2), have even more latitude than public institutions do in promulgating disciplinary rules. Courts are likely to recognize a broad right to discipline that is inherent in the private student-institution relationship or to find such a right implied in some contractual relationship between student and school. Under this broad construction, private institutional rules will not be held to specificity standards such as those in *Soglin* above. Thus, in *Dehaan* v. *Brandeis University*, 150 F. Supp. 626 (D.Mass. 1957), the court upheld the plaintiff's suspension for misconduct under a policy where the school "reserves the right to sever the connection of any student with the university for appropriate reason"; and in *Carr* v. *St. John's University, New York*, 17 App.Div.2d 632, 231 N.Y.S.2d 410, affirmed 12 N.Y.2d 802, 187 N.E.2d 18 (1962), the court upheld the dismissal of four students for off-campus conduct under a regulation providing that "in conformity with the ideals of Christian education and conduct, the University reserves the right to dismiss a student at any time on whatever grounds the University judges advisable."

Despite the breadth of such cases, the private school administrator, like his or her public counterpart, should not assume a legally free hand in promulgating disciplinary rules. Under one developing theory or another (see Section 1.4.3), courts can now be expected to protect private school students from clearly arbitrary disciplinary actions. When a school has disciplinary rules, courts may overturn actions taken in derogation of the rules. And when there is no rule or the applicable rule provides no standard of behavior, courts may overturn suspensions for conduct which the student could not reasonably have known was wrong. Thus in *Slaughter* v. *Brigham Young University*, 514 F.2d 622 (10th Cir. 1975), though the court upheld the expulsion of a graduate student for dishonesty under the student code of conduct, it first asked "whether the . . . [expulsion] was arbitrary" and indicated that the university's findings would be accorded a presumption of correctness only "if the regulations concerned are reasonable [and] if they are known to the student or should have been." To avoid such situations, it is wise for private institutions to adhere to much the same guidelines for promulgating rules as are suggested above for public institutions.

Sec. 4.5. Grades, Credits, and Degrees

Fewer legal restrictions pertain to both public and private institutions' application of academic standards to students than to their application of behavioral standards. Courts are more deferential to academia when evaluation of academic work is the issue, believing such evaluation to reside in the expertise of the faculty rather than the court.

The leading case is *Connelly* v. *University of Vermont,* 244 F. Supp. 156 (D.Vt. 1965), where a medical student challenged his dismissal from medical school. He had failed the pediatrics-obstetrics course and was excluded under a College of Medicine rule for having failed 25 percent or more of his major third-year courses. The court described its role, and the institution's legal obligation, in such cases as follows:

> Where a medical student has been dismissed for a failure to attain a proper standard of scholarship, two questions may be involved; the first is, was the student in fact delinquent in his studies or unfit for the practice of medicine? The second question is, were the school authorities motivated by malice or bad faith in dismissing the student, or did they act arbitrarily or capriciously? In general, the first question is not a matter for judicial review. However, a student dismissal motivated by bad faith, arbitrariness, or capriciousness may be actionable. . . .
>
> This rule has been stated in a variety of ways by a number of courts. It has been said that courts do not interfere with the management of a school's internal affairs unless "there has been a manifest abuse of discretion or where [the school officials'] action has been arbitrary or unlawful," *State ex rel. Sherman* v. *Hyman,* 180 Tenn. 99, 171 S.W.2d 822, cert. den. 319 U.S. 748, 63 S. Ct. 1158, 87 L. Ed. 1703 (1942), or unless the school authorities have acted "arbitrarily or capriciously," *Frank* v. *Marquette University,* 209 Wis. 372, 245 N.W. 125 (1932), or unless they have abused their discretion, *Coffelt* v. *Nicholson,* 224 Ark. 176, 272 S.W.2d 309 (1954), *People ex rel. Bluett* v. *Board of Trustees of University of Illinois,* 10 Ill.App.2d 207, 134 N.E.2d 635, 58 A.L.R.2d 899 (1956), or acted in "bad faith," *Barnard* v. *Inhabitants of Shelburne,* . . . [216 Mass. 19, 102 N.E. 1095 (1913)] and see 222 Mass. 76, 109 N.E. 818 (same case).
>
> The effect of these decisions is to give the school authorities absolute discretion in determining whether a student has been delinquent in his studies, and to place the burden on the student of showing that his dismissal was motivated by arbitrariness, capriciousness, or bad faith. The reason for this rule is that in matters of scholarship, the school authorities are uniquely qualified by training and

> experience to judge the qualifications of a student, and
> efficiency of instruction depends in no small degree upon
> the school faculty's freedom from interference from other
> noneducational tribunals. It is only when the school
> authorities abuse this discretion that a court may interfere
> with their decision to dismiss a student [244 F. Supp. at
> 159–60].

Because the plaintiff had alleged that his instructor decided before
completion of the course to fail him regardless of the quality of his
work, the court found that he met these requirements. His
complaint thus stated a cause of action which if proven at trial
would justify the entry of appropriate relief against the college.

In 1975 the U.S. Court of Appeals for the Tenth Circuit
issued an important reaffirmation of the principles underlying the
Connelly case. *Gaspar* v. *Bruton*, 513 F.2d 843 (10th Cir. 1975),
concerned a practical nurse student who had been dismissed for
deficient performance in clinical training. In rejecting the student's
suit against the school, the court held that:

> Courts have historically refrained from interfering
> with the authority vested in school officials to drop a
> student from the rolls for failure to attain or maintain
> prescribed scholastic rating (whether judged by objective
> and/or subjective standards), absent a clear showing that
> the officials have acted arbitrarily or have abused the
> discretionary authority vested in them. . . .
>
> The courts are not equipped to review academic
> records based upon academic standards within the particu-
> lar knowledge, experience, and expertise of academicians.
> Thus, when presented with a challenge that the school
> authorities suspended or dismissed a student for failure re
> academic standards, the court may grant relief, as a
> practical matter, only in those cases where the student
> presents positive evidence of ill will or bad motive [513 F.2d
> at 850–51].

Although the U.S. Supreme Court has not expressly adopted
the judicial review standards of cases such as *Connelly* and *Gaspar,*
it did address the issue briefly in *Board of Curators of the
University of Missouri* v. *Horowitz*, 98 S. Ct. 948 (1978) (discussed
in Section 4.6.3). A dismissed medical student claimed that the
school applied stricter standards to her because of her sex, religion,
and physical appearance. Referring particularly to *Gaspar* v.

Bruton, the Court rejected the claim in language inhospitable to substantive judicial review of academic decisions:

> [A] number of lower courts have implied in dictum that academic dismissals from state institutions can be enjoined if "shown to be clearly arbitrary or capricious." . . . Even assuming that the courts can review under such a standard an academic decision of a public educational institution, we agree with the District Court that no showing of arbitrariness or capriciousness has been made in this case. Courts are particularly ill-equipped to evaluate academic performance. The factors discussed . . . with respect to procedural due process [see Section 4.6.3] speak *a fortiori* here and warn against any such judicial intrusion into academic decision-making [98 S. Ct. at 956.]

Sec. 4.6. Procedures for Suspension, Dismissal, and Other Sanctions

4.6.1. In general. As Sections 4.4 and 4.5 indicate, both public and private postsecondary institutions have the clear right to dismiss, suspend, or impose lesser sanctions on students for behavioral misconduct or academic deficiency. But just as that right is limited by the principles set out in those sections, so it is also circumscribed by a body of procedural requirements which institutions must follow in effecting disciplinary or academic sanctions. These procedural requirements tend to be more specific and substantial than the requirements set out above, although they do vary depending on whether behavior or academics is involved and whether the institution is public (see Section 1.4) or private.

At the threshold level, whenever an institution has established procedures which apply to the imposition of sanctions, the law will usually require that they be followed. In *Woody* v. *Burns,* 188 So.2d 56 (Fla. 1966), for example, the court invalidated an expulsion from a public institution because a faculty committee had "circumvented . . . [the] duly authorized [disciplinary] committee and arrogated unto itself the authority of imposing its own penalty for Appellant's misconduct." And in *Kwiatkowski* v. *Ithaca College,* 368 N.Y.S.2d 973 (Sup. Ct. 1975), the court granted a suspended private school student a new hearing before the school's appeal board because the school had violated its own judicial code in refusing to permit the student or his representative to appear before that board.

There are two exceptions, however, to this "follow-the-rules" principle. An institution may be excused from following its own procedures if the student knowingly and freely waives his or her right to them, as in *Yench* v. *Stockmar*, 483 F.2d 820 (10th Cir. 1973), where the student neither requested that the published procedures be followed nor objected when they were not. Second, deviations from established procedures may be excused when they do not disadvantage the student, as in *Winnick* v. *Manning*, 460 F.2d 545 (2d Cir. 1972), where the student contested the school's use of a panel other than that required by the rules, but the court held that the "deviations were minor ones and did not affect the fundamental fairness of the hearing."

4.6.2. Public institutions: disciplinary sanctions. State institutions may be subject to state administrative procedure acts, state board of higher education rules, or other state statutes or administrative regulations specifying particular procedures for suspensions or expulsions. In *Mull* v. *Oregon Institute of Technology*, 538 P.2d 87 (Ore. 1975), the court applied that state's administrative procedure act to a suspension for misconduct and remanded the case to the college with instructions to enter findings of fact and conclusions of law as required by the act. But for public institutions the primary source of procedural requirements is the due process clause of the federal Constitution. Since the early 1960s the concept of procedural due process has been one of the primary legal forces shaping the administration of postsecondary education.

A landmark 1961 case on suspension procedures, *Dixon* v. *Alabama State Board of Education*, 294 F.2d 150 (5th Cir. 1961), is still very instructive. Several black students at Alabama State College had been expelled during a period of intense civil rights activity in Montgomery, Alabama. The students, supported by the National Association for the Advancement of Colored People (NAACP), sued the state board, and the court faced the question "whether [the] due process [clause of the Fourteenth Amendment] requires notice and some opportunity for hearing before students at a tax-supported college are expelled for misconduct." On appeal this question was answered in the affirmative, with the court establishing standards by which to measure the adequacy of a public institution's expulsion procedures:

> The notice should contain a statement of the specific charges and grounds which, if proven, would justify expulsion under the regulations of the Board of Education. The nature of the hearing should vary depending upon the circumstances of the particular case. The case before us requires something more than an informal interview with an administrative authority of the college. By its nature, a charge of misconduct, as opposed to a failure to meet the scholastic standards of the college, depends upon a collection of the facts concerning the charged misconduct, easily colored by the point of view of the witnesses. In such circumstances, a hearing which gives the Board or the administrative authorities of the college an opportunity to hear both sides in considerable detail is best suited to protect the rights of all involved. This is not to imply that a full-dress judicial hearing, with the right to cross-examine witnesses, is required. Such a hearing, with the attending publicity and disturbance of college activities, might be detrimental to the college's educational atmosphere and impractical to carry out. Nevertheless, the rudiments of an adversary proceeding may be preserved without encroaching upon the interests of the college. In the instant case, the student should be given the names of the witnesses against him and an oral or written report on the facts to which each witness testifies. He should also be given the opportunity to present to the Board, or at least to an administrative official of the college, his own defense against the charges and to produce either oral testimony or written affidavits of witnesses in his behalf. If the hearing is not before the Board directly, the results and findings of the hearing should be presented in a report open to the student's inspection. If these rudimentary elements of fair play are followed in a case of misconduct of this particular type, we feel that the requirements of due process of law will have been fulfilled [294 F.2d at 158–59].

Since the *Dixon* case, courts at all levels have continued to recognize and extend the due process safeguards available to students charged by college officials with misconduct. Such safeguards must now be provided for all students in publicly

supported schools not only before expulsion, as in *Dixon*, but
before suspension and other serious disciplinary action as well. In
1975 the U.S. Supreme Court itself recognized the vitality and clear
national applicability of such developments when it held that even
a secondary school student faced with a suspension of less than ten
days is entitled to "oral or written notice of the charges against him
and, if he denies them, an explanation of the evidence the
authorities have and an opportunity to present his side of the
story" (*Goss* v. *Lopez*, 419 U.S. 565 (1975)).

Probably the case which has set forth due process requirements in greatest detail is *Estaban* v. *Central Missouri State
College*, 277 F. Supp. 649 (W.D. Mo. 1967), affirmed 415 F.2d 1077
(8th Cir. 1969), discussed in Section 4.4 above. The plaintiffs had
been suspended for two semesters for engaging in protest
demonstrations. The lower court held that the students had not
been accorded procedural due process and ordered the school to
provide the following protections for them: (1) a written statement
of the charges, for each student, made available at least ten days
before the hearing; (2) a hearing before the person(s) having power
to expel or suspend; (3) the opportunity for advance inspection of
any affidavits or exhibits the college intends to submit at the
hearing; (4) the right to bring counsel to the hearing to advise them
(but not to question witnesses); (5) the opportunity to present their
own version of the facts, by personal statements as well as affidavits
and witnesses; (6) the right to hear evidence against them and
question (personally, not through counsel) adverse witnesses; (7) a
determination of the facts of each case by the hearing officer solely
on the basis of the evidence presented at the hearing; (8) a written
statement of the hearing officer's findings of fact; and (9) the right,
at their own expense, to make a record of the hearing. Although
the appellate court set forth its due process requirements in less
detail, it did speak approvingly of the district court's list and did
not invalidate it in any way.

The judicial imposition of such specific due process
requirements rankles many administrators. By and large, courts
have been sufficiently sensitive to avoid such detail in favor of
administrative flexibility. Yet for the internal guidance of an
administrator responsible for disciplinary procedures, the *Esteban*

requirements provide a very useful checklist. The listed items not
only suggest the outer limits of what a court might require but also
identify those procedures most often considered valuable for
ascertaining facts where they are in dispute. Within this framework
of concerns, the constitutional focus remains on the notice-and-
opportunity-for-hearing concept of *Dixon.*

    4.6.2.1. Notice. Notice should be given of both the
conduct with which the student is charged and the rule or policy
which allegedly proscribes that conduct. The charges need not be
drawn with the specificity of a criminal indictment, but they
should be "in sufficient detail to fairly enable . . . [the student] to
present a defense" at the hearing (*Jenkins* v. *Louisiana State Board
of Education,* 506 F.2d 992 (5th Cir. 1975), holding notice in a
suspension case to be adequate, particularly in light of information
provided by the defendant subsequent to the original notice).
Factual allegations not enumerated in the notice may be developed
at the hearing if the student could reasonably have expected them
to be included.

    There is no clear constitutional requirement concerning
how much advance notice the student must have of the charges. As
little as two days before the hearing has been held adequate (*Jones*
v. *Tennessee State Board of Education,* 279 F. Supp. 190 (M.D.
Tenn. 1968), affirmed 407 F.2d 834 (6th Cir. 1969)). *Esteban*
required ten days, however, and in most other cases the time has
been longer than two days. In general, courts handle this issue case
by case, asking whether the amount of time was fair under all the
circumstances.

    4.6.2.2. Hearing. The minimum requirement is that
the hearing provide the student an opportunity to speak in her
own defense and explain her side of the story. Since due process
apparently does not require an open or public hearing, the
institution has the discretion to close or partially close the hearing
or to leave the choice to the accused student. But courts usually
will accord students the right to hear the evidence against them and
to present oral testimony, or, at minimum, written statements,
from witnesses. Formal rules of evidence need not be followed.
Cross-examination, the right to counsel, the right to a transcript,

and an appellate procedure have generally not been constitutional essentials, but where institutions have voluntarily provided these procedures, courts have often cited them approvingly as enhancers of the hearing's fairness. The hearing officer or panel and the decision maker(s) must of course be impartial and must decide the case on the basis of the evidence. Generally the student must show malice, bias, or conflict of interest on the part of the officer or panel member before a court will make a finding of partiality. In *Blanton v. State University of New York,* 489 F.2d 377 (2d Cir. 1973), the court held that—at least where students had a right of appeal—due process was not violated when a dean who had witnessed the incident at issue also sat on the hearing committee. And in *Jones* v. *Tennessee State Board* (Section 4.6.2.1), the court even permitted a member of the hearing committee to give evidence against the accused student, in the absence of proof of malice or personal interest. But other courts may be less hospitable to such practices, and it would be wise to avoid them where possible.

The hearing must normally take place before the suspension or expulsion goes into effect. The leading case on this point has been *Stricklin* v. *Regents of University of Wisconsin,* 297 F. Supp. 416 (W.D. Wis. 1969), where the court limited the use of interim suspensions pending a final decision to situations where "the appropriate university authority has reasonable cause to believe that danger will be present if a student is permitted to remain on campus pending a decision following a full hearing." The court also noted that "an interim suspension may not be imposed without a prior preliminary hearing, unless it can be shown that it is impossible or unreasonably difficult to accord it prior to an interim suspension," in which case "procedural due process requires that . . . [the student] be provided such a preliminary hearing at the earliest practical time." These requirements would protect a student from being "suspended in ex parte proceedings . . . without any opportunity, however brief and however limited, to persuade the suspending authority that there is a case of mistaken identity or that there was extreme provocation or that there is some other compelling justification for withholding or terminating the interim suspension." While case law on these points has been sparse, the U.S. Supreme Court's 1975 ruling in *Goss* v. *Lopez* (Section 4.6.2) affirms that at least part of *Stricklin* applies nationwide:

> [A]s a general rule notice and hearing should precede removal of the student from school. We agree . . . , however, that there are recurring situations in which prior notice and hearing cannot be insisted upon. Students whose presence poses a continuing danger to persons or property or an ongoing threat of disrupting the academic process may be immediately removed from school . . . [and notice and hearing] should follow as soon as practicable.

The extent to which the notice and hearing procedures set forth above apply to disciplinary sanctions less severe than suspension or expulsion is unclear. On the one hand, a pre-*Goss* case, *Yench* v. *Stockmar* (discussed in Section 4.6.1), held the due process clause inapplicable to disciplinary probation cases. On the other hand, any penalty which deprives the student of substantial educational benefits or seriously affects his reputation is, under *Goss,* arguably subject to at least the "rudimentary" protections of due process. In general, an institution should provide increasingly more formal and comprehensive due process procedures as the severity of the potential penalty increases and should gear its procedures to the *maximum* penalty which can be meted out in each type of proceeding it authorizes.

4.6.3. Public institutions: academic sanctions. The Fourteenth Amendment's due process clause also applies to students facing suspension or dismissal from publicly supported schools for deficient academic performance. But due process affords substantially less protection in this context. This lesser protection results not because academic dismissal is less damaging to a student than disciplinary dismissal—it may be even more damaging—but because courts recognize they are less competent to review academic evaluative judgments than factually based determinations of misconduct and because hearings and the attendant formalities of witnesses and evidence are less meaningful in the grading context than in determining misconduct.

Gaspar v. *Bruton,* 512 F.2d 843 (10th Cir. 1975), was

apparently the first case to provide any procedural due process rights to a student facing an academic suspension or dismissal. The plaintiff was a forty-four-year-old high school graduate pursuing practical nurse training in a vocational-technical school. After completing more than two-thirds of the program she was dismissed for deficient performance in clinical training. She had been on probation for two months owing to such deficiencies and had been informed she would be dismissed if they were not corrected. When they were not, she was notified of dismissal in a conference with the superintendent and some of her instructors and was subsequently offered a second conference and an opportunity to question other staff-faculty members who had participated in the dismissal decision.

The trial and appellate courts upheld the dismissal, rejecting the student's contention that before dismissal she should have been confronted with and allowed to challenge the evidence supporting the dismissal and allowed to present evidence in her defense. Although the appellate court recognized a "property interest" in continued attendance, it held that school officials had only minimal due process obligations in this context:

> Gaspar was provided much more due process than that which we hold must be accorded in cases involving academic termination or suspension. We hold that school authorities, in order to satisfy due process prior to termination or suspension of a student for deficiencies in meeting minumum academic performance, need only advise that student with respect to such deficiencies in any form. All that is required is that the student be made aware prior to termination of his failure or impending failure to meet those standards [513 F.2d at 850–51].

More significant protection was afforded in *Greenhill* v. *Bailey*, 519 F.2d 5 (8th Cir. 1975), where another U.S. court of appeals invalidated a medical student's dismissal because he had not been accorded procedural due process. The school had dismissed the student for "lack of intellectual ability or insufficient preparation" and had conveyed that information to the Liaison Committee of the Association of American Medical Colleges, where it was available to all other medical schools. The court ruled that "the action by the school in denigrating Greenhill's intellectual ability, as distinguished from his performance, deprived him of a significant interest in liberty, for it admittedly 'imposed on him a stigma or other disability that foreclose[s] his freedom to take advantage of other . . . opportunities.'" In such circumstances, due process required that

> [a]t the very least, Greenhill should have been notified in writing of the alleged deficiency in his intellectual ability, since this reason for his dismissal would potentially stigmatize his future as a medical student elsewhere, and should have been accorded an opportunity to appear personally to contest such allegation.
>
> We stop short, however, of requiring full trial-type procedures. . . . But an "informal give-and-take" between the student and the administrative body dismissing him— and foreclosing his opportunity to gain admission at all comparable institutions—would not unduly burden the educational process and would, at least, give the student "the opportunity to characterize his conduct and put it in what he deems proper context" (*Goss* v. *Lopez,* 419 U.S. at 584, 95 S. Ct. at 741) [519 F.2d at 9].

The next year the same U.S. court of appeals extended its *Greenhill* ruling in another medical school case, *Horowitz* v. *Board of Curators of University of Missouri,* 538 F.2d 1317 (8th Cir. 1976). But on appeal the U.S. Supreme Court clipped this court's wings and put an apparent halt to the development of procedural due process in academic disputes (*Board of Curators of the University of Missouri* v. *Horowitz,* 98 S. Ct. 948 (1978)). The university had dismissed the student, who had received excellent grades on written exams, for deficiencies in clinical performance, peer and patient relations, and personal hygiene. After several faculty members repeatedly expressed dissatisfaction with her clinical work, the school's Council on Evaluation recommended that Horowitz not be allowed to graduate on time and that, "absent radical improvement" in the remainder of the year, she be dropped from the program. She was then allowed to take a special set of oral and practical exams, administered by practicing physicians in the area, as a means of appealing the Council's determination. After receiving the results of these exams, the Council reaffirmed its recommendation. At the end of the year, after receiving further clinical reports on Horowitz, the Council recommended that she be dropped from school. The school's Coordinating Committee, then the dean, and finally the provost for health sciences, all affirmed the decision.

Though there was no evidence that the reasons for the dismissal were conveyed to the Liaison Committee, as in *Greenhill,* the court of appeals found it to be "uncontroverted that Horowitz's dismissal from medical school will make it difficult or impossible for her to obtain employment in a medically related field or to enter another medical school." The court concluded that dismissal would so stigmatize the student as to deprive her of liberty under the Fourteenth Amendment and that, under the circumstances, the student could not be dismissed without providing "a hearing before the decision making body or bodies, at which she shall have an opportunity to rebut the evidence being relied upon for her dismissal and accorded all other procedural due process rights."

The Supreme Court found it unnecessary to decide whether Horowitz had been deprived of a liberty or property interest. Even assuming she had, Horowitz had no right to a hearing:

> Respondent has been awarded at least as much due process as the Fourteenth Amendment requires. The School fully informed respondent of the faculty's dissatisfaction with her clinical progress and the danger that this posed to timely graduation and continued enrollment. The ultimate decision to dismiss respondent was careful and deliberate. These procedures were sufficient under the Due Process Clause of the Fourteenth Amendment. We agree with the District Court that respondent
>
>> was afforded full procedural due process by the [school]. In fact, the Court is of the opinion, and so finds, that the school went beyond [constitutionally required] procedural due process by affording [respondent] the opportunity to be examined by seven independent physicians in order to be absolutely certain that their grading of the [respondent] in her medical skills was correct [98 S. Ct. at 952].

The Court relied on the distinction between academic and disciplinary cases that lower courts had developed in cases prior to *Horowitz*, finding that distinction to be consistent with its own due process pronouncements, especially *Goss* v. *Lopez* (discussed in Section 4.6.2):

> The Court of Appeals apparently read *Goss* as requiring some type of formal hearing at which respondent could defend her academic ability and performance. . . . But we have frequently emphasized that "[t]he very nature of due process negates any concept of inflexible procedures universally applicable to every imaginable situation." *Cafeteria Workers* v. *McElroy*, 367 U.S. 886, 895 (1961). The need for flexibility is well illustrated by the significant difference between the failure of a student to meet academic standards and the violation by a student of valid rules of conduct. This difference calls for far less stringent procedural requirements in the case of an academic dismissal. . . .
>
> A school is an academic institution, not a courtroom or administrative hearing room. In *Goss*, this Court felt that suspensions of students for disciplinary reasons have a sufficient resemblance to traditional judicial and administrative factfinding to call for a "hearing" before the relevant school authority. . . .
>
> Academic evaluations of a student, in contrast to disciplinary determinations, bear little resemblance to the judicial and administrative factfinding proceedings to which we have traditionally attached a full hearing requirement. In *Goss*, the school's decision to suspend the students rested on factual conclusions that the individual students had participated in demonstrations that had disrupted classes, attacked a police officer, or caused physical damage to school property. The requirement of a hearing, where the student could present his side of the factual issue, could under such circumstances "provide a meaningful hedge against erroneous action." The decision to dismiss respondent, by comparison, rested on the academic judgment of school officials that she did not have the necessary clinical ability to perform adequately as a medical doctor and was making insufficient progress toward that goal. Such a judgment is by its nature more subjective and evaluative than the typical factual questions presented in the average disciplinary decision. Like the decision of an individual professor as to the proper grade

for a student in his course, the determination whether to dismiss a student for academic reasons requires an expert evaluation of cumulative information and is not readily adapted to the procedural tools of judicial or administrative decisionmaking [98 S. Ct. at 952–55].

While *Horowitz* clearly indicates the Court's lack of receptivity to procedural requirements for academic dismissals, the case does not say that *no* due process is required. It is clear that an adversary hearing is not required. Nor are all the procedures used by the university in *Horowitz* required, since the Court suggests that Horowitz received *more* due process than she was entitled to. But some minimal procedural protections do appear to be required; the exact character of them is not yet clear. Probably due process requires the institution to inform the student of the inadequacies in performance and their consequences on academic standing. Apparently due process also generally requires that the institution's decision-making be "careful and deliberate." For the former requirements, courts are likely to be lenient on how much information or explanation the student must be given and also on how far in advance of formal dismissal the student must be notified. For the latter requirement, courts are likely to be very flexible, not demanding any particular procedure but rather accepting any decision-making process that, overall, supports reasoned judgments concerning academic quality. Even these minimal requirements would be imposed on institutions only when their academic judgments infringe on a student's "liberty" or "property" interests, and it is not yet clear what constitutes such infringements in the postsecondary context. (The court of appeals opinions in *Gaspar* and *Greenhill* noted earlier are the best analyses thus far; see generally Note, "Due Process in Academic Dismissals from Post Secondary Schools," 26 *Catholic Univ. L. Rev.* 111 (1976).)

Since courts attach markedly different due process requirements to academic sanctions than to disciplinary sanctions, it is crucial to be able to place particular cases in one category or the other. The characterization required is not always easy. The *Horowitz* case is a good example. The student's dismissal was not a typical case of inadequate scholarship, such as poor grades on written exams; rather she was dismissed at least partly for inadequate peer and patient relations and personal hygiene. It is arguable that such a decision involves "factfinding" as in a disciplinary case more than an "evaluative," "academic judgment." Indeed, the Court split on this issue: five judges applied the "academic" label to the case, two judges applied the "disciplinary" label or argued that no labeling was appropriate, and two judges refused to determine either which label to apply or "whether such a distinction is relevant."

Another illustration of the categorization difficulty is provided by a pre-*Horowitz* case, *Brookins* v. *Bonnell*, 362 F. Supp. 379 (E.D. Pa. 1973). A nursing student was dismissed from a community college for (1) failing to submit a state-required physical examination report, (2) failing to inform the college he had previously attended another nursing school, and (3) failing to attend class regularly. The student disputed these charges and argued he should have been afforded a hearing before he was dismissed. The court indicated that the right to a hearing depended on whether the student had been dismissed "because of disciplinary misconduct" or "solely because of an academic failure." After noting that the situation "does not fit neatly" into either category, the court decided the issue as follows:

> This case is not the traditional disciplinary situation where a student violates the law or a school regulation by actively engaging in prohibited activities. Plaintiff has allegedly failed to act and comply with school regulations for admission and class attendance by passively ignoring these regulations. These alleged failures do not constitute misconduct in the sense that plaintiff is subject to disciplinary procedures. They do constitute misconduct in the sense that plaintiff was required to do something. Plaintiff contends that he did comply with the requirements. Like the traditional disciplinary case, the determination of whether plaintiff did or did not comply with the school regulations is a question of fact. Most importantly, in determining this factual question, reference is not made to a standard of achievement in an esoteric academic field. Scholastic standards are not involved, but rather disputed facts concerning whether plaintiff did or did not comply with certain school regulations. These issues adapt them-

selves readily to determination by a fair and impartial "due process" hearing.

This court's key to distinction is sound and is generally supported in the various justices' opinions in *Horowitz*. When dismissal or other serious sanctions depend more on disputed factual issues concerning conduct than on expert evaluation of academic work, the student should be accorded procedural rights akin to those for disciplinary cases (Section 4.6.2) rather than the lesser rights for academic deficiency cases. Of course, even when the academic label is clearly appropriate, administrators may choose to provide more procedural safeguards than the Constitution requires. Indeed, there may be good reason to provide some form of hearing prior to academic dismissal whenever the student has some basis for claiming that the academic judgment was arbitrary, in bad faith, or discriminatory. (See Section 4.5.) The question for the administrator, therefore, is not merely what procedures are constitutionally required but also what procedures would make the best policy for the particular institution.

4.6.4. Private institutions. Federal constitutional guarantees of due process do not bind private institutions unless their imposition of sanctions falls under the state action doctrine explained in Section 1.4.2. But the inapplicability of constitutional protections, as Sections 4.4 and 4.5 suggest, does not necessarily mean that the student stands procedurally naked before the authority of the school.

The old view is illustrated by *Anthony* v. *Syracuse University*, 224 App. Div. 487, 231 N.Y.S. 435 (1928), where a private school student's dismissal was upheld even though "no adequate reason [for it] was assigned by the university authorities." The court held that "no reason for dismissing need be given," though the institution "must . . . have a reason" which falls within its dismissal regulation. "Of course, the university authorities have wide discretion in determining what situation does and what does not fall within . . . [its regulation], and the courts would be slow indeed in disturbing any decision of the university authorities in this respect."

In more recent times, however, many courts have become

faster on the draw with private schools. In *Carr* v. *St. John's University, New York* (see Section 4.4.2)—a case limiting the impact of *Anthony* within New York State—the court indicated that a private institution dismissing a student must act "not arbitrarily but in the exercise of an honest discretion based on facts within its knowledge that justify the exercise of discretion." In subsequently applying this standard to a discipline case, another New York court ruled that "it is imperative that the college or university's decision to discipline that student be predicated on procedures which are fair and reasonable and which lend themselves to a reliable determination" (*Kwiatkowski* v. *Ithaca College;* see Section 4.6.1).

A U.S. court of appeals has recently taken a similar approach. *Slaughter* v. *Brigham Young University,* 514 F.2d 622 (9th Cir. 1975), concerned a student who was dismissed for violating the honesty provision of the student code, having made unauthorized use of a professor's name as co-author of an article. After the lower court had awarded $88,000 in damages to the student, the appellate court set aside the judgment and upheld the dismissal. But in doing so it tested "whether the action was arbitrary" by investigating both the "adequacy of the procedure" and the substantiality of the evidence supporting the institution's determination. In judging the procedures, the court used *constitutional* due process as a guide, holding that the "proceedings met the requirements of the constitutional procedural due process doctrine as it is presently applied to public universities," and it is therefore unnecessary "to draw any distinction, *if there be any,* between the requirements in this regard for private and for public institutions" (emphasis added).

Cases such as these indicate a judicial trend toward increased protections for private school students. As is true of public institutions, this trend is much more evident in the misconduct area than in the academic sphere. In the 1970 case of *Militana* v. *University of Miami,* 236 So.2d 162 (Fla. App. 1970), for example, the court upheld the dismissal of a medical student, stating flatly that notice and opportunity to be heard, though required in discipline cases, are "not required when the dismissal is for academic failure." Yet even here, the contract theory (see Section 4.1.3) may provide some lesser procedural protections for students in academic jeopardy at private institutions.

While the doctrinal bases for procedural rights in the public and private sectors are different, and while the law accords private institutions greater flexibility, a rough similarity of treatment nevertheless appears to be developing in the courts. The *Slaughter* case above provides a good illustration. It may thus be prudent for private school administrators to use constitutional due process principles (Sections 4.6.2 and 4.6.3) as general guides in implementing their own procedural systems. And if a private school makes a conscious policy choice not to use certain procedures which due process would require for public schools, that choice should be clearly reflected in its rules and regulations so as to inhibit a court from finding such procedures implicit in the rules or in the student-institution relationship.

Sec. 4.7. Student Protest and Demonstrations

4.7.1. General principles. In a line of cases arising mainly from the campus unrest of the late sixties and early seventies, courts have affirmed that students have a right to peacefully protest and demonstrate—a right which public institutions may not infringe. This right stems from the free speech clause of the First Amendment as reinforced by that amendment's freedom of assembly and freedom to petition for redress of grievances. The keystone case is *Tinker* v. *Des Moines Independent School District,* 393 U.S. 503 (1969). Several high school students had been suspended for wearing black armbands to school to protest the United States' Vietnam War policy. The U.S. Supreme Court ruled that the protest was a nondisruptive exercise of free speech which could not be punished by suspension from school. The court made clear that "First Amendment rights, applied in light of the special characteristics of the school environment, are available to teachers and students" and that students "are possessed of fundamental rights which the state must respect, just as they themselves must respect their obligations to the state." The court also made clear that the First Amendment protects more than just words; it also protects certain "symbolic acts" which are done "for the purpose of expressing certain views."

Though *Tinker* involved secondary school students, the Supreme Court soon applied its principles to postsecondary education in *Healy* v. *James*, 408 U.S. 169 (1972), discussed further in Section 4.8.1. The *Healy* opinion carefully notes the First Amendment's important place on campus:

> State colleges and universities are not enclaves immune from the sweep of the First Amendment. . . . Of course, as Mr. Justice Fortas made clear in *Tinker*, First Amendment rights must always be applied "in light of the special characteristics of the . . . environment" in the particular case. And, where state-operated educational institutions are involved, this Court has long recognized "the need for affirming the comprehensive authority of the states and of school officials, consistent with fundamental constitutional safeguards, to prescribe and control conduct in the schools" [*Tinker* at 507]. Yet, the precedents of this Court leave no room for the view that, because of the acknowledged need for order, First Amendment protections should apply with less force on college campuses than in the community at large. Quite to the contrary, "[t]he vigilant protection of constitutional freedoms is nowhere more vital than in the community of American schools" (*Shelton* v. *Tucker*, 364 U.S. 479, 487 (1960)). The college classroom with its surrounding environs is peculiarly the "'marketplace of ideas,'" and we break no new constitutional ground in reaffirming this Nation's dedication to safeguarding academic freedom [408 U.S. at 180].

Despite occasional rhetoric to the contrary, *Tinker* and *Healy* clearly do not create the total permissive society on campus. The *Tinker* opinion repeats many times that freedom to protest does not constitute freedom to disrupt: "conduct by the student, in class or out of it, which for any reason—whether it stems from time, place, or type of behavior—materially disrupts classwork or involves substantial disorder or invasion of the rights of others is . . . not immunized by the constitutional guarantee of freedom of speech." *Healy* makes the same point.

4.7.2. Regulation of student protest. Postsecondary institutions may promulgate student conduct rules which prohibit group demonstrations or other forms of group or individual protest falling within the *Tinker/Healy* guidelines above. Students who violate such rules by actively participating in a disruptive demonstration may be suspended. An example would be students entering the stands during a college football game and "by abusive and disorderly acts and conduct" depriving the spectators "of the right to see and enjoy the game in peace and with safety to themselves" (*Barker* v. *Hardway,* 283 F. Supp. 228 (S.D. W.Va.), affirmed 399 F.2d 638 (4th Cir. 1968)). Another example would be a situation in which students physically block entrances to campus buildings and prevent personnel or other students from using the buildings (*Buttney* v. *Smiley,* 281 F. Supp. 280 (D. Colo. 1968)).

The critical problem in enforcing rules prohibiting disruptive protest activity is determining when the activity has become sufficiently disruptive to lose its protection under *Tinker* and *Healy.* It is clearly not sufficient that administrators suspect or fear that there will be disruption:

> [U]ndifferentiated fear or apprehension of disturbance is not enough to overcome the right to freedom of expression. Any departure from absolute regimentation may cause trouble. Any variation from the majority's opinion may inspire fear. Any word spoken, in class, in the lunchroom, or on the campus, that deviates from the views of another person may start an argument or cause disturbance. But our Constitution says we must take this risk, *Terminiello* v. *Chicago,* 337 U.S. 1 (1949); and our history says that it is this sort of hazardous freedom—this kind of openness—that is the basis of our national strength and of the independence and vigor of Americans who grow up and live in this relatively permissive, often disputatious, society [*Tinker;* 393 U.S. at 508–09].

Yet substantial disruption need not be a fait accompli before administrators can take action. It is sufficient that administrators have actual evidence on which they can "reasonably . . . forecast" (*Tinker* at 514) that substantial disruption is imminent.

The administrator should also determine whether the

disruption is created by the protesters themselves or by the onlookers' reaction to their presence. In striking down an off-campus-speakers regulation for Mississippi state colleges, the court in *Stacy* v. *Williams,* 306 F. Supp. 963 (N.D. Miss. 1969), emphasized that "one simply cannot be restrained from speaking, and his audience cannot be prevented from hearing him, unless the feared result is likely to be engendered by what the speaker himself says or does." Either the protesters' own conduct must be disruptive, as in *Barker* and *Buttney* above, or their words and acts must be "directed to inciting or producing imminent" disruption by others and "likely to produce" such disruption (*Brandenburg* v. *Ohio,* 395 U.S. 444 (1969)) before an administrator may stop the protest or discipline the protesters. Where the onlookers rather than the protesters have created the disruption, the administrator's proper recourse is against the onlookers.

Besides adopting regulations prohibiting disruptive protest, public institutions may also promulgate "reasonable regulations with respect to the time, the place, and the manner in which student groups conduct their speech-related activities" (*Healy* at 192–93). Students who violate such regulations may be disciplined even if their violation did not create substantial disruption. To be valid, however, such regulations must cover only times, places, or manners of expressions which are "basically incompatible with the normal activity of a particular place at a particular time" (*Grayned* v. *Rockford,* 408 U.S. 104, 116 (1972)). Incompatibility must be determined by the physical impact of the speech-related activity on its surroundings and not by the content of the speech; "above all else, the First Amendment means that government has no power to restrict expression because of its message, its ideas, its subject matter, or its content" (*Police Department* v. *Mosley,* 408 U.S. 92, 95 (1972)). Time, place, and manner regulations must also be drafted "with narrow specificity" so that students are clearly informed about what the institution requires or prohibits (see *Hynes* v. *Mayor and Council of Oradell,* 425 U.S. 610 (1976)).

The source of these requirements concerning time, place, and manner regulations is the doctrines of "overbreadth" and "vagueness," also discussed in Sections 3.4 and 4.4.1. The overbreadth doctrine provides that regulation of speech-related activities must be "necessary to further significant governmental interests" and "narrowly tailored" to further those interests in a way which has the least restrictive impact on free expression (*Grayned* v. *Rockford*, 408 U.S. 104, 115 (1972)). The vagueness doctrine provides that regulations of conduct must be sufficiently clear to be understandable by persons of common intelligence. Vagueness principles apply more stringently when the regulations deal with speech-related activity: "'[S]tricter standards of permissible statutory vagueness may be applied to a statute having a potentially inhibiting effect on speech; a man may the less be required to act at his peril here, because the dissemination of ideas may be the loser'" (*Hynes* at 620, quoting *Smith* v. *California*, 361 U.S. 147, 151 (1959)). Both doctrines have a general application to all the regulations governing student protest discussed in Sections 4.7.2, 4.7.3, and 4.7.4. The *Grayned* case contains an excellent discussion, in the school context, of the interrelationship between the two doctrines.

   4.7.3. Prior approval of protest activities. Sometimes institutions have attempted to avoid disruption and disorder on campus by requiring that protest activity be approved in advance and by approving only those activities that will not pose problems. Under this strategy a protest would be halted, or its participants disciplined, not because the protest was in fact disruptive or violated reasonable time, place, and manner requirements but merely because it had not been approved in advance. Administrators of public institutions should be extremely leery of such a strategy. A prior approval system constitutes a "prior restraint" on free expression, that is, a temporary or permanent prohibition of expression imposed before the expression has occurred rather than a punishment imposed afterward. Prior restraints "are the most serious and the least tolerable infringement of First Amendment rights" (*Nebraska Press Ass'n* v. *Stuart*, 427 U.S. 539, 559 (1976)).

   Hammond v. *South Carolina State College*, 272 F. Supp. 947 (D.S.C. 1967), provides a classic example of prior restraint. The defendant college had a rule providing that "the student body is not to celebrate, parade, or demonstrate on the campus at any time without the approval of the Office of the President." Several students were expelled for violating this rule after they held a demonstration for which they had not obtained prior approval. The court found the rule to be "on its face a prior restraint on the right to freedom of speech and the right to assemble" and held the rule and the expulsions under it to be invalid.

The courts have not asserted, however, that all prior restraints on expression are invalid. *Healy* v. *James* (Sections 4.7.1 and 4.7.2) summarizes the current judicial attitude: "While a college has a legitimate interest in preventing disruption on campus, which under circumstances requiring the safeguarding of that interest may justify . . . [a prior] restraint, a 'heavy burden' rests on the college to demonstrate the appropriateness of that action." It is extremely difficult to determine what prior restraints would be valid under *Healy*. Probably prior approval requirements could be imposed on student protest activities to assure that such activities will not violate time, place, or manner regulations meeting the guidelines in Section 4.7.2. They probably could also be imposed for the limited purpose of determining that, under those guidelines, protest activities will not cause substantial disruption. In either case, however, it is questionable whether prior approval requirements would be appropriate if applied to small-scale protests that have no reasonable potential for disruption. Also in either case, prior approval regulations would have to contain a clear definition of the protest activity to which they apply, precise standards to limit the administrator's discretion in making approval decisions, and procedures for assuring an expeditious and fair decision-making process. The administrator must always assume the burden of proving that the protest activity would violate a reasonable time, place, or manner regulation or would cause substantial disruption.[9]

Given these complexities, prior approval requirements may invite substantial legal challenges. Administrators should carefully

[9]These prior restraint requirements have been established in bits and pieces in various court cases. *Healy* is a leading case on burden of proof. *Kunz* v. *New York*, 340 U.S. 290 (1951), and *Shuttlesworth* v. *Birmingham*, 394 U.S. 147 (1969), are leading cases on standards to guide administrative discretion. *Southeastern Promotions* v. *Conrad*, 420 U.S. 546 (1975), is a leading case on procedural requirements.

consider whether and when the prior approval strategy is worth the risk. There are always alternatives—the disciplining of students who violate regulations prohibiting disruptive protest or establishing time, place, or manner requirements, as set out in Section 4.7.2, or the use of injunctive or criminal processes, as set out in Section 4.7.4.

4.7.4. Court injunctions and criminal prosecutions. When administrators are faced with a mass disruption which they cannot end by discussion, negotiation, or threat of disciplinary action, they may want to seek judicial assistance. A court injunction terminating the demonstration is one option. Arrest and criminal prosecution is the other. Although both options involve critical tactical considerations and risks, commentators favor the injunction for most situations, primarily because it provides a more immediate judicial forum for resolving disputes and because it shifts the responsibility for using law enforcement officials from administrators to the court. Injunctions may also be used in some instances to enjoin future disruptive conduct, whereas criminal prosecutions are limited to punishing past conduct. The use of the injunctive process does not legally foreclose the possibility of later criminal prosecutions, nor do either injunctive orders or criminal prosecutions legally prevent the institution from initiating student disciplinary proceedings. Under U.S. Supreme Court precedents, none of these combinations would constitute double jeopardy. (For other problems regarding the relationship between criminal prosecutions and disciplinary proceedings, see Section 4.13.3.)

The legality of injunctions or criminal prosecutions depends on two factors. First, the conduct at issue must be unlawful under state law. In the case of an injunction, the conduct must be an imminent or continuing violation of property or civil rights protected by state law; in the case of a criminal arrest and prosecution, the conduct must violate the state criminal code. Second, the conduct at issue must not constitute expression protected by the First Amendment. Both injunctive orders and criminal convictions are restraints on speech-related activity and would be tested by the same principles that apply to campus regulations under Section 4.7.2 above. Since injunctions act to restrain future demonstration activity, they may operate as prior restraints on expression and would also be subject to the First Amendment principles described in Section 4.7.3.

When the assistance of the court is requested, public and private institutions are on the same footing. Since the court, rather than the institution, will ultimately impose the restraint, and since the court is clearly a public entity subject to the Constitution, both public and private institutions' use of judicial assistance must comply with First Amendment requirements. Also, for both public and private institutions, judicial assistance depends on the same technical requirements regarding the availability and enforcement of injunctions and the procedural validity of arrests and prosecutions.

Sec. 4.8. Student Organizations

4.8.1. Right to organize. It is clear that students in public postsecondary institutions have a general right to organize, to be officially recognized whenever the school has a policy of recognizing student groups, and to use meeting rooms, bulletin boards, and similar campus facilities. Such rights are protected by the freedom of association and freedom of expression concepts of the First Amendment. It is also clear, however, that public institutions retain authority to withhold or revoke recognition in certain instances and to evenhandedly regulate the organizational use of campus facilities. The balance between the organization's rights and the institution's authority was struck in *Healy* v. *James,* 408 U.S. 169 (1972), the leading case in the field.

Healy arose after a student request at Central Connecticut State College for recognition as a local Students for a Democratic Society (SDS) organization had been approved by the college's Student Affairs Committee. But the college's president denied recognition, asserting that the organization's philosophy was antithetical to the college's commitment to academic freedom and that the organization would be a disruptive influence on campus. The denial of recognition had the effect of prohibiting the student group from using campus meeting rooms and campus bulletin boards and placing announcements in the student newspaper. The U.S. Supreme Court found these reasons insufficient under the facts to justify the extreme effects of nonrecognition on the organization's ability to "remain a viable entity" on campus and "participate in the intellectual give and take of campus debate." The Court therefore overruled the president's decision and remanded the case to the lower court, ruling that the college had to recognize the student group if the lower court determined the group was willing to abide by all reasonable campus rules.

The associational rights recognized in *Healy* are not limited to situations where recognition is the issue. In *Gay Students Organization of the University of New Hampshire v. Bonner*, 509 F.2d 652 (1st Cir. 1974), for instance, the plaintiff (GSO) was an officially recognized campus organization. After it sponsored a dance on campus, the state governor criticized the university's policy regarding GSO and, in reaction, the university announced that GSO could no longer hold social functions on campus. GSO filed suit, and the court of appeals found that the university's new policy violated the students' freedom of association and expression. *Healy* was the controlling precedent even though GSO had not been denied recognition:

> [T]he Court's analysis in *Healy* focused not on the technical point of recognition or nonrecognition, but on the practicalities of human interaction. While the Court concluded that the SDS members' right to further their personal beliefs had been impermissibly burdened by nonrecognition, this conclusion stemmed from a finding that the "primary" impediment to free association flowing from nonrecognition is the denial of use of campus facilities for meetings and other appropriate purposes." The ultimate issue at which inquiry must be directed is the effect which a regulation has on organizational and associational activity, not the isolated and for the most part irrelevant issue of recognition per se [509 F.2d at 658–59].

Healy and related cases reveal three broad bases on which administrators may exert authority over student organizations without violating associational rights. First,

> [a] college administrator may impose a requirement
> . . . that a group seeking official recognition affirm in
> advance its willingness to adhere to reasonable campus law.
> Such a requirement does not impose an impermissible
> condition on the students' associational rights. Their
> freedom to speak out, to assemble, or to petition for
> changes in school rules is in no sense infringed. It merely
> constitutes an agreement to conform to reasonable stan-
> dards respecting conduct. This is a minimal requirement,
> in the interest of the entire academic community, of any
> group seeking the privilege of official recognition [*Healy;*
> 408 U.S. at 193].

Such standards of conduct, of course, must not themselves violate the First Amendment or other constitutional safeguards. Recognition, for instance, could not be conditional on the organization's willingness to abide by a rule prohibiting all peaceful protest demonstrations on campus (see Section 4.7) or requiring all campus newspaper announcements to be approved in advance by the administration (see Section 4.9). But so long as campus rules avoid such pitfalls, student organizations must comply with them, just as individual students must. If the organization refuses to agree in advance to obey campus law, recognition may be denied until such time as the organization does agree. If a recognized organization violates campus law, its recognition may be suspended or withdrawn for a reasonable period of time.

Second, "associational activities need not be tolerated where they . . . interrupt classes . . . or substantially interfere with the opportunity of other students to obtain an education" (*Healy* at 189). Thus administrators may also deny recognition to a group which would create substantial disruption on campus and may revoke the recognition of a group which has created such disruption. In either case the institution has the burden of demonstrating with reasonable certainty that substantial disrup-tion will or did in fact result from the organization's actions—a burden which the college failed to meet in *Healy*. This burden is a heavy one because "denial of recognition . . . [is] a form of prior restraint" of First Amendment rights (*Healy* at 184).

Third, the institution may act to prevent organizational activity which is itself illegal under local, state, or federal laws, as well as activity which is "directed to inciting or producing imminent lawless action and . . . likely to incite or produce such action" (*Brandenburg* v. *Ohio*, 395 U.S. 444, 447 (1969), quoted in *Healy* at 188). While the *GSO* case specifically supported this basis for regulation, the court found that the institution had not met its burden of demonstrating that the group's activities were illegal or inciting. A similar conclusion was reached in *Gay Lib* v. *University of Missouri*, 558 F.2d 848 (8th Cir. 1977), reversing 416 F. Supp. 1350 (W.D. Mo. 1976). The trial court found, on the basis of the university's expert evidence, that recognition of the student group "would predictably lead to increased homosexual activities, which include sodomy [a felony under state law] as one of the most prevalent forms of sexual expression in homosexuality." Relying on this finding and on the fact that sodomy is an illegal activity that can be prohibited, the trial court upheld the university's refusal to recognize the group. Overruling the trial court, the appellate court held that the university's proof was insufficient to demonstrate that the student organization intended to breach university regulations or advocate or incite imminent lawless acts. At most, the group intended to peaceably advocate the repeal of certain criminal laws—expression that constitutionally could not be prohibited. Thus the appellate court concluded that the university's denial of recognition impermissibly penalized the group's members because of their status rather than their conduct.

All rules and decisions regarding student organizations should be supportable on one or more of these three regulatory bases. Rules should be applied evenhandedly, carefully avoiding selective applications to particular groups whose philosophy or activities are repugnant to the institution. Decisions under the rules should be based on a sound factual assessment of the impact of the group's activity rather than on speculation or on what the Supreme Court calls "undifferentiated fear or apprehension." Decisions denying organizational privileges should be preceded by "some reasonable opportunity for the organization to meet the university's contentions" or "to eliminate the basis of the denial" (*Wood* v. *Davison*, 351 F. Supp. 543, 548 (N.D. Ga. 1972)). Keeping these points in mind, administrators can retain substantial yet sensitive authority over student groups.

4.8.2. Right not to organize. The right-to-organize concept has a flip side. Often students are organized into some large campus-wide or college-wide association recognized by the institution as a student government or similar representational organization. Sometimes mandatory student activities fees are collected by the institution and channeled to the student association. Where such circumstances pertain at a public institution, may students argue that their constitutional rights are violated either by a requirement that they be members of the association or by a requirement that their activity fees be used to support the association? Or, where nonrepresentational, special-purpose student organizations are concerned, may a public institution channel funds from a mandatory student activities fee to such an organization when other students object to supporting the organization's beliefs or statements?

Although the law on these questions is still fairly sparse, a recent case provides substantial guidance in developing answers. In *Good* v. *Associated Students of the University of Washington*, 86 Wash.2d 94, 542 P.2d 762 (1975), some students challenged the university's support of the ASUW, a nonprofit corporation purporting to represent all students at the university but with whose political viewpoints the plaintiff students disagreed. All university students were required to be members of the ASUW, and the ASUW was the recipient of part of a mandatory student activities fee which the university collected from all students. After finding that the university had authority under state law to support such a corporation so long as it is "in essence an agency of the university and subject to ultimate control by the board [of regents]," the court asked whether compulsory membership and financial support violated the students' "freedom to associate, [which] carries with it a corresponding right to not associate."

The court first held that mandatory *membership* was unconstitutional:

> Notwithstanding the convolutions of the . . . opinions of the United States Supreme Court, we have no hesitancy in holding that the state, through the university, may not compel membership in an association, such as the ASUW, which purports to represent *all* the students at the university, including these plaintiffs. That association

expends funds for political and economic causes to which the dissenters object and promotes and espouses political, social, and economic philosophies which the dissenters find repugnant to their own views. There is no room in the First Amendment for such absolute compulsory support, advocation, and representation [542 P.2d at 768].

The court was not willing, however, to place an absolute ban on the mandatory *fee*. This issue called for a delicate balance:

We must balance the plaintiff's First Amendment rights against the traditional need and desirability of the university to provide an atmosphere of learning, debate, dissent, and controversy. Neither is absolute. If we allow mandatory financial support to be unchecked, the plaintiffs' rights may be meaningless. On the other hand if we allow dissenters to withhold the nominal financial contributions required we would permit a possible minority view to destroy or cripple a valuable learning adjunct of university life. . . .

When a student enrolls at a university, he or she enters an academic community—a world which allows the teaching, advocacy, and dissemination of an infinite range of ideas, theories, and beliefs. They may be controversial or traditional, radical or conformist. But the university is the arena in which accepted, discounted—even repugnant— beliefs, opinions, and ideas challenge each other [*Good* at 768–69].

Considering these factors, the court concluded that "dissenting students should not have the right to veto every event, speech, or program with which they disagree." Accordingly, student associations like the ASUW may use mandatory fees so long as (1) such use does "not exceed the statutory purposes" for which fees may be spent, and (2) the group does not "become the vehicle for the promotion of one particular viewpoint, political, social, economic, or religious" (542 P.2d at 769).[10]

[10]Although the U.S. Supreme Court has not addressed the problem of student activity fees, lawyers will want to consult *Abood* v. *Detroit Board of Education*, 431 U.S. 209 (1977), a case involving similar issues respecting mandatory service fees charged teachers by the collective

A similar approach can be taken toward the validity of mandatory fee allocations to special-purpose organizations (such as minority or foreign student groups, social action groups, academic or honorary societies). If students have no "right to veto every event, speech, or program" they disagree with, then neither should students be able to veto university support for every organization with which they disagree. Thus, unlike broad representational groups such as the ASUW, special-purpose groups can promote a "particular viewpoint." In *Larson* v. *Board of Regents of the University of Nebraska,* 204 N.W.2d 568 (Neb. 1973), for instance, the court rejected student challenges to mandatory fee allocations for the student newspaper and the visiting-speakers program, whose views the plaintiffs opposed. The limit appears to be that the institution's fee allocations, as a whole, must provide a forum for a broad spectrum of viewpoints rather than selectively supporting particular ones with which the institution feels comfortable. Each special-purpose organization, of course, must use the funds only for purposes permitted under any state statutes or regulations governing the use of student activity fees.

Thus, in overseeing student organizations, administrators should avoid imposing compulsory membership requirements. In allocating mandatory student fees, they should develop evenhanded processes devoid of artificial limits on the number or type of viewpoints which may be supported. To the extent the process includes limits on which purposes or groups may be supported, these limits should be demonstrably consistent with the three bases for regulation set out in Section 4.8.1 above or with some other substantial and evenly applied educational priority of the institution.

4.8.3. Principle of nondiscrimination. While the law prohib-

---

bargaining representative for teachers. The Court permits such fees but allows individual teachers to get rebates for fees used for ideological activities unrelated to collective bargaining. Apparently, the *Abood* reasoning can be applied to support mandatory student fees in the university setting. When students could get rebates is less apparent since it is unclear when a fee expenditure would be unrelated to the university's purpose in establishing the fee system. Overall, the *Good* approach appears consistent with *Abood.*

its administrators from imposing certain kinds of restrictions on student organizations, as Sections 4.8.1 and 4.8.2 indicate, there are other kinds of restrictions which administrators may be *required* to impose. The primary example concerns discrimination, particularly on the basis of race or sex. Just as the institution usually cannot discriminate on grounds of race or sex, neither can the student organization discriminate either as the agent of (see generally Section 2.1), or with the substantial support of, the institution. The institution generally has an affirmative obligation either to prohibit discrimination by student organizations in these circumstances or to withhold institutional support from those which do discriminate.

In public institutions, student organizations may be subject to constitutional equal protection principles under the state action doctrine (Section 1.4.2) if they act as agents of the institution or make substantial use of institutional facilities, resources, or funds. Thus in *Joyner* v. *Whiting,* 477 F.2d 456 (4th Cir. 1973) (also discussed in Section 4.9.2), a black-oriented student newspaper allegedly had a segregationist editorial policy and had discriminated by race in staffing and in accepting advertising. Although prohibiting the university president from permanently cutting off the paper's funds because of the restraining effect of such a cut off on free press, the court did hold that the president could and must prohibit the discrimination in staffing and advertising: "The equal protection clause forbids racial discrimination in extracurricular activities of a state-supported institution . . . and freedom of the press furnishes no shield for discrimination."

Similarly, *Uzzell* v. *Friday,* 547 F.2d 801 (4th Cir. 1977), concerned certain rules of student organizations at the University of North Carolina. The Campus Governing Council, legislative branch of the student government, was required under its constitution to have at least two minority students, two males, and two females among its eighteen members. The student Honor Court, under its rules, permitted defendants to demand that a majority of the judges hearing the case be of the same race or the same sex as the defendant. Eschewing the need for any extended analysis, the court invalidated each of the provisions as race discrimination: "Without either reasonable basis or compelling interest, the composition of the Council is formulated on the basis of race. This form of constituency blatently fouls the letter and the spirit of both the Civil Rights Act [42 U.S.C. sec. 2000d] and the Fourteenth Amendment." (The sex discrimination aspects of the provisions were not challenged by the plaintiff students or addressed by the court.) The U.S. Supreme Court, seeing possible affirmative action issues underlying this use of racial considerations, vacated the court of appeals' judgment and remanded the case for further consideration in light of the *Bakke* decision (see Section 4.2.5). 98 S. Ct. 3139 (1978).

In private institutions as well as public, federal civil rights laws (see Section 7.4) may require institutions to assure, as a condition to receiving federal funds, that student organizations do not discriminate. The Title VI regulations (Section 7.4.2) contain several provisions broad enough to cover student organizations; in particular, 45 C.F.R. sec. 80.3(b)(1) prohibits institutions from discriminating by race either "directly or through contractual or other arrangements," and 45 C.F.R. sec. 80.3(b)(4) prohibits discrimination respecting any service or benefit provided "in or through a facility" constructed or operated in whole or part with federal funds. And the Title IX regulations (Section 7.4.3) prohibit institutions from "providing significant assistance" to any organization "which discriminates on the basis of sex in providing any aid, benefit or service to students" (45 C.F.R. sec. 86.31(b)(7)). Section 86.6(c) makes clear that the institution's obligation to comply with Title IX is not lessened in situations where an organization has a rule or regulation which, on the basis of sex, limits a student's participation in an institutional program or activity which "receives or benefits from" federal aid. Title IX does not apply, however, to the membership practices of tax-exempt social fraternities and sororities (sec. 86.14(a)).

The clear lesson of such principles is that administrators cannot avoid all legal problems by simply giving free reign to student organizations. In some areas, discrimination being the primary example (see Section 4.9.4 and the *Wallace* case in Section 2.3.1 for another example), administrators must be actively concerned with student organizations in order to fulfill their institution's obligations under the law.

Sec. 4.9. Student Press

4.9.1. General perspectives. A public institution's relationships with student newspapers, magazines, and other publications should be viewed in the first instance under the same principles that are set out in the preceding section on student organizations. Often student publications are under the auspices of some student organization (such as the newspaper staff) which may be recognized by the school or funded from mandatory student activity fees. Such organizations can claim the same freedom of association as the organizations discussed in the preceding section, and a public institution's recognition and regulation of such organizations is limited to the three regulatory options set out in that section. Objecting students, moreover, have no more right to challenge the allocation of mandatory student fees to student newspapers which express a particular viewpoint than they have to challenge such allocations to other student organizations expressing particular viewpoints. In *Arrington* v. *Taylor*, 380 F. Supp. 1348 (M.D. N.C. 1974), affirmed 526 F.2d 587 (4th Cir. 1975), for example, the court rejected a challenge to the University of North Carolina's use of mandatory fees to subsidize its campus newspaper, *The Daily Tar Heel*. Since the paper did not purport to speak for the entire student body nor did its existence inhibit students from expressing or supporting opposing viewpoints, the subsidy did not infringe First Amendment rights.

However, student publications must also be viewed from an additional perspective not directly involved in the section on student organizations: the perspective of freedom of the press. As perhaps the most staunchly guarded of all First Amendment rights, the right to a free press protects student publications from virtually all encroachments on their editorial prerogatives by public institutions. In a series of forceful recent cases, courts have implemented this student press freedom using First Amendment principles akin to those that would apply to a big city daily published by a private corporation.

The chief concern of the First Amendment's free press guarantee is censorship. Thus, whenever a public institution seeks to control or coercively influence the *content* of a student publication, it will have a legal problem on its hands. The problem will be exacerbated if the institution imposes a prior restraint on publication, that is, a prohibition imposed in advance of publication rather than a sanction imposed subsequently (see Section 4.7.3). Conversely, the institution's legal problems will be alleviated to the extent the institution's regulations (concerning, for example, the allocation of office space or limitations on the time, place, or manner of distribution) do not affect the message, ideas, or subject matter of the publication and do not permit prior restraints on publication.

   4.9.2. Permissible scope of regulation. Joyner v. *Whiting,* 477 F.2d 456 (4th Cir. 1973), arose after the president of North Carolina Central University permanently terminated university financial support for the campus newspaper. The president asserted that the newspaper had printed articles urging segregation and had advocated the maintenance of an all-black university. The court of appeals held that the president's action violated the student staff's First Amendment rights:

> It may well be that a college need not establish a campus newspaper, or, if a paper has been established, the college may permanently discontinue publication for reasons wholly unrelated to the First Amendment. But if a college has a student newspaper, its publication cannot be suppressed because college officials dislike its editorial comment. . . .
>
> The principles reaffirmed in *Healy* [v. *James,* Section 4.7.1] have been extensively applied to strike down every form of censorship of student publications at state-supported institutions. Censorship of constitutionally protected expression cannot be imposed by suspending the editors, suppressing circulation, requiring imprimatur of controversial articles, excising repugnant materials, withdrawing financial support, or asserting any other form of censorial oversight based on the institution's power of the purse [477 F.2d at 460].

The president had also asserted, as grounds for terminating the paper's support, that the newspaper would employ only blacks and would not accept advertising from white-owned businesses. While such practices were not protected by the First Amendment and could be enjoined, the court held the permanent cut-off of funds to be an inappropriate remedy for such problems because of its broad effect on all future ability to publish.

Bazaar v. *Fortune*, 476 F.2d 570, rehearing 489 F.2d 225 (5th Cir. 1973), is also illustrative. The University of Mississippi had halted publication of an issue of *Images*, a student literary magazine written and edited with the advice of a professor from the English department, because a university committee had found two stories objectionable on grounds of "taste." While the stories concerned interracial marriage and black pride, the university disclaimed objection on this basis and relied solely on the stories' inclusion of "earthy" language. The university argued that the stories would stir an adverse public reaction and, since the magazine had a faculty advisor, their publication would reflect badly on the university. The court held that the involvement of a faculty advisor did not enlarge the university's authority over the magazine's content. The university's action violated the First Amendment because "speech cannot be stifled by the state merely because it would perhaps draw an adverse reaction from the majority of people, be they politicians or ordinary citizens, and newspapers. To come forth with such a rule would be to virtually read the First Amendment out of the Constitution and, thus, cost this nation one of its strongest tenets."

Schiff v. *Williams*, 519 F.2d 257 (5th Cir. 1975), concerned the firing of the editors of the *Atlantic Sun*, the student newspaper of Florida Atlantic University. The university's president based his action on the poor quality of the newspaper and on the editors' failure to respect university guidelines regarding the publication of the paper. The court characterized the president's action as a form of direct control over the paper's content and held that such action violated the First Amendment. Poor quality, even though it "could embarrass, and perhaps bring some element of disrepute to the school," was not a permissible basis on which to limit free speech. The university president in *Schiff* attempted to bolster his case by arguing that the student editors were employees of the state. The court did not give the point the attention it deserved. Presumably if a public institution chose to operate its own publication (such as an alumni magazine) and hired a student editor, the institution could fire that student if the technical quality of his or her work was inadequate. The situation in *Schiff* did not fit this model, however, because the newspaper was not set up as the university's own publication. Rather it was recognized by the university as a publication primarily by and for the student body, and the student editors were paid from a special student activities fee fund under the general control of the student government association. While such arrangements may insulate the student newspaper from university control, might it also be said that use of mandatory student fees and university facilities constitutes state action (see Section 1.4.2) such that student editors must themselves comply with the First Amendment when dealing with other students and with outsiders? See *Mississippi Gay Alliance* v. *Goudelock*, 536 F.2d 1073 (5th Cir. 1976) (state action argument rejected over strong dissent), discussed in item no. 2, sec. 4.9, of this chapter's Selected Annotated Bibliography.

   Joyner, Bazaar, and *Schiff* clearly illustrate the very substantial limits on an administrator's authority to control the student press in public institutions. Though each case involves a different regulatory technique and a different rationale for regulation, the administrators lost each time. Yet even these cases suggest grounds on which student publications can be subjected to some regulation. The *Joyner* case indicates that the student press can be prohibited from racial discrimination in its staffing and advertising policies. *Bazaar* indicates that institutions may dissociate themselves from student publications to the extent of requiring or placing a disclaimer on the cover or format of the publication. (The court specifically approved the following disclaimer after it reheard the case: "This is not an official publication of the University.") *Schiff* suggests enigmatically that there may be "special circumstances" where administrators may regulate the press to prevent "significant disruption on the university campus or within its educational processes."

   In these and other student press cases, the clear lesson is not "don't regulate" but rather "don't censor." So long as administrators avoid direct or indirect control of content, they may regulate publications by student organizations or individual students in much the same way they may regulate organizations (Section 4.8) or students generally (Section 4.7). Even content need not be totally beyond an administrator's concern. A disclaimer requirement can be imposed to avoid confusion concerning the publication's status within the institution. And, as the next two sections discuss, content which is illegal under state law because it is obscene or libelous may be regulated. Advertising in a publication also can be controlled to some extent. *Pittsburgh Press Co.* v. *Pittsburgh Commission on Human Relations*, 413 U.S. 376 (1973), upheld a regulation prohibiting newspapers from publishing "help-wanted" advertisements in sex-designated columns. And *Virginia State Board of Pharmacy* v. *Virginia Citizens Consumer Council*, 425 U.S. 748 (1976), while invalidating a statutory ban on advertising prescription drug prices, did affirm the state's authority to regulate false or misleading advertising and advertising which proposes illegal transactions.

4.9.3. Obscenity. It is clear that institutions may discipline students or student organizations for having published obscene material. Institutions may even halt the publication of such material *if* they do so under carefully constructed and conscientiously followed procedural safeguards. A leading case is *Antonelli* v. *Hammond*, 308 F. Supp. 1329 (D.Mass. 1970), which invalidated a system of prior review and approval by a faculty advisory board. The system's major defects were the failure to place the burden of proving obscenity on the board, the failure to provide for a prompt review and internal appeal of the board's decisions, and the failure to provide for a prompt final judicial determination. *Baughman* v. *Freimuth*, 478 F.2d 1345 (4th Cir. 1973), which sets out prior review requirements in the secondary school context, is also illustrative. Clearly, the constitutional requirements for prior review are stringent, and the creation of a constitutionally acceptable system is a very difficult and delicate task. (The most recent U.S. Supreme Court teaching on prior review is in *Southeastern Promotions, Ltd.* v. *Conrad*, 420 U.S. 546 (1975).)

Moreover, institutional authority extends only to material which is actually obscene, and the definition and identification of obscenity is, at best, an exceedingly difficult proposition. In a leading Supreme Court case, *Papish* v. *Board of Curators of the University of Missouri*, 410 U.S. 667 (1973), the plaintiff was a graduate student who had been expelled for violating a board of curators bylaw prohibiting distribution of newspapers "containing forms of indecent speech." The newspaper at issue had a political cartoon on its cover which "depicted policemen raping the Statute of Liberty and the Goddess of Justice. The caption under the cartoon read: 'With Liberty and Justice for All.'" The newspaper also "contained an article entitled 'M----- F----- Acquitted,' which discussed the trial and acquittal on an assault charge of a New York City youth who was a member of an organization known as 'Up Against the Wall, M----- F-----.'" After being expelled, the student sued the university alleging a violation of her First Amendment rights.

The Supreme Court ruled unanimously in favor of the student:

> We think *Healy* [v. *James*, Section 4.7.1] makes it clear that the mere dissemination of ideas—no matter how offensive to good taste—on a state university campus may not be shut off in the name alone of "conventions of decency." Other recent precedents of this Court make it equally clear that neither the political cartoon nor the headline story involved in this case can be labeled as constitutionally obscene or otherwise unprotected [410 U.S. at 670].

Obscenity, then, is not definable in terms of an institution's or an administrator's own personal conceptions of taste, decency, or propriety. Obscenity can be defined only in terms of the guidelines courts have constructed to prevent the concept from being used to choke off controversial social or political dialogue:

> [W]e now confine the permissible scope of . . . regulation [of obscenity] to works which depict or describe sexual conduct. That conduct must be specifically defined by the applicable state law, as written or authoritatively construed. A state offense must also be limited to works which, taken as a whole, appeal to the prurient interest in sex, which portray sexual conduct in a patently offensive way, and which, taken as a whole, do not have serious literary, artistic, political, or scientific value [*Miller* v. *California*, 413 U.S. 15, 24 (1973)].

Although these guidelines were devised for the general community, the Supreme Court made clear in *Papish* that "the First Amendment leaves no room for the operation of a dual standard in the academic community with respect to the content of speech." Administrators devising campus rules are thus bound by the same obscenity guidelines that bind the legislators promulgating obscenity laws. Under these guidelines the permissible scope of regulation is very narrow, and the drafting or application of rules is a technical exercise which administrators should undertake with the assistance of counsel, if at all.

4.9.4. Libel. As they may for obscenity, institutions may discipline students or organizations who publish libelous matter and probably may, subject to stringent procedural safeguards, halt the publication of libelous matter. Here again, however, the authority of public institutions extends only to matter which is libelous according to technical legal definitions. It is not sufficient that a particular statement be false or misleading. Common law and constitutional doctrines require that (1) the statement be false; (2) the publication cause at least nominal injury to the person libeled, usually including but not limited to injury to reputation; and (3) the falsehood be attributable to some fault on the part of the person or organization publishing it. The degree of fault which must exist depends on the subject of the alleged libel. If the subject is a public official or what the courts call a "public figure," the statement must have been made with "actual malice," that is, with knowledge of its falsity or with reckless disregard for its truth or falsity. In all other situations governed by the First Amendment, the statement need only have been made negligently. Courts make this distinction in order to give publishers extra breathing space when reporting on certain matters of high public interest.[11]

Given the complexity of the libel concept, administrators should approach it most cautiously. Because of the need to assess both injury and fault, as well as identify the defamatory falsehood, libel may be even more difficult to combat than obscenity. Suppression in advance of publication is particularly perilous, since injury can only be speculated about at that point, and facts

---

[11]The U.S. Supreme Court has developed the constitutional boundaries of libel law in a progression of decisions beginning with *New York Times* v. *Sullivan*, 376 U.S. 254 (1964). See also *Curtis Pub. Co.* v. *Butts*, 388 U.S. 130 (1967); *Associated Press* v. *Walker*, 388 U.S. 162 (1967); *Gertz* v. *Robert Welch, Inc.*, 418 U.S. 323 (1974); and *Time, Inc.* v. *Firestone*, 424 U.S. 448 (1976).

concerning fault may be difficult to uncover. Much of the material in campus publications, moreover, may involve public officials or public figures and thus be protected by the higher fault standard of actual malice.

Though these factors might reasonably lead administrators to forgo any regulation of libel, there is a countervailing consideration: Institutions or administrators may occasionally be held liable in court for libelous statements in student publications. (See Sections 2.3.1 and 2.4.1 for a general discussion of tort liability.) Such liability could exist where the institution sponsors a publication (such as a paper operated by the journalism department as a training ground for its students), employs the editors of the publication, establishes a formal committee to review material in advance of publication, or otherwise exercises some control (constitutionally or unconstitutionally) over the publication's content. In any case, liability would exist only for statements deemed libelous under the criteria set out above.

Such potential liability, however, need not necessarily prompt increased surveillance of student publications. Increased surveillance would demand regulations which stay within constitutional limits yet are strong enough to weed out all libel—an unlikely combination. And since institutional control of the publication is the predicate to the institution's liability, increased regulation increases the likelihood of liability should a libel be published. Thus administrators may choose to handle liability problems by lessening rather than enlarging control. The privately incorporated student newspaper operating independently of the institution would be the clearest example of a no control/no liability situation.

4.9.5. Obscenity and libel in private institutions. Since the First Amendment does not apply to private institutions not engaged in state action (Section 1.4.2), such institutions have a freer hand in regulating obscenity and libel. Yet private institutions should devise their regulatory role cautiously: Regulations broadly construing libel and obscenity based on lay concepts of those terms could stifle the flow of dialogue within the institution, while attempts to avoid this problem with narrow regulations may lead the institution into the same definitional complexities that public institutions face when seeking to comply with the First Amendment. Moreover, private institutions will want to consider the potential impact of state law in devising its policy on obscenity and libel. Violation of state obscenity or libel law by student publications could subject the responsible students to injunctions, damage actions, and even criminal prosecutions, causing unwanted publicity for the institution. But if the institution regulates the student publications to prevent such problems, it could be held liable along with the students if it exercises sufficient control over the publication. (See Sections 2.1 and 4.9.4.)

Sec. 4.10. Student Housing

4.10.1. Housing regulations. Postsecondary institutions with residential campuses usually have policies specifying which students may, and which students must, live in campus housing. Institutions also typically have policies regulating living conditions in campus housing. Several such housing policies have been challenged in recent court cases by students in public institutions.

Where institutional regulations require students to live on campus, such regulations sometimes apply only to certain groups of students. The classifications may be based on the student's age, sex, class, or marital status. In *Prostrollo* v. *University of South Dakota,* 507 F.2d 775 (8th Cir. 1974), students claimed that the university's regulation requiring all single freshmen and sophomores to live in university housing was unconstitutional because it denied them equal protection under the Fourteenth Amendment and infringed their constitutional rights of privacy and freedom of association. The university admitted that one purpose of the regulation was to maintain a certain level of dormitory occupancy to secure revenue to repay dormitory construction costs. But the university also offered testimony that the regulation was instituted to ensure that younger students would educationally benefit from the experience in self-government, community living, and group discipline, and the opportunities for relationships with staff members that dormitory life provides. In addition, university officials believed dorm living provided easy access to study facilities and to films and discussion groups.

After evaluating these justifications, the lower court determined that the primary purpose of the housing regulation was financial and that the regulation's differentiation of freshmen and sophomores from upperclass students had no rational relationship to the purpose of ensuring housing income. The lower court therefore held the regulation unconstitutional under the equal protection clause. The court of appeals reversed the lower court decision. It reasoned that, even if the regulation's primary purpose was financial, there was no denial of equal protection because there was another rational basis for differentiating freshmen and sophomores from upperclass students: the university officials' belief that the regulation contributed to the younger students' adjustment to college life. The appellate court also rejected the students' right-to-privacy and freedom-of-association challenges. The court gave deference to school authorities' traditionally broad powers in formulating educational policy.

A similar housing regulation which used an age classification to prohibit certain students from living off campus was at issue in *Cooper* v. *Nix*, 496 F.2d 1285 (5th Cir. 1974). The regulation required all unmarried full-time undergraduate students, regardless of age and whether or not emancipated, to live on campus. The regulation contained an exemption for certain older students which in practice the school enforced by simply exempting all undergraduates age twenty-three and over. Neither the lower court nor the court of appeals found any justification in the record for a distinction between twenty-one-year-old students and twenty-three-year-old students. Though the lower court had enjoined the school from requiring students twenty-one and older to live on campus, the court of appeals narrowed the remedy to require only that the school not automatically exempt all twenty-three-year-olds. Thus the school could continue to enforce the regulation if it exempted students over twenty-three only on a case-by-case basis.

A regulation which allowed male students but not female students to live off campus has also been challenged. In *Texas Woman's University* v. *Chayklintaste*, 521 S.W.2d 949 (Tex. Civ. App. 1975), the court found such a regulation to be unconstitutional. Though the university convinced the court that it did not have the space or money to provide on-campus male housing, the court held that mere financial reasons could not justify the discrimination. The court held that the university was unconstitutionally discriminating against its male students by not providing them any housing facilities and also unconstitutionally discriminating against its female students by not permitting them to live off campus.

The university subsequently made housing available to males and changed its regulations to require both male and female undergraduates under twenty-three to live on campus. Although the regulation was now like the one found unconstitutional in *Cooper,* above, the Texas Supreme Court upheld its constitutionality in a later appeal of *Texas Woman's University* v. *Chayklintaste,* 530 S.W.2d 927 (1975). In this case the university justified the age classification with reasons similar to those used in *Prostrollo,* above, which upheld the freshman and sophomore classification. The university argued that on-campus dormitory life added to the intellectual and emotional development of its students and supported this argument with evidence from two professional educational journals and the testimony of a vice-president of student affairs, a professor of education, and an instructor of social work.

In *Bynes* v. *Toll,* 512 F.2d 252 (2d Cir. 1975), another challenge was brought against a university concerning a housing regulation which permitted married students to live on campus but barred their children from living on campus. The court found that there was no denial of equal protection since the university had several very sound safety reasons for not allowing children to reside in the dorms. The court also found that the regulation did not interfere with the marital privacy of the students or their natural right to bring up their children.

Housing regulations limiting dormitory visitation privileges have also been challenged. In *Futrell* v. *Ahrens,* 88 N.M. 284, 540 P.2d 214 (1975), students claimed that a regulation prohibiting visitation by members of the opposite sex in dormitory bedrooms violated their rights of privacy and free association. The regulation did not apply to the lounges or lobbies of the dorms. The court held for the institution, reasoning that even if the regulation affected rights of privacy and association, it was a reasonable time and place restriction upon exercise of those rights which served legitimate educational interests and conformed with accepted standards of conduct.

Taken together, these cases indicate that the Constitution affords public universities broad leeway in regulating on-campus student housing. An institution may require some students to live on campus; may regulate living conditions to fulfill legitimate health, safety, or educational goals; and may apply its housing policies differently to different student groups. In treating students differently, however, the Constitution does require that the basis for classifying students be reasonable. The cases above suggest that classification based solely on financial considerations may not meet that test. Administrators should thus be prepared to offer sound nonfinancial justifications for classifications in their residence rules—such as the promotion of educational goals, the protection of the health and safety of students, or the protection of other students' privacy interests. Differing treatment of students based upon sex may require a relatively stronger showing of justification, and differing treatment based on race would require a justification so compelling that perhaps none exists.

Besides these limits on administrators' authority over student housing, the Constitution also limits public administrators' authority with regard to the entry of student rooms (see Section 4.10.2) and regulation of political canvassing and voter registration in student residences (see Section 5.4.3).

For private institutions as well as public, federal civil rights regulations also limit administrators' authority to treat students differently on grounds of race or sex, or because they are handicapped. The Title VI regulations (see Section 7.4.2) apparently prohibit any and all different treatment of students by race (45 C.F.R. secs. 80.3(b)(1)–(b)(5) and 80.4(d)). The Title IX regulations (see Section 7.4.3) have specific provisions on student housing which require that the institution provide amounts of housing for female and male students proportionate to the number of housing applicants of each sex, that such housing be comparable in quality and in cost to the student, and that the institution not have different housing policies for each sex (45

C.F.R. secs. 86.32 and 86.33). The Section 504 regulations on discrimination against the handicapped (see Section 7.4.4) require institutions to provide "comparable, convenient, and accessible" housing for handicapped students at the same cost as for nonhandicapped students (45 C.F.R. sec. 84.45). In addition, the forthcoming regulations for the Age Discrimination Act of 1973 (see Section 4.2.4.4) may limit administrators' authority to make distinctions in housing policies based on the age of the student.

4.10.2. Searches and seizures. The Fourth Amendment secures an individual's expectation of privacy against government encroachment by providing that "[t]he right of the people to be secure in their persons, houses, papers, and effects, against unreasonable searches and seizures, shall not be violated, and no warrants shall issue, but upon probable cause, supported by oath or affirmation, and particularly describing the place to be searched, and the persons or things to be seized." Searches or seizures conducted pursuant to a warrant meeting the requirements of this provision are deemed reasonable. Warrantless searches may also be found reasonable if they are conducted with the consent of the individual involved, if they are incidental to a lawful arrest, or if they come within a few narrow judicial exceptions, such as an emergency situation.

The applicability of these Fourth Amendment mandates to postsecondary institutions has not always been clear. In the past, when administrators' efforts to provide a "proper" educational atmosphere resulted in noncompliance with the Fourth Amendment, the deviations were defended by administrators and often upheld by courts under a variety of theories. While the previously common justification of in loco parentis is no longer appropriate (see Section 4.1), several remaining theories retain vitality. The leading case of Piazzola v. Watkins, 442 F.2d 284 (5th Cir. 1971), provides a good overview of these theories and their validity.

Piazzola involved the dean of men at a state university, who was informed by the police that they had evidence that marijuana was in the dormitory rooms of certain students. In response to a police request, the dean pledged the cooperation of university officials in searching the rooms. At the time of the search the university had the following regulation in effect: "The college reserves the right to enter rooms for inspection purposes. If the administration deems it necessary, the room may be searched and the occupant required to open his personal baggage and any other personal material which is sealed." Both defendants' rooms were searched without their consent and without a warrant by police officers and university officials. When police found marijuana in each room, the defendants were arrested, tried, convicted, and sentenced to five years in prison. The court of appeals reversed the convictions, holding that "a student who occupies a college dormitory room enjoys the protection of the Fourth Amendment" and that the warrantless searches were unreasonable and therefore unconstitutional under that amendment.

Piazzola and similar cases establish that administrators of public institutions cannot avoid the Fourth Amendment simply by asserting that a student has no reasonable expectation of privacy in institution-sponsored housing. Similarly, administrators can no longer be confident of avoiding the Fourth Amendment by asserting the in loco parentis concept or by arguing that the institution's landlord status, standing alone, authorizes it to search to protect its property interests. Nor does the landlord status, by itself, permit the institution to consent to a search by police, since it has been held that a landlord has no authority to consent to a police search of a tenant's premises. (See, for example, *Chapman* v. *United States,* 365 U.S. 610 (1961).)

However, two limited bases remain on which administrators of public institutions or their delegates can enter a student's premises uninvited and without the authority of a warrant. Under the first approach the institution can obtain the student's consent to entry by including such consent in a written housing agreement or in housing regulations incorporated in the housing agreement. *Piazzola* explains the substantial limits on this approach. Citing the regulation quoted above, the court explained that

> [T]he University retains broad supervisory powers which permit it to adopt . . . [this regulation], provided that regulation is reasonably construed and is limited in its application to further the University's function as an educational institution. The regulation cannot be construed or applied so as to give consent to a search for evidence for

the primary purpose of a criminal prosecution. Otherwise, the regulation itself would constitute an unconstitutional attempt to require a student to waive his protection from unreasonable searches and seizures as a condition to his occupancy of a college dormitory room [442 F.2d at 289].

Thus housing agreements or regulations must be narrowly construed to permit only such entry and search as is expressly provided, and in any case to permit only entries undertaken in pursuit of an educational purpose rather than a criminal enforcement function.

Under the second approach to securing entry to a student's premises, the public institution can sometimes conduct searches (sometimes called "administrative searches") whose purpose is the protection of health and safety. Unconsented administrative searches to enforce health regulations or fire and safety codes usually require a warrant, under this second approach, but it may be obtained under less stringent standards than those for obtaining a criminal search warrant. The leading case is *Camara* v. *Municipal Court*, 387 U.S. 523 (1967), where the U.S. Supreme Court held that a person cannot be prosecuted for refusing to permit city officials to conduct a warrantless code-enforcement inspection of his residence. The Court held that such a search required a warrant that could be obtained "if reasonable legislative or administrative standards for conducting an area inspection are satisfied," which standards need "not necessarily depend upon specific knowledge of the condition of the particular dwelling."

In emergency situations where there is insufficient time to obtain a warrant, health and safety searches may be conducted without one. The U.S. Supreme Court emphasized in the *Camara* case (387 U.S. at 539) that "nothing we say today is intended to foreclose prompt inspections, even without a warrant, that the law has traditionally upheld in emergency situations." In other cases courts have recognized police officers' authority to "enter a dwelling without a warrant to render emergency aid and assistance to a person whom they reasonably believe to be in distress and in need of that assistance" (*Root* v. *Gauper*, 438 F.2d 361 (8th Cir. 1971); and see also *United States* v. *Barone*, 330 F.2d 543 (2d Cir. 1964)).

For genuine health and safety searches, it may often be possible to obtain the specific consent of the student(s) whose premises will be entered. Administrators should obtain such consent whenever feasible for reasons of courtesy as well as because it reinforces the validity of the entry. (The same might be said for searches provided for in the housing agreement, even though the student has already consented generally by entering the agreement.) As *Camara* suggests, administrators may not take disciplinary action against a student for refusing to consent where such consent was not previously required in the housing agreement or regulations.

Administrators at private institutions are generally not subject to Fourth Amendment restraints, since their actions are usually not "state action" (Section 1.4.2). But if local, state, or federal law enforcement officials are in any way involved in a search at a private institution, such involvement may be sufficient to make the search state action subject to the Fourth Amendment. In *People* v. *Boettner,* 362 N.Y.S.2d 365 (Sup. Ct. 1974), affirmed 50 App.Div.2d 1074, 376 N.Y.S.2d 59 (1975), for instance, the question was whether a dormitory room search by officials at the Rochester Institute of Technology, a private institution, was state action. The court answered in the negative only after establishing that the police had not expressly or implicitly requested the search; that the police were not aware of the search; and that there was no evidence of any implied participation of the police by virtue of a continuing cooperative relationship between university officials and the police. Thus a private institution's authority to conduct searches unshackled by the Fourth Amendment depends on the absence of direct or indirect involvement of public law enforcement officials in such searches.

Sec. 4.11. Athletics

4.11.1. General principles. Athletics, as a subsystem of the postsecondary institution, is governed by the general principles set forth elsewhere in this chapter and this book. These principles, however, must be applied in light of the particular characteristics and problems of curricular, extracurricular, and intercollegiate athletics programs. A student-athlete's eligibility for financial aid, for instance, would be viewed under the general principles in Section 4.3, but aid conditions related to the student's eligibility for or performance in intercollegiate athletics may create a special focus for the problem. In *Taylor* v. *Wake Forest*, 191 S.E.2d 379 (N. Car. Ct. App. 1972), for instance, the court held that a student-athlete's refusal to participate in practice was a breach of his contractual obligations under his athletic scholarship. Similarly, the due process principles in Section 4.6 above may apply when a student-athlete is disciplined, and the First Amendment principles in Section 4.7 may apply when student-athletes engage in protest activities. But in each case the problem may have a special focus.

In a discipline situation, the penalty may be suspension from the team, thus raising the issue whether the procedural protections accompanying suspension from school are also applicable to suspension from a team. For institutions engaging in state action (see Sections 1.4.2 and 4.11.4), the constitutional issue is whether the student-athlete has a "property interest" or "liberty interest" in continued intercollegiate competition sufficient to make suspension of that interest a deprivation of "liberty or property" within the meaning of the due process clause. (The same general issue arises with respect to due process's applicability to faculty dismissals (see Section 3.5.2) as well as to suspension of students from school (Section 4.6.2).) Three lower court cases have addressed the question, two answering affirmatively and one negatively.

In *Behagen* v. *Intercollegiate Conference of Faculty Representatives*, 346 F. Supp. 602 (D.Minn. 1972), a suit brought by University of Minnesota basketball players suspended from the team for participating in an altercation during a game, the court reasoned that participation in intercollegiate athletics has "the potential to bring [student athletes] great economic rewards" and is thus as important as continuing in school. The court therefore held the students' interest in intercollegiate participation to be protected by procedural due process and granted the suspended athletes the protections established in the *Dixon* case (Section 4.6.2). In *Regents of University of Minnesota* v. *NCAA*, 422 F. Supp. 1158 (D. Minn. 1976), the same U.S. district court reaffirmed and further explained its analysis of student athletes' due process rights. The court reasoned that the opportunity to participate in intercollegiate competition was a property interest entitled to due process protection not only because of the possible remunerative careers that result but also because such participation was an important part of the student athlete's educational experience. (Although the appellate court reversed this decision, 560 F.2d 352 (8th Cir. 1977), it did so on other grounds and did not question the district court's due process analysis.)

In contrast, the court in *Colorado Seminary* v. *NCAA*, 417 F. Supp. 885 (D.Colo. 1976), relying on an appellate court opinion involving high school athletes (*Albach* v. *Odle*, 531 F.2d 983 (10th Cir. 1976)), held that college athletes had no property or liberty interests in either participating in intercollegiate sports, participating in postseason competition, or appearing on television. The court did suggest, however, that revocation of an athletic scholarship would infringe property or liberty interests of the student and require due process safeguards. (See Section 4.3.1.) The appellate court affirmed (570 F.2d 320 (10th Cir. 1978)). Given this disagreement among the courts, the extent of student athletes' procedural due process protections remains an open question, and administrators should tread cautiously in this area.

In a protest situation, the First Amendment rights of protesting athletes must be viewed in light of the institution's particular interest in maintaining order and discipline in its athletic programs. An athlete's protest which disrupts an athletics program would no more be protected by the First Amendment than any other student protest which disrupts institutional functions. While the case law regarding athletes' First Amendment rights is as sparse as that regarding their due process rights, *Williams* v. *Eaton*, 468 F.2d 1079 (10th Cir. 1972), does specifically apply the *Tinker* case (Section 4.7.1) to a protest by intercollegiate football players. Black football players had been suspended from the team for insisting on wearing black armbands during a game to protest the alleged racial discrimination of the opposing church-related school. The court held that the athletes' protest was unprotected by the First Amendment because it would interfere with the religious freedom rights of the opposing players and their church-related institution. The *Williams* opinion is unusual in that it mixes considerations of free speech and freedom of religion. The court's analysis would have little relevance to situations where religious freedom is not involved. Since the court did not find that the athletes' protest was disruptive, it relied solely on the seldom-used "interference with the rights of others" branch of the *Tinker* case.

Tort law is another area where athletics programs present special problems. Because of the physical nature of athletics and because athletics programs often require travel to other locations, the danger of injury to students and the possibilities for institutional liability are greater than those resulting from other institutional functions. These problems are subject to the same tort liability principles that are set out in Sections 2.3.1 and 2.4.1, applied in light of the special characteristics of athletics programs. In *Scott* v. *State,* 158 N.Y.S.2d 617 (Ct. Claims 1956), for instance, a student collided with a flag pole while chasing a fly ball during an intercollegiate baseball game; the student was awarded $12,000 damages because the school had negligently maintained the playing field in a dangerous condition, and the student had not assumed the risk of such danger. But in *Rubtchinsky* v. *State University of New York at Albany,* 260 N.Y.S.2d 256 (Ct. Claims 1965), discussed in Section 2.3.1, a student injured in an extracurricular pushball game did not collect damages; the student was injured when clipped by another player, and the court held the student had assumed the risk of such injury. When the alleged negligence is that of a public institution (as in the two cases above), the general principles of tort immunity may also apply to athletic injury cases. In *Lowe* v. *Texas Tech University,* 530 S.W.2d 337 (Tex. Civ. App. 1975), for instance, a varsity football player with a knee injury had his damages suit dismissed by the intermediate appellate court because the university had sovereign immunity; but on further appeal the suit was reinstituted because it fell within a specific statutory waiver of immunity (540 S.W.2d 297 (1976)).

4.11.2. Sex discrimination. Sex discrimination has become a major issue in athletics programs. Before the passage of Title IX, 20 U.S.C. secs. 1681 *et seq.* (see Section 7.4.3), the legal aspects of this controversy centered on the Fourteenth Amendment's equal protection clause. In recent years courts have held that certain governmental actions violate this clause because they classify and treat persons differently on the basis of their sex. As in the case of admissions (Section 4.2.4.2), courts have been searching for an appropriate standard by which to ascertain the validity of sex-based classifications in athletics. Most of the cases have concerned female high school athletes seeking the opportunity to try out for male teams. Although the decisions are not all in agreement, a consensus appears to be developing on one point: When the sport is a "noncontact sport," that is, a sport involving little bodily contact among participants, the female athlete must be afforded an equal opportunity to compete for the traditionally male team *if* there is no comparable athletic activity provided for females.[12]

Since the implementation in 1975 of the Title IX regulations (45 C.F.R. Part 86), the equal protection aspects of sex discrimination in high school and college athletics have been playing second fiddle to Title IX. Since Title IX applies to both public and private institutions receiving federal aid, it has a broader reach than equal protection, which applies only to public institutions. (See Section 1.4.2.) Moreover, Title IX has several provisions on athletics which establish requirements more extensive than anything yet devised under the banner of equal protection. Thus in most situations the Title IX regulations, rather than the equal protection clause, will provide the primary legal guidance for administrators dealing with sex discrimination in their institutions' athletics programs.

Section 86.41 of the Title IX regulations is the primary provision on athletics; it establishes various equal opportunity requirements applicable to "interscholastic, intercollegiate, club, or intramural athletics." Section 86.37(c) establishes equal opportunity requirements regarding the availability of athletic scholarships. Physical education classes are covered by section 86.34, and extracurricular activities related to athletics, such as cheerleading

---

[12]The cases are collected in Annot., "Validity, Under Federal Law, of Sex Discrimination in Athletics," 23 A.L.R. Fed. 664 (1975 and periodic supp.).

and booster clubs, are covered generally under section 86.31. Institutional activities falling within these various categories are subject to Title IX whether or not they directly receive federal funds (45 C.F.R. 86.2(h), 86.11). The U.S. Department of Health, Education, and Welfare has issued a memorandum (40 Fed. Reg. 52655 (Nov. 11, 1975)) titled "Elimination of Sex Discrimination in Athletic Programs" which will be helpful to administrators attempting to understand these various requirements. Postsecondary institutions must have achieved full compliance with sections 86.41, 86.37(c), and 86.34 by July 21, 1978, or earlier if possible (45 C.F.R. 86.41(d), 86.37(c)(2), 86.34(a); HEW memorandum). With respect to 86.31, full compliance must have been achieved by July 21, 1976 (45 C.F.R. 86.3(c)).

Probably the greatest controversy stirred by Title IX concerns the issue of sex-segregated versus unitary (integrated) athletic teams. The regulations develop a compromise approach to this issue which roughly parallels the equal protection principles emerging from the court cases discussed above.[13] Under section 86.41(b),

> [an institution] may operate or sponsor separate teams for members of each sex where selection for such teams is based upon competitive skill or the activity involved is a contact sport. However, where a recipient operates or sponsors a team in a particular sport for members of one sex but operates or sponsors no such team for members of the other sex, and athletic opportunities for members of that sex have previously been limited, members of the excluded sex must be allowed to try out for the team

[13]It is still an open question whether Title IX's athletic regulations fully comply with constitutional equal protection and due process requirements. There is some basis for arguing that the Title IX regulations do not fully meet the equal protection requirements that courts have constructed or will construct in this area. See W. Kaplin and S. Marmur, "Validity of the 'Separate but Equal' Policy of the Title IX Regulations on Athletics," a memorandum reprinted in the *Congressional Record* S777–779 (daily ed., Jan. 23, 1975). One court has ruled on the question, holding Title IX regulation 86.41(b) unconstitutional as applied to exclude physically qualified girls from competing with boys in contact sports; *Yellow Springs Exempted Village School District* v. *Ohio High School Athletic Association*, 443 F. Supp. 753 (S.D. Ohio 1978).

offered unless the sport involved is a contact sport. For the purposes of this part, contact sports include boxing, wrestling, rugby, ice hockey, football, basketball, and other sports the purpose or major activity of which involves bodily contact.

This regulation requires institutions to operate unitary teams only for noncontact sports where selection is not competitive. Otherwise the institution may operate either unitary or separate teams and may even operate a team for one sex without having any team in the sport for the opposite sex, so long as the institution's overall athletics program "effectively accommodate[s] the interests and abilities of members of both sexes" (45 C.F.R. 86.41(c)(1); HEW Memorandum at 52656). In a noncontact sport, however, if an institution operates only one competitively selected team, it must be open to both sexes whenever the "athletic opportunities" of the traditionally excluded sex "have previously been limited" (45 C.F.R. 86.41(b)).

Institutions similarly retain wide discretion in devising administrative structures for their athletic programs. An institution may have either "separate administrative structures for men's and women's sports (if separate teams exist) or a unitary structure," so long as the structure or coaching assignments do not "have a disproportionately adverse effect on the employment opportunities of employees of one sex" (HEW Memorandum at 52655. HEW has taken the same position with respect to the institution's physical education department (*Chronicle of Higher Education,* p. 10, col. 4 (Nov. 8, 1976)).

Regardless of whether its teams are separate or unitary, the institution must "provide equal athletic opportunity for members of both sexes" (45 C.F.R. 86.41(c)). This requirement "addresses the totality of the athletic program of the institution rather than each sport offered" (HEW Memorandum at 52656). While equality of opportunity does not require either equality of "aggregate expenditures for members of each sex" or equality of "expenditures for male and female teams," an institution's "failure to provide necessary funds for teams for one sex" is a relevant factor in determining compliance (45 C.F.R. 86.41(c)). Postsecondary administrators grappling with this slippery equal opportunity concept will be helped by section 86.41(c)'s list of ten nonexclusive factors by which to measure overall equality:

> 1. Whether the selection of sports and levels of competition effectively accommodate the interests and abilities of members of both sexes
> 2. The provision of equipment and supplies
> 3. Scheduling of games and practice time
> 4. Travel and per diem allowance
> 5. Opportunity to receive coaching and academic tutoring
> 6. Assignment and compensation of coaches and tutors
> 7. Provision of locker rooms, practice and competitive facilities
> 8. Provision of medical and training facilities and services
> 9. Provision of housing and dining facilities and services
> 10. Publicity

The equal opportunity focus of the regulations also applies to athletic scholarships. Institutions must "provide reasonable opportunities for such awards for members of each sex in proportion to the number of each sex participating in . . . intercollegiate athletics" (45 C.F.R. 86.37(c)(1)). If the institution operates separate teams for each sex, as permitted in section 86.41, it may allocate athletic scholarships on the basis of sex to implement its separate team philosophy, so long as the overall allocation achieves equal opportunity. If athletic scholarships are not allocated by sex, the institution must assure that its criteria for awarding such scholarships "do not inherently disadvantage members of either sex" (HEW Memorandum at 52656).

4.11.3. Discrimination on the basis of handicap. Under HEW's regulations implementing Section 504 of the Rehabilitation Act of 1973 (see Section 7.4.4), handicapped students must be given an opportunity to participate in physical education and athletics programs:

> (1) In providing physical education courses and athletics and similar programs and activities to any of its

students, a recipient to which this subpart applies may not discriminate on the basis of handicap. A recipient that offers physical education courses or that operates or sponsors intercollegiate, club, or intramural athletics shall provide to qualified handicapped students an equal opportunity for participation in these activities.

(2) A recipient may offer to handicapped students physical education and athletic activities that are separate or different only if separation or differentiation is consistent with the requirements . . . [that the programs and activities be operated in "the most integrated setting appropriate"] and only if no qualified handicapped student is denied the opportunity to compete for teams or to participate in courses that are not separate or different [45 C.F.R. sec. 84.47(a)].

4.11.4. Athletic associations and conferences. Often legal issues regarding athletics will arise from the activity of the various athletics conferences and associations which participate in regulating intercollegiate athletics. Individual institutions have become involved in such legal issues in two ways. Student-athletes penalized for violating conference or association rules have sued both the conference or association and the institution over the enforcement of these rules. And institutions themselves have sued conferences or associations over their rules, policies, or decisions. Either situation presents the difficult threshold problem of determining what legal principles apply to the dispute.

The bulk of such disputes have involved the National Collegiate Athletic Association (NCAA), the primary regulator of intercollegiate athletics in the United States. In a series of recent cases courts have held that the NCAA, an institutional membership association for both public and private collegiate institutions, is engaged in "state action" (see Section 1.4.2) and thus subject to the constraints of the U.S. Constitution such as due process and equal protection. The leading case, *Parish* v. *NCAA,* 506 F.2d 1028 (5th Cir. 1975), concerned sanctions applied against Centenary College for granting athletic eligibility to several basketball players who did not meet the NCAA academic requirement. The players, later joined by the college, challenged the constitutionality of the academic requirement (then known as the "1.600 rule"). The court rejected the NCAA's argument that it is a private association not subject to the Constitution:

> We see no reason to enumerate again the contacts and the degree of participation of the various states, through their colleges and universities, with the NCAA. Suffice it to say that state-supported educational institutions and their members and officers play a substantial, although admittedly not pervasive, role in the NCAA's program. State participation in or support of nominally private activity is a well-recognized basis for a finding of state action. . . . Moreover, we cannot ignore the states'—as well as the federal government's—traditional interest in all aspects of this country's educational system. Organized athletics play a large role in higher education, and improved means of transportation have made it possible for any college, no matter what its location, to compete athletically with other colleges throughout the country. Hence, meaningful regulation of this aspect of education is now beyond the effective reach of any one state. In a real sense, then, the NCAA by taking upon itself the role of coordinator and overseer of college athletics—in the interest both of the individual student and of the institution he attends—is performing a traditional governmental function [506 F.2d at 1032-33].

The court here is using first the "government contacts" theory and second the "public function" theory of state action, both of which are explained in Section 1.4.2. (Most other cases holding the NCAA engaged in state action, such as *Howard Univ.* v. *NCAA*, 510 F.2d 213 (D.C. Cir. 1975), rely only on the government contacts theory.) Having found the NCAA to be engaged in state action, the court proceeded to examine the NCAA's rule under due process and equal protection principles, finding the rule valid in both respects.

Besides the Constitution, relevant legal principles can be found in what is called the common law of "voluntary, private associations."[14] Primarily these principles would require the

---

[14]This same body of common law also applies to private

NCAA and other conferences and associations to adhere to their own rules and procedures, fairly and in good faith, in their relations with their member institutions. *California State University, Hayward* v. *NCAA,* 47 Cal.App.3d 533, 121 Cal. Rptr. 85 (1975), for instance, arose after the NCAA had declared the university's athletic teams indefinitely ineligible for postseason play. The university argued that the NCAA's decision was contrary to the NCAA's own constitution and bylaws. The court issued a preliminary injunction against the NCAA, holding the following principle applicable to the NCAA:

> [C]ourts will intervene in the internal affairs of associations where the action by the association is in violation of its own bylaws or constitution. "It is true that courts will not interfere with the disciplining or expelling of members of such associations where the action is taken in good faith and in accordance with its adopted laws and rules. But if the decision of the tribunal is contrary to its laws or rules, or it is not authorized by the bylaws of the association, a court may review the ruling of the board and direct the reinstatement of the member" [quoting another case] [47 Cal.App.3d at 539, 121 Cal. Rptr. at 88, 89].

Thus postsecondary administrators should keep in mind that they have two legal weapons to use against the NCAA in disputes with that association: the United States Constitution and the common law. Conversely, administrators should be aware that these weapons are two-edged: student-athletes may also claim constitutional and common law protections when the NCAA and the institution are jointly engaged in enforcing NCAA rules against such students. In these circumstances even private institutions may be so involved with the NCAA's "state action" that they are themselves engaged in state action; and institutions may also be acting on the NCAA's behalf sufficiently to be subject to the

---

accrediting associations, as discussed in Sections 8.1 and 8.2. Regarding the application of voluntary private association law to the NCAA, see Note, "Judicial Review of Disputes Between Athletes and the National Collegiate Athletic Association," 24 *Stanford L. Rev.* 903, 909–916 (1972).

common law principles binding the NCAA. The same legal principles would be relevant to other athletic associations and conferences in which postsecondary institutions hold memberships, although state action may or may not exist, depending on whether the particular association meets the requirements of *Parish* and similar cases.

Sec. 4.12. Student Files and Records

4.12.1. The Buckley Amendment. The Family Educational Rights and Privacy Act of 1974, 20 U.S.C. 1232g, popularly known as the Buckley Amendment, has created a very substantial role for the federal government with respect to student records. The act and its implementing regulations, 45 C.F.R. Part 99 (1976), apply to all public and private educational agencies or institutions which receive federal funds from the U.S. Office of Education or whose students receive such funds (under the Guaranteed Student Loan Program, for example) and pay them to the agency or institution (45 C.F.R. sec. 99.1). While the Buckley Amendment does not invalidate common law or state statutory law applicable to student records (see Section 4.12.2), the regulations are so extensive that they are clearly the predominant legal consideration in dealing with student records.[15]

The Buckley Amendment and regulations establish requirements pertaining to (1) students' right of access to their education records (45 C.F.R. 99.11–99.13); (2) students' right to challenge the content of their records (45 C.F.R. 99.20–99.22); (3) disclosure of

---

[15]Section 99.61 of the Buckley regulations, 45 C.F.R. 99.61, provides that "an educational agency or institution which determines that it cannot comply with the requirements . . . [of the act or regulations] because a state or local law conflicts with . . . [their] provisions . . . shall so advise the . . . [Family Educational Rights and Privacy Act Office] within forty-five days of any such determination, giving the text and legal citation of the conflicting law." Where such conflict exists, the federal law will take precedence unless the institution is willing to relinquish federal funding; see generally *Rosado* v. *Wyman*, 397 U.S. 397, 420–23 (1970). The federal government would, however, allow a period of negotiation and encourage the institution to seek an official interpretation of the state law compatible with Buckley or an amendment of the state law.

"personally identifiable" information from these records to personnel of the institution or to outsiders (45 C.F.R. 99.30–99.37); (4) the
institution's obligation to notify students of their rights under the
act and regulations (45 C.F.R. 99.5–99.6); and (5) recourse for
students and the federal government when an institution may have
violated the act or regulations (45 C.F.R. 99.60–99.67). Recourse
includes a formal system for receipt, investigation, and adjudication of complaints by the Family Educational Rights and Privacy
Act Office of HEW and by a review board (45 C.F.R. 99.60).[16] All
students enrolled or formerly enrolled in postsecondary institutions
have rights under the act and regulations regardless of whether
they are eighteen and regardless of whether they are dependent on
their parents (45 C.F.R. 99.1(d), 99.4). (If students are dependents
for federal income tax purposes, however, they cannot prevent their
parents from seeing their education records (99.31(a)(8)).)

Students have rights with respect to all "those records which
(1) are directly related to a student, and (2) are maintained by an
educational agency or institution or by a party acting for the
agency or institution" (20 U.S.C. 1232g(a)(4)(A); 45 C.F.R. sec.
99.3). This section of the regulations contains five exceptions to
this definition which exclude from coverage certain personal and
private records of institutional personnel, certain campus law
enforcement records, certain student employment records, certain
records regarding health care, and "records . . . [such as alumni
records] which contain only information relating to a person after
that person was no longer a student at the . . . institution." There
is also a partial exception for "directory information," which is
exempt from the regulations' nondisclosure requirements under
certain conditions (45 C.F.R. 99.37).

The key to success in dealing with the Buckley Amendment
is a thorough understanding of the implementing regulations.
Administrators should keep copies of the regulations at their

[16]It is not yet clear whether courts will permit students injured by
an institution's violation of the Buckley Amendment to sue the institution
in court. Nor is it clear, if such a "private cause of action" (see Section
7.4.9) is recognized, whether the complainant must first pursue the
complaint process within HEW. See the legal memo on this point printed
in the *Congressional Record*, S8482–8486, June 3, 1976 (daily ed.).

fingertips and should not rely on secondary sources to resolve particular problems. Counsel should review the institution's record-keeping policies and practices, and every substantial change in them, to assure compliance with the regulations. Administrators and counsel should work together to maintain appropriate legal forms to use in implementing the regulations, such as forms for a student's waiver of his rights under the act or regulations (45 C.F.R. 99.7), forms for securing a student's consent to release personally identifiable information from his records (45 C.F.R. 99.30), and forms for notifying parties to whom information is disclosed of the limits on the use of that information (45 C.F.R. 99.33). Questions concerning the interpretation or application of the regulations may be directed to the Family Educational Rights and Privacy Act Office at HEW.

4.12.2. *State law.* In a majority of states, courts now recognize a common law tort of invasion of privacy which, in some circumstances, protects individuals against the public disclosure of damaging private information about them and against intrusions in their private affairs. A few states have similarly protected privacy with a statute or constitutional provision. Although this body of law has seldom been applied to educational record-keeping practices, the basic legal principles appear applicable to record-keeping abuses by postsecondary institutions. This body of right-to-privacy law could protect students against abusive collection and retention practices where clearly intrusive methods are used to collect information concerning private affairs. In *White* v. *Davis*, 120 Cal. Rptr. 94, 533 P.2d 222 (1975) (see Section 5.5), for example, the court held that undercover police surveillance of university classes and meetings violated the right to privacy because "no professor or student can be confident that whatever he may express in class will not find its way into a police file." Similarly, right-to-privacy law could protect students against abusive dissemination practices which result in unwarranted public disclosure of damaging personal information.

In addition to this developing right-to-privacy law, many states also have statutes or administrative regulations dealing specifically with record-keeping. These include subject access laws, open or public records laws, and confidentiality laws. Such laws usually apply only to state agencies, and a state's postsecondary institutions may or may not be considered state agencies subject to record-keeping laws. Occasionally a state statute deals specifically with postsecondary education records. Massachusetts, for instance, has a statute making it an "unfair educational practice" for any "educational institution," including public and private postsecondary institutions, to request information or make or keep records concerning certain arrests or misdemeanor convictions of students or applicants (Mass. Gen. Laws, ch. 151C, sec. 2(f)(1972)).

Since state laws on privacy and records vary greatly from state to state, administrators should check with counsel to determine the law in their particular state. Since state records requirements may occasionally conflict with the Buckley Amendment regulations, it is especially important for counsel to determine whether any such conflict exists (see Section 4.12.1, note 15). Regarding right-to-privacy concepts, an institution which is in compliance with the Buckley Amendment regulations is not likely to be violating any state right to privacy. The two exceptions concern information collection practices and the particular types of records kept, which are not treated in the Buckley regulations (except that Buckley requires that a "record of disclosures" of information be kept—99.32). In these situations, developing state law may carve out requirements, as in the *White* case and the Massachusetts statute above, independent of and supplementary to Buckley.

4.12.3. The federal Privacy Act. The Privacy Act of 1974, 88 Stat. 1896, partly codified in 5 U.S.C. sec. 552a, applies directly to federal government agencies and, with two exceptions discussed below, does not restrict postsecondary educational institutions. The act accords all persons, including students, faculty members, and staff members, certain rights enforceable against the federal government regarding information about them in federal agency files, whether collected from a postsecondary institution or from any other source. The act grants the right to inspect, copy, and correct such information and limits its dissemination by the agency.

The first situation where the act applies to postsecondary institutions concerns social security account numbers: Section 7 of the act prohibits federal, state, and local government agencies from requiring persons to disclose their social security numbers. This provision applies to public but not to private postsecondary institutions and thus prevents public institutions from requiring either students or employees to disclose their social security numbers. The two exceptions to this nondisclosure requirement permit an institution to require disclosure (1) where it is required by federal statute, and (2) where the institution maintains "a system of records in existence and operating before January 1, 1975, if such disclosure was required under statute or regulation adopted prior to such date to verify the identity of an individual" (88 Stat. 1896 at 1903).

The second provision of the act potentially relevant to some postsecondary institutions is section 3(m), 5 U.S.C. sec. 552a(m), which applies the act's requirements to government contractors who operate record-keeping systems on behalf of a federal agency pursuant to the contract.

Sec. 4.13. Disciplinary and Grievance Systems

4.13.1. Establishment of systems. It is clear from much of the material in this chapter that postsecondary institutions have extensive authority to regulate both the academic and nonacademic activities and behavior of students. This power is delineated in an often-cited judicial statement:

> In the field of discipline, scholastic and behavioral, an institution may establish any standards reasonably relevant to the lawful missions, processes, and functions of the institution. It is not a lawful mission, process, or function of . . . [a public] institution to prohibit the exercise of a right by the Constitution or a law of the United States to a member of the academic community in the circumstances. Therefore, such prohibitions are not reasonably relevant to any lawful mission, process or function of . . . [a public] institution.
>
> Standards so established may apply to student behavior on and off the campus when relevant to any lawful mission, process, or function of the institution. By such standards of student conduct the institution may prohibit any action or omission which impairs, interferes

with, or obstructs the missions, processes, and functions of
the institution.

Standards so established may require scholastic
attainments higher than the average of the population and
may require superior ethical and moral behavior. In
establishing standards of behavior, the institution is not
limited to the standards or the forms of criminal laws
[*General Order on Judicial Standards of Procedure and
Substance in Review of Student Discipline in Tax-
Supported Institutions of Higher Education*, 45 F.R.D. 133,
145 (W.D. Mo., 1968)].

It is not enough, however, for an administrator to understand the extent and limits of institutional authority. The
administrator must also skillfully implement this authority
through various systems for the resolution of disputes concerning
students. Such systems should include procedures for processing
and resolving disputes; substantive standards or rules to guide the
judgment of the persons responsible for dispute resolution; and
mechanisms and penalties with which decisions are enforced. The
procedures, standards, and enforcement provisions should be
written and made available to all students. Dispute-resolution
systems, in their totality, should create a two-way street; that is,
they should provide for complaints *by* students *against* other
members of the academic community as well as complaints *against*
students *by* other members of the academic community.

The choice of structures for resolving disputes depends on
policy decisions made by administrators, preferably in consultation
with representatives of various interests within the institution.
Should a single system cover both academic and nonacademic
disputes, or should there be separate systems for separate kinds of
disputes? Should there be a separate disciplinary system for
students, or should there be a broader system covering other
members of the academic community as well? Will the systems use
specific and detailed standards of student conduct, or will they
operate on the basis of more general rules and policies? To what
extent will students participate in establishing the rules governing
their conduct? To what extent will students, rather than administrators or faculty members, be expected to assume responsibility for
reporting or investigating violations of student conduct codes or

honor codes? To what extent will students take part in adjudicating complaints by or against students? What kinds of sanctions can be levied against students found to have been engaged in misconduct? Can they be fined, be made to do volunteer work on campus, be expelled from the institution, be given a failing grade in a course or be denied a degree, or be required to make restitution? To what extent will the president, provost, or board of trustees retain final authority to review decisions concerning student misconduct?

Devices for creating dispute-resolution systems may include honor codes or codes of academic ethics; codes of student conduct; bills of rights, or rights and responsibilities, for students or for the entire academic community; the use of various legislative-type bodies such as a student or university senate; a formal judiciary system for resolving disputes concerning students; and the establishment of grievance mechanisms for students, such as an ombudsman system or a grievance committee. On most campuses security guards or some other campus law enforcement system will also be involved in the resolution of disputes and regulation of student behavior.

Occasionally, specific procedures or mechanisms will be required by law. Constitutional due process, for instance, requires the use of certain procedures before a student is suspended or dismissed. (See Section 4.6.) Similarly, both the Title IX regulations (Section 7.4.3) and the Buckley Amendment regulations (Section 4.12.1) require institutions to establish certain procedures for resolving disputes under those particular statutes. Even when specific mechanisms or procedures are not required by law, the procedures or standards adopted by an institution will sometimes be affected by existing law. A public institution's rules regarding student protest, for instance, must comply with First Amendment strictures protecting freedom of speech (Section 4.7). And its rules regarding administrative access to or search of student rooms, and the investigatory techniques of its campus police, must comply with Fourth Amendment strictures regarding search and seizure (Section 4.10.2). Though an understanding of the law is thus crucial to the establishment of disciplinary and grievance systems, the law by no means rigidly controls their form and operation. To a large extent the kind of systems adopted will depend on the institution's notions of good administrative practice.

Fair and accessible dispute-resolution systems, besides being useful administrative tools in their own right, can also serve to insulate institutions from lawsuits. Students who feel their arguments or grievances will be fairly considered within the institution may forestall or forgo resort to the courts. If students ignore internal mechanisms in favor of immediate judicial action, the courts may refer the students to the institution. Under the "exhaustion of remedies" doctrine (see Section 3.5.3), courts may require plaintiffs to exhaust available remedies within the institution before bringing the complaint to court.

4.13.2. Codes of student conduct. If a code of conduct defines the offenses for which a student may be penalized by a public institution, that code must comply with constitutional due process requirements concerning vagueness. The requirement is a minimal one, generally requiring the code to be sufficiently clear that students can understand the standards with which their conduct must comply and that the code is not susceptible to arbitrary enforcement. (See Section 4.4.) A public institution's code of conduct must also comply with the constitutional doctrine of overbreadth in any area where the code could affect First Amendment rights. Basically this doctrine requires that the code not be drawn so broadly and vaguely as to include protected First Amendment activity along with behavior subject to legitimate regulation. (See Section 4.7.2.) And finally, a public institution's student conduct code must comply with a general requirement of evenhandedness. This means that the code cannot arbitrarily discriminate in the range and type of penalties, or in the procedural safeguards, afforded various classes of offenders. *Paine* v. *Board of Regents of the University of Texas System,* 355 F. Supp. 199 (W.D. Texas 1972), affirmed per curiam, 474 F.2d 1397 (5th Cir. 1973), concerned such discriminatory practices. The institution had treated students convicted of drug offenses differently from all other code offenders, including those charged with equally serious offenses, giving them a harsher penalty and fewer procedural safeguards. The court found this differential treatment to violate the equal protection and due process clauses.

As noted in the judicial statement quoted in Section 4.13.1, codes of conduct can apply to the off-campus actions as well as the on-campus activity of students. But the extension of a code to off-campus activity can pose significant legal and policy questions. In the *Paine* case above, the institution automatically suspended students who had been put on probation by the criminal courts for possession of marijuana. The court invalidated the suspensions partly because they were based on an off-campus occurrence—court probation—which did not automatically establish a threat to the institution. To avoid such a problem, administrators should ascertain that an off-campus act has some detrimental impact on the campus before using that act as a basis for disciplining students.

Private institutions not subject to the state action doctrine (see Section 1.4.2) are not constitutionally required to follow these principles regarding student codes. Yet these principles reflect basic notions of fairness which can be critical components of good administrative practice; thus administrators of private institutions may wish to use them as policy guides in formulating their codes.

4.13.3. Judicial systems. Judicial systems which adjudicate complaints of student misconduct must be very sensitive to procedural safeguards. The membership of judicial bodies, the procedures they use, the extent to which their proceedings are open to the academic community, the sanctions they may impose, the methods by which they may initiate proceedings against students, and provisions for appealing their decisions should be set out in writing and made generally available within the institution.

Whenever the charge could result in a punishment as serious as suspension, a public institution's judicial system must provide the procedures required by the due process clause. (See Section 4.6.2.) The focal point of these procedures is the hearing at which the accused student may present evidence and argument concerning the charge. The institution, however, may wish to include preliminary stages in its judicial process for more informal disposition of complaints against students. The system may provide for negotiations between the student and the complaining party, for instance, or for preliminary conferences before designated representatives of the judicial system. Full due process safeguards need not be provided at every such preliminary stage. *Andrews* v. *Knowlton*, 509 F.2d 898 (2d Cir. 1975), dealt with the procedures required at a stage preceding an honor code hearing. The court held that due process procedures were not required at that time because it was not a "critical stage" which could have a "prejudicial impact" on the final honor code determination. Thus administrators have broad authority to construct informal preliminary proceedings so long as a student's participation in such stages does not adversely affect his or her ability to defend the case in the final stage.

Occasionally a campus judicial proceeding may involve an incident which is also the subject of criminal court proceedings. The same student may thus be charged in both forums at the same time. In such circumstances, the public postsecondary institution is not legally required to defer to the criminal courts by canceling or postponing its proceedings. As held in *Paine* (Section 4.13.2) and other cases, dual prosecution is not double jeopardy because the two proceedings impose different kinds of punishment to protect different kinds of state interests. The Constitution's double jeopardy clause applies only to successive *criminal* prosecutions for the same offense. Nor will the existence of two separate proceedings necessarily violate the student's privilege against self-incrimination. Several courts have rejected student requests to stay campus proceedings on this ground pending the outcome of criminal trials, such as in *Grossner* v. *Trustees of Columbia University*, 287 F. Supp. 535 (S.D.N.Y. 1968). One court emphasized, however, that if students in campus proceedings "are forced to incriminate themselves . . . and if that testimony is offered against them in subsequent criminal proceedings, they can then invoke . . . [Supreme Court precedents] in opposition to the offer" (*Furutani* v. *Ewigleben*, 297 F. Supp. 1163 (N.D. Cal. 1969)). A student's claim that being identified in campus disciplinary proceedings would increase the possibility of misidentification by witnesses at his criminal trial was rejected as speculative in *Nzuve* v. *Castleton State College*, 335 A.2d 321 (Vermont 1975).

While neither double jeopardy nor self-incrimination need tie the administrator's hands, administrators may nevertheless choose, for policy reasons, to delay or dismiss particular campus proceedings when the same incident is in the criminal courts. It is possible that the criminal proceedings will adequately protect the institution's interests. Or, as *Furutani* and *Nzuve* suggest, student testimony at a campus proceeding could create evidentiary problems for the criminal court.

If the outcome of a criminal proceeding is subsequently used as the basis for disciplinary action, a public institution must be careful not to violate the student's due process rights. In the *Paine* case, also discussed above, a university rule required the automatic two-year suspension of any student convicted of a narcotics offense. The court held that the students must be given an opportunity to show that, despite their conviction and probation, they posed "no substantial threat of influencing other students to use, possess, or sell drugs or narcotics." Thus a criminal conviction does not automatically provide the basis for suspension; administrators should still ascertain that the conviction has a detrimental impact on the campus, and the affected student should have the opportunity to make a contrary showing.

4.13.4. Security officers. The powers and responsibilities of campus security officers should be carefully delineated. Administrators must determine whether such officers should be permitted to carry weapons, and under what conditions. They must determine the security officers' authority to investigate crime on campus or to investigate violations of student codes of conduct. Record-keeping practices must be devised.[17] The relationship which security officers will have with local and state police must be cooperatively worked out with local and state police forces. Because campus security officers may play dual roles, partly enforcing public criminal laws

---

[17]For a general discussion of the legal restrictions on record-keeping, see Section 4.12. The Buckley Amendment, discussed there, has a specific provision relating to campus law enforcement records. Section 99.3 of the regulations exempts from the amendment all the records of a law enforcement unit of an educational agency or institution that are (1) maintained apart from student education records, (2) maintained solely for law enforcement purposes, and (3) not disclosed to individuals other than law enforcement officials of the same jurisdiction, provided that the education records maintained by the agency or institution are not disclosed to the personnel of the law enforcement unit (45 C.F.R. sec. 99.3, definition of "education records," paragraph (b)(2)).

and partly enforcing the institution's codes of conduct, administrators should carefully delineate the officers' relative responsibilities in each role.

Administrators must also determine whether security guards are, or should be, "peace officers" with full arrest powers under state or local law. In *People* v. *Wesley*, 365 N.Y.S.2d 593 (City Ct., Buffalo, 1975), for instance, the court determined that security officers at a particular state campus were peace officers under the terms of section 355(2)(m), N.Y. Education Law. State law in other states may also designate certain security guards of public institutions as peace officers. For private institutions and public institutions not covered by state law, deputization under city or county law or the use of "citizens' arrest" powers may be an option. Administrators should carefully consider the extent, if any, to which security officers should employ either of these options.

Police work is subject to a variety of constitutional restraints concerning such matters as investigations, arrests, and searches and seizures of persons or private property. Security officers for public institutions are subject to all these restraints. In private institutions, security officers who have arrest powers or who are operating in conjunction with local or state police forces may also be subject to constitutional restraints under the state action doctrine (see Sections 4.10.2 and 1.4.2). In devising the responsibilities of such officers, therefore, administrators should be sensitive to the constitutional requirements regarding police work.

Administrators should also be sensitive to the tort law principles applicable to security work (see generally Sections 2.3.1, 2.4.1, and 2.5). Like athletic activities (Section 4.11), campus security actions are particularly likely to involve the institution in tort liability. Using physical force or weapons, detaining or arresting persons, entering or searching private property can all occasion tort liability if they are undertaken without justification or accomplished carelessly. *Jones* v. *Wittenberg University*, 534 F.2d 1203 (6th Cir. 1976), for example, dealt with a university security guard who had fired a warning shot at a fleeing student. The shot pierced the student's chest and killed him. The guard and the university were held liable for the student's death, even though the guard did not intend to hit the student and may have had justification for firing a shot to frighten a fleeing suspect. The appellate court reasoned that the shooting could nevertheless constitute negligence "if it was done so carelessly as to result in foreseeable injury."

Although the *Jones* case is a dramatic reminder of the perils in providing campus security, not all liability arises from such a specific, affirmative act as the negligent use of a firearm. As the owner of property onto which it invites students, a postsecondary institution may also have a more general responsibility to protect or at least warn students against foreseeable dangers on campus. In a District of Columbia case which attracted national headlines, for instance, a jury held a university liable for injury to a student who was raped in a locker room in the campus gym (*P.D.* v. *Catholic University*, Civ. No. 75-2198 (D.D.C. 1976). The extent of this institutional obligation to protect students remains unclear, given the absence of a written opinion in the *P.D.* case and a lack of other judicial opinions. There will probably be additional court cases and a better delineation of institutional responsibility in future years.

Selected Annotated Bibliography

General

1. *Joint Statement on Rights and Freedoms of Students*, 52 AAUP Bull. 365 (1967), provides a set of model guidelines for implementing students' rights on campus, drafted by the Association of American Colleges, the American Association of University Professors, the National Student Association, the National Association of Student Personnel Administrators, and the National Association of Women Deans and Counsellors, and endorsed by a number of other professional organizations. This document should be read in conjunction with W. Van Alstyne's discussion of the Joint Statement in G. W. Holmes (ed.), *Student Protest and the Law* 181–186 (Institute of Continuing Legal Education, Ann Arbor, 1969).
2. Laudicina, R., and Tramutola, J., Jr., *A Legal Overview of the New Student as Educational Consumer, Citizen, and Bar-*

gainer (Thomas, 1976), is a survey of recent legal developments concerning students and their impact on postsecondary administration; suggests legal and administrative models for dealing with legal and policy developments. Written by an administrator and a lawyer, with commentary by many other contributors.

3. Tice, T. N., *Student Rights, Decisionmaking, and the Law* (ERIC/Higher Education Research Report no. 10, American Association for Higher Education, 1976), includes an essay on the impact of laws and morals on campus administration, a set of guidelines for administrative decisions concerning students, and an extensive annotated bibliography on student rights and responsibilities.

4. Young, D. P., and others (eds.), *The College Student and the Courts* (1973 and periodic supplements), provides briefs and supporting comments on court cases concerning students, with the addition of new cases by quarterly supplements.

Sec. 4.1 (The Legal Status of Students)

1. Comment, "Consumer Protection and Higher Education—Student Suits Against Schools," 37 *Ohio State L. J.* 608 (1976), surveys the types of problems being addressed as part of the new student consumerism movement, the legal theories courts use in student consumerism cases, and the steps institutions might take to alleviate the problems and attendant lawsuits.

2. Hanson, D. J., *The Lowered Age of Majority: Its Impact on Higher Education* (Association of American Colleges, 1975), provides a very helpful overview of how the lowered age of majority affects a range of legal issues regarding student status, such as determining dependency for financial aid purposes, determining residency for tuition purposes, and devising residence hall regulations; written by a lawyer but primarily for laypersons.

3. University of Denver College of Law, "Legal Aspects of Student Institutional Relationships," 45 *Denver L. J.* 497 (1968), is a series of papers and commentaries from an invitational con-

ference. Though some of the case law discussion is outdated, the work provides interesting perspectives and useful conceptual principles concerning the status of students.

Sec. 4.2 (Admissions)

1. Gellhorn, E., and Hornby, D. B., "Constitutional Limitations on Admissions Procedures and Standards—Beyond Affirmative Action," 60 *Virginia L. Rev.* 975 (1974), discusses legal issues concerning law school admissions procedures and, more generally, analyzes due process and equal protection limitations on postsecondary admissions; includes a general analysis of courts' treatment of educational administration questions and gives specific recommendations for law school admissions procedures.

2. Hornby, D. B., *Higher Education Admission Law Service* (Educational Testing Service, 1973 and subsequent additions), is a looseleaf service revised and updated annually. Particularly useful for admissions officers in both public and private institutions.

3. Institute for the Study of Educational Policy, *Equal Educational Opportunity for Blacks in U.S. Higher Education* (Howard University Press, 1976), a statistical and analytical assessment, includes chapters on "Access, Distribution, and Persistence of Blacks in College," "Barriers to Equal Educational Opportunity for Blacks," and "Federal Policies Related to Equal Educational Opportunity."

4. Karst, K. L., and Horowitz, H. W., "Affirmative Action and Equal Protection," 60 *Virginia L. Rev.* 955 (1974), discusses the legal and social implications of employing racial preferences in higher education admissions.

5. O'Neil, R. M., *Discriminating Against Discrimination: Preferential Admissions and the DeFunis Case* (Indiana University Press, 1975), provides a detailed examination of the *DeFunis* case and the continuing issues emerging from it. The author, a lawyer and university vice-president, argues in favor of special admissions programs for minorities, considering and rejecting various nonracial alternatives in the process.

6. Tollett, K. S., "Black Institutions of Higher Learning: Inadvert-
   ent Victims or Necessary Sacrifices?" 3 *Black L. J.* 162 (1974),
   sets forth the background of black higher education and provides a legal and policy analysis of the application of integration principles to black higher education. The author
   argues for both maintaining the identity of black institutions and providing minority admissions programs in predominantly white institutions.

Sec. 4.3 (Financial Aid)

1. Hopkins, B., "Scholarships and Fellowship Grants: Current Tax
   Developments and Problems," 3 *J. of College and University Law* 54 (1976), traces recent trends concerning the federal taxability of various financial aid awards to students,
   including research or teaching stipends, tuition remissions,
   and loan forgivenesses.
2. Jenkins, H., "Regulation of Colleges and Universities Under the
   Guaranteed Student Loan Program," 4 *J. of College and
   University Law* 13 (1977), explains and defends the federal
   regulations of a major student loan program and compares
   them with provisions in the Education Amendments of
   1976, which impose similar regulatory requirements on the
   other major federal student aid programs.

Sec. 4.4 (Disciplinary Rules and Regulations)

See the bibliography for Section 4.13 below.

Sec. 4.5 (Grades, Credits, and Degrees)

Mancuso, J., "Legal Rights to Reasonable Rules, Fair Grades,
   and Quality Courses," in J. S. Stark (ed.), *Promoting Consumer Protection for Students* 75–89 (Jossey-Bass, 1976),
   examines the judicial precedents, current legal and policy
   trends, and future prospects regarding student academic
   grievances, such as unfair grading and inferior educational
   services.

*Sec. 4.6 (Procedures for Suspension, Dismissal,
and Other Sanctions)*

See the bibliography for Section 4.13 below.

Sec. 4.7 (Student Protest and Demonstrations)

1. Blasi, V., "Prior Restraints on Demonstrations," 68 *Michigan L. Rev.* 1482 (1970), is a comprehensive discussion of First Amendment theory and case law and the specific manner in which the law bears upon the various components of a student demonstration.
2. Herman, J., "Injunctive Control of Disruptive Student Demonstrations," 56 *Virginia L. Rev.* 215 (1970), analyzes strategic, constitutional, and procedural issues concerning the use of injunctions to control disruptive student protest.
3. Holmes, G. W., *Student Protest and the Law* (Institute of Continuing Legal Education, Ann Arbor, 1969), is a collection of papers, panel discussions, and supporting documents (such as pleadings and injunctive orders) presented at a national conference; covers a broad range of topics relevant to student protest and to student affairs generally. Useful and practical resource for both lawyers and administrators.

Sec. 4.8 (Student Organizations)

Fishbein, E. A., "Legal Aspects of Student Activities Fees," 1 *J. of College and University Law* 190 (1974), provides an overview of the cases and issues regarding a postsecondary institution's imposition and management of mandatory student activities fees.

Sec. 4.9 (Student Press)

1. Duscha, J., and Fischer, T., *The Campus Press: Freedom and Responsibility* (American Association of State Colleges and Universities, 1973), is a handbook that provides historical, philosophical, and legal information on college newspapers.

Not only discusses case law that affects the campus press but also illustrates the variety of ways the press may be organized on campus and the responsibilities the institution may have for its student publications.

2. Newell, L., "A Right of Access to Student Newspapers at Public Universities," 4 *J. of College and University Law* 209 (1977), considers the application of the state action doctrine to student newspapers and the possibility of a First Amendment right of access to the newspaper's pages.

3. Note, "Tort Liability of a University for Libelous Material in Student Publications," 71 *Michigan L. Rev.* 1061 (1973) provides the reader with a general understanding of libel law and discusses the various theories under which a university may be held liable for the torts of its student press. The author also recommends preventive measures to minimize university liability.

Sec. 4.10 (Student Housing)

1. Delgado, R., "College Searches and Seizures: Students, Privacy and the Fourth Amendment," 26 *Hastings L. J.* 57 (1975), provides a broad view of the legal issues involved in dormitory searches and analyzes the validity of the various legal theories used to justify such searches.

2. Note, "Admissibility of Evidence Seized by Private University Officials in Violation of Fourth Amendment Standards," 56 *Cornell L. Rev.* 507 (1971), discusses the applicability of Fourth Amendment standards to actions by private universities; addresses the degree of involvement by school and police authorities that may render private university actions subject to the state action doctrine.

Sec. 4.11 (Athletics)

1. Appenzeller, H., *Athletics and the Law* (Michie, 1975), provides a basic and easy-to-read overview of legal issues arising in athletics programs, including good conduct rules for ath-

letes, travel and transportation, sex discrimination, relations with the NCAA and other athletics associations, and tort liability. Primarily for athletic directors and coaches.

2. Cross, H. M., "The College Athlete and the Institution," 38 *Law and Contemporary Problems* 151 (1973), provides a legal analysis of the student-athlete's status within the institution; discusses admissions, recruitment, athletic eligibility, and the athlete's status as a member of the student body. Written by a law professor and former NCAA president.

3. Note, "Sex Discrimination and Intercollegiate Athletics," 61 *Iowa L. Rev.* 420 (1975), provides a comprehensive analysis of the current status of sex discrimination in athletics under the equal protection clause, Title IX, and the proposed Equal Rights Amendment; includes related historical and social background on sex discrimination.

Sec. 4.12 (Student Files and Records)

1. American Association of Collegiate Registrars and Admissions Officers, Task Force on Buckley Amendment, *A Guide to Postsecondary Institutions for Implementation of the Family Educational Rights and Privacy Act of 1974 As Amended* (AACRAO, 1975), explains the act and its regulations, as well as the procedures and strategies for compliance, and provides sample forms for use in complying and a copy of the act and its regulations.

2. Michigan Law Review Editorial Board, "Government Information and the Rights of Citizens," 73 *Michigan L. Rev.* 971 (1975), provides an exhaustive review of federal and state constitutional, statutory, and common law protections of the right to privacy; includes lengthy discussions of the Privacy Act of 1974 and state law applicable to education records, as well as a brief discussion of the Buckley Amendment; focuses primarily on the limitations applicable to public agencies and institutions.

3. Schatken, S., "Student Records at Institutions of Postsecondary Education: Selected Issues Under the Family Educational

Rights and Privacy Act of 1974," 4 *J. of College and University Law* 147 (1977), identifies the major Buckley issues, explains why they are issues, suggests resolutions, and gives practical advice for administrators and counsel dealing with student records.

Sec. 4.13 (Disciplinary and Grievance Systems)

1. Beaney, W. M., and Cox, J. C. S., "Fairness in University Disciplinary Proceedings," 22 *Case-Western L. Rev.* 390 (1971), provides legal and policy analyses, and suggested guidelines, concerning the development of fair disciplinary proceedings on campus.

2. Blumer, D. H., and Witsil, J. L., "Security on the Campus," in D. H. Blumer (ed.), *Legal Issues for Postsecondary Education: Briefing Papers II* 35–44 (American Association of Community and Junior Colleges, 1976), reviews the legal and policy problems regarding campus security and provides possible solutions.

3. Cazier, S., *Student Discipline Systems in Higher Education* (ERIC/American Association for Higher Education Research Rpt. No. 7, 1973), synthesizes the literature since 1961 relating to disciplinary policies and practices and applicable legal principles.

4. Sims, O. S., Jr. (ed.), *New Directions in Campus Law Enforcement: A Handbook for Administrators* (University of Georgia Center for Continuing Education, 1971), is a series of papers setting forth case studies, proposals, and advice concerning law enforcement on campus.

5. U.S. District Court, Western District of Missouri *(en banc)*, *General Order on Judicial Standards of Procedure and Substance in Review of Student Discipline in Tax-Supported Institutions of Higher Education*, 45 *Federal Rules Decisions* 133 (1968), provides a set of guidelines promulgated for the guidance of that court in deciding students' rights cases. The guidelines are similarly useful to administrators and counsel seeking to comply with federal legal requirements.

Chapter V

✂✂✂✂✂✂✂✂✂✂✂✂✂✂✂✂✂✂✂✂✂✂

The College
and the Community

Sec. 5.1. General Principles

Postsecondary institutions are typically subject to the regulatory authority of one or more local government entities, such as a city, village, town, or county government. Sometimes this authority is relatively noncontroversial, as in the case of some fire and safety codes. In other situations, the regulation may be highly controversial, as when Cambridge, Massachusetts, attempted in 1976–77 to regulate genetic experimentation on the Harvard and MIT campuses. When dealing with these issues, postsecondary administrators should be aware of the extent of, and limits on, each local government's regulatory authority.

A local government has only that authority which the state has delegated to it by state law. When a local government has been delegated "home rule" powers, its authority will usually be broadly interpreted; otherwise, its authority will usually be narrowly construed. Even where a local body has general authority, it cannot exercise that authority in a way that conflicts with state law, which generally prevails over local law in case of conflict.[1] Nor can a local government regulate matters which the state otherwise has "preempted" by its own extensive regulation of the field or matters which are considered protected by the state's sovereign immunity. Nor, of course, can local governments regulate in a way which violates the federal Constitution.

Both public and private institutions will be bound by local government regulations which are interpreted to apply to them and which satisfy the foregoing principles concerning authority. Public institutions, however, are more likely than private institutions to escape the local regulatory net. Although the preemption doctrine applies to both public and private institutions, public institutions are more heavily regulated by the states (see Section 6.2) and thus more likely in particular cases to have preemption defenses. Public institutions may also defend against local regulation by asserting sovereign immunity, a defense not available to private institutions.

The preemption doctrine governs situations in which state and local regulatory activities overlap. If a local government ordinance regulates the same kind of activity as a state law, the institution may only be bound by the state law. Courts will resolve any apparent overlapping of state law and local ordinances by a case-by-case determination whether state law has preempted the field and precluded local regulation. In *Hall* v. *City of Taft*, 47 Cal.2d 177, 302 P.2d 574 (1956), the court held that detailed state regulation of public school construction preempted the field, so that public schools built in the municipality did not have to conform with local building codes. But in *Port Arthur Independent School District* v. *City of Groves*, 376 S.W.2d 330 (Tex. 1974), the court held that local public school buildings were subject to

[1]Occasionally state laws may be held invalid because they regulate matters of "purely local concern" which the state constitution reserves to local "home rule" governments or because they constitute "local" or "special" legislation prohibited by the state constitution. In such a case, there is no conflict, and local law may prevail.

municipal building codes, in the absence of explicit state regulation of construction standards, because "[t]o hold otherwise would be to leave a hiatus in regulation necessary to the health and safety of the community."

A rather unusual case concerning colleges and universities illustrates the application of these principles. *Board of Trustees* v. *City of Los Angeles*, 49 Cal.App.3d 45, 122 Cal. Rptr. 361 (1975), arose after a state university leased one of its facilities to a circus and claimed that the municipal ordinance regulating circus operations was preempted by a state statute authorizing the board of regents to promulgate rules for the governance of state colleges. In upholding the ordinance, the court found as follows:

> The general statutory grant of authority (Ed Code, secs. 23604, 23604.1, 23751) to promulgate regulations for the governing of the state colleges and the general regulations promulgated pursuant to that authority (Cal. Admin. Code, tit. 5, secs. 4000 *et seq.*) contain no comprehensive state scheme for regulating the conduct of circuses or similar exhibitions with specific references to the safety, health, and sanitary problems attendant on such activities. Nor can the board point to any attempt by it to control the activities of its lessees for the purpose of protecting the public, the animals, or the neighboring community.
>
> In the absence of the enforcement of the city's ordinance there would be a void in regulating circuses and similar exhibitions when those activities were conducted on university property, thereby creating a status for tenants of the university which would be preferential to tenants of other landowners. This preferential status, under the circumstances, serves no governmental purpose. The subject matter of Los Angeles Municipal Code section 53.50 has not been preempted by the state [122 Cal. Rptr. at 365].

The sovereign immunity doctrine holds that state institutions, as arms of state government, cannot be regulated by a lesser governmental authority which has only those powers delegated to it by the state. In order to claim sovereign immunity, the public institution must be performing state "governmental" functions, not acting in a merely "proprietary" capacity. In *Board of Trustees*

v. *City of Los Angeles,* above, the court rejected the board's
sovereign immunity defense by using this distinction:

> In the case at bar the board leases . . . [its facilities]
> as a revenue-producing activity. The activities which are
> conducted thereon by private operators have no relation to
> the governmental function of the university. "[T]he state is
> acting in a proprietary capacity when it enters into
> activities . . . to amuse and entertain the public. The
> activities of [the board] do not differ from those of private
> enterprise in the entertainment industry." The doctrine of
> sovereign immunity cannot shield the university from local
> regulation in this case. Even less defensible is the univer-
> sity's attempt here to extend its immunity to private
> entrepreneurs who are involved in the local commercial
> market where their competitors are subject to local
> regulation. By the terms of the lease the university
> specifically disavowed any governmental status for its lessee
> [122 Cal. Rptr. at 364].

In contrast, a sovereign immunity defense was successful in
Board of Regents of Universities v. *City of Tempe,* 88 Ariz. 299, 356
P.2d 399 (1960). The board sought an injunction to prohibit
the city from applying its local construction codes to the board. In
granting the board's request, the court reasoned:

> The essential point is that the powers, duties, and
> responsibilities assigned and delegated to a state agency
> performing a governmental function must be exercised free
> of control or supervision by a municipality within whose
> corporate limits the state agency must act. The ultimate
> responsibility for higher education is reposed by our
> Constitution in the State. The legislature has empowered
> the Board of Regents to fulfill that responsibility subject
> only to the supervision of the legislature and the governor.
> It is inconsistent with this manifest Constitutional and
> legislative purpose to permit a municipality to exercise its
> own control over the Board's performance of these func-
> tions. A central, unified agency, responsible to State officials
> rather than to the officials of each municipality in which a
> university or college is located, is essential to the efficient
> and orderly administration of a system of higher education

responsive to the needs of all the people of the State [356 P.2d at 406–07].

Sec. 5.2. Zoning and Land Use Regulation

5.2.1. *Overview.* The zoning and other land use regulations of local governments can influence the operation of postsecondary institutions in many ways.[2] Where the institution is located, the size of its campus, the institution's ability to expand its facilities, the density and character of its building, the traffic and parking patterns of its campus can all be affected by zoning laws. Although zoning problems are not the typical daily fare of administrators, when problems do arise they can be critical to the institution's future development. Building programs, the expansion of the campus area, the development of branch campuses or additional facilities in other locations (see especially the *New York Institute of Technology* case in Section 5.2.4), program changes that affect the size and character of the student body or the times during which the campus is heavily used (see especially the *Marjorie Webster Junior College* case in Section 5.2.4)—all can be limited, even prevented, by local zoning laws. Thus, administrators should be careful not to underestimate the formidable challenge that zoning laws can present in such circumstances. Since successful maneuvering through zoning laws involves many legal strategy choices and technical considerations, administrators should involve counsel at the beginning of any zoning problem.

Local governments that have the authority to zone typically do so by enacting zoning ordinances that are administered by a local zoning board. Ordinances may altogether exclude educational uses of property from certain zones (called exclusionary zoning). Where educational uses are permitted, the ordinances may impose general regulations—such as architectural and aesthetic standards, set-back requirements, and height and bulk controls—which limit the way educational property may be used (called regulatory

[2]The relevant cases and authorities are collected in Annot., "Zoning Regulations As Applied to Colleges, Universities, or Similar Institutions for Higher Education," 64 A.L.R.3d 1138 (1975 and periodic supp.).

zoning). Public postsecondary institutions are more protected from zoning, just as they are from other types of local regulation, than are private institutions because public institutions often have sovereign immunity.

5.2.2. *Sovereign immunity of public institutions.* The courts have employed three tests to determine whether a unit of government, such as a state university, is subject to another government's local zoning law. As summarized in *City of Temple Terrace* v. *Hillsborough Association,* 322 So.2d 571 (Fla. App. 1975), these tests are (1) the superior sovereign test, (2) the governmental/proprietary distinction, and (3) the balancing test. The court's opinion summarizes the case law on the first two tests:

> One approach utilized by a number of courts is to rule in favor of the superior sovereign. Thus, where immunity from a local zoning ordinance is claimed by an agency occupying a superior position in the governmental hierarchy, it is presumed that immunity was intended in the absence of express statutory language to the contrary. . . . A second test frequently employed is to determine whether the institutional use proposed for the land is "governmental" or "proprietary" in nature. If the political unit is found to be performing a governmental function, it is immune from the conflicting zoning ordinance. . . . On the other hand, when the use is considered proprietary, the zoning ordinance prevails. . . . Where the power of eminent domain has been granted to the governmental unit seeking immunity from local zoning, some courts have concluded that this conclusively demonstrates the unit's superiority where its proposed use conflicts with zoning regulations. . . . Other cases are controlled by explicit statutory provisions dealing with the question of whether the operation of a particular governmental unit is subject to local zoning. . . .
>
> When the governmental unit which seeks to circumvent a zoning ordinance is an arm of the state, the application of any of the foregoing tests has generally resulted in a judgment permitting the proposed use. This has accounted for statements of horn-book law to the effect that a state agency authorized to carry out a function of the state is not bound by local zoning regulations [322 So.2d at 576; citations omitted].

In applying these tests to postsecondary education, the court in *City of Newark* v. *University of Delaware*, 304 A.2d 347 (Del. Ch. 1973), used a traditional sovereign immunity analysis combining tests (1) and (2): "[I]t has generally been held that a state agency is immune from local zoning ordinances. . . . The University of Delaware is an agency of the State of Delaware. . . . Its function is governmental. . . . It has the power of eminent domain. . . . Traditionally these characteristics and/or power have been cited as establishing immunity" (304 A.2d at 348).

Rutgers, State University v. *Piluso*, 60 N.J. 142, 286 A.2d 697 (1972), is the leading case on the third and newest test of balancing. A balancing approach weighs the state's interest in providing immunity for the institution against the local interest in land use regulation. In determining the strength of the state's interest, the *Rutgers* court analyzed the implied legislative intent to confer immunity on the university.

> The rationale which runs through our cases and which we are convinced should furnish the true test of immunity in the first instance, albeit a somewhat nebulous one, is the legislative intent in this regard with respect to the particular agency or function involved. That intent, rarely specifically expressed, is to be divined from a consideration of many factors, with a value judgment reached on an overall evaluation. All possible factors cannot be abstractly catalogued. The most obvious and common ones include the nature and scope of the instrumentality seeking immunity, the kind of function or land use involved, the extent of the public interest to be served thereby, the effect local land use regulation would have upon the enterprise concerned and the impact upon legitimate local interests. . . . In some instances one factor will be more influential than another or may be so significant as to completely overshadow all others. No one, such as the granting or withholding of the power of eminent domain, is to be thought of as ritualistically required or controlling. And there will undoubtedly be cases, as there have been in the past, where the broader public interest is so important that immunity must be granted even though the local interests may be great. The point is that there is no precise formula or set of criteria

which will determine every case mechanically and automatically [286 A.2d at 702–03].

On the facts of the *Rutgers* case, the court decided that the legislative intent was to immunize the university from local zoning laws:

> With regard to a state university . . . there can be little doubt that, as an instrumentality of the state performing an essential governmental function for the benefit of all the people of the state, the Legislature would not intend that its growth and development should be subject to restriction or control by local land use regulation. Indeed, such will generally be true in the case of all state functions and agencies [286 A.2d at 703].

The court emphasized, however, that immunity is not absolute and may be conditioned by local needs:

> Even where . . . [immunity] is found to exist, it must not . . . be exercised in an unreasonable fashion so as to arbitrarily override all important legitimate local interests. This rule must apply to the state and its instrumentalities as well as to lesser governmental entities entitled to immunity. For example, it would be arbitrary, if the state proposed to erect an office building in the crowded business district of a city where provision for off-street parking was required, for the state not to make some reasonable provision in that respect. And, at the very least, even if the proposed action of the immune governmental instrumentality does not reach the unreasonable stage for any sufficient reason, the instrumentality ought to consult with the local authorities and sympathetically listen and give every consideration to local objections, problems, and suggestions in order to minimize the conflict as much as possible [286 A.2d at 703].

The court then held that, under the facts of the case, the local interests did not outweigh the university's claim of immunity:

> As far as Rutgers' proposal here, to erect the student family housing on the Kilmer tract, is concerned, we fail to

see the slightest vestige of unreasonableness as far as
Piscataway's local interests are concerned or in any other
respect. (The university did present the proposal to the local
authorities by its variance application.) The possible
additional local cost of educating children living in the
housing is clearly not a legitimate local interest from any
proper land use impact point of view [286 A.2d at 703].

State institutions may be in a stronger position to successfully assert sovereign immunity than are community colleges
sponsored by local governments. In confrontations with a local
zoning board, a state institution is clearly the superior sovereign,
whereas an institution of another local government may not be.
Moreover, the legislature's intent regarding immunity may be
clearer for state institutions than for local ones. For an example of
a case where a community college was subjected to local zoning
laws, see *Appeal of Community College of Delaware County*, 435
Pa. 264, 254 A.2d 641 (1969).

5.2.3. *Private institutions and zoning regulations.* In seeking
redress against a local government's zoning regulations, private
postsecondary institutions may challenge the zoning board's
interpretation and application of the zoning ordinance or may
argue that the ordinance conflicts with the federal Constitution or
some state law limitation on the local government's zoning
authority. Where those arguments are unavailing, the institution
may seek an exception (Section 5.2.4), a variance (Section 5.2.5), or
an amendment to the zoning ordinance (Section 5.2.6).

A leading case dealing with the constitutional argument is
Nectow v. *Cambridge*, 277 U.S. 183 (1928), where the Court stated
that "[t]he governmental power to interfere by zoning regulations
with the general rights of the land owner by restricting the
character of his use is not unlimited, and other questions aside,
such restriction cannot be imposed if it does not bear a substantial
relation to the public health, safety, morals, or general welfare"
(277 U.S. at 188). Despite this precedent, however, constitutional
challenges of zoning laws seldom succeed. One major success is
Prentiss v. *American University*, 94 App. D.C. 204, 214 F.2d 282
(1954), where a U.S. Court of Appeals overturned a rezoning action
of the local zoning board because it did not bear a substantial

relation to the public welfare and therefore constituted an unconstitutional taking of property without due process.

In several cases educational institutions have challenged zoning ordinances which exclude educational uses of land in residential zones. In *Yanow* v. *Seven Oaks Park*, 11 N.J. 341, 94 A.2d 482 (1953), a postsecondary religious training school challenged the reasonableness of an ordinance which excluded schools of higher or special education from residential zones where elementary and secondary schools were permitted. The court, determining that the former schools could be "reasonably placed in a separate classification" from the latter, upheld the exclusion. But in *Long Island University* v. *Tappan*, 202 Misc. 956, 113 N.Y.S.2d 795, affirmed 305 N.Y. 893, 114 N.E.2d 432 (1952), the institution won its battle against an exclusionary ordinance. After the university had obtained a certificate of occupancy from the local township, a nearby village annexed the tract of land where the university was located. The village then passed a zoning ordinance which would have prohibited the operation of the university. The court concluded that "[i]nsofar as the Zoning Ordinance seeks to prohibit entirely the use of plaintiff's lands in the village for the purposes for which it is chartered, the Zoning Ordinance is void and ineffectual, as beyond the power of the Village Board to enact and as bearing no reasonable relation to the promotion of the health, safety, morals, or general welfare of the community" (113 N.Y.S.2d at 799).

Even when the zoning ordinance permits all or particular kinds of educational institutions to operate in a residential or other zone, the zoning board may not consider all the institution's uses of its land and buildings to be educational use.[3] The distinction is much the same as that drawn in local taxation law (see Section 5.3), where the tax status of an educational institution's property depends not only on the character of the institution but also

[3]The relevant cases and authorities are collected in Annot., "What Constitutes 'School,' 'Educational Use,' or the Like Within Zoning Ordinance," 64 A.L.R.3d 1087 (1975 and periodic supp.); and in Annot., "Zoning Regulations as Applied to Colleges, Universities, or Similar Institutions for Higher Education," 64 A.L.R.3d 1138, secs. 9–11 (1975 and periodic supp.).

on whether the particular property is being used for educational purposes. When there are no specific definitions or restrictions in the ordinance itself, courts tend to broadly interpret "educational use" and similar phrases to permit a wide range of uses. In *Scheuller* v. *Board of Adjustment,* 95 N.W.2d 731 (Iowa 1959), the court held that a seminary's dormitory building was an educational use under an ordinance that permitted educational uses but did not permit apartment houses or multiple dwellings. And in *Property Owners Association* v. *Board of Zoning Appeals,* 123 N.Y.S.2d 716 (Sup. Ct. 1953), the court held that seating to be constructed adjacent to a college's athletic field was an educational use.

Where a zoning ordinance prohibits or narrowly restricts educational uses in a particular zone, an educational institution may be able to argue that its proposed use is a permissible noneducational use under some other part of the ordinance. In *Application of LaPorte,* 2 App.Div.2d 710, 152 N.Y.S.2d 916, affirmed 2 N.Y.2d 921, 161 N.Y.S.2d 886, 141 N.E.2d 917 (1956), a college was allowed to construct a residence to accommodate more than sixty students because the residence came within the ordinance's authorization of single-family dwelling units:

> The city's legislative body has the right to define the term "family." It has done so, placing no limitation on the number of persons constituting a family, nor does it require that the members thereof be related by blood or marriage. We may not impose any restrictions not contained in the ordinance. The petition does not allege, nor does the record disclose, facts from which it can be determined that the proposed building does not constitute a single dwelling unit, or that the members of the order will occupy the dwelling unit other than as a "single, nonprofit housekeeping unit," with the purview of the ordinance [152 N.Y.S.2d at 918].

Fraternity houses may be excluded from residential districts or may be a permissible educational or noneducational use, depending on the terms of the ordinance and the facts of the case.[4]

[4]The relevant cases and authorities are collected in Annot., "Application of Zoning Regulations to College Fraternities and Sororities," 25 A.L.R.3d 921 (1969 and periodic supp.).

In *City of Baltimore* v. *Poe*, 224 Md. 428, 168 A.2d 193 (1961), a fraternity was permitted in a zone which excluded any "club, the chief activity of which is a service customarily carried on as a business." The court found that "the chief activities carried on at this fraternity house . . . have clearly been established to be social and educational functions for the benefit of the whole membership." But in *Theta Kappa, Inc.* v. *City of Terre Haute*, 226 N.E.2d 903 (Ind. 1967), the court found that a fraternity did not come within the term "dwelling" as defined by the zoning ordinance and was therefore not a permissible use in the residential district in which it was located.

Other problems concerning zoning ordinances arise not because the ordinances exclude a particular use of property but because they regulate the way in which permitted uses are effected. The validity of such "regulatory zoning" also often depends on the interpretation and application of the ordinance and its consistency with state law.

In *Sisters of Holy Cross* v. *Brookline*, 347 Mass. 486, 198 N.E.2d 624 (1969), a local zoning authority attempted to apply construction requirements for single-family homes to the facilities of a private college. A state statute provided that "no ordinance or bylaw which prohibits or limits the use of land for any church or other religious purpose or for any educational purpose . . . shall be valid." The court rejected the town's claim that the statute did not cover ordinances regulating the dimensions of buildings: "We think that this bylaw, as applied to Holy Cross, 'limits the use' of its land and, therefore, we think such application invalid."

The same state statute was involved in *Radcliffe College* v. *City of Cambridge*, 350 Mass. 613, 215 N.E.2d 892 (1966). A Cambridge zoning ordinance required the college to provide off-street parking for newly constructed facilities. This time the court held that the ordinance did not conflict with the state statute:

> Providing for the parking or housing of the automobiles of students, instructors, and employees of an educational institution is within the broad scope of the educational powers of the institution, just as is providing for the feeding and housing of such personnel. These are secondary functions incidental to the main educational

purpose. Hence, a regulation that requires that some
of the college land be used for parking does not lessen
the availability of all or any of the institution's land
for some appropriate educational purpose. We think
the statute does not bar such regulation. Plainly the
statute does not do so in express terms. At most the
Cambridge ordinance requires choices among the proper educational purposes of the institution. In so doing
it does not impede the reasonable use of the college's land
for its educational purposes. We rule, therefore, that it does
not limit "the use of [its] land for any . . . educational
purpose" within the meaning of . . . [the statute] [215
N.E.2d at 895–96].

5.2.4. Special exceptions. Particular educational or noneducational uses may be permitted as "conditional uses" in an
otherwise restricted zone. In this situation, the institution must
apply for a special exception, "a special use which is considered by
the local legislative body to be essential or desirable for the welfare
of the community and its citizenry and not essentially incompatible
with basic uses in the zone involved, but not at every or any
location therein or without restrictions or conditions being
imposed on such use" (*Piscatelli* v. *Township of Scotch Plains*, 103
N.J. Super. 589, 248 A.2d 274, 277 (1968)). An educational
institution may seek a special exception by demonstrating that it
satisfies the conditions which the zoning board imposes. If it
cannot do so, it may challenge the conditions as being unreasonable or beyond the zoning board's authority under the ordinance or
state law.

The plaintiff in *Marjorie Webster Junior College* v. *District
of Columbia Board of Zoning Adjustment*, 309 A.2d 314 (D.C.
1973), had operated a girls' finishing school in a residential zone
under a special exception granted by the zoning board. The
discretion of the zoning board was limited by a regulation which
specified that exceptions would be granted only where "in the
judgment of the board such special exceptions will be in harmony
with the general purpose and intent of the zoning regulations and
maps and will not tend to affect adversely the use of neighboring
property in accordance with said zoning regulations and maps."
Another regulation specifically authorized exceptions for colleges

and universities, but only if "such use is so located that it is not likely to become objectionable to neighboring property because of noise, traffic, number of students, or other objectionable conditions." The college was sold to new owners who instituted new programs (mostly short-term continuing education programs) which altered the curriculum of the school and attracted a new clientele to the campus. After a citizens' group complained that this new use was outside the scope of the college's special exception, the college filed an amendment to the campus plan which constituted the basis for its special exception. The zoning board rejected the amendment after extensive hearings, concluding that, under the applicable regulations, the new use of the college property would not be in harmony with the general purpose and intent of the zone and would adversely affect neighboring property by attracting large numbers of transient men and women to the campus and increasing vehicular traffic in the neighborhood. On appeal by the college, the court held that the zoning regulations contained adequate standards to control the board's discretion and that the board's decision was supported by sufficient evidence.

New York Institute of Technology v. *LeBoutillier*, 33 N.Y.2d 125, 350 N.Y.S.2d 263, 305 N.E.2d 754 (1973), took up a similar issue. A private college had entered an agreement with the local government regarding the use of the college's existing property. Subsequent to the agreement, the college acquired property not contiguous with the main campus, in a residential zone which permitted educational use by special exception. The college's application for a special exception was denied by the zoning board, and the court upheld the board's decision in an interesting opinion combining fact, policy, and law:

> Several factors persuade us that there should be an affirmance in this case. To begin with, the institute seeks to expand an existing educational use without a demonstrable need to expand. Need, of course, is not a criterion for granting a special exception permit. But a reading of the cases dealing with the expansion of existing educational or religious uses clearly indicates that need was apparent. . . .
>
> The institute already owns in excess of four hundred acres in Old Westbury. To date it has built on only about 1 percent of its land, whereas, pursuant to the 1965 agreement, it is permitted to build on up to 10 percent.

Moreover, its master plan contemplates building on only about 8 percent of its acreage, again less than the allowable percentage. Then, too, student enrollment is only about three thousand, whereas the permissible enrollment under the agreement is seventy-five hundred. Need to expand, it seems, is highly questionable.

The institute contends, however, that it is more feasible economically to purchase the Holloway estate and to renovate the existing structures for its teacher education program than to undertake new construction at its main campus. It also contends that certain aspects of the planned teacher education program make separation from the main campus desirable. There is force to the argument that these judgments should be made by college administrators, not zoning boards of appeal or courts. But at some point, probably not definable with precision, a college's desire to expand, here by the path of least economic resistance, should yield to the legitimate interests of village residents. The village has, in the past, acceded to the incorporation of after-acquired properties into the site plan for the campus. But the right to expand is not absolute. . . .

Here, the 1965 agreement becomes relevant. That agreement, although not expressly applicable to after-acquired property, governs the relationship between the institute and the village. By its adoption it became part of the village's comprehensive plan. Approval of this application would constitute a substantial departure from that agreement. The property is not contiguous with the existing campus. It is located in the center of the village in a single-family residential district with two-acre minimum building lots, one-half mile straight-line distance from the main campus, and about four miles over interior village roads. Approval of the institute's application would negate village planning objectives of keeping college uses on the perimeter of the village in an area buffered by golf courses, thereby minimizing the impact on area residents. Approval would also negate the planning objective of routing traffic to and from the colleges over perimeter county roads, rather than interior village routes. There is ample evidence that a traffic problem already exists on Wheatley Road, which the planning board found would be aggravated by students commuting between the main campus and the proposed one at the Holloway estate.

Finally, it should be quite evident that Old Westbury, containing parts of four college campuses occupying substantial acreage in the village, is not pursuing a policy of exclusion or insularism. On the contrary, it has attempted to accommodate these uses to the essentially residential character of the community by placing reasonable restrictions upon them. Moreover, it has, in the past, approved incorporation of contiguous properties into the institute's campus. However, having approved expansion of the institute on previous applications does not require the board to grant the institute's present request to expand its existing educational use irrespective of the effect it may have on the overall character of the community [305 N.E.2d at 758–59].

5.2.5. Variances. If a proposed use by an educational institution conforms neither to the general standards of the zone nor to the terms of a special exception, the institution may seek a variance. "A variance is an exercise of the power of the governmental authority to grant relief, in a proper case, from the liberal application of the terms of an ordinance. It is to be used where strict application of the ordinance would cause unnecessary and substantial hardship to the property holder peculiar to the property in question, without serving a warranted and corresponding benefit to the public interest" (*Arcadia Development Corp.* v. *Bloomington,* 267 Minn. 211, 125 N.W.2d 846, 851 (1964)).

Zoning boards may grant variances only in these narrow circumstances and only on the basis of standards created by state or local law. Variances which constitute substantial changes in the zoning plan or alter the boundaries of established zones may be considered in excess of the zoning board's authority. The defendant in *Ranney* v. *Institute Pontificio Delle Maestre Filippini,* 20 N.J. 189, 119 A.2d 142 (1955), a private educational institution, had applied for a variance to expand its existing facilities located in a restrictive residential zone. The zoning board granted the variance, but the Supreme Court of New Jersey reversed in an opinion taking a restrictive stance on the grant of a variance:

> The record does not support the finding that the variance may be granted "without substantial detriment to the public good" which "will not substantially impair the intent and purpose of the zone plan and zoning ordinance," N.J.S.A. 40:55-39(d), despite the recitation to that effect in

the resolutions of the township bodies. The existing use and structure cannot justify an enlargement in the face of a zoning plan which has prescribed and fostered the overwhelmingly residential character of the area in which Villa Walsh is located. . . . A variance here would be directly antagonistic to the design and purpose of the ordinance and sound zoning. The "disintegrating process would be set in motion," *Beirn* v. *Morris* . . . [14 N.J. 529, 103 A.2d 365]. "The zoning act does not contemplate variations which would frustrate the general regulations and impair the overall scheme which is set up for the general welfare of the several districts and the entire community," *Dolan* v. *DeCapua*, 16 N.J. 599, 611, 109 A.2d 615, 621 (1954) [119 A.2d at 147].

5.2.6. Amendment of zoning ordinances. If an educational institution's proposed use is prohibited within a zone, and the institution cannot obtain an exception or variance, it may petition the local government to amend the zoning ordinance. Unlike an exception or variance, an amendment is designed to correct an intrinsic flaw in the zoning ordinance rather than to relieve individual hardship imposed by zoning requirements. An institution seeking an amendment should be prepared to demonstrate that the proposed change is in the public interest rather than just for its own private advantage.

Jurisdictions vary in the presumptions and standards applied to zoning amendments. Some jurisdictions give amendments a presumption of reasonableness. Others presume that the original ordinance was reasonable and require that any amendment be justified. Many jurisdictions require that an amendment conform to the comprehensive zoning plan. "Spot zoning," which reclassifies a small segment of land, is frequently overturned for nonconformance with a comprehensive plan.

Bidwell v. *Zoning Board of Adjustment*, 4 Pa. Cmwlth. 327, 286 A.2d 471 (1972), illustrates many of the important legal considerations regarding zoning amendments. An amendment reclassified a tract of land from single-family to multi-family residential and granted an exception to a college to allow the construction of a library, a lecture hall, and off-street parking. The court upheld the amendment:

From the very nature of the proposed use as a library
and lecture hall, it is not unreasonable to conclude that
commercial activity will not intensify. Nor is there evidence
that danger to residents will be significantly increased.
Excessive congestion is also not a factor since off-street
parking is to be provided. The ordinance in question here
merely extended a preexisting zone in accordance with the
legislative judgment. . . .

Appellants have not borne their burden of proving
that the amendments in question were not in accordance
with a comprehensive plan. . . . Public hearings regarding
the proposed changes were held and the well-contemplated
decision of the legislative body was to amend the zoning
ordinance. Considering the presumption afforded this
judgment, and taking into account the tenor of the general
area, we are of the opinion that this legislation reflects and
implements the "totality of a municipality's program of
land utilization, considering both the land resources
available and the needs and desires of the community" [286
A.2d at 473, 474].

5.2.7. *Rights of other property owners.* In considering
various approaches to zoning problems, administrators should be
aware that other property owners may challenge zoning decisions
favorable to the institution or may intervene in disputes between
the institution and the zoning board. The procedures of the zoning
board may require notice to local property owners and an
opportunity for a hearing before certain zoning decisions are made.
Thus zoning problems may require administrators to "do battle"
with the local community in a very real and direct way.

A landowner usually can challenge a zoning decision if she
has suffered some special loss different from that suffered by the
public generally. Adjacent landowners almost always are considered to have suffered such loss and thus to have "standing" (that is,
a legal capacity) to challenge zoning decisions regarding the
adjacent land. Property owners' associations may or may not have
standing based on their special loss or that of their members,
depending on the jurisdiction. In *Pierce Junior College* v.
Schumaker, 333 A.2d 510, neighboring landowners were denied
permission to intervene in a local college's appeal of a zoning
decision because they were not the owners or tenants of the

property directly involved. But in *Citizens Association of George-town* v. *District of Columbia Board of Zoning Adjustment*, 365 A.2d 372 (D.C. 1976), a citizens' association from the neighboring area was successful in challenging and overturning, on procedural grounds, a special exception granted to Georgetown University.

Sec. 5.3. Local Government Taxation

5.3.1. General tax concepts. Local government taxation is one of the most traditional problems in postsecondary education law. Although the basic concepts are more settled here than they are in many areas, these concepts often prove difficult to apply in particular cases. Moreover, in an era of tight budgets, where local governments seek new revenue sources and postsecondary institutions attempt to minimize expenditures, the sensitivity of local tax questions is increasing.

The real property tax is the most common tax which local governments impose on educational institutions. Sales taxes and admissions taxes are also imposed in a number of jurisdictions. A local government's authority to tax is usually grounded in state enabling legislation which delegates various types of taxing power to various types of local governments. Most local tax questions involving postsecondary institutions concern the interpretation of this state legislation, particularly its exemption provisions. A local government must implement its taxing power by local ordinance, and questions may also arise concerning the interpretation of these ordinances.

A public institution's defenses against local taxation may differ from those of a private institution. State property is exempt from taxation in most states by constitutional provision or statute; in these states public institutions are shielded from local real property taxation to the extent their property is that of the state. Public institutions may also make sovereign immunity claims (see Section 5.1) against local government attempts to impose taxes or tax collection responsibilities on them. Private institutions, on the other hand, depend on state constitutional or statutory exemptions which limit the local government's authority to tax. Although the provisions vary, most tax codes contain some form of tax exemption for religious, charitable, and educational organizations. These exemptions are usually "strictly construed to the end that such concessions will be neither enlarged nor extended beyond the plain meaning of the language employed" (*Cedars of Lebanon Hospital* v. *Los Angeles County*, 35 Cal.2d 729, 221 P.2d 31, 34 (1950)). The party requesting the exemption has the burden of proving that the particular activity for which it seeks exemption is covered by the exemption provision. The strictness with which exemptions are construed depends on the state and the type of exemption involved.

   5.3.2. Property taxes. In order for state property, including that of state educational institutions, to be exempt from local taxation, the property must be used for public purposes. The use of the property itself, rather than the income derived from the property, is the critical issue. Since the exemption of state property from taxation may create an economic hardship for the local community, the state sometimes makes payments in lieu of taxes to compensate the local government.

   Most tax codes exempt private nonprofit educational institutions from property taxation. The general standard is that the institution must be organized for an educational purpose and the property in question must be used for that purpose. Jurisdictions vary in the tests applied to implement this standard. Some require that the property be used "exclusively" for educational purposes in order to qualify for any exemption. Others require only that the property be used "primarily" for educational purposes.

   A series of cases on the exemption of houses which educational institutions provide for their presidents illustrates the different results obtained under different standards of "use" and different facts. In *Appeal of University of Pittsburgh*, 407 Pa. 416, 180 A.2d 760 (1962), the court allowed an exemption under a lenient standard of use:

> The head of such an institution, whether he be called president or chancellor, represents to the public eye the "image" of the institution. Both an educator and an administrator of the tremendous "business" which any university or college now is, he must also be the official

representative to host those who, for one reason or the other, find the university or college a place of interest and, if he is to assume the full scope and responsibility of his duties to the university or college, he must be universal in his contacts. Many years ago the Supreme Court of Massachusetts in *Amherst College* v. *Assessors*, 193 Mass. 168, 169, 170, 79 N.E. 248 stated: "At the same time the usage and customs of the college impose upon the president certain social obligations. . . . The scope, observations, and usage of the character mentioned are not matters of express requirement or exaction. They are, however, required of a president in the use of the house, and noncompliance with them unquestionably would subject him to unfavorable comment from the trustees and others, or, at least, be regarded as a failure on his part to discharge the obligations and hospitality associated with his official position." . . . The residence of the head of a university or college necessarily renders a real function, tangibly and intangibly, in the life of the institution. While its utility to the purposes and objectives of the institution is incapable of *exact* measurement and evaluation, it is nonetheless real and valuable [180 A.2d at 763].

A subsequent case, citing the *Pittsburgh* case, denied an exemption for a president emeritus' house using the same lenient test. The court made a finding of fact that the house was not actually used for institutional purposes:

University of Pittsburgh Tax Exemption Case, 407 Pa. 416, 180 A.2d 760 (1962), held that a president's or chancellor's residence could enjoy tax exemption, where the record showed that the majority of the events for which the residence was utilized bore a direct relationship to the proper functioning of the University of Pittsburgh and served its aims and objectives. In this appeal the record does not support the test laid down in the *University of Pittsburgh Tax Exemption Case*. This record reflects that the president emeritus is retained on a consultative basis in development and public relations. The residence provided the president emeritus by the trustees appears to properly afford him an appropriate dwelling house commensurate with his past worthy service to Albright College. The record does not support, as in the case of the chancellor's residence

of the University of Pittsburgh, that the residence in fact
was used for the general purposes of Albright College [*In
Re Albright College,* 213 Pa. Super. 479, 249 A.2d at 835
(1968)].

In *Cook County Collector* v. *National College of Education,*
41 Ill. App. 633, 354 N.E.2d 507 (1976), the institution introduced
extensive evidence of the institutional use of the president's house.
The vice-president for business affairs testified that the house,
"although used as the residence of the president, . . . is used as well
for a number of educational, fund raising, business, alumni and
social activities of the College," citing many examples. The
exemption was denied, however, because the evidence did not
satisfy the more stringent "primary use" test applied in that
jurisdiction:

> On cross-examination . . . [the vice-president] stated
> that classes are not held in the home; that access to the
> home is by invitation only; and that the primary use of the
> premises is to house the president and his family.
>   The trial court found that the property was not
> exempt, stating that it is used primarily for residential
> purposes as an accommodation for the president and only
> incidentally for college-related purposes [354 N.E.2d at 508].

Cases dealing with faculty and staff housing illustrate a
similar split of opinions, depending on the facts of the case and the
test applied. *MacMurray College* v. *Wright,* 38 Ill.2d 272, 230
N.E.2d 846 (1967), is illustrative. The court denied a tax exemption
for faculty and staff housing using a primary use test:

> The colleges have failed to demonstrate clearly that
> the faculty and staff housing was primarily used for
> purposes which were reasonably necessary for the carrying
> out of the schools' educational purposes. The record does
> not show that any of the faculty or staff members of either
> college were required, because of their educational duties, to
> live in these residences or that they were required to or did
> perform any of their professional duties there. Also, though
> both records before us contain general statements that there
> were associations between the concerned faculty and

students outside the classroom, there was no specific proof presented, aside from one isolated example, to show that student, academic, faculty, administrative, or any other type of college-connected activities were ever actually conducted at home by any member of the faculty or staff of either of the colleges [230 N.E.2d at 850].

Student dormitories are usually exempt from property taxation, even if the institution charges students rent. Sorority houses, fraternity houses, and other property used for mixed social and residential purposes may not qualify for an exemption as property used by an educational institution for educational purposes. If the institution itself owns the property, it must prove that the property is used for the educational purposes of the institution. In *Alford* v. *Emory University*, 216 Ga. 391, 116 S.E.2d 596 (1960), the court held that fraternity houses operated by the university as part of its residential program were entitled to a tax exemption:

> Under the evidence in this case, these fraternity buildings were built by the university; they are regulated and supervised by the university; they are located in the heart of the campus, upon property owned by the university, required to be so located and to be occupied only by students of the university; adopted as a part of the dormitory and feeding system of the college, and an integral part of the operation of the college. In our opinion these fraternity houses are buildings erected for and used as a college, and not used for the purpose of making either private or corporate income or profit for the university, and our law says that they shall be exempt from taxes [116 S.E.2d at 601].

In *Cornell University* v. *Board of Assessors*, 24 App. Div. 526, 260 N.Y.S.2d 197 (1965), however, the court focused on the social uses of university-owned fraternity houses to deny an exemption under an "exclusive use" test:

> It is true, of course, that the fraternities perform the essential functions of housing and feeding students, but it is clear that, in each case, the use of the premises is also

devoted, in substantial part, to the social and other personal objectives of a privately organized, self-perpetuating club, controlled by graduate as well as student members. The burden of demonstrating these objectives to be educational purposes was not sustained and thus . . . [the lower court] properly found that the premises were not used "exclusively" for educational purposes, within the intendment of the exemption statute [260 N.Y.S.2d at 199].

If an independently incorporated fraternity or sorority seeks its own property tax exemption, it must demonstrate an educational, religious, or charitable purpose independent of the university and prove that the property is used for that purpose. Greek letter and other social fraternities usually do not qualify for exemptions. In *Kappa Alpha Educational Foundation* v. *Holliday*, 226 A.2d 825 (Del. 1967), the court found that a fraternity house was being held as an investment by the corporation which owned it and therefore did not qualify for exemption. Professional fraternities have been somewhat more successful in establishing the educational purpose and use of their property in order to qualify for exemption. In *City of Memphis* v. *Alpha Beta Welfare Association*, 174 Tenn. 440, 126 S.W.2d 323 (1939), the court of appeals upheld a district court's finding of fact that a medical fraternity's house was used exclusively for educational purposes:

It is shown in proof that the student members of the fraternity by reason of being housed together receive medical, ethical, and cultural instruction that they otherwise would not get. The acquisition of the property in order that the students might be housed together was but the means to the end that the purpose of the Phi Chi Medical Fraternity to promote the welfare of medical students morally and scientifically might be more effectively carried out [126 S.W.2d at 326].

Even if a campus sorority or fraternity does not qualify for an educational exemption, it may qualify under a general statutory exemption for social organizations. In *Gamma Phi Chapter of Sigma Chi Building Fund Corp.* v. *Dade County*, 199 S.2d 717 (Fla. 1967), the court held that the property of a national college fraternity was eligible for a statutory exemption designed for fraternal lodges. The exemption was denied on a technicality, however, because the fraternity, missed the filing date.

Athletic and recreational facilities owned by an educational institution may be exempt if the institution can prove that the facilities are used for educational purposes. Facilities far in excess of the institution's potential use may be subject to judicial scrutiny. In *Trustees of Rutgers University* v. *Piscataway Township*, 134 N.J.L. 85, 46 A.2d 56 (1946), the court held that a stadium with a seating capacity of twenty thousand owned by an institution with a student body of seventeen hundred was not entitled to a property tax exemption.

Dining facilities that are located on the property of an educational institution and whose purpose is to serve the college community rather than to generate a profit have long been recognized as part of the educational program and therefore entitled to a property tax exemption. An early case, *People ex rel. Mt. Pleasant Academy* v. *Mezger*, 98 App. Div. 237, 90 N.Y.S. 488, affirmed, 181 N.Y. 511, 73 N.E. 1130 (1904), held that the dining hall of an academy was exempt under an exclusive use test. A later case, *People ex rel. Goodman* v. *University of Illinois Foundation*, 388 Ill. 363, 58 N.E.2d 33 (1944), upheld an exemption for dining halls (as well as dormitory and recreational facilities) even though the university derived incidental income by charging for the services. Dining facilities may be tax exempt even if the institution contracts with a private caterer to provide food services. In *Blair Academy* v. *Blairstown*, 95 N.J. Super. 583, 232 A.2d 178 (1967), the court held:

> The use of a catering system to feed the students and faculty of this boarding school cannot be regarded as a commercial activity or business venture of the school. Blair pays for this catering service an annual charge of $376 per person. It has been found expedient by the management of the school to have such a private caterer, in lieu of providing its own personnel to furnish this necessary service. The practice has been carried on for at least ten years. Nor do we find material as affecting Blair's nonprofit status that the catering system uses Blair's kitchen equip-

ment and facilities in its performance or that some of the caterer's employees were permitted by the school to occupy quarters at the school, rent-free [232 A.2d at 181–82].

Exemptions of various other kinds of institutional property also depend on the particular use of the property and the particular test applied in the jurisdiction. In *Princeton University Press* v. *Borough of Princeton*, 35 N.J. 209, 172 A.2d 420 (1961), a university press was denied exemption under an "exclusive use" test.

> There is no question that the petitioner has been organized exclusively for the mental and moral improvement of men, women, and children. The Press's publication of outstanding scholarly works, which the trade houses would not be apt to publish because of insufficient financial returns, carries out not only the purposes for which it was organized but also performs a valuable public service. It cannot be likewise concluded, however, that the property is *exclusively used* for the mental and moral improvement of men, women, and children as required by the statute. A substantial portion of the Press's activity consists of printing work taken in for the purpose of offsetting the losses incurred in the publication of scholarly books. Such printing, which includes work done for educational and nonprofit organizations other than Princeton University, is undertaken for the purpose of making a profit. Hence, in this sense the printing takes on the nature of a commercial enterprise and, therefore, it cannot be said that the property is *exclusively used* for the statutory purpose [172 A.2d at 424].

But in *District of Columbia* v. *Catholic Education Press*, 199 F.2d 176 (D.C. Cir. 1952), an exemption was granted.

> [T]he Catholic Education Press does not stand alone. It is a publishing arm of the University. It is an integral part of it. It has no separate life except bare technical corporate existence. It is not a private independent corporation, but to all intents and purposes it is a facility of the University. . . .
> If the Catholic University of America, in its own name, should engage in activities identical with those of its

> subsidiary, the Catholic Education Press, we suppose its
> right to exemption from taxation on the personal property
> used in such activities would not be questioned. We see no
> reason for denying the exemption to the University merely
> because it chooses to do the work through a separate
> nonprofit corporation [199 F.2d at 178–79].

If an otherwise eligible institution leases some of its property, the property may still be exempt from property taxation. Exemption again depends on the use of the property and the exemption test applied in the jurisdiction.[5]

If institutional property is denied an exemption and subjected to property taxation, the institution's administrators must then deal with the problem of valuation. After a property tax assessor makes the initial assessment, the institution may challenge the assessment through procedures established by the local government. The assessment of institutional property may be difficult because of the absence of comparable market values. In *Dartmouth Corp. of Alpha Delta* v. *Town of Hanover*, 332 A.2d 390 (N.H. 1975), an independent fraternity challenged the assessment of its property. The town had compared the fraternity property to dormitory facilities to arrive at an evaluation. The court upheld the assessor's estimate, reasoning that "[i]n view of the functional similarity between fraternities and dormitories and considering that the college regulates the rents of both types of facilities, it was not unlawful for the board to consider the income and costs of the fraternity buildings if used as dormitories in ascertaining their assessed value."

5.3.3. Sales and admission taxes. A local government may impose a sales tax on the sales or purchases of an educational institution. The institution may claim a specific exemption based on a particular provision of the sales tax ordinance or a general exemption provided by a state statute or the state constitution. The language of the provision may limit the exemption only to the sales or the purchases of an educational institution or may cover both. The institution's eligibility for exemption from these taxes,

[5]Cases dealing with leased property are collected in Annot., "Tax Exemption—Leased Property," 55 A.L.R.3d 430 (1974 and periodic supp.).

as from property taxes, depends on the language of the provision creating the exemption, as interpreted by the courts, and the particular factual circumstances.

New York University v. *Taylor,* 251 App. Div. 444, 296 N.Y.S. 848 (1937), arose after the Comptroller of the City of New York tried to impose a sales tax on both the sales and purchases of a nonprofit educational institution. The law in effect at that time provided that "receipts from sales or services . . . by or to semi-public institutions . . . shall not be subject to tax hereunder." Semi-public institutions were defined as "those charitable and religious institutions which are supported wholly or in part by public subscriptions or endowment and are not organized or operated for profit." The court made a finding of fact that the university was a "semi-public institution" within the meaning of the statute and therefore was not subject to taxation on its sales or purchases.

Sales by an educational institution may be exempt even if some of the institution's activities generate a profit. The exemption will depend on the use of the profits and the language of the exemption. In *YMCA* v. *City of Philadelphia,* 139 Pa. Super. 332, 11 A.2d 529 (1940), the court held that the sale was not subject to taxation under an ordinance that exempted sales by or to semi-public institutions:

> [C]ertainly, the ordinance contemplated a departure by such institutions from the activities of a public charity, which, in its narrowest sense, sells nothing and is supported wholly by public subscriptions and contributions or endowment; and may be said to recognize that many institutions organized for charitable purposes and supported in part by public subscriptions or endowment do engage in certain incidental activities, of a commercial nature, the proceeds of which, and any profits derived therefrom, are devoted to the general charitable work of the institution and applied to no alien or selfish purpose [11 A.2d at 531].

City of Boulder v. *Regents of the University of Colorado,* 501 P.2d 123 (Colo. 1972), concerned the attempt of the local government to impose an admissions tax on various events, including intercollegiate football games, held on the University of

Colorado campus. The court held that the city could not impose tax collection responsibilities on the university because the university as a branch of the state government could claim sovereign immunity. The Supreme Court of Colorado quoted the trial court's opinion with approval:

> "[I]n the instant case the City is attempting to impose duties on the Board of Regents which would necessarily interfere with the Regents' control of the University. The Constitution establishes a statewide University and vests control in the Board of Regents. The Board of Regents has *exclusive* control and direction of all funds of, and appropriations to, the University. . . . Thus, the City of Boulder cannot force the Regents to apply any funds toward the collection of the tax in question. Even if the City claims that sufficient funds would be generated by the tax to compensate the Regents for collection expense and, arguably, such funds could be paid to the Regents by the City, the Regents are still vested with the 'general supervision' of the University. The University would necessarily be required to expend both money and manpower for the collection, identification, and payment of such funds to the City. This interferes with the financial conduct of the University and the allocation of its manpower for its statewide educational duties. . . .
>
> "Thus, since the Constitution has established a statewide University at Boulder and vested general supervisory control in a statewide Board of Regents and management in control of the state, a city, even though a home rule city, has no power to interfere with the management or supervision of the activities of the University of Colorado. If the City of Boulder was allowed to impose duties on the University, such duties would necessarily interfere with the functions of the state institution. There is no authority to permit the City of Boulder to force a state institution to collect such a local tax. Consequently, the City of Boulder cannot require the Board of Regents of the University of Colorado to become involuntary collectors of the City of Boulder's admission tax" [501 P.2d at 125].

The court also held, over two dissents, that the admissions tax was itself invalid as applied to various university functions.

> When academic departments of the University, or

> others acting under the auspices of the University, sponsor
> lectures, dissertations, art exhibitions, concerts and dra-
> matic performances, whether or not an admission fee is
> charged, these functions become a part of the educational
> process. This educational process is not merely for the
> enrolled students of the University, but it is a part of the
> educational process for those members of the public
> attending the events. In our view the home rule authority of
> a city does not permit it to tax a person's acquisition of
> education furnished by the State. We hold that the tax is
> invalid when applied to University lectures, dissertations,
> art exhibitions, concerts, and dramatic performances [501
> P.2d at 126].

With respect to football games, however, the tax's validity was
affirmed because the university had not made "a showing that
football is so related to the educational process that its devotees
may not be taxed by a home rule city." This latter ruling is
"probably academic," as the court acknowledged, since under
sovereign immunity the university cannot be required to collect the
tax, even if it is valid.

Sec. 5.4. Student Voting in the Community

The passage of the Twenty-Sixth Amendment to the U.S.
Constitution, lowering the voting age to eighteen, created several
new problems for postsecondary administrators. On some voting
issues, administrators may at most play an intermediary or
advocate role in disputes between students and the community.
Other issues require positive action by administrators to establish
guidelines for voting activities on campus.

5.4.1. Registering to vote. The extension of the franchise did
not automatically give every citizen over eighteen the right to vote.
All potential voters must register with the board of elections of
their legal residence in order to exercise their right. Determining
the legal residence of students attending residential institutions has
created major controversies. Some small communities near colleges
and universities, fearful of the impact of the student vote, have
tried to limit student registration, while students eager to

participate in local affairs and to avoid the inconveniences of absentee voting have pushed for local registration.

The trend of recent cases has been to overturn statutes or practices which impede student registration. In *Jolicoeur* v. *Mihaly*, 5 Cal.3d 565, 488 P.2d 1 (1971), the court held that a statute which created an almost conclusive presumption that an unmarried minor's residence was her parents' home violated the equal protection clause and the Twenty-Sixth Amendment:

> Sophisticated legal arguments regarding a minor's presumed residence cannot blind us to the real burden placed on the right to vote and associated rights of political expression by requiring minor voters residing apart from their parents to vote in their parents' district. . . .
>
> An unmarried minor must be subject to the same requirements in proving the location of his domicile as is any other voter. Fears of the way minors may vote or of their impermanency in the community may not be used to justify special presumptions—conclusive or otherwise—that they are not bona fide residents of the community in which they live.
>
> It is clear that respondents have abridged petitioners' right to vote in precisely one of the ways that Congress sought to avoid—by singling minor voters out for special treatment and effectively making many of them vote by absentee ballot. . . .
>
> Respondents' policy would clearly frustrate youthful willingness to accomplish change at the local level through the political system. Whether a youth lives in Quincy, Berkeley, or Orange County, he will not be brought into the bosom of the political system by being told that he may not have a voice in the community in which he lives, but must instead vote wherever his parents live or may move to. Surely as well, such a system would give any group of voters less incentive "in devising responsible programs" in the town in which they live [488 P.2d at 4, 7].

In Michigan a statute created a rebuttable presumption that students are not voting residents of the district where their institution is located. The statute was implemented through elaborate procedures applicable only to students. The court invalidated the statute on equal protection grounds as a penalty on the right to vote (*Williams* v. *Bentley*, 385 Mich. 670, 189 N.W.2d 423 (1971)).

In contrast, statutory provisions neutralizing attendance at a local college or university as a factor in determining a student's residence have been upheld. In *Whittingham* v. *Board of Elections*, 320 F. Supp. 889 (N.D.N.Y. 1970), a special three-judge court upheld a "gain or loss provision" of the New York constitution. This provision, found in many state constitutions and statutes, requires a student to prove residency by indicia other than student status. The *Whittingham* case was followed by *Gorenberg* v. *Onondaga County Board of Elections*, 38 A.D.2d 145, 328 N.Y.S.2d 198 (1972), upholding a New York State statute specifying criteria for determining student residence, including dependency, employment, marital status, age, and location of property.

A few general rules for determining student residency emerge. Mere presence as a student is not sufficient to establish residency. A student must manifest intent to establish residency in the community. Present intent to establish residency is probably sufficient. Students who intend to leave the community after graduation do not have such intent. Students who are uncertain about their postgraduation plans, but consider the home community their home for the time, probably do have such intent. A statute which required proof of intent to remain *indefinitely* in the community after graduation was held a denial of equal protection in *Whatley* v. *Clark*, 482 F.2d 1230 (5th Cir. 1973).

Uncertainties concerning future plans and the difficulties of proving intent complicate the application of these general rules. The indicia used by boards of election to determine whether a student intends to establish residency include vacation activity, the type of home established, the location of property, the choice of banks and other services, membership in community groups, and the declaration of residence for other purposes such as tax payment and auto registration.

5.4.2. Scheduling elections. The only reported case which deals with the timing of an election in a district with a substantial student population is *Walgren* v. *Board of Selectmen of Town of*

Amherst, 519 F.2d 1364 (1st Cir. 1975). The appellate court opinion lays out the special facts of the case.

> The controversy arises from events which took place over a ten-day period in December 1972, during which the town selectmen, at plaintiff Walgren's urging, endeavored to change the scheduled date for the town caucus, the primary election in which nominees for the positions of town officer and town meeting member are selected. On December 10, 1972, Walgren protested the then recently published schedule for the 1973 elections on the ground that the caucus date of January 19 would be during the winter recess of the University of Massachusetts, when some ten thousand dormitory students would be out of town. On December 11, the board voted to reconsider the schedule at its December 18 meeting. After a week of public reaction, both pro and con, a long and animated meeting was held on December 18, at the end of which the board voted to establish a new calendar. But the dates for the caucus and the final election proposed by Walgren, January 29 and March 1, raised the possibility of a conflict with a state requirement that thirty-one days separate the two dates. The board, being of the opinion that statutory notice for the proposed new dates would have to be published by the following day, provisionally adopted them, subject to advice of counsel. When, on December 19, the advice was received that the dates would be illegal, the board, at a special meeting in the evening, turned down its counsel's proposal that the town meeting itself be moved ahead by a week, and reinstated the original calendar [519 F.2d at 1365].

The lower court refused to set aside the election. Although disagreeing with the lower court's finding that the burden on students' and faculty members' right to vote was insignificant, the appellate court relied on the good-faith efforts of the selectmen to schedule an appropriate date:

> In short, we would be disturbed if, given time to explore alternatives and given alternatives which would satisfy all reasonable town objectives, a town continued to insist on elections during vacations or recess, secure in the

conviction that returning to town and absentee voting would be considered insignificant burdens.

The critical element which in our view serves to sustain the 1973 election is the foreshortened time frame within which the selectmen were forced to face up to and resolve a problem which was then novel. . . .

We would add that, under the circumstances of this case, even if we had found the burden impermissible, we would have looked upon the novelty and complexity of the issue, the shortness of time, and the good faith efforts of the defendants as sufficient justification for refusing to order a new election at this late date [519 F.2d at 1368].

The special facts of the case and the narrowness of the court's holding limit *Walgren*'s authority as precedent. But *Walgren* does suggest that purposefully scheduling an election so as to disenfranchise an identifiable segment of the student electorate can be successfully challenged under some circumstances.

5.4.3. Canvassing and registration on campus. The regulation of voter canvassing and registration on campus is the voting issue most likely to require the direct involvement of college and university administrators. Any regulation must accommodate the First Amendment rights of the canvassers, the First Amendment rights of the students who may be potential listeners, the Twenty-Sixth Amendment rights of registrars, the privacy interests of those students who may not wish to be canvassed, the requirements of local election law, and the institution's interests in order and safety. Not all of these considerations have been explored in litigation.

James v. *Nelson,* 349 F. Supp. 1061 (N.D. Ill. 1972), arose after Northern Illinois University prohibited all canvassing in student living areas. A proposed regulation, which would have had to be adopted by two-thirds of the students of each dormitory, would have allowed canvassing under specified conditions. The court held that the referendum requirement unconstitutionally infringed the freedom of association and expression rights of the canvassers. The basis for the *James* decision is difficult to discern. The court specifically did not hold that the proposed canvassing regulation was "in any way unreasonable or beyond the powers of the university administration to impose in the interests of good order and the safety and comfort of the student body." If the proposed regulation was reasonable, a referendum adopting it would not infringe anyone's constitutional rights. The court's implicit ruling must be that the university's blanket prohibition on canvassing was an infringement of First Amendment rights, and a referendum which could reject a liberalization of that rule and uphold the original prohibition was therefore unconstitutional.

National Movement for the Student Vote v. *The Regents of the University of California,* 50 Cal.App.3d 131, 123 Cal. Rptr. 141 (1975), was decided on statutory grounds. A local statute permitted registrars to register voters at their residences. University policy, uniformly enforced, did not allow canvassing in student living areas. Registrars were permitted to canvass in public areas of the campus and in the lobbies of the dormitories.

The court held that the privacy interest of the students limited the registrars' right to canvass to reasonable times and places and that the limitations imposed by the university were reasonable and in compliance with the law. In determining reasonableness, the court emphasized the following facts:

> [T]here was evidence and findings to the effect that dining and other facilities of the dormitories are on the main floor; the private rooms of the students are on the upper floors; the rooms do not contain kitchen, washing, or toilet facilities; each student must walk from his or her room to restroom facilities in the halls of the upper floors in order to bathe or use the toilet facilities; defendants, in order to "recognize and enhance the privacy" of the students and to minimize assaults upon them and thefts of their property, have maintained a policy and regulations prohibiting solicitation, distribution of materials, and recruitment of students in the upper-floor rooms; students in the upper rooms complained to university officials about persons coming to their rooms and canvassing them and seeking their registrations; defendants permitted signs regarding the election to be posted throughout the dormitories and permitted deputy registrars to maintain tables and stands in the main lobby of each dormitory for registration of students; students in each dormitory had to pass through the main lobby thereof in order to go to and from their rooms; a sign encouraging registration to vote was at each

table, and students registered to vote at the tables [123 Cal.
Rptr. at 146].

Though the *National Student Movement* decision is based
on a statute, the court's language suggests that similar principles
and factors would be used in considering the constitutionality of a
public institution's canvassing regulations under the First Amendment. Though a public institution could not completely prohibit
voter canvassing on campus, it might impose reasonable restrictions upon the "time, place, and manner" of canvassing. (Compare
Section 4.7.2.)

Sec. 5.5. Relations with Local Police

Since the academic community is part of the surrounding
community, it will generally be within the geographical jurisdiction of one or more local (town, village, city, county) police forces.
The circumstances under which local police may and will come
onto the campus, and their authority once on campus, are thus of
concern to every administrator. Their role on campus depends on a
mixture of considerations: the state and local law of the
jurisdiction, federal constitutional limitations on police powers,
the adequacy of the institution's own security services, and the
terms of any explicit or implicit understanding between local
police and campus authorities.

If the institution has its own uniformed security officers, it
will be important to determine what working relationships they
will have with local police. This decision will depend partly on the
extent of the security officers' authority, especially regarding arrests,
searches, and seizures, authority which should also be carefully
delineated. (See generally Section 4.13.4.) Similarly, it is important
for administrators to understand the relationship between arrest
and prosecution in local courts, on the one hand, and campus disciplinary proceedings on the other. (See Section 4.13.3.) Although
administrators cannot make crime an internal affair by hiding
evidence of crime from local police, they may be able to assist local
law enforcement officials in determining prosecution priorities.
Campus and local officials may also be able to cooperate in

determining whether a campus proceeding should be stayed pending the outcome of a court proceeding, or vice versa.

The powers of local police are circumscribed by various federal constitutional provisions, particularly the Fourth Amendment strictures on arrests, searches, and seizures. These provisions limit local police authority on both public and private campuses. Under the Fourth Amendment, local police must often obtain a warrant before arresting or searching a member of the academic community or searching or seizing any private property on the campus. (See Section 4.10.2.) On a private institution's campus nearly all the property may be private, and local police may need a warrant or the consent of whoever effectively controls the property before entering most areas of the campus. On a public institution's campus, it is more difficult to determine which property would be considered public and which private, and thus more difficult to determine when local police must have a warrant or consent prior to entry. In general, for both public and private institutions, police will need a warrant or consent before entering any area in which members of the academic community have a "reasonable expectation of privacy." (See generally *Katz* v. *United States*, 389 U.S. 347 (1967).) The constitutional rules and concepts are especially complex in this area, however; and administrators should consult counsel whenever questions arise concerning the authority of local police on campus.

A different problem arises when local police enter a campus not to make an arrest or conduct a search but to engage in surveillance of members of the institutional community. In *White* v. *Davis*, 120 Cal.2d 94, 533 P.2d 222 (1975), a history professor at UCLA sued the Los Angeles police chief to enjoin the use of undercover police agents for generalized surveillance in the university. Unidentified police agents had registered at the university and compiled dossiers on students and professors based on information obtained during classes and public meetings. The California Supreme Court held that such action was a prima facie violation of students' and faculty members' First Amendment freedoms of speech, assembly, and association, as well as the "right to privacy" provision of the California constitution. The case was returned to the trial court to determine whether the police were acting on any compelling state interest which would justify the infringement of constitutional rights.

The court's opinion differentiates the First Amendment surveillance problem from the more traditional Fourth Amendment search and seizure problem:

> The most familiar limitations on police investigatory and surveillance activities, of course, find embodiment in the Fourth Amendment of the federal Constitution and article I, section 13 (formerly art. I, sec. 19) of the California Constitution. On numerous occasions in the past, these provisions have been applied to preclude specific ongoing police investigatory practices. Thus, for example, the court in *Wirin* v. *Parker,* supra, 48 Cal.2d 890, 313 P.2d 844, prohibited the police practice of conducting warrantless surveillance of private residences by means of concealed microphones. . . .
>
> Unlike these past cases involving the limits on police surveillance prescribed by the constitutional "search and seizure" provisions, the instant case presents the more unusual question of the limits placed upon police investigatory activities by the guarantees of freedom of speech. (U.S. Const. 1st and 14th Amends.; Cal. Const., art. I, sec. 2.) As discussed below, this issue is not entirely novel; to our knowledge, however, the present case represents the first instance in which a court has confronted the issue in relation to ongoing police surveillance of a university community.
>
> Our analysis of the limits imposed by the First Amendment upon police surveillance activities must begin with the recognition that with respect to First Amendment freedoms "the Constitution's protection is not limited to direct interference with fundamental rights" (*Healy* v. *James* (1972) 408 U.S. 169, 183, 92 S. Ct. 2338, 2347, 33 L.Ed.2d 266). Thus, although police surveillance of university classrooms and organizations' meetings may not constitute a direct prohibition of speech or association, such surveillance may still run afoul of the constitutional guarantee if the effect of such activity is to chill constitutionally protected activity. . . .
>
> As a practical matter, the presence in a university classroom of undercover officers taking notes to be preserved in police dossiers must inevitably inhibit the exercise of free speech both by professors and students [533 P.2d at 228–29].

The court also emphasized the special danger that police surveillance poses for academic freedom:

> The threat to First Amendment freedoms posed by any covert intelligence gathering network is considerably exacerbated when, as in the instant case, the police surveillance activities focus upon university classrooms and their environs. As the United States Supreme Court has recognized time and again: "The vigilant protection of constitutional freedoms is nowhere more vital than in the community of American schools." . . .
>
> The police investigatory conduct at issue unquestionably poses . . . [a] debilitating . . . threat to academic freedom. . . . According to the allegations of the complaint, which for purposes of this appeal must be accepted as true, the Los Angeles Police Department has established a network of undercover agents which keeps regular check on discussions occurring in various university classes. Because the identity of such police officers is unknown, no professor or student can be confident that whatever opinion he may express in class will not find its way into a police file. . . .
>
> The crucible of new thought is the university classroom; the campus is the sacred ground of free discussion. Once we expose the teacher or the student to possible future prosecution for the ideas he may express, we forfeit the security that nourishes change and advancement. The censorship of totalitarian regimes that so often condemns developments in art, science, and politics is but a step removed from the inchoate surveillance of free discussion in the university; such intrusion stifles creativity and to a large degree shackles democracy [533 P.2d at 229–31].

The principles of *White* v. *Davis* would apply equally to local police surveillance at a private institution. As an agency of government, the police are prohibited from violating any person's freedom of expression or right to privacy, whether on a public campus or a private one.[6]

[6]The case's right-to-privacy reasoning would apply only to states which recognize an individual right to privacy similar to that created under the California constitution. The applicability of the case's First Amendment reasoning may be limited to states whose courts would grant

Sec. 5.6. Community Access to Institutional Property

5.6.1. Public versus private institutions. Postsecondary institutions have often been the location for many types of events which attract people from the surrounding community and sometimes from other parts of the state, country, or world. Because of their capacity for large audiences and the sheer numbers of students and faculty and staff members on campus every day, postsecondary institutions provide an excellent forum for speakers, conferences, exhibits, pamphleteering, and other kinds of information exchanges. In addition, cultural, entertainment, and sporting events attract large numbers of outside persons. Whether public or private, postsecondary institutions have considerable authority to determine how and when their property will be used for such events and to regulate access to such events by outside persons. In some respects, however, a public institution's authority is more limited than that of a private institution.

Both private and public institutions customarily have ownership or leasehold interests in their campuses and buildings which are protected by the property law of the state. Subject to this statutory and common law, both types of institution have authority to regulate how and by whom their property is used. Typically, an institution's authority to regulate use by its students and faculty members is limited by the contractual commitments it has made to these groups. (See Sections 3.1 and 4.1.) Thus, for instance, students may have contractual rights to the reasonable use of dormitory rooms and the public areas of residence halls or of campus libraries and study rooms; and faculty members may have contractual rights to the reasonable use of office space or classrooms. With respect to the outside community, however, such contractual rights usually do not exist.

A public institution's authority to regulate the use of its

---

professors or students standing to raise illegal surveillance claims. The *White* plaintiffs obtained standing under a California "taxpayer standing" statute. They apparently would not have succeeded in the federal court, since the U.S. Supreme Court has held, in *Laird* v. *Tatum,* 408 U.S. 1 (1972), that government surveillance does not cause the type of specific harm necessary to establish federal court standing.

property is further limited by the federal Constitution, in particular the First Amendment, and may also be affected by state statutes or regulations applicable to state property in general or specifically to the property of state educational institutions. Unlike contract law limitations, these limitations on institutional authority may provide rights of access and use not only to faculty members and students (see, for example, Sections 4.7.1, 4.7.2, and 4.8.1 on the First Amendment usage rights of students) but also to the outside community. The following subsections explore various statutes, regulations, and First Amendment considerations which affect outsiders' access to the property of public institutions.

5.6.2. *Speaker bans.* Administrators who seek to avoid disruption by banning particular speakers or events have inevitably clashed not only with the participants but with those on campus who demand the right to hear the speaker or attend the event. These clashes have often resulted in litigation. Most of the cases on access to campus facilities have involved regulations on off-campus speakers, commonly referred to as "speaker bans."

Since rules regulating off-campus speakers provide a convenient target for a First Amendment attack, such rules should be drafted with extreme care. Much of the law which has developed concerning faculty members' and students' free speech rights on campus also applies to the off-campus speaker issue. (See Sections 3.6 and 4.7.)

It is clear under the First Amendment that administrators may reasonably regulate the time, place, and manner of speeches and other communicative activities, whether engaged in by on- or off-campus persons. Problems arise when these basic rules of order are expanded to include regulations under which a speaker can be banned because of the content of his speech or his political affiliation or persuasion. Such regulations are particularly susceptible to judicial invalidation because they are prior restraints on speech (Section 4.7.3). *Stacy* v. *Williams*, 306 F. Supp. 963 (N.D. Miss. 1969), is a leading example. The Board of Trustees of the Institutions of Higher Learning of the State of Mississippi promulgated rules which provided, in part, that "all speakers invited to the campus of any of the state institutions of higher learning must first be investigated and approved by the head of the institution involved and when invited the names of such speakers must be filed with the Executive Secretary of the Board of Trustees." The regulations were amended several times to prohibit "speakers who will do violence to the academic atmosphere," "persons in disrepute from whence they come," persons "charged with crime or other moral wrongs," any person "who advocates a philosophy of the overthrow of the United States," and any person "who has been announced as a political candidate or any person who wishes to speak on behalf of a political candidate." In addition, political or sectarian meetings sponsored by any outside organization were prohibited.

Under the authority of these regulations, the board prevented political activists Aaron Henry and Charles Evers from speaking on any Mississippi state campus. Students at several schools joined faculty members and other persons as plaintiffs in an action to invalidate the regulations. The court struck down the regulations because they created a prior restraint on the students' and faculties' First Amendment right to hear speakers. Not all speaker bans, however, are unconstitutional under the court's opinion. When the speech "presents a 'clear and present danger' of resulting in serious substantive evil," a ban would not violate the First Amendment:

> For purpose of illustration, we have no doubt that the college or university authority may deny an invitation to a guest speaker requested by a campus group if it reasonably appears that such person would, in the course of his speech, advocate (1) violent overthrow of the government of the United States, the State of Mississippi, or any political subdivision thereof; (2) willful destruction or seizure of the institution's buildings or other property; (3) disruption or impairment, by force, of the institution's regularly scheduled classes or other educational functions; (4) physical harm, coercion, or intimidation or other invasion of lawful rights of the institution's officials, faculty members, or students; or (5) other campus disorder of violent nature. In drafting a regulation so providing, it must be made clear that the "advocacy" prohibited must be of the kind which prepares the group addressed for imminent action and steels it to such action, as opposed to the abstract espousal of the moral propriety of a course of

action by resort to force; and there must be not only
advocacy to action but also a reasonable apprehension of
imminent danger to the essential functions and purposes of
the institution, including the safety of its property and the
protection of its officials, faculty members and students [306
F. Supp. at 973–74].

The court also promulgated a set of "Uniform Regulations
for Off-Campus Speakers" which it determined to comply with the
First Amendment (306 F. Supp. at 979–80). These regulations
provide that all speaker requests come from a recognized student or
faculty group, thus precluding any outsider's insistence on using
the campus as a forum. This approach accords with the court's
basis for invalidating the regulations: the rights of students or
faculty members to hear a speaker.

Besides meeting a "clear and present danger" or comparable
test, speaker ban regulations must use language that is sufficiently
clear and precise to be understood by the average reader.
Ambiguous or vague regulations run the risk of being struck down,
under the First and Fourteenth Amendments, as "void for
vagueness." (See Sections 4.4.1 and 4.7.2.) In *Dickson* v. *Sitterson*,
280 F. Supp. 486 (M.D. N.Car. 1968), the court relied on this
ground to invalidate a state statute and regulations which
prohibited a person from speaking at state colleges or universities
if he was a "known member of the Communist Party," was
"known to advocate the overthrow of the Constitution of the
United States or the State of North Carolina," or had "pleaded the
Fifth Amendment" in response to questions relating to the
Communist Party or other subversive organizations.

The absence of rules can be just as risky as poorly drafted
ones, since either situation leaves administrators and affected
persons with insufficient guidance. *Brooks* v. *Auburn University*,
412 F.2d 1171 (5th Cir. 1969), is illustrative. A student organization,
the Human Rights Forum, had requested that the Reverend
William Sloan Coffin speak on campus. After the request was
approved by the Public Affairs Seminar Board, the president of
Auburn overruled the decision because the Reverend Coffin was "a
convicted felon and because he might advocate breaking the law."
Students and faculty members filed suit contesting the president's

action, and the U.S. court of appeals upheld their First Amendment claim:

> Attributing the highest good faith to Dr. Philpott in his action, it nevertheless is clear under the prior restraint doctrine that the right of the faculty and students to hear a speaker, selected as was the speaker here, cannot be left to the discretion of the university president on a pick and choose basis. As stated, Auburn had no rules or regulations as to who might or might not speak and thus no question of a compliance with or a departure from such rules or regulations is presented. This left the matter as a pure First Amendment question; hence the basis for prior restraint. Such a situation of no rules or regulations may be equated with a licensing system to speak or hear and this has been long prohibited. . . .
>
> It is strenuously urged on behalf of Auburn that the president was authorized in any event to bar a convicted felon or one advocating lawlessness from the campus. This again depends upon the right of the faculty and students to hear. We do not hold that Dr. Philpott could not bar a speaker under any circumstances. Here there was no claim that the Reverend Coffin's appearance would lead to violence or disorder or that the university would be otherwise disrupted. There is no claim that Dr. Philpott could not regulate the time or place of the speech or the manner in which it was to be delivered. The most recent statement of the applicable rule by the Supreme Court, perhaps its outer limits, is contained in the case of *Brandenburg* v. *Ohio,* decided June 9, 1969, 395 U.S. 444, 89 S. Ct. 1927, 23 L.Ed.2d 430:
>
> " . . . These later decisions have fashioned the principle that the constitutional guarantees of free speech and free press do not permit a State to forbid or proscribe advocacy of the use of force or of law violation except where such advocacy is directed to inciting or producing imminent lawless action and is likely to incite or produce such action." . . .
>
> There was no claim that the Coffin speech would fall into the category of this exception [412 F.2d at 1172–73].

Under these cases, off-campus speaker regulations present sensitive legal issues for public institutions. If such regulations are determined to be necessary, they should be drafted with the aid of counsel. The cases clearly permit reasonable regulation of "the time or place of the speech or the manner in which it . . . [is] delivered," as the *Brooks* opinion notes. But regulating a speech because of its content is permissible only in narrow circumstances such as those set out in *Stacy* and in *Brooks*. The regulations promulgated by the court in *Stacy* provide useful guidance in drafting legally sound regulations.

5.6.3. Trespass statutes and regulations. Many states have trespass statutes which limit the use of a public institution's facilities by nonstudents, and sometimes students as well. Such statutes usually provide that a violation will result in excluding the offender from the campus. The violation of an order to leave made pursuant to the statute is usually a misdemeanor.

In *Kristel* v. *State*, 13 Md. App. 482, 284 A.2d 12 (1971), the plaintiff was an artist who had received an offer to display his work at Towson State College. The administration later withdrew the offer, and when the artist arrived on campus, the college notified him that he had ten minutes in which to leave or he would be arrested for violating a state trespass statute which said, in part:

> The highest official or governing body of the University of Maryland, any of the State colleges, any community college or public school may deny access to the buildings or grounds of the institution to persons who are not bona fide, currently registered students, staff, or faculty at the institution, and who have no lawful business to pursue at the institution, or who are acting in a manner disruptive or disturbing to the normal educational functions of the institution [Md. Ann. Code art. 27, sec. 577B].

The court upheld the statute against the claim that it was void for vagueness and that it encroached on the artist's First Amendment rights. On the vagueness claim, the court stated:

> Certainly the language of the act that a person who refuses or fails to leave after being requested to do so is guilty of a misdemeanor conveys sufficiently definite warning as to what conduct is prescribed when measured by common understanding and practices. . . . Nor do we find

vague the standard required for the request. We construe
"lawful business" within the meaning of sec. 577B as . . .
any constitutionally protected activity [284 A.2d at 16].

Regarding the First Amendment freedoms of speech and assembly,
the court stated: "The state may enact and enforce reasonable,
nondiscriminatory laws governing conduct in its buildings and on
its grounds. We find that the provisions of sec. 577B are reasonable
and nondiscriminatory" (284 A.2d at 17).

The opinion in *Kristel* is not well reasoned. Since the court
conceded that the artist was not disruptive of the orderly processes
of the college, the artist could only have violated the statute if he
had "no lawful business to pursue at the institution." But it
remains unclear, under the opinion and thus under the statute,
what kinds of nondisruptive activities are lawful (which the court
defines as "constitutionally protected") and what kinds are not. It
is questionable whether other courts, faced with similar statutes,
would construe them in such a manner.

One case which does strike down a trespass statute is *Grady*
v. *State*, 278 N.E.2d 280 (Ind. 1972), where the law at issue provided
that

> [i]t shall be a misdemeanor for any person to refuse
> to leave the premises of any institution established for the
> purpose of the education of students enrolled therein when
> so requested, regardless of the reason, by the duly consti-
> tuted officials of any such institution [Ind. Ann. Code Sec.
> 10-4533].

The court held that the law was void on its face owing to
vagueness and overbreadth in violation of the First and Fourteenth
Amendments:

> This statute attempts to grant to some undefined
> school "official" the power to order cessation of *any* kind of
> activity whatsoever, by *any* person whatsoever, and the
> official does not need to have any special reason for the
> order. The official's power extends to teachers, employees,
> students, and visitors and is in no way confined to
> suppressing activities that are interfering with the orderly

use of the premises. This statute empowers the official to
order any person off the premises because he does not
approve of his looks, his opinions, his behavior, no matter
how peaceful, or *for no reason at all.* Since there are *no*
limitations on the reason for such an order, the official can
request a person to leave the premises solely because the
person is engaging in expressive conduct even though that
conduct may be clearly protected by the First Amendment.
If the person chooses to continue the First Amendment
activity he can be prosecuted for a crime under sec. 10-4533.
This statute is clearly overbroad [278 N.E.2d at 282–83].

Even if a regulation or statute is neither vague nor
overbroad, it may be vulnerable to a procedural due process attack.
There is some authority for the proposition that a notice and a
hearing are required before a noncampus person can be expelled
from a public campus. In *Dunkel* v. *Elkins,* 325 F. Supp. 1235
(D.Md. 1971), the court construed the same Maryland statute which
was upheld in *Kristel* v. *State.* The court held that the institution
must afford a notice and an opportunity for a hearing before
excluding an "outsider" from campus. If a prior hearing is not
feasible because of emergency conditions, then a prompt post-
expulsion hearing must be held. The burden of proof is on the
institution to establish that the person to be excluded fell within
the terms of the statute.

A notice and a hearing were also required in *Watson* v.
Board of Regents of the University of Colorado, 182 Colo. 307, 512
P.2d 1162 (1973). The plaintiff, a consultant to the University of
Colorado Black Student Alliance with substantial ties to the
campus, was rejected for admission to the university. Believing the
decision to be that of a particular admissions committee member,
the plaintiff threatened his safety. The university president then
notified the plaintiff in writing that he would no longer be allowed
on campus. Nevertheless, the plaintiff returned to campus and was
arrested for trespass. Relying on *Dunkel* v. *Elkins,* the court agreed
that the exclusion violated procedural due process:

Where students have been subjected to disciplinary
action by University officials, courts have recognized that
procedural due process requires—prior to imposition of the

disciplinary action—adequate notice of the charges, reasonable opportunity to prepare to meet the charges, an orderly
administrative hearing adapted to the nature of the case,
and a fair and impartial decision. . . . The same protection
must be afforded nonstudents who may be permanently
denied access to University functions and facilities.

As part of a valid Regent's regulation of this type, in
addition to providing for a hearing, there should be a
provision for the person or persons who will act as
adjudicator(s).

In the present posture of this matter we should not
attempt to "spell out" all proper elements of such a
regulation. This task should be undertaken first by the
Regents. We should say, however, that when a genuine
emergency appears to exist and it is impractical for
University officials to grant a prior hearing, the right of
nonstudents to access to the University may be suspended
without a prior hearing, so long as a hearing is thereafter
provided with reasonable promptness [512 P.2d at 1165].

Sec. 5.7. Community Activities of Faculty Members and Students

Not only are faculty members and students part of the
academic community; they are also private citizens whose private
lives may involve them in the broader local community. Thus, a
postsecondary institution may be concerned not only with its
authority over matters arising when the community comes onto the
campus, as in Section 5.6, but also with its authority over matters
arising when the campus goes out into the community.

Generally an institution has much less authority over a
student's or faculty member's activities in the community than on
the campus. The faculty-institution contract (Section 3.1) and
student-institution contract (Section 4.1.3) may have little or no
application to the off-campus activities which faculty or students
engage in as private citizens or may affirmatively protect faculty
members or students from institutional interference in their private
lives. In public institutions, both faculty members (Section 3.6.4)
and students (Section 4.13.2) have constitutional rights which
protect them from undue institutional interference in their private
lives.

In relation to First Amendment rights, a landmark teacher

case, *Pickering* v. *Board of Education*, 391 U.S. 563 (1968) (see Section 3.6.1), created substantial protection for teachers against being disciplined for expressing themselves in the community on issues of public concern. A U.S. court of appeals case, *Pickings* v. *Bruce*, 430 F.2d 595 (8th Cir. 1970), establishes similar protections for students. The issue in *Pickings* was that Southern State College had placed SURE (Students United for Rights and Equality), an officially recognized campus group, on probation for writing a letter to a local church criticizing its racial policies. SURE claimed that the college's action deprived the group's members of their First Amendment rights. In holding for the students, the court made this general statement concerning campus involvement in the community:

> Students and teachers retain their rights to freedom of speech, expression, and association while attending or teaching at a college or university. They have a right to express their views individually or collectively with respect to matters of concern to a college or to a larger community. They are neither required to limit their expression of views to the campus or to confine their opinions to matters that affect the academic community only. It follows that here the administrators had no right to prohibit SURE from expressing its views on integration to the College View Baptist Church or to impose sanctions on its members or advisors for expressing these views. Such statements may well increase the tensions within the College and between the College and the community, but this fact cannot serve to restrict freedom of expression. *Tinker* v. *Des Moines Community School Dist.*, 393 U.S. at 508–09, 89 S. Ct. 733 [430 F.2d at 598].

Selected Annotated Bibliography

General

1. Antieau, C. J., *Local Government Law* (Matthew Bender, 1975, with periodic supplements), is a seven-volume treatise, which comprehensively covers the legal concepts and principles regarding municipal and town governments, counties,

and independent local districts and authorities. Section 5.41 covers the preemption doctrine; sections 19A.09–19A.13 and 44.05–44.11 cover state immunities from local regulation and taxation; sections 7.00–8.15 and 35.07–35.15 cover local land use regulation; sections 21.00–21.28 and 41.00–41.17 cover local tax powers; and sections 17.00–17.30 and 45.00–45.19 cover local elections. Primarily a resource for lawyers, but can also provide a useful general knowledge base for laypersons.

Sec. 5.2 (Zoning and Land Use)

1. Johnston, R., "Recent Cases in the Law on Intergovernmental Zoning Immunity: New Standards Designed to Maximize the Public Interests," 8 *Urban Lawyer* 327 (1976), provides a concise analysis of traditional zoning immunity concepts and new trends in the case law.
2. "Special Project: The Private Use of Public Power: The Private University and the Power of Eminent Domain," 27 *Vanderbilt L. Rev.* 681 (1974), is a lengthy study of eminent domain as a land use planning technique to benefit private universities. Emphasis is on the use of eminent domain in conjunction with federal urban renewal programs. A case study involving Nashville, Tennessee, is included.

Sec. 5.3 (Local Government Taxation)

Sierk, C. H., "State Tax Exemptions of Nonprofit Organizations," 19 *Cleveland State L. Rev.* 281 (1970), is a brief summary of trends in exemptions of nonprofit organizations from real property, sales, use, and income taxes.

Sec. 5.5 (Relations with Local Police)

1. Bickel, R., "The Relationship Between the University and Local Law Enforcement Agencies in Their Response to the Problem of Drug Abuse on the Campus," in D. P. Young (ed.), *Higher Education: The Law and Campus Issues* 17–27 (Institute of Higher Education, University of Georgia, 1973),

provides a practical discussion of the general principles of search and seizure, double jeopardy, and confidentiality in the campus drug abuse context; also discusses the necessity of administrators' having the advice of counsel.

2. Cowen, L., "The Campus and the Community: Problems of Dual Jurisdiction," in D. P. Young (ed.), *Proceedings of a Conference on Higher Education: The Law and Student Protest* 28–32 (Institute of Higher Education, University of Georgia, 1970), is a brief discussion of the policy considerations governing the division of authority between the institution and local law enforcement agencies.

3. Ferdico, J. N., *Ferdico's Criminal Procedure for the Law Enforcement Officer* (West, 1975), is an introductory text on police and criminal court procedure, including arrest, search, admissions, investigation, and evidence.

4. Kalaidjian, E., "Problems of Dual Jurisdiction of Campus and Community," in G. Holmes (ed.), *Student Protest and the Law* 131–148 (Institute of Continuing Legal Education, University of Michigan, 1969), addresses issues arising out of concurrent criminal and disciplinary proceedings and police entry onto campus.

Sec. 5.6 (Community Access to Institutional Property)

"Comment: The University and the Public: The Right of Access by Nonstudents to University Property," 54 *California L. Rev.* 132 (1966), discusses the appropriateness and constitutionality of using state trespass laws to limit the public's access to state university and college campuses; California's criminal trespass law designed for state colleges and universities (Cal. Penal Code sec. 602-7, 1965), since amended and recodified as Cal. Penal Code sec. 626.6 (West, supplement, 1977), is highlighted.

Sec. 5.7 (Community Activities of Faculty Members and Students)

McKay, R., "The Student as Private Citizen," 45 *Denver L.J.* 558 (1968), with three responding commentaries by other authors, provides a legal and policy overview of students' status as private citizens of the larger community.

Chapter VI

❧❧❧❧❧❧❧❧❧❧❧❧❧❧

The College
and the State
Government

Sec. 6.1. General Background

Unlike the federal government (see Section 7.1) and local governments (Section 5.1), state governments have general rather than limited powers and can claim all power not denied them by the federal Constitution or their own state constitution. Thus the states have the greatest reservoir of legal authority over postsecondary education, although the extent to which this source is tapped varies greatly from state to state. The states' functions include planning, coordinating, operating, regulating, and funding. These functions are performed through myriad agencies, including boards of regents; statewide planning or coordinating boards; departments of education or higher education; "1202 Commissions" formed for planning purposes under Title X of the Higher Education Act of 1965, as amended in 1972 (20 U.S.C. 1142a); institutional licensure boards or commissions; State Approval Agencies (SAAs), which operate under contract to the federal Veterans' Administration to approve courses for which veterans' benefits may be expended; and various professional and occupational licensure boards which indirectly regulate postsecondary education by evaluating programs of study and establishing educational prerequisites for taking licensure exams.

Other state agencies whose primary function is not education (such as workers' compensation boards and labor boards) may also regulate postsecondary education as part of a broader class of covered institutions, corporations, or government agencies. States also have broad authority to tax postsecondary education. All private institutions, or their property, within the state are presumed subject to taxation under the existing tax statutes unless a specific statutory or constitutional provision grants an exemption. The principles and problems regarding state taxation of postsecondary institutions are similar to those related to local government taxation, discussed in Section 5.3.

Much as is now the case with the federal government, postsecondary administrators can increasingly expect to bump into state government in the course of their daily institutional duties. State governmental presence is particularly apparent whenever administrators plan to add new departments or degree programs, to establish new institutions, or to operate branch campuses or off-campus programs in other states—in which case some form of state approval is likely to be required. Postsecondary administrators should keep abreast of all state approval processes which may affect institutional planning and should make the approval process itself an integral part of their planning. Administrators should also encourage their legal counsel or their government relations office to monitor the growing body of state law and keep key institutional personnel apprised of such developments.

Sec. 6.2. State Systems of Public Postsecondary Education

Public postsecondary educational systems vary in type and organization from state to state. Such systems may be established by the state constitution, by legislative acts, or by a combination of the two, and may encompass a variety of institutions from the large state university to smaller state colleges or teachers' colleges, to community colleges, technical schools, and vocational schools. Major governance concerns include the coordination of public postsecondary education activities within the state; the legal status and autonomy granted to particular institutions; and the division of authority among the individual institution, the statewide governing or coordinating body, the legislature, and the governor. High-level administrators of public institutions should be familiar with these issues as they affect their particular schools and, to effectively handle these issues when they arise, should have a firm understanding of their state's superstructure for postsecondary governance.

6.2.1. Governance or coordination systems for public postsecondary institutions. Every state has at least one designated body which bears statewide responsibility for some aspect of public postsecondary education.[1] These bodies are known by such titles as the Board of Higher Education, the Commission on Higher Education, the Board of Regents, the Regents, the Board of Educational Finance, or the Board of Governors. Most such boards are involved in some phase of planning, program review and approval, and budget development for the institutions under their control or within their sphere of influence. Other responsibilities might also be imposed, such as the development of data bases and management information systems or the establishment of new degree-granting institutions. Depending on their functions, boards are classifiable into two groups: governing and coordinating. Governing boards have the legal responsibility for the management

[1]The information which follows in this section is drawn heavily from R. M. Millard, *State Boards of Higher Education* (American Association for Higher Education, ERIC Higher Educ. Research Rpt. No. 4, 1976).

and operation of the institutions under their control. Coordinating boards have the lesser responsibilities which their name implies. Most governing boards work directly with the institutions for which they are responsible. Coordinating boards may or may not do so. Although community colleges are closely tied to their locales, most come within the jurisdiction of some state board or agency.

    6.2.2. Legal status of individual public institutions. Public institutions are established either by a provision in the state constitution or by statute. Constitutionally established institutions have more freedom from legislative control because the state legislature cannot interfere with the terms and conditions of the constitutional grant. For legal purposes public institutions have been variously characterized as "state agencies," "public trusts," or "autonomous universities," depending on the language of the constitutional or statutory provision establishing the institution and any other relevant state law.

    A "state agency" is legally part of the state government. As such, it may be subject to the state administrative law applicable to state agencies and is able to assert the legal defenses available to the state, such as sovereign immunity. In *Board of Trustees of Howard Community College* v. *John K. Ruff, Inc.,* 278 Md. 580, 366 A.2d 360 (1976), for instance, the court's holding that the board of trustees of a regional community college was a state agency enabled the board to assert sovereign immunity as a defense against a suit for breach of contract. A "public trust," on the other hand, may not be subject to state administrative law and may not share all the defenses of the state. The trustees of such an institution must fulfill the special fiduciary duties of public trustees under state law in administering the trust for the educational benefit of the public. An "autonomous university" is established as a separate entity by the state constitution. It may be a public corporation; it may be a public trust, as in the California constitutional provision (Cal. Const. art. 9, sec. 9); or it may have some other independent public status under state law. The autonomy is with reference to the legislature, not the public.

    Constitutional and statutory provisions vary in the responsibilities and restrictions they place on the institutions they establish.

Sometimes the provisions reserve certain authority for a state governing board or other state agency or officer apart from the institution. There has been increasing litigation in a number of states over who bears the ultimate authority for certain decisions which affect public postsecondary institutions: the legislature, a state governing board, the governor, the commissioner of education, or the individual institution. The litigated issues include the registration of doctoral programs (*Moore* v. *The Board of Regents of the University of the State of New York,* 390 N.Y.S.2d 582 (Sup. Ct. 1977), affirmed 59 A.D. 44, 397 N.Y.S.2d 449 (1977); the establishment of tuition rates (*Kowalski* v. *Board of Trustees of Macomb County Community College,* 67 Mich. App. 74, 240 N.W.2d 272 (1976)); the ability to make binding agreements with faculties (*Busboom* v. *S.E. Nebraska Technical Community College,* 194 Neb. 488, 232 N.W.2d 24 (1975)); the authority to authorize expenditures by a constitutionally established university (*The Regents of the University of Michigan* v. *The State of Michigan,* 395 Mich. 52, 235 N.W.2d 1 (1975); *Board of Regents of University of Nebraska* v. *Exxon,* 199 Neb.. 146, 256 N.W.2d 330 (1977); *State of New Mexico* v. *Kirkpatrick,* 86 N.Mex. 359, 524 P.2d 975 (1974)); the approval of budget amendments and the appropriation of funds for the university system (*Board of Regents of Higher Education* v. *Judge,* 543 P.2d 1323 (Mont. 1975)); and the power to determine the residency requirements for in-state tuition rates (*Schmidt* v. *The Regents of the University of Michigan,* 63 Mich. App. 54, 233 N.W.2d 855 (1975)). Which entity does have the final authority depends on the language of the relevant constitutional and statutory provisions and on the particular facts of the situation. The following cases are illustrative.

In *Moore* v. *The Board of Regents of the University of the State of New York,* 390 N.Y.S.2d 582 (Sup. Ct. 1977), affirmed 59 App. Div. 44, 397 N.Y.S.2d 449 (1977), the State University of New York trustees and chancellor, together with several professors and doctoral students in the affected departments, sought a declaratory judgment that the university trustees were responsible under the law for providing the standards and regulations for the organization and operation of university programs, courses, and curricula in accordance with the state's master plan. The defendants were the state Board of Regents and the state Commissioner of Education. The case concerned the commissioner's deregistration of the doctoral programs in history and English at the State University of New York at Albany. In statements for the news media, each of the opposing litigants foresaw an ominous impact from a decision for the other side: if the commissioner and the state board won, the institution would continue to be subjected to "unprecedented intervention"; if the trustees won, the university would be placed beyond public accountability (*The Chronicle of Higher Education*, March 8, 1976, p. 3, cols. 1–2).

On the basis of its analysis of the state's constitution, Education Law, and administrative regulations, the court concluded that the commissioner, acting for the board of regents, which was established by the state constitution, had the authority to make the decision:

> In support of this conclusion, the court points out that the Board of Regents is a constitutional body which was created in 1784 under the name of the Regents of the University of the State of New York (N.Y. Const. art. XI, sec. 2). The University of the State of New York (not to be confused with the State University of New York) is the name given to the entire educational community under the jurisdiction of the Board of Regents. It includes "all institutions of higher education which are now or may hereafter be incorporated in this state" (L. 1892, ch. 378; see Education Law sec. 214).
>
> As of 1784, the regents were vested with full power and authority to make ordinances for the government of the colleges which should compose the University. In 1892, prior to the adoption of the 1894 Constitution, the Legislature granted broad powers to the regents; these powers included the power to charter institutions and colleges, and the legislation prohibited institutions not holding university or college degree-conferring powers from assuming the appellation of college or university or conferring degrees. These and other powers were, in effect, confirmed by the Constitution of 1894 [references omitted].
>
> In its *amicus curiae* brief, the Commission on Independent Colleges and Universities notes that since 1787 the regents have registered programs and since 1910 they

have conducted such registration through the commissioner. In construing the statute to allow the regents,
through the commissioner, to register programs, the court
relies not only on the historical grants of extensive power to
the regents, but also on the rule that a long continued
course of action by those administering a statute is entitled
to great weight (see McKinney's *Cons. Laws of N.Y.*, Book
1, Statutes, sec. 129). Moreover, it would appear that the
Legislature has recognized the existence and exercise of this
authority (Education Law, sec. 224, subd. 4). . . .

The court also rejects plaintiffs' contention that
notwithstanding the existence of any power the regents and
the commissioner may have to register programs in other
institutions, they have no power to approve programs in
the State University of New York. The State University of
New York was created by the Legislature on July 1, 1948 (L.
1948, ch. 695 [Education Law, sec. 352]), as a corporation
within the State Education Department and the University
of the State of New York. In 1961, chapter 388 of the Laws
of 1961 gave the Board of Trustees of the State University of
New York the authority to administer the internal affairs of
the State University. Nothing contained in that statute, or
in the legislative history leading to its passage, indicates
that the State University was to become *sui generis* and not
subject to the same requirements imposed by the regents
and commissioner on private institutions of higher education in this state [390 N.Y.S. at 585–86].

In contrast, the authority of individual institutions was
upheld in *The Regents of the University of Michigan* v. *The State
of Michigan*, 395 Mich. 52, 235 N.W.2d 1 (1975). The issue was the
relative responsibilities for public higher education of the legislature and governor, the governing boards of the universities, and
the State Board of Education. The institutions challenged the
constitutionality of statutes requiring legislative approval for
certain expenditures and contract arrangements. The court asserted
that the state constitution prohibits the legislature from imposing
conditions upon its appropriations which interfere with the
governing boards' control of their institutions, but then held the
statute in question to be constitutional because it required only
that the university notify the legislature as to how its funds were
spent. Because the university retained sole authority to enter into

contracts and need not obtain legislative approval of its actions, the reporting requirement did not impinge upon its authority.

The institutions also challenged the State Board of Education's authority over higher education. The State Board of Education argued that it had the authority to approve program changes of the universities. Relying on the express terms of the constitutional provision, the court held that the State Board of Education's authority over higher education is advisory only. The institutions are required only to inform the board of program changes so it can "knowledgeably carry out its advisory duties." Thus, although constitutionally created governing boards may have exclusive authority over the operation of their universities, some requirements may be imposed upon them to accommodate the authority given other state agencies or branches of government. (See also *Regents of the University of Michigan* v. *Michigan Employment Relations Commission*, 389 Mich. 96, 204 N.W.2d 218 (1973) (University of Michigan is a public employer and subject to the Public Employees Relations Act).)

Sec. 6.3. State Chartering and Licensure of Private Postsecondary Institutions

The authority of states to regulate private postsecondary education is not as broad as their authority over their own public institutions. (See Section 1.4.1.) Nevertheless, under their police powers, states do have extensive regulatory authority. In a leading case, *Shelton College* v. *State Board of Education*, 48 N.J. 501, 226 A.2d 612 (1967), the court reviewed the authority of New Jersey to license degree-granting institutions and approve the basis and conditions on which they grant degrees. The State Board of Education had refused to approve the granting of degrees by the plaintiff college, and the college challenged the board's authority on a variety of grounds. In an informative opinion the New Jersey Supreme Court rejected all the challenges and broadly upheld the board's decision and the validity of the statute under which the board had acted. Another leading case at the other end of the spectrum, *State* v. *Williams*, 253 N.Car. 337, 117 S.E.2d 444 (1960), narrowly construed state authority over private education. But the attitude reflected in *Shelton College* is more likely to prevail in future cases than is that in *Williams.*

Authority over postsecondary education is exercised, in varying degrees depending on the state, in two basic ways. The first is incorporation or chartering, a function performed by all states. In some states postsecondary institutions are subject to the nonprofit corporation laws applicable to all nonprofit corporations; in others, postsecondary institutions come under corporation statutes designed particularly for charitable institutions; and in a few states there are special statutes for incorporating educational institutions. Proprietary (profit-making) schools often fall under general business corporation laws. The states also have laws applicable to "foreign" corporations (that is, those chartered in another state) under which states may "register" or "qualify" out-of-state institutions which seek to do business in their jurisdiction.

The second method for regulating private postsecondary institutions is licensure. Imposed as a condition to offering education within the state or to granting degrees or using a collegiate name, licensure is a more substantial form of regulation than chartering. An overview of the kinds of provisions that are or can be included in state licensing systems, as well as some of the policy choices involved, can be found in *Model State Legislation: Report of the Task Force on Model State Legislation for Approval of Postsecondary Educational Institutions and Authorization to Grant Degrees* (Ed. Comm'n. of the States, Rpt. No. 39, June 1973).

There are three basic types of requirements which represent three different approaches to licensure:

> First, a state can license on the basis of *minimum standards.* The state may choose to specify, for example, that all degree-granting institutions have a board, administration, and faculty of certain characteristics, an organized curriculum with stipulated features, a library of given size and facilities defined as adequate to the instruction offered. Among states pursuing this approach, the debate centers on what and in what detail the state should prescribe—some want higher levels of prescription to assure "quality," others want to allow room for "innovation."
>
> A second approach follows models developed in contemporary regional accreditation and stresses *realization*

of objectives. Here the focus is less on a set of standards applicable to all than on encouragement for institutions to set their own goals and realize them as fully as possible. The role of the visiting team is not to inspect on the basis of predetermined criteria but to analyze the institution on its own terms and suggest new paths to improvement. This help-oriented model is especially strong in the eastern states with large numbers of well-established institutions; in some cases, a combined state-regional team will be formed to make a single visit and joint recommendation.

A third model would take an *honest practice* approach. The essence of it is that one inspects to verify that an institution is run with integrity and fulfills basic claims made to the public. The honesty and probity of institutional officers, integrity of the faculty, solvency of the balance sheet, accuracy of the catalogue, adequacy of student records, equity of refund policies—these related matters would be the subject of investigation. If an institution had an occupation-related program, employment records of graduates would be examined. It is unclear whether any state follows this model in its pure form, though it is increasingly advocated, and aspects of it do appear in state criteria. A claimed advantage is that, since it does not specify curricular components or assess their strengths and weaknesses (as the other two models might), an "honest practice" approach avoids undue state "control" of education [*Approaches to State Licensing of Private Degree-Granting Institutions,* at 17–19 (Postsecondary Education Convening Authority, George Washington University, 1975)].

Although almost all states have some form of licensing laws applicable to proprietary institutions, only about two-thirds have licensing laws for nonprofit degree-granting institutions. Among those states the strength of the laws and the effectiveness of their enforcement vary considerably. Often, by statutory mandate or the administrative practice of the licensing agency, regionally accredited institutions (see Section 8.1) are exempted from all or most licensing requirements.

State corporation laws will usually not pose significant problems for postsecondary institutions, since their requirements can usually be met easily and routinely. Although licensing laws contain more substantial requirements, even in the more rigorous states these laws present few problems for established institutions, either because they are exempted by accreditation or because their established character makes compliance easy. For these institutions, problems with licensing laws are most likely to arise if they establish new programs in other states and must therefore comply with the various licensing laws of those other states (see Section 6.4). The story is quite different for new institutions, especially if they have innovative (nontraditional) structures, programs, or delivery systems, or if they operate across state lines (Section 6.4). For these institutions, licensing laws can be quite burdensome because such laws may not be adapted to the particular characteristics of nontraditional education or receptive to out-of-state institutions.

When an institution does encounter problems with state licensing laws, administrators may have several possible legal arguments to raise, which generally stem from state administrative law or the due process clauses of state constitutions or the federal Constitution. Administrators should insist that the licensing agency proceed according to written standards and procedures, that it make them available to the institution, and that it scrupulously follow its own standards and procedures. If any standard or procedure appears to be outside the authority delegated to the licensing agency by state statute, it may be questioned before the licensing agency and challenged in court. Occasionally, even if standards and procedures are within the agency's delegated authority, the authorizing statute itself may be challenged as an unlawful delegation of legislative power. In *Packer Collegiate Institute* v. *University of the State of New York*, 298 N.Y. 184, 81 N.E.2d 80 (1948), the court invalidated New York's licensing legislation because "the legislature has not only failed to set out standards or tests by which the qualifications of the schools might be measured, but has not specified, even in most general terms, what the subject matter of the regulations is to be." *State* v. *Williams*, referred to at the beginning of this section, used similar reasoning to invalidate a North Carolina law. However, a much more hospitable approach to legislative delegations of authority is found in the *Shelton College* case, also discussed earlier in this section, which upholds a New Jersey law against a charge that it was an unlawful delegation of authority.

Perhaps the soundest legal argument for an institution involved with a state licensing agency is that the agency must follow the procedures in the state's administrative procedure act (where applicable) or the constitutional requirements of procedural due process. *Blackwell College of Business* v. *Attorney General,* 454 F.2d 928 (D.C. Cir. 1971), a case involving a federal agency function analogous to licensing, provides a good illustration. The case involved the withdrawal by the Immigration and Naturalization Service (INS) of Blackwell College's status as a school approved for attendance by nonimmigrant alien students under section 1101(a)(15)(F) of the Immigration and Nationality Act. The INS had not afforded the college a hearing on the withdrawal of its approved status, but only an interview with agency officials and an opportunity to examine agency records concerning the withdrawal. The appellate court found that "the proceedings . . . were formless and uncharted" and did not meet the requirements of either the federal Administrative Procedure Act or constitutional due process. Invalidating the INS withdrawal of approval because of this lack of procedural due process, the court established guidelines for future government proceedings concerning the withdrawal of a school's license or approved status:

> [T]he notice of intention to withdraw approval . . . should specify in reasonable detail the particular instances of failure to . . . [comply with agency requirements]. The documentary evidence the school is permitted to submit . . . can then be directed to the specific grounds alleged. In addition, if requested, the school should be granted a hearing before an official other than the one upon whose investigation the [agency] has relied for initiating its withdrawal proceedings. If the evidence against the school is based upon authentic records, findings may be based thereon, unless the purport of the evidence is denied, in which event the school may be required to support its denial by authentic records or live testimony. If, however, the data presented in support of noncompliance is hearsay evidence, the college, if it denies the truth of the evidence, shall have opportunity, if it so desires, to confront and

cross-examine the person or persons who supplied the evidence, unless the particular hearsay evidence is appropriate for consideration under some accepted exception to the hearsay rule. In all the proceedings the school, of course, shall be entitled to representation and participation by counsel. The factual decision of the [agency] shall be based on a record thus compiled; and the record shall be preserved in a manner to enable review of the decision. . . . We should add that we do not mean that each and every procedural item discussed constitutes by itself a prerequisite of procedural due process. Rather our conclusion of unfairness relates to the totality of the procedure. . . . The ultimate requirement is a procedure that permits a meaningful opportunity to test and offer facts, present perspective, and invoke official discretion [454 F.2d at 936].

Although state incorporation and licensing laws are often sleeping dogs, they can sometimes bite hard. Institutional administrators—especially in new, expanding, or innovating institutions—should remain aware of the potential impact of these laws and the legal arguments available should problems arise.

Sec. 6.4. State Regulation of Out-of-State Institutions

Postsecondary institutions are increasingly departing from the traditional mold of a campus-based organization existing at a fixed location within a single state.[2] Nowadays both established and new institutions, public as well as private, are establishing branch campuses, off-campus programs, colleges without walls, learning "clusters" or centers, TV and other media-based programs, and other innovative systems for delivering education to a wider audience. See K. P Cross, J. R. Valley, and associates, *Planning Non-Traditional Programs: An Analysis of the Issues for Postsecondary Education* (Jossey-Bass, 1974). This nontraditional

[2]The material in this section is drawn from prior work of the author included in Chapter Nine of *Nova University's Three National Doctoral Degree Programs* (Nova/N.Y.I.T. Press, 1977) and in section 4.3 of *Legal and Other Constraints to the Development of External Degree Programs* (report done under Grant NE-G-00-3-0208, National Institute of Education, Jan. 1975).

education (NTE) movement often takes institutions into states other than their home states where they were incorporated, and subjects institutions to the regulatory jurisdiction of those other states.

For these multistate institutions, whether public or private, legal problems increase both in number and in complexity. Not only must they meet the widely differing and possibly conflicting legal requirements of the various states, but they must also be prepared to contend with laws or administrative practices which are not suited to or hospitable to either out-of-state or nontraditional programs. Institutional administrators contemplating the development of any program which will cross state lines should be sensitive to this added legal burden and to the legal arguments which may be used to lighten it.

A multistate institution may seek to apply the legal arguments in Section 6.3 to states which prohibit or limit the operation of the institution's programs within their boundaries; these legal arguments apply to all state regulation whether it concerns out-of-state institutions or not. Out-of-state institutions may also raise particular questions concerning the state's authority over out-of-state, as opposed to in-state, institutions. Is the state licensing agency authorized under state law to license out-of-state schools which award degrees under the authority of their home states? Is the licensing agency authorized to apply standards to an out-of-state school which are higher than or different from the standards it applies to in-state schools? And, most intriguing, can the agency's authority be challenged on the basis of the commerce clause of the U.S. Constitution?

In addition to being a rich lode of power for the federal government (see Section 7.1), the commerce clause has another, less understood, role: it limits the authority of states to use their regulatory powers in ways which interfere with the free movement of goods and people across state lines. As the U.S. Supreme Court recently reemphasized, "the very purpose of the commerce clause was to create an area of free trade among the several states. . . . [B]y its own force [the clause] created an area of trade free from interference by the states" (*Great A&P Tea Co.* v. *Cottrell*, 424 U.S. 366 (1976)). The term *commerce* has been very broadly construed by the courts. It includes both business and nonbusiness, profit and nonprofit activities. It encompasses the movement of goods or people, the communication of information or ideas, the provision of services which cross state lines, and all component parts of such transactions. Interstate educational activities were specifically found to fall within the category of commerce as far back as 1910 in *International Textbook Co. v. Pigg*, 217 U.S. 91 (1910), where the Supreme Court held that an out-of-state correspondence school could not constitutionally be subjected to Kansas's foreign corporation requirements.[3]

What protection, then, might the commerce clause yield for multistate institutions? The zone of protection has been clearly identified in one circumstance: when the out-of-state program is subjected to requirements which are different from and harsher than those the state applies to in-state (domestic) programs. Such differentiation is clearly unconstitutional. For one hundred years it has been settled that states may not discriminate against interstate commerce, or goods or services from other states, in favor of their own intrastate commerce, goods, and services.

Beyond this principle of nondiscrimination or evenhandedness, the commerce clause's umbrella of protection against state regulation becomes more uncertain and more dependent on the facts of each particular case. It covers only the genuinely interstate activities of a particular program or institution. Many activities can become sufficiently fixed within particular states—such as the ownership or rental of real estate, the regular use of agents or employees in the state, and entering contracts within the state—to be considered intrastate. Owing to "this element of localization," as the Supreme Court calls it (*Allenberg Cotton Co. v. Pittman*, 419 U.S. 20 (1974)), such activities can be regulated by the state without raising serious commerce clause problems.

[3]Lawyers will want to compare the *Pigg* case with *Eli Lilly and Co. v. Sav-On Drugs*, 366 U.S. 276 (1961), where the Supreme Court distinguished between the *intrastate* and *interstate* activities of a foreign corporation engaged in interstate commerce and permitted the state to regulate the corporation's intrastate activities. See generally Annot., "Regulation and Licensing of Correspondence Schools and Their Canvassers or Solicitors," 92 A.L.R.2d 522 (1963 plus periodic supp.).

The extent to which interstate activities are actually
protected from state regulation also depends on further refine-
ments. The courts engage in a delicate balancing process,
attempting to preserve the right of states to protect their
governmental interests while protecting the principle of free trade
and intercourse among the states. After a long period of feeling its
way, the Supreme Court in 1970 finally agreed unanimously on
this general approach:

> Where the statute regulates evenhandedly to effectu-
> ate a legitimate local public interest, and its effects on
> interstate commerce are only incidental, it will be upheld
> unless the burden imposed on such commerce is clearly
> excessive in relation to the putative local benefits. If a
> legitimate local purpose is found, then the question
> becomes one of degree. And the extent of the burden that
> will be tolerated will, of course, depend on the nature of the
> local interest involved, and on whether it could be
> promoted as well with a lesser impact on interstate activities
> [*Pike* v. *Bruce Church*, 397 U.S. 137, 142 (1970)].

Under this test the state's interest must be "legitimate"—a
label which courts have sometimes refused to apply to parochial,
internal economic interests prompted by a state's desire to protect
its own economy from out-of-state competition. In one famous
case, the Supreme Court unanimously invalidated a state regulation of an interstate sales transaction because it had "the aim and
effect of establishing an economic barrier against competition with
the products of another state or the labor of its residents" (*Baldwin*
v. *Seelig*, 294 U.S. 511 (1935)). In another famous case, which arose
after a state had refused to license an out-of-state business because
the in-state market was already adequately served, the Court said
the state's decision was "imposed for the avowed purpose and with
the practical effect of curtailing the volume of interstate commerce
to aid local economic interests" and held that "the State may not
promote its own economic advantages by curtailment or burdening
of interstate commerce" (*H. P. Hood & Sons* v. *DuMond*, 336 U.S.
525 (1949)). While an economically based regulation is not

invariably invalid, it is usually suspect and may be accorded little or no weight as a legitimate state interest.

These various principles are most likely to get their test run in the education field in a situation where a state denies entry to an out-of-state program or places such burdensome restrictions on its entry that it is excluded in effect. A state might, for instance, deny entry to an out-of-state program by using academic standards higher than those applied to in-state programs. Or a state might impose a "need requirement" to which in-state programs are not subjected or a need requirement which is newly applied to both out-of-state and in-state programs but which serves to freeze and preserve a market dominated by in-state schools. A state might also deny entry for lack of approval by a regional or statewide coordinating council dominated by in-state institutions. All these possibilities, save perhaps the first, are difficult. But the relevant commerce clause principles point to the possible vulnerability of state authority in each instance. Although states undoubtedly can regulate the localized activities of both out-of-state and in-state programs to promote such legitimate interests as safety, fair dealing, accountability, and institutional competence, it is doubtful that they can completely exclude an interstate program for reasons such as those presented.

These legal arguments (state authority, due process, commerce clause) have not yet been thoroughly tested in litigation, and not all of them would have a clear application to every state regulatory problem faced by an out-of-state institution. But such arguments do present sufficient ammunition for institutional administrators to make it quite likely they can hit the mark in cases where state regulation stifles the development of legitimate interstate postsecondary programs.

Sec. 6.5. Other State Regulatory Laws Affecting Postsecondary Education Programs

Aside from the body of state law specifically designed for postsecondary education, discussed in Sections 6.2 and 6.3, public and private postsecondary institutions are subject to a variety of state statutes and regulations which are not specifically tailored to educational operations. Most of this law concerns the institution's role either as employer or, in the case of public schools, as a government agency.

In some regulatory areas, especially with regard to private institutions, federal legislation has "preempted the field," thus leaving no room for state law. Private sector collective bargaining is a major example. (See Section 7.2.2.) The federal government has the power to preempt and thereby to exclude state law in any field of concern encompassed by its constitutional powers. (See Section 7.1.) In other areas, where there is little or no federal legislation, state legislation is primary. Major examples include public sector collective bargaining laws and wage and hour laws; workers' compensation laws; deceptive practices laws (for nonprofit entities); and open meeting laws, ethics codes, civil service laws, and contract and competitive bidding procedures for public agencies. In yet other areas, federal and state governments may share regulatory responsibilities, with some overlap and coordination of federal and state laws; fair employment laws and occupational health and safety laws are major examples. In this latter area federal law will prevail over state law in case of conflict so long as the subject being regulated is within the federal government's constitutional powers.

Open meeting laws provide a particularly good illustration of the controversy and litigation that can be occasioned by applying general state law to the particular circumstances of postsecondary education. In an era of skepticism about public officials and institutions, public postsecondary administrators must be especially sensitive to laws whose purpose is to promote openness and accountability in government. As state entities, public postsecondary institutions are often subject to open meeting laws and similar legislation, and the growing body of legal actions under such laws indicates that the public intends to assure that public institutions comply.

Litigation to enforce or to clarify the effect of open meeting laws on public institutions has been initiated by the media, faculty members, students, education associations, and members of the general public. In *Arkansas Gazette Co.* v. *Pickens*, 522 S.W.2d 350

(Ark. 1975), for instance, a newspaper and one of its reporters argued that committees of the University of Arkansas Board of Trustees, and not just the full board itself, were subject to the Arkansas Freedom of Information Act. The reporter had been excluded from a committee meeting on a proposed rule change that would have allowed students of legal age to possess and consume intoxicating beverages in university-controlled facilities at the Fayetteville campus. The Arkansas Freedom of Information Act provided in part that "[i]t is vital in a democratic society that public business be performed in an open and public manner so that the electors shall be advised of the performance of public officials and of the decisions that are reached in public activity and in making public policy. Toward this end this act is adopted, making it possible for them or their representatives to learn and to report fully the activities of the public officials" (Ark. Stat. Ann. sec. 12-2802). The board of trustees contended, and the lower court agreed, that meetings of the board's committees were not "public meetings" within the meaning of the act. The Arkansas Supreme Court reversed, reasoning that the "intent of the legislature, as so emphatically set forth in its statement of policy, [was] that *public business* be performed in an open and public manner" (522 S.W.2d at 353). The court could find no distinction between the board's business and that of its committees and thus applied the open meeting requirement to both.

Not all cases, however, have been resolved in favor of openness. In *The Associated Students of the University of Colorado v. The Regents of the University of Colorado*, 543 P.2d 59 (Colo. 1975), the plaintiffs sought to enjoin the regents from holding executive sessions barred to the public. After the trial court applied the state's open meeting law to the board of regents and enjoined it from holding executive sessions except when matters covered by the attorney-client privilege would be discussed, the Colorado Supreme Court reversed. It held that the board was not subject to the open meeting law because it was a constitutional body corporate (see Section 6.2.2) with broad powers under the state constitution and statutes to supervise its own affairs.

One problem created by open meeting statutes and similar laws is how to balance the public's right to know with an individual's right to privacy or an institution's need for confidentiality. Administrators must consider the complex interplay of all these interests. Sometimes the legislation provides guidelines or rules for striking this balance. Even in the absence of such provisions, some courts have narrowly construed open meeting laws to avoid intrusion on compelling interests of privacy or confidentiality.

Selected Annotated Bibliography

Sec. 6.1 (General Background)

1. Schwartz, B., *Administrative Law* (Little, Brown, 1976), is a comprehensive overview of the principles of administrative law. Although the book does not focus on education, its analyses can be applied to state postsecondary systems (to the extent they are considered state agencies), to state agencies that charter or license private institutions, and to other state agencies whose regulatory authority extends to postsecondary institutions.

Sec. 6.2 (State Systems of Public Postsecondary Education)

1. Millard, R. M., *State Boards of Higher Education* (American Association for Higher Education, ERIC/Higher Education Research Rpt. No. 4, 1976), discusses the history, structure, functions, and future directions of state governing and coordinating boards for higher education; includes state-by-state tables and a bibliography.
2. Schaefer, H., "The Legal Status of the Montana University System Under the New Montana Constitution," 35 *Montana Law Review* 189 (1974), compares and analyzes the new and old Montana constitutional provisions and discusses comparable provisions in other state constitutions; considers the impact of such provisions on the state institution's relationships with other branches of state government.

Sec. 6.3 (State Chartering and Licensure of Private Postsecondary Institutions)

1. Postsecondary Education Convening Authority, *Approaches to State Licensing of Private Degree-Granting Institutions* (George Washington University, Institute for Educational Leadership Rpt. No. 8, 1975), is the conference report on the first conference of state officials who license private degree-granting institutions; explores the concepts of chartering and licensing, the current status of licensing in the fifty states, and the policy and legal problems facing licensing officials; makes recommendations for the future.

Sec. 6.4 (State Regulation of Out-of-State Institutions)

1. Hughes, E., Simco, E., Nelson, F., and Fischler, A., *Nova University's Three National Doctoral Degree Programs* (Nova University, 1977), is a Ford Foundation funded case study on the development of multistate education programs. Chap. 9 (by F. Nelson and W. Kaplin) provides a discussion of "Legal and Political Constraints on Nova University's External Degree Programs."

Sec. 6.5 (Other State Regulatory Laws Affecting Postsecondary Education Programs)

1. Hopkins, B., "Regulation of Interstate Charitable Solicitations: Implications for Colleges and Universities," 2 *J. of College and University Law* 289 (1975), analyzes the various state laws regulating charitable solicitations and discusses the legal and policy problems such laws present for colleges and universities; includes appendices categorizing the various state laws and giving addresses in each state for information.
2. Simon, A. M., "The Application of State Sunshine Laws to Institutions of Higher Education," 4 *J. of College and University Law* 83 (1977), explores the state sunshine laws from every angle of concern to postsecondary administrators

and their counsel. Includes extensive citations to cases and statutes, three appendices collecting and categorizing state laws, and a bibliography.

Chapter VII

The College
and the Federal
Government

Sec. 7.1. Federal Constitutional Powers over Education

It is a basic constitutional principle that the federal government is a government of limited powers. It has only those powers which are expressly conferred by the U.S. Constitution or can reasonably be implied from those conferred, the remaining powers being "reserved to the States respectively, or to the people" under the Tenth Amendment. Because the Constitution does not mention education, let alone delegate power over it to the federal government, it is sometimes argued that the Tenth Amendment reserves the handling of education to the states or the people. That

argument is a misconception. Many federal constitutional powers
—particularly the spending power, the taxing power, the commerce power, and the civil rights enforcement power—are broad
enough to extend to many matters concerning education. Whenever an activity falls within the scope of such federal powers (such
as making conditional grants to, or contracting with, postsecondary institutions; regulating unfair labor practices or unfair trade
practices that affect interstate commerce; taxing graduate assistantships; prohibiting sex discrimination in postsecondary employment practices), the federal government may regulate it. (See, for
example, *Case* v. *Bowles*, 327 U.S. 92 (1946), rejecting a Tenth
Amendment challenge to federal emergency price controls on sales
of property owned by the states and used for school purposes.)

The Tenth Amendment affects the scope of federal power in
only one narrow respect: When the federal government undertakes
to directly regulate the states or their political subdivisions, it may
not, at least under the commerce power, enact regulations which
would impair state sovereignty by "directly displac[ing] the states'
freedom to structure integral operations in areas of traditional
governmental functions" (*National League of Cities* v. *Usery*, 426
U.S. 833, 852 (1976)). As the discussion later in this section
indicates, the application of this vague principle to public
postsecondary education is unclear.

The current federal involvement in education stems primarily from the "spending power," that is, Congress's power under
Article I, section 8, clause 1, to spend its funds for the "general
welfare of the United States." The spending power is the basis of
the federal aid-to-education programs discussed in Section 7.3 and
the civil rights requirements discussed in Section 7.4. It is also the
basis of the student records (Buckley Amendment) requirements
analyzed in Section 4.12.1. The practice of placing conditions on
grants to postsecondary education was approved as long ago as
1907, when in *Wyoming ex rel. Wyoming Agricultural College* v.
Irvin, 206 U.S. 278 (1907), the U.S Supreme Court upheld a
condition attached to grants under the land grant college acts.
Since then, especially after the Supreme Court's validation of
innovative spending legislation passed during Roosevelt's New
Deal, the spending power has been broadly construed to permit

virtually any spending program Congress believes will further the general welfare (see *Helvering* v. *Davis,* 301 U.S. 619 (1937)), and any condition on spending, whether imposed on governmental or private entities, which is "reasonable" and "relevant to federal interest in the project and the overall objective thereof" (*Ivanhoe Irrigation District* v. *McCracken,* 357 U.S. 275, 295 (1958)). The spending power, however, does not give the federal government a roving commission to regulate postsecondary education. What leverage the federal government exerts through the spending power arises from its establishment of the purposes and conditions for its expenditure of funds. Though fund recipients are subject to federal requirements, they can avoid the requirements by not accepting the funds.

The federal taxing power also comes from Article I, section 8, clause 1, which authorizes Congress "to lay and collect taxes" in order to raise the money it spends for the general welfare. The tax power is the basis for the laws discussed in Section 7.2.8. Though the purpose of the tax power is to raise revenue rather than to regulate, as such, the power has been broadly construed to permit tax measures with substantial regulatory effects. The application of the tax power to postsecondary education was upheld in *Allen* v. *Regents,* 304 U.S. 439 (1938), which concerned an admissions tax that the federal government had levied on state college football games. The tax power may be somewhat greater over private than over public institutions, since public institutions may enjoy a constitutional immunity from federal taxation of their basic sovereign functions (see G. Burke, "Federal Taxation of State Colleges and Universities: Recent Developments Call for Reconsideration of Theories of Exemption," 4 *J. of College and University Law* 43 (1977)).

The federal commerce power stems from Article I, section 8, clause 3 of the Constitution, which authorizes Congress "to regulate commerce with foreign nations, and among the several States." This is the major regulatory power which has been applied to postsecondary education and is the basis for most of the laws discussed in Section 7.2. The commerce power has been broadly construed to permit the regulation of activities which either are *in* interstate or foreign commerce or *affect* it. As the U.S. Supreme

Court has often acknowledged, "Congress's power under the Commerce Clause is very broad. Even activity that is purely intrastate in character may be regulated by Congress, where the activity, combined with like conduct by others similarly situated, affects commerce among the States or with foreign nations" (*Fry* v. *United States,* 421 U.S. 542, 547 (1975)).

Recently, however, the U.S. Supreme Court did confine the commerce power somewhat as a basis for regulating state government activities. In *National League of Cities* v. *Usery,* the Court relied on the Tenth Amendment to invalidate federal wage and hours laws as applied to state and local government employees, reasoning that "their application will significantly alter or displace the States' abilities to structure employer-employee relationships . . . in areas of traditional governmental functions." The Court premised this decision on a general principle that "Congress may not exercise . . . [the commerce] power so as to force directly upon the States its choices as to how essential decisions regarding the conduct of integral governmental functions are to be made." Though this principle would pose some limit on the federal authority to regulate public postsecondary institutions, the principle's breadth is uncertain. It is unclear how the principle would extend to state functions other than public employment relations or to powers other than the commerce power. In a case decided after *National League of Cities,* for instance, *Fitzpatrick* v. *Bitzer,* 427 U.S. 445 (1976), the Court upheld the 1972 extension of the Title VII employment discrimination law (see Section 3.3.2.1) to state and local government employers because the law was based on the civil rights enforcement power rather than on the commerce power. And in *Usery* v. *Allegheny County Institution District,* 544 F.2d 148 (3d Cir. 1976), a court of appeals upheld the application of the Equal Pay Act (see Section 3.3.2.4) to state and local employers, the Tenth Amendment notwithstanding, because that act is based on the civil rights enforcement power.

The civil rights enforcement power is the fourth major federal power applicable to education. Its source is the enforcement clauses of various constitutional amendments, particularly the Fourteenth Amendment (due process and equal protection), whose fifth section provides that "the Congress shall have power to

enforce, by appropriate legislation, the provisions of this article."
In *Katzenbach* v. *Morgan*, 384 U.S. 641 (1966), the U.S. Supreme
Court held that section 5 of the Fourteenth Amendment empowers
Congress to "exercise its discretion in determining whether and
what legislation is needed to secure the [amendment's] guarantees,"
so long as the legislation is "adapted to carry out the objects the
. . . [amendment has] in view" and not otherwise prohibited by the
Constitution.

The civil rights enforcement powers are the basis for the
Title VII and Equal Pay Act employment discrimination laws
upheld in the *Fitzpatrick* and *Allegheny County* cases discussed in
this section. They are also the basis for various civil rights
regulatory statutes which have some application to postsecondary
education, such as 42 U.S.C. section 1981 (discussed above in
Sections 3.3.2.7 and 4.2.4.1) and 42 U.S.C. section 1983 (discussed
in Section 2.4.3). Although the enforcement powers clearly apply to
public institutions, and although Section 1981 has been extended
to private institutions in the area of race discrimination (see
Fairfax-Brewster v. *Gonzales*, 427 U.S. 160 (1976), discussed in
Section 4.2.4.1), there is some question concerning the validity of
other applications to private institutions.[1]

Sec. 7.2. Federal Regulation of Postsecondary Education

The federal government asserts varying amounts of control
over postsecondary institutions under federal legislation that is not
specifically, or at least not exclusively, designed for such institutions. This section briefly discusses several such laws. While many
of these laws are based on Congress's commerce power (see Section
7.1) and thus apply only to activities which are in or which affect
interstate commerce under the particular formulation of each
statute, current interpretations of these formulations are broad
enough to include most postsecondary institutions.

[1]The question is complex and varies with the civil rights statute at
issue and the constitutional amendment which the statute purports to
enforce. For an extended analysis of the issues, see Note, "Federal Power to
Regulate Private Discrimination: The Revival of the Enforcement Clauses
of the Reconstruction Era Amendments," 74 *Columbia L. Rev.* 449 (1974).

7.2.1. Occupational Safety and Health Act. Private postsecondary institutions must conform to the federal Occupational Safety and Health Act of 1970 (OSHA), 29 U.S.C. secs. 651 *et seq.* Under this act, a private institution must "furnish to each of [its] employees employment and a place of employment which are free from recognized hazards that are causing or are likely to cause death or serious physical harm" (29 U.S.C. sec. 654). Violations may result in fines or imprisonment (sec. 666). The act does not preempt any rights employees may have to pursue civil actions or other remedies under state laws (sec. 653(b)(4)).

Though public postsecondary institutions are not subject to OSHA, they may be required to conform to state occupational safety and health laws or equivalent state legislation or administrative regulations.

7.2.2. Labor Management Relations Act. The Labor Management Relations Act, 29 U.S.C. secs. 141 *et seq.,* protects the employees of covered employers in "the exercise . . . of full freedom of association, self-organization, and designation of representatives of their own choosing, for the purpose of negotiating the terms and conditions of their employment or other mutual aid or protection" (29 U.S.C. sec. 151). The LMRA's application to faculty members is discussed in Section 3.2.

The act defines "employee" to exclude "any individual employed as a supervisor" (29 U.S.C. sec. 152(3)); a "supervisor" is defined as "any individual having authority, in the interest of the employer, to hire, transfer, suspend, lay off, recall, promote, discharge, assign, reward, or discipline other employees, or responsibly to direct them, or to adjust their grievances, or effectively to recommend such action, if in connection with the foregoing the exercise of such authority is not of a merely routine or clerical nature, but requires the use of independent judgment" (sec. 152 (11)). The act defines "employer" to exclude "any state or political subdivision thereof," thereby removing public employers, including public postsecondary institutions, from the act's coverage (29 U.S.C. sec. 152 (2)). The LMRA thus applies only to private postsecondary institutions and, under current National Labor Relations Board rules, only to those with gross annual revenues of at least one million dollars (29 C.F.R. sec. 103.1).

Public institutions, though not subject to the LMRA, are often subject to similar legislation at the state level. (See Section 3.2.)

7.2.3. Employee Retirement Income Security Act. The Employee Retirement Income Security Act of 1974, also known as "The Pension Reform Act" or "ERISA," codified in part at 26 U.S.C. secs. 401 *et seq.* and 29 U.S.C. secs. 1001 *et seq.*, establishes "standards of conduct, responsibility, and obligation for fiduciaries of employee benefit plans" (29 U.S.C. sec. 1001(b)). The act alters both federal tax laws and federal labor laws insofar as it identifies the possible ways in which certain retirement plans may be arranged, including those established for employees of private postsecondary institutions. The retirement plans of public institutions are excluded from coverage as "governmental plan[s]" under 29 U.S.C. sec. 1002(32) and 26 U.S.C. sec. 414(d). Rules and regulations have been issued covering reporting and disclosure requirements, minimum standards, and fiduciary responsibilities. (See 29 C.F.R. Parts 2510, 2520, 2530, and 2550.) Interpretive bulletins explaining the act and its regulations have also been issued and reprinted at 29 C.F.R. Part 2509.

Some special rules apply to benefit plans for teachers and other employees of tax-exempt organizations. The employees of an educational institution may, under some circumstances, delay their participation in a benefit plan until they reach thirty. (See 26 U.S.C. sec. 410(a)(1)(B); 29 U.S.C. sec. 1052(a)(1)(B)(ii).) The rules regarding the investment of funds in tax-sheltered annuities also provide for different treatment of such employees. (See 26 U.S.C. sec. 403(b); 26 U.S.C. sec. 415(c)(4).)

7.2.4. Fair Labor Standards Act. The Fair Labor Standards Act (FLSA), 29 U.S.C. secs. 201 *et seq.*, establishes the minimum hourly wage and the piecework rates as well as the maximum hours allowed for certain nonsupervisory employees, including those of private postsecondary institutions. The FLSA once applied to public postsecondary institutions under a 1966 amendment extending coverage to state hospitals and schools. But the case which upheld this amendment, *Maryland* v. *Wirtz*, 392 U.S. 183 (1968), was expressly overruled by the U.S. Supreme Court in *National League of Cities* v. *Usery*, 426 U.S. 833 (1976) (discussed in Section 7.1), thus cutting off coverage of public postsecondary educational institutions.

In situations where an applicable state law establishes a minimum wage rate which conflicts with the federal standard, the higher rate must prevail (29 U.S.C. sec. 218).

7.2.5. *Antitrust laws.* Federal antitrust laws, in particular the Sherman Act, 15 U.S.C. secs. 1 *et seq.*, and the Clayton Act, 15 U.S.C. secs. 12 *et seq.*, may apply to the business or commercial practices of private postsecondary institutions. Public institutions, however, are exempt from federal antitrust laws. In *Parker* v. *Brown,* 317 U.S. 341 (1943), and *Cantor* v. *Detroit Edison,* 428 U.S. 579, 96 S. Ct. 3110 (1976), the U.S. Supreme Court held that the Sherman Act does not apply to the governmental actions of state officials and agents. In *Saenz* v. *University Inter-scholastic League,* 487 F.2d 1026 (5th Cir. 1973), the *Parker* v. *Brown* doctrine was applied to exempt public postsecondary education activities from antitrust coverage.

The antitrust provision most likely to trouble postsecondary education is section 1 of the Sherman Act, under which "[e]very contract, combination . . . , or conspiracy, in restraint of trade or commerce . . . is declared illegal." While it has sometimes been agreed that this language does not cover "the liberal arts and learned professions" because they are not business or commercial ventures, in 1975 the Supreme Court refuted the existence of any such absolute exemption from antitrust coverage (*Goldberg* v. *Virginia State Bar,* 421 U.S. 773 (1975)). Under *Goldberg,* "the nature of an occupation, standing alone, does not provide sanctuary from the Sherman Act," although the "public service aspect" or other unique aspects of particular activities may require that their treatment under antitrust laws be different from that of typical business activities.

In these days of shrinking dollars and of diversity and innovation in postsecondary education, it is increasingly likely that postsecondary institutions with common interests will join together in associations or organizations part of whose purpose is to enhance the institutions' position in the education or political world. Administrators should be cautious about such "combinations" because, under *Goldberg,* they can present antitrust problems if they have the effect of restraining some other institution's operations. But if such a restraint arises from the association's pursuit of valid educational goals, it is not likely to be illegal under the antitrust laws. In *Marjorie Webster Junior College* v. *Middle States Association,* 432 F.2d 650 (D.C. Cir. 1970) (discussed in Section 8.2), for example, the defendant's accreditation activities escaped antitrust liability because they were not undertaken with a "commercial motive" and went "to the heart of the concept of education itself." Moreover, lobbying activities engaged in by combinations of institutions will usually not be illegal under the antitrust laws, even if the government action sought would result in a restraint of trade. (See *Eastern Railroads Presidents Conference* v. *Noerr,* 365 U.S. 127 (1961), and *United Mineworkers* v. *Pennington,* 381 U.S. 657 (1965).)

7.2.6. *Federal Trade Commission Act.* The Federal Trade Commission Act, 15 U.S.C. secs. 41 *et seq.,* prohibits covered entities (sec. 45(a)(2)) from "using unfair methods of competition in or affecting commerce and unfair or deceptive acts or practices in or affecting commerce" (sec. 45(a)(1)). The act applies to proprietary postsecondary institutions but not to private nonprofit institutions or public institutions. The Federal Trade Commission has been developing a trade regulation rule to regulate unfair and deceptive practices by proprietary vocational schools. (See 40 Fed. Reg. 44582 (Sept. 29, 1975).)

7.2.7. *Copyright laws.* In 1976, after many years of effort inside and outside government, Congress revised the federal copyright law. Effective as of January 1, 1978, the General Revision of the Copyright Law, 17 U.S.C. secs. 101 *et seq.,* has particular relevance to educational institutions because it addresses the question of what kinds of copying of copyrighted materials may be done for teaching and scholarship. This question, previously governed by the judicially created "fair use" doctrine, is now governed by the codification of that doctrine in sections 107 and 108 of the new act. Unfortunately, these sections do not provide a clear guide to what may and may not be copied for teaching and scholarship. Some further help is contained in two documents included as part of the new act's legislative history: (1) an "Agreement on Guidelines for Classroom Copying in Not-for-

Profit Educational Institutions," in House Report No. 94-1476
(94th Cong., 2d Sess.); and (2) "Guidelines for the Proviso of
Subsection 108(g)(2)" (interlibrary arrangements), in Conference
Report No. 94-1733 (94th Cong., 2d Sess.).

7.2.8. *Tax laws.* To qualify for and maintain federal tax-
exempt status, a postsecondary educational institution must
conform to the following description:

> [It must be an institution] organized and operated
> exclusively for . . . educational purposes, . . . no part of the
> net earnings of which inures to the benefit of any private
> shareholder or individual, no substantial part of the
> activities of which is carrying on propaganda, or otherwise
> attempting to influence legislation (except as otherwise
> provided . . .), and which does not participate in, or
> intervene in . . . any political campaign on behalf of any
> candidate for public office [26 U.S.C. sec. 501(c)(3)].

A public institution may also qualify for tax exemption under two
alternate theories, either (1) that it is a political subdivision of a
state under 26 U.S.C. sec. 115 and related provisions or (2) that it is
immune from taxation under the constitutional doctrine of
intergovernmental immunities.

Through these requirements for tax exemption, the federal
government influences the organizational structures and activities
of educational institutions. The Internal Revenue Service, for
instance, regulates an institution's involvement in lobbying efforts
and political activities. (See 26 U.S.C. sec. 501(c)(3), above, and 26
U.S.C. sec. 501(h).) It also requires that private schools maintain a
policy of nondiscrimination on the basis of race, color, and
national or ethnic origin. (See Rev. Proc. 75-50, 1975–2 Cum. Bull.
587; Rev. Rul. 75-231, 1975–1 Cum. Bull. 158, setting out illustrative situations regarding church-affiliated schools.) The loss of tax-
exempt status can severely affect an institution's financial resources. In addition to incurring tax liability, the institution may
lose financial support from donors, because donations to an
institution which is not tax-exempt are not deductible for federal
tax purposes.

Other tax provisions also can exert a substantial influence

on postsecondary institutions. Provisions on the taxability of fellowships and scholarships, for instance, may affect an institution's financial aid policy. And provisions on the taxability of an institution's unrelated business income may affect the extent and character of the institution's noneducational ventures.

7.2.9. *Employment discrimination laws.* Aside from the nondiscrimination requirements which it imposes as conditions on federal spending (see Section 7.4), the federal government also directly regulates employment discrimination under several other statutes. Primary among them is Title VII of the Civil Rights Act of 1964, 42 U.S.C. sec. 2000e *et seq.* These statutes are discussed in Section 3.3.2.

Sec. 7.3. Federal Aid-to-Education Programs

The federal government's major function regarding postsecondary education is to establish national spending priorities and to provide funds in accordance with those priorities. In establishing and administering its priorities, the federal government attaches a wide and varied range of conditions to the funds it makes available and enforces these conditions against postsecondary institutions and other aid recipients. Some of these conditions are specific to the program for which funds are given. Others apply across a range of programs, such as the civil rights requirements discussed in Section 7.4 and the privacy-of-student-records requirements discussed in Section 4.12. Cumulatively, these conditions exert a most substantial influence on postsecondary institutions, often leading to institutional cries of economic coercion and federal control. In light of this growing institutional criticism, refining national policy and the role of federal funding in relation to postsecondary education will likely be a major issue for the foreseeable future.

Although some current criticisms of the federal spending role are new, and although the level of federal expenditure has increased vastly since the early sixties, federal spending for education has a long history. Shortly after the founding of the United States, the federal government began endowing public higher education institutions with public lands. In 1862 Congress passed the first Morrill Act, providing grants of land or land scrip to the states for the support of agricultural and mechanical colleges, and later provided continuing appropriations for these colleges. The second Morrill Act, providing money grants for instruction in various branches of higher education, was passed in 1890. In 1944 Congress enacted the first G.I. Bill, which was followed in later years by successive programs providing funds to veterans to further their education. The National Defense Education Act, passed in 1958 after Congress was spurred by Russia's launching of Sputnik, included a large-scale program of low-interest loans for students in institutions of higher education. The Higher Education Facilities Act of 1963 authorized grants and low-interest loans to public and private nonprofit institutions of higher education for constructing and improving various educational facilities. Then, in 1965, Congress finally jumped broadly into subsidizing higher education with the passage of the Higher Education Act of 1965 (20 U.S.C. secs. 1001 *et seq.*). The act's various titles authorized federal support for a range of postsecondary education activities, including community educational services; resources, training, and research for college libraries and personnel; strengthening developing institutions; and student financial aid programs. As later amended, the act now contains most of the student financial aid programs and provisions discussed in Section 4.3.

Financial assistance for postsecondary education is disbursed by a number of federal agencies. Aside from the agencies involved in procurement activities (such as U.S. Department of Defense research contracts) which are for the government's own purposes, the major financial aid agencies are the U.S. Office of Education and the Veterans' Administration.

The Office of Education (OE), created in 1867 and headed by the Commissioner of Education, is now a constituent agency of the Department of Health, Education, and Welfare. Under a 1972 statute, 20 U.S.C. secs. 1221a–1221c, the Office of Education, together with the National Institute of Education (NIE), constitutes the Education Division of HEW, which is headed by an assistant secretary for education. The Commissioner of Education has considerable autonomy within this framework, however, because most federal aid-to-education legislation vests administrative authority directly in the commissioner. The administrators and legal counsel of postsecondary institutions will therefore often deal with the commissioner and his designees rather than with the secretary of HEW or the assistant secretary. A notable exception is civil rights legislation (Section 7.4), which is administered directly by the secretary and the Office for Civil Rights (OCR), which is under the secretary's authority.

The Veterans' Administration (VA) administers the veterans' educational benefits programs found in 38 U.S.C. secs. 1673 *et seq.* (See *Max Cleland, Administrator of VA* v. *National College of Business*, 98 S. Ct. 1024 (1978), upholding various federal statutory restrictions (the "85-15" rule and the "two-year" rule) on veterans' use of VA benefits.) The VA contracts with the State Approving Agencies, which review courses and determine whether to approve them as courses for which veterans can expend veterans' benefits. The State Approving Agencies must follow criteria and procedures for course approval which are set out in 38 U.S.C. secs. 1775–1776. (See Section 4.3.2 above.)

Federal aid to postsecondary education is dispensed in a variety of ways. The federal government may make grants or loans directly to individual students; it may guarantee loans made to individual students by third parties; it may make grants or loans directly to postsecondary institutions; it may award contracts to postsecondary institutions; or it may provide grants, loans, or contracts to state agencies which in turn aid institutions or students. Whether an institution is eligible to receive federal aid, either directly from the federal agency or a state agency or indirectly from the student recipient, depends on the requirements of the particular aid program. Typically, however, the institution must be accredited by a recognized accrediting agency or demonstrate compliance with one of the few statutorily prescribed substitutes for accreditation. (See Sections 8.1 and 8.3.)

The "rules of the game" regarding eligibility, application procedures, the selection of recipients, allowable expenditures, conditions on spending, records and reports requirements, and other federal aid requirements are set out in a variety of sources. Administrators will want to be familiar with these sources in order to maximize the institution's ability to obtain and effectively utilize federal money. Legal counsel will want to be familiar with these sources in order to protect the institution from challenges to its eligibility or to its compliance with applicable requirements.

The starting point is the statute which authorizes the particular federal aid program, along with the statute's legislative history. Occasionally the appropriations legislation funding the program for a particular fiscal year will also contain some requirement applicable to the expenditure of the appropriated funds. The next source, adding specificity to the statutory base, is the regulations for the program. The regulations, which are published in the *Federal Register* and then codified in the *Code of Federal Regulations*, are usually the primary source of program requirements. Regulations may be backed up by federal program manuals, guidelines, or policy memoranda, which are also sometimes used in lieu of formal regulations. Published regulations have the force of law and bind the government, the aid recipients, and all the outside parties. Manuals, guidelines, and memoranda generally do not have the status of law; they may only bind recipients who had actual notice of them before receiving federal funds, or they may be treated as agency suggestions rather than requirements and thus not bind anyone. (See 5 U.S.C. sec. 552(a)(1).) Additional requirements or suggestions may be found in the grant award documents or contracts under which the aid is awarded, in agency manuals on grant and contract policies applicable across a range of programs, or in Office of Management and Budget (OMB) circulars which set government-wide policy on such matters as allowable cost principles and the establishment of indirect cost rates. In addition, the civil rights statutes and regulations (see Section 7.4) establish nondiscrimination requirements applicable to all federal aid programs.

The U.S. Office of Education is subject to federal statutes which place additional restrictions on its rules of the game. The General Education Provisions Act, 20 U.S.C. secs. 1221 *et seq.*, establishes numerous organizational, administrative, and other requirements applicable to OE spending programs. Under section 431 of the act, no OE rule or regulation "of general applicability" can become effective until thirty days after it has been published in the *Federal Register*. The General Education Provisions Act has been implemented by extensive regulations codified in 45 C.F.R. Parts 100–100d; Appendices A-D to these regulations set forth standard grant terms and conditions, and cost principles applicable to grantee expenditures under OE grant programs.

The federal government has several methods for enforcing compliance. The responsible agency may periodically audit the institution's expenditures of federal money and may take an "audit exception" for funds not spent in compliance with program requirements. The institution then owes the federal government the amount specified in the audit exception. Alternatively, or in addition to audit exceptions, the agency may limit, suspend, or terminate the institution's funding under the program or programs in which noncompliance is found. Under section 133(a) of the Education Amendments of 1976, 20 U.S.C. sec. 1088f-1(a)(4), for instance, the Commissioner of Education has the authority to prescribe regulations for

> the limitation, suspension, or termination of the eligibility for any program under this title [that is, the title containing OE's major student financial aid programs] of any otherwise eligible institution, whenever the Commissioner has determined, after reasonable notice and opportunity for hearing on the record, that such institution has violated or failed to carry out any provision of this title or any regulation prescribed under this title, except that no period of suspension under this section shall exceed sixty days unless the institution and the Commissioner agree to an extension or unless limitation or termination proceedings are initiated by the Commissioner within that period of time.

Federal funding agencies also apparently have the authority to sue institutions in court to obtain compliance with grant and contract conditions, although they seldom exercise this power. In *United States* v. *Frazer*, 297 F. Supp. 319 (M.D. Ala. 1968), a suit against the administrators of the Alabama state welfare system, the court held that the United States had standing to sue to enforce welfare grant conditions requiring that personnel for federally financed programs be hired on a merit basis. And in *United States* v. *Institute of Computer Technology*, 403 F. Supp. 922 (E.D. Mich.

1975), the court permitted the United States to sue a school which had allegedly breached a contract with the Office of Education under which the school disbursed funds for the Basic Educational Opportunity Grant program.

Given the number and complexity of the conditions attached to federal spending programs, and the federal government's substantial enforcement power, postsecondary institutions will want to keep attuned to all the procedural rights, legal arguments, and negotiating leverage they may utilize in case of disputes with federal funding agencies. The institution's legal position and negotiating strength will depend on the provisions of the particular funding program, on the particular facts of the case, and on whether the institution is applying for aid or being threatened with a fund cut-off. Typically, applicants have fewer procedural rights than do recipients.

The funding statutes or program regulations often provide a right to a hearing before funding is cut off, as does the 20 U.S.C. sec. 1088(f) provision quoted earlier in this section. (See 20 U.S.C. sec. 1232c(c); and 45 C.F.R. sec. 100a.495.) In other cases the institution may have a right to a hearing before a grants review board or contract review board of the agency. When no hearing is provided under agency statutes or regulations, the federal Administrative Procedure Act, 5 U.S.C. secs. 551 *et seq.*, may provide either a right to a hearing or a right to judicial review of the agency's decision. The due process clause of the Fifth Amendment may also guarantee a right to a hearing regarding fund termination. It is questionable whether *public* postsecondary institutions would be protected by the Fifth Amendment, however; that amendment protects only "persons," and as government agencies, public institutions probably would not fall into that category.

While such procedural protections can be very important, often the critical issue will concern the substance of what the federal agencies are doing to institutions rather than the procedures by which they do it. In particular, in times charged with claims of federal control over education, institutions may seek to challenge the substantive validity of particular conditions that federal agencies attach to the expenditure of federal funds. In 1976–77, for instance, a furor arose over a congressional requirement (since repealed) that, as a condition for receiving capitation grants, medical schools had to reserve a number of places for American students transferring from foreign medical schools. But because the federal government's constitutional power to tax and spend is so broad (see Section 7.1), substantive challenges to such spending conditions are difficult and speculative. Arguments that particular conditions violate the principles of academic freedom (First Amendment) or substantive due process (Fifth Amendment) may sometimes be possible. (See P. Lacovara, "How Far Can the Federal Camel Slip Under the Academic Tent?" 4 *J. of College and University Law*, in press.) When the condition is created by an agency rule or regulation rather than by the funding statute itself, it may be possible to argue that the rule or regulation is *ultra vires*, that is, beyond the authority delegated to the agency under the funding statute. Such substantive legal challenges, even more than procedural challenges, provide an area ripe for creative activity by postsecondary institutions and their legal counsel.

Sec. 7.4. Civil Rights Compliance

7.4.1. General. Postsecondary institutions receiving assistance under federal aid programs are obligated to follow not only the programmatic and technical requirements of each program under which aid is received (see Section 7.3) but also various civil rights requirements which apply generally to federal aid-to-education programs. These requirements are a major focus of federal spending policy, importing substantial social goals into education policy and making equality of educational opportunity a clear national priority in education. The implementation and enforcement of civil rights have often been steeped in controversy— some arguing the federal role is too great, and some that it is too small; some arguing that the federal government proceeds too fast, and some too slow; and others arguing that the compliance process is too cumbersome or costly for the affected institutions. Despite the controversy, it is clear that the federal civil rights efforts in education have been a major force for social change in America.

As conditions on spending, the civil rights requirements represent an exercise of Congress's spending power (see Section 7.1) implemented through delegating authority to the various federal departments and agencies which administer federal aid programs. As nondiscrimination principles promoting equal educational opportunity, the civil rights requirements may also be justifiable as exercises of Congress's power to enforce the Fourteenth Amendment's equal protection clause (see Section 7.1).

Three different federal statutes prohibit discrimination in education programs receiving federal financial assistance. Title VI of the Civil Rights Act of 1964 prohibits discrimination on the basis of race, color, or national origin. Title IX of the Education Amendments of 1972 prohibits discrimination on the basis of sex. Section 504 of the Rehabilitation Act of 1973, as amended in 1974, prohibits discrimination against the handicapped. (A fourth statute on age discrimination, not due to be implemented by regulations until late 1978, is briefly discussed in Section 7.4.5.) Title IX is specifically limited to education programs receiving federal financial assistance, while Title VI and Section 504 apply to all programs receiving such assistance. Each statute delegates enforcement responsibilities to each of the federal agencies disbursing federal financial assistance. Postsecondary institutions may thus be subject to the civil rights regulations of several federal agencies, the most important one being the Department of Health, Education, and Welfare.

Although the language of the three statutes is similar, each statute protects a different group of beneficiaries, and an act which constitutes discrimination against one group does not necessarily constitute discrimination if directed against another group. "Separate but equal" treatment of the sexes is sometimes permissible under Title IX, for instance, but such treatment of the races is never permissible under Title VI. Administrative regulations, particularly those of HEW, have considerably fleshed out the meaning of the statutes. Since the spring of 1978, HEW's Office for Civil Rights has also published policy interpretations of HEW regulations in the *Federal Register*. Judicial decisions occasionally contribute additional interpretive gloss on major points, but the administrative regulations remain the primary source for understanding the civil rights requirements.

7.4.2. Title VI. Title VI of the Civil Rights Act of 1964, 42 U.S.C. sec. 2000d, declares:

> No person in the United States shall, on the ground of race, color, or national origin, be excluded from participation in, be denied the benefits of, or be subjected to discrimination under any program or activity receiving federal financial assistance.

Early judicial interpretation held that Title VI incorporated the standards developed under the equal protection clause for identifying unlawful discrimination (*Goodwin* v. *Wyman,* 330 F. Supp. 1038 note 3 (D.C.N.Y. 1971), affirmed 406 U.S. 964 (1972)). In *Washington* v. *Davis,* 426 U.S. 229 (1976), however, the Supreme Court held that a finding of discriminatory intent must be made in order for a discriminatory act to constitute an equal protection violation, but suggested that discriminatory intent need not necessarily be proved under civil rights statutes. The HEW Title VI regulations, 45 C.F.R. Part 80, especially at sec. 80.3(b)(2), suggest that only a discriminatory effect must be shown to establish a Title VI violation.

Section 80.3(b) of the HEW regulations provides the best guidance for administrators of postsecondary institutions:

> (b) *Specific discriminatory actions prohibited.*
>
> (1) A recipient under any program to which this part applies may not, directly or through contractual or other arrangements, on ground of race, color, or national origin:
>
> (i) Deny an individual any service, financial aid, or other benefit provided under the program;
>
> (ii) Provide any service, financial aid, or other benefit to an individual which is different, or is provided in a different manner, from that provided to others under the program;
>
> (iii) Subject an individual to segregation or separate treatment in any matter related to his receipt of any service, finanical aid, or other benefit under the program;
>
> (iv) Restrict an individual in any way in the enjoyment of any advantage or privilege enjoyed by others receiving any service, financial aid, or other benefit under the program;

(v) Treat an individual differently from others in determining whether he satisfies any admission, enrollment, quota, eligibility, membership, or other requirement or condition which individuals must meet in order to be provided any service, financial aid, or other benefit provided under the program;

(vi) Deny an individual an opportunity to participate in the program through the provision of services or otherwise or afford him an opportunity to do so which is different from that afforded others under the program (including the opportunity to participate in the program as an employee but only to the extent set forth in paragraph (c) of this section).

(vii) Deny a person the opportunity to participate as a member of a planning or advisory body which is an integral part of the program.

(2) A recipient, in determining the types of services, financial aid, or other benefits, or facilities which will be provided under any such program, or the class of individuals to whom, or the situations in which such services, financial aid, other benefits, or facilities will be provided under any such program, or the class of individuals to be afforded an opportunity to participate in any such program, may not directly or through contractual or other arrangements utilize criteria or methods of administration which have the effect of subjecting individuals to discrimination because of their race, color, or national origin, or have the effect of defeating or substantially impairing accomplishment of the objectives of the program as respect individuals of a particular race, color, or national origin.

(3) In determining the site or location of facilities, an applicant or recipient may not make selections with the effect of excluding individuals from, denying them the benefits of, or subjecting them to discrimination under any programs to which this regulation applies, on the ground of race, color, or national origin; or with the purpose or effect of defeating or substantially impairing the accomplishment of the objectives of the Act or this regulation.

(4) As used in this section, the services, financial aid, or other benefits provided under a program receiving federal financial assistance shall be deemed to include any service, financial aid, or other benefits provided in or through a facility provided with the aid of federal financial assistance.

(5) The enumeration of specific forms of prohibited discrimination in this paragraph and paragraph (c) of this

section does not limit the generality of the prohibition in
paragraph (a) of this section.

The application of Title VI to traditionally black colleges
and universities poses a special problem. Black institutions may be
charged with Title VI violations or may be included in a statewide
remedy for Title VI violations in a state system of postsecondary
education. Commentators have suggested, however, that the
integration of traditionally black institutions, as long as access for
minority students to traditionally white institutions remains
limited, will further limit opportunities for minority students.
Commentators have also emphasized the intrinsic value of
traditionally black institutions as a source of pride in the minority
community and a source of role models for minority youths. In
Adams v. *Richardson*, 480 F.2d 1159 (D.C. Cir. 1973), discussed
further in Section 7.4.7, the U.S. court of appeals recognized the
importance of traditionally black institutions in training black
professionals:

> The problem of integrating higher education must
> be dealt with on a statewide rather than a school-by-school
> basis. Perhaps the most serious problem in this area is the
> lack of statewide planning to provide more and better
> trained minority group doctors, lawyers, engineers, and
> other professionals. A predicate for minority access to
> quality postgraduate programs is a viable, coordinated
> statewide higher education policy that takes into account
> the special problems of minority students and of black
> colleges. As *amicus* points out, these black institutions
> currently fulfill a crucial need and will continue to play an
> important role in black higher education [480 F.2d at
> 1164–65].

As Title VI law develops at the postsecondary level,
institutional administrators should be sensitive to these possible
differences between, and the interrelation between, traditionally
black and traditionally white institutions. A recent development in
this regard is HEW's issuance of desegregation criteria for states
found to have *de jure* segregated systems of higher education. In
general the criteria, a result of the *Adams* v. *Richardson* litigation,

require the affected states to take various affirmative steps,
including enhancing the quality of black state-supported colleges
and universities, placing new "high demand" programs on
traditionally black campuses, eliminating unnecessary program
duplication between black and white institutions, increasing the
percentage of black academic employees in the system, and increasing the enrollment of blacks at traditionally white public colleges.
See *Revised Criteria Specifying the Ingredients of Acceptable Plans
to Desegregate State Systems of Public Higher Education* (Feb. 2,
1978), a historical overview, legal analysis, and explanation
available from HEW's Office for Civil Rights.

7.4.3. *Title IX.* The central provision of Title IX of the
Education Amendments of 1972, 20 U.S.C. secs. 1681 *et seq.*,
declares:

(a) No person in the United States shall, on the basis of
sex, be excluded from participation in, be denied the
benefits of, or be subjected to discrimination under any
education program or activity receiving federal financial
assistance, except that:

(1) in regard to admissions to educational institutions,
this section shall apply only to institutions of vocational
education, professional education, and graduate higher
education, and to public institutions of undergraduate
higher education;

(2) in regard to admissions to educational institutions,
this section shall not apply (A) for one year from June 23,
1972, nor for six years after June 23, 1972, in the case of an
educational institution which has begun the process of
changing from being an institution which admits only
students of one sex to being an institution which admits
students of both sexes, but only if it is carrying out a plan
for such a change which is approved by the Commissioner
of Education or (B) for seven years from the date an
educational institution begins the process of changing from
being an institution which admits only students of only one
sex to being an institution which admits students of both
sexes, but only if it is carrying out a plan for such a change
which is approved by the Commissioner of Education,
whichever is the later;

(3) this section shall not apply to an educational
institution which is controlled by a religious organization if

the application of this subsection would not be consistent with the religious tenets of such organization;

(4) this section shall not apply to an educational institution whose primary purpose is the training of individuals for the military services of the United States, or the merchant marine;

(5) in regard to admissions this section shall not apply to any public institution of undergraduate higher education which is an institution that traditionally and continually from its establishment has had a policy of admitting only students of one sex.

Title IX also excludes from its coverage the membership practices of tax-exempt social fraternities and sororities (20 U.S.C. sec. 1681(a)(6)(A)); the membership practices of the YMCA, YWCA, Girl Scouts, Boy Scouts, Campfire Girls, and other tax-exempt, traditionally single-sex "youth service organizations" (20 U.S.C. sec. 1681(a)(6)(B)); American Legion, Boys State, Boys Nation, Girls State, and Girls Nation activities (20 U.S.C. sec. 1681(a)(7)); and father-son and mother-daughter activities if provided on a reasonably comparable basis for students of both sexes (20 U.S.C. sec. 1681(a)(8)).

HEW's regulations implementing Title IX, 45 C.F.R. Part 86, include provisions paralleling the language of the previously quoted Title VI regulations. (See 45 C.F.R. sec. 86.31.) Additional Title IX regulations specify in much greater detail the acts of discrimination prohibited in programs and activities receiving federal financial aid. Educational institutions may not discriminate on the basis of sex in admissions and recruitment (with certain exceptions) (see Section 4.2.4.2); in awarding financial assistance (Section 4.3.3); in athletics programs (Section 4.11.2); or in the employment of faculty and staff members (Section 3.3.2.3) or students (see 45 C.F.R. sec. 86.38). Section 86.32 prohibits sex discrimination in housing accommodations with respect to fees, services, or benefits, but does not prohibit separate housing by sex (Section 4.10.1 above). Section 86.33 requires that separate facilities for toilets, locker rooms, and shower rooms be comparable. Section 86.34 prohibits sex discrimination in student access to course offerings. Sections 86.36 and 86.38 require that counseling services and employment placement services be offered to students in such a way that there is no discrimination on the basis of sex. Section 86.39 prohibits sex discrimination in health and insurance benefits and services, including any medical, hospital, accident, or life insurance policy or plan which the recipient offers to its students. Under Section 86.40, an institution may not "apply any rule concerning a student's actual or potential parental, family, or marital status" which would have the effect of discriminating on the basis of sex, nor may the recipient discriminate against any student on the basis of pregnancy or childbirth.

7.4.4. *Section 504.* Section 504 of the Rehabilitation Act of 1973, as amended, 29 U.S.C. sec. 794, states:

> No otherwise qualified handicapped individual in the United States . . . shall, solely by reason of his handicap, be excluded from participation in, be denied the benefits of, or be subjected to discrimination under any program or activity receiving federal financial assistance.

After an extended period of controversy, revision, and maneuvering, HEW issued regulations in the spring of 1977 implementing Section 504 for all recipients of HEW financial assistance (42 Fed. Reg. 22676-22701 (May 4, 1977), codified in 45 C.F.R. Part 84). Like Titles VI and IX, Section 504 is administered by the HEW Office for Civil Rights.

The regulations contain specific provisions which establish standards for postsecondary institutions to follow with regard to "qualified handicapped" students and applicants, as well as "qualified handicapped" employees, applicants for employment, and members of the public seeking to take advantage of institutional programs and activities open to the public. A "handicapped person" is "any person who (i) has a physical or mental impairment which substantially limits one or more major life activities, (ii) has a record of such an impairment, or (iii) is regarded as having such an impairment" (45 C.F.R. sec. 84.3(j)). In the context of postsecondary and vocational education services, a "qualified" handicapped person is someone who "meets the academic and technical standards requisite to admission or participation in the recipient's education program or activity" (45 C.F.R. sec. 84.3(k)(3)). Whether a handicapped person is "qualified" in other situations depends on different criteria. In the context of employment, a qualified handicapped person is one who, "with reasonable accommodation, can perform the essential functions of the job in question" (45 C.F.R. sec. 84.3(k)(1)). With regard to other services, it is someone who "meets the essential eligibility requirements for the receipt of such services" (45 C.F.R. sec. 84.3(k)(4)).

Although HEW's Section 504 regulations resemble those for Title VI and Title IX in the types of programs and activities considered, they differ in some of the means used for achieving nondiscrimination. These differences exist because "different or special treatment of handicapped persons, because of their handicaps, may be necessary in a number of contexts in order to ensure equal opportunity" (42 Fed. Reg. 22676, May 4, 1977). Institutions receiving federal funds may not discriminate on the basis of handicap in admission and recruitment of students (see Section 4.2.4.3); in providing financial assistance (Section 4.3.3); in athletics programs (Section 4.11.3); in housing accommodations (Section 4.10.1); or in the employment of faculty and staff members (Section 3.3.2.6) or students (see 45 C.F.R. sec. 84.46(c)). The regulations also prohibit discrimination on the basis of handicap in a number of other programs and activities of postsecondary institutions.

Section 84.43 requires nondiscriminatory "treatment" of students in general. Besides prohibiting discrimination in the institution's own programs and activities, this section requires that when "education programs or activities not operated wholly by the . . . [institution are] part of, or equivalent to, an education program or activity operated by the . . . [institution], . . . the other education program or activity, as a whole, . . . [must provide] opportunity for the participation of qualified handicapped persons." In a student-teaching program, for example, the "on the whole" concept allows the institution to make use of a particular external program or activity which discriminates, provided that the recipient's entire student-teaching program, taken as a whole, offers handicapped student teachers "the same range and quality of choice in student-teaching assignments afforded nonhandicapped students" (42 Fed. Reg. at 22692 (comment 30)). Furthermore, the institution must operate its programs and activities in "the most integrated setting appropriate," that is, by integrating handicapped persons with nonhandicapped persons to the maximum extent appropriate.

The HEW regulations recognize that certain academic adjustments may be necessary to protect against discrimination on the basis of handicap:

> (a) *Academic requirements.* A recipient to which this subpart applies shall make such modifications to its academic requirements as are necessary to ensure that such requirements do not discriminate or have the effect of discriminating, on the basis of handicap, against a qualified handicapped applicant or student. Academic requirements that the recipient can demonstrate are essential to the program of instruction being pursued by such student or to any directly related licensing requirement will not be regarded as discriminatory within the meaning of this section. Modifications may include changes in the length of time permitted for the completion of degree requirements, substitution of specific courses required for the completion of degree requirements, and adaptation of the manner in which specific courses are conducted.
>
> (b) *Other rules.* A recipient to which this subpart applies may not impose upon handicapped students other rules, such as the prohibition of tape recorders in classrooms or of dog guides in campus buildings, that have the effect of limiting the participation of handicapped students in the recipient's education program or activity.
>
> (c) *Course examinations.* In its course examinations or other procedures for evaluating students' academic achievement in its program, a recipient to which this subpart applies shall provide such methods for evaluating the achievement of students who have a handicap that impairs sensory, manual, or speaking skills as will best ensure that the results of the evaluation represent the student's achievement in the course, rather than reflecting the student's impaired sensory, manual, or speaking skills (except where such skills are the factors that the test purports to measure).
>
> (d) *Auxiliary aids.* (1) A receipient to which this subpart applies shall take such steps as are necessary to ensure that no handicapped student is denied the benefits of, excluded from participation in, or otherwise subjected to discrimination under the education program or activity

operated by the recipient because of the absence of educational auxiliary aids for students with impaired sensory, manual, or speaking skills. (2) Auxiliary aids may include taped texts, interpreters, or other effective methods of making orally delivered materials available to students with hearing impairments, readers in libraries for students with visual impairments, classroom equipment adapted for use by students with manual impairments, and other similar services and actions. Recipients need not provide attendants, individually prescribed devices, readers for personal use or study, or other devices or services of a personal nature [45 C.F.R. sec. 84.44].

Section 84.47(b) provides that counseling and placement services be offered on the same basis to handicapped and nonhandicapped students. The institution is specifically charged with ensuring that job counseling is not more restrictive for handicapped students. Under section 84.47(c), an institution that supplies significant assistance to student social organizations must determine that these organizations do not discriminate against handicapped students in their membership practices.

Discrimination on the basis of handicap must not result from the physical inaccessibility of the institution's programs or activities or the unusability of the institution's facilities. The regulations applicable to existing facilities differ from those applied to new construction:

(a) *Program accessibility*. A recipient shall operate each program or activity to which this part applies so that the program or activity, when viewed in its entirety, is readily accessible to handicapped persons. This paragraph does not require a recipient to make each of its existing facilities or every part of a facility accessible to and usable by handicapped persons.

(b) *Methods*. A recipient may comply with the requirements of paragraph (a) of this section through such means as redesign of equipment, reassignment of classes or other services to accessible buildings, assignment of aids to beneficiaries, home visits, delivery of health, welfare, or other services at alternate accessible sites, alteration of existing facilities and construction of new facilities in conformance with the requirements of sec. 84.23, or any

> other methods that result in making its program or activity accessible to handicapped persons. A recipient is not required to make structural changes in existing facilities where other methods are effective in achieving compliance with paragraph (a) of this section. In choosing among available methods for meeting the requirement of paragraph (a) of this section, a recipient shall give priority to those methods that offer programs and activities to handicapped persons in the most integrated setting appropriate [45 C.F.R. sec. 84.22].

If a structural change in existing facilities is necessary to make a program or activity accessible, the change must be completed by June 3, 1980. All new construction on the other hand—that is, construction for which ground is broken after June 3, 1977—must be readily accessible when it is completed.[2]

   7.4.5. Age Discrimination Act of 1973. The newcomer on the civil rights scene, this act provides that:

> No person in the United States shall, on the basis of age, be excluded from participation in, or be subject to discrimination under, any program or activity receiving federal financial assistance [42 U.S.C. sec. 6102].

While this language parallels Titles VI and IX and Section 504, the introductory provision of the Age Discrimination Act (42 U.S.C. sec. 6101) indicates that its purpose is to prohibit only *"unreasonable* discrimination on the basis of age" (emphasis added). This additional language, having no counterpart in the other civil

---

   [2]Compliance with accessibility requirements is attained by conforming to the "American National Standard Specifications for Making Buildings and Facilities Accessible to, and Usable by, the Physically Handicapped," American National Standards Institute, Inc., 1430 Broadway, New York, N.Y. 10018. "Under section 2122 of the Tax Reform Act of 1976, recipients that pay federal income tax are eligible to claim a tax deduction of up to $25,000 for architectural and transportation modifications made to improve accessibility for handicapped persons" (42 Fed. Reg. at 22689 (comment 20)). See also 42 U.S.C. secs. 4151 *et seq.* (Architectural Barriers Act of 1968) and 29 U.S.C. sec. 792 (the act's federal Compliance Board) for further requirements applicable to buildings constructed, altered, or leased with federal aid funds.

rights acts, suggests that this act is less stringent and will permit "reasonable" forms of age discrimination. Section 6103(b) also excludes some considerations of age from the act's coverage when necessary to fulfill the statutory objective of a program or when a statute provides for selection of recipients or determination of benefits by age.

Administrators can understand the act's coverage only by studying HEW's implementing regulations, which were due to be published the latter part of 1978.

7.4.6. Affirmative action. Affirmative action poses a special problem under the federal civil rights statutes. The HEW Title VI regulations both require and permit affirmative action under certain circumstances:

> (i) In administering a program regarding which the recipient has previously discriminated against persons on the ground of race, color, or national origin, the recipient must take affirmative action to overcome the effects of prior discrimination.
>
> (ii) Even in the absence of such prior discrimination, a recipient in administering a program may take affirmative action to overcome the effects of conditions which resulted in limiting participation by persons of a particular race, color, or national origin [45 C.F.R. sec. 80.3(b)(6)].

The Title IX regulations also permit affirmative action for voluntary correction of conditions which resulted in limited participation by the members of one sex in the institution's programs and activities (45 C.F.R. sec. 86.3(b)). However, both Title IX and Section 504 require a recipient to engage in "remedial action" rather than "affirmative action" to overcome the effects of its own prior discrimination (45 C.F.R. sec. 86.3(a); 45 C.F.R. sec. 84.6(a)). In addition, Section 504 suggests that the recipient take only "voluntary action" rather than "affirmative action" to correct conditions which resulted in limited participation by the handicapped (45 C.F.R. sec. 84.6(b)). But none of the regulations defines "affirmative action," "remedial action," or "voluntary action," or sets out the limits of permissible action. One federal district court has ruled that in a Title VI case some "affirmative action" may itself constitute a Title VI violation. In *Flanagan* v. *President and Directors of Georgetown College*, 417 F. Supp. 377 (D.D.C. 1976), the issue was that Georgetown Law Center had allocated 60 percent of its scholarship funds to minority students, who constituted only 11 percent of the class. The university claimed that the program was permissible under 45 C.F.R. sec. 80.3(b)(6)(ii). The court disagreed, holding that the scholarship program was not administered on a "racially neutral basis" and was "reverse discrimination on the basis of race, which cannot be justified by a claim of affirmative action." Subsequently, in *University of California Regents* v. *Bakke*, 46 *U.S. Law Week* 4896 (see Section 4.2.5), the first U.S. Supreme Court case on affirmative action under Title VI, a 5-4 majority of the Court agreed that Title VI did not require complete racial neutrality in affirmative action. But no majority of justices could agree on the extent to which Title VI and its regulations permit racial or ethnic preferences to be used as one part of an affirmative action program.

Thus, the federal regulations give postsecondary administrators little guidance concerning the affirmative or remedial actions they must take to maintain compliance, or may take without jeopardizing compliance. Insufficient guidance, however, is not a justification for avoiding affirmative action when it is required by the regulations, nor should it deter administrators from taking voluntary action when it is their institution's policy to do so. Rather administrators should proceed carefully, seeking the assistance of legal counsel and of HEW and keeping abreast of the developing case law on affirmative action. (See Sections 3.4 and 4.2.5.)

7.4.7. Scope and coverage problems. The scope and coverage of the civil rights statutes still have not been precisely defined. The statutes prohibit recipients of federal funds from discriminating in any "program or activity receiving Federal financial assistance." The statutes do not define "recipient," "Federal financial assistance," or "program or activity," however, leaving those terms to be defined by administrative regulations and court decisions.

HEW's Title VI, Title IX, and Section 504 regulations define "recipient" in similar but not identical language. Under Title VI "recipient" means any State, political subdivision of any State, or instrumentality of any State or political subdivision, any public or private agency, institution, or organization, or other entity, or any individual, in any State, to whom Federal financial assistance is extended, directly or through another recipient, for any program, including any successor, assign, or transferee thereof, but such term does not include any ultimate beneficiary under any such program [45 C.F.R. sec. 80.13(i)].

While the Section 504 definition contains only minor variations (45 C.F.R. sec. 84.3(f)), Title IX varies in one major respect: The definition is potentially broader because it includes any recipient operating a program or activity which receives *or benefits from* federal financial assistance (45 C.F.R. sec. 86.2(h)).

The type of federal assistance received also helps determine whether a postsecondary institution is covered by the civil rights statutes. All three sets of HEW regulations define "federal financial assistance" very broadly. Under the HEW Title IX regulations, for instance,

"[f]ederal financial assistance" means any of the following, when authorized or extended under a law administered by the Department:

(1) A grant or loan of Federal financial assistance, including funds made available for:

(i) The acquisition, construction, renovation, restoration, or repair of a building or facility or any portion thereof; and

(ii) Scholarships, loans, grants, wages or other funds extended to any entity for payment to or on behalf of students admitted to that entity, or extended directly to such students for payment to that entity.

(2) A grant of Federal real or personal property or any interest therein, including surplus property, and the proceeds of the sale or transfer of such property, if the Federal share of the fair market value of the property is not, upon such sale or transfer, properly accounted for to the Federal Government.

(3) Provision of the services of Federal personnel.

(4) Sale or lease of Federal property or any interest therein at nominal consideration, or at consideration reduced for

the purpose of assisting the recipient or in recognition of
public interest to be served thereby, or permission to use
Federal property, or any interest therein without consideration.

(5) Any other contract, agreement, or arrangement which
has as one of its purposes the provision of assistance to any
education program or activity, except a contract of insurance or guaranty [45 C.F.R. sec. 86.2(g)].

The definitions under Title VI (45 C.F.R. sec. 80.13) and Section
504 (45 C.F.R. secs. 84.3(h) and (i)) are similar.

In *Bob Jones University* v. *Johnson*, 396 F. Supp. 597
(D.C.S.C. 1974), affirmed 529 F.2d 514 (4th Cir. 1975), the court
broadly interpreted the phrase "federal financial assistance" in
reviewing a Veterans' Administration decision that the university
had violated Title VI. The educational benefits paid by the
Veterans' Administration under its G.I. Bill program to some of
the university's students constituted the university's sole source of
federal funding. The court held that the university was a recipient
of federal financial assistance within the meaning of Title VI.

In applying the regulations, the VA has determined
that the educational benefits statutes which it administers
are covered by Title VI, and that the educational institutions schooling veterans subsidized under these statutes are
recipients of federal financial assistance within the meaning
of Title VI. Accordingly, Bob Jones, in common with all
other participating schools, is prohibited by Section 601
from discriminating on the basis of race with respect to its
federally assisted educational programs. . . . The method of
payment does not determine the result; the literal language
of Section 601 requires only federal assistance—not payment to a program or activity—for Title VI to attach. The
appropriate questions are (1) whether the federally subsidized veteran participates in a "program or activity" and if
so, (2) whether that program or activity is "receiving federal
financial assistance." The facts in this case project an
affirmative answer to both questions [396 F. Supp. at
601–02].

The third pertinent coverage concept, "program or activity,"
is incompletely defined in HEW regulations. The Title VI

regulations do define "program" in a way which also encompasses the concept of "activity":

> The term "program" includes any program, project, or activity for the provision of services, financial aid, or other benefits to individuals (including education or training, health, welfare, rehabilitation, housing, or other services, whether provided through employees of the recipient of Federal financial assistance or provided by others through contracts or other arrangements with the recipient, and including work opportunities and cash or loan or other assistance to individuals), or for the provision of facilities for furnishing services, financial aid, or other benefits to individuals. The services, financial aid, or other benefits provided under a program receiving Federal financial assistance shall be deemed to include any services, financial aid, or other benefits provided with the aid of Federal financial assistance or with the aid of any non-Federal funds, property, or other resources required to be expended or made available for the program to meet matching requirements or other conditions which must be met in order to receive the Federal financial assistance, and to include any services, financial aid, or other benefits provided in or through a facility provided with the aid of Federal financial assistance or such non-Federal resources [45 C.F.R. sec. 80.13(g)].

Neither the Title IX nor the Section 504 regulations include separate definitions of either "program" or "activity." However, the Title IX regulations do indicate that discrimination is prohibited "under any academic, extracurricular, research, occupational training, or other education program or activity" (45 C.F.R. sec. 86.31(a)). The Section 504 regulations contain similar but more detailed language in a section having specific reference to postsecondary education institutions (45 C.F.R. sec. 84.43(a)).

Most of the controversy over the scope of the civil rights statutes has concerned fund termination. Title VI provides that any termination of a recipient's federal funding for failure to comply with civil rights requirements "shall be limited in its effect to the particular program, or part thereof, in which such noncompliance has been so found" (42 U.S.C. sec. 2000d-1). Title IX contains the same language (20 U.S.C. sec. 1682). By Executive Order No. 11914, 41 Fed. Reg. 17871 (1976), Section 504 has a somewhat more exacting "pinpoint" provision, limiting terminations to the "particular program or activity or part thereof" which is not complying.

The leading case on the fund termination remedy is *Board of Public Instruction of Taylor County* v. *Finch*, 414 F.2d 1068 (5th Cir. 1969). HEW had cut off the recipient's federal funds under three different federal programs without making individual findings of discrimination for each program. Although HEW had found faculty and student segregation in the school system,.the court indicated that, under Title VI's fund termination provision, it could not assume "that defects in one part of a school system automatically infect the whole." Rather, in order to comply with the termination provision, "the administrative agency seeking to cut off federal funds must make findings of fact indicating either that a particular program is itself administered in a discriminatory manner, or is so affected by discriminatory practices elsewhere in the school system that it thereby becomes discriminatory." Under this test, federal funding for a program can be terminated not only if the program is discriminatory but also if it is "infected" by discrimination elsewhere in the school system or institution. The federal funding agency can thus exert leverage over nonfederally subsidized programs by claiming that discrimination in those programs infects the system's or institution's federally funded programs.

Special problems of scope and coverage are posed by the application of the civil rights statutes to employment discrimination and to discrimination in athletics programs. (See, for example, J. Kuhn, "Title IX—Employment and Athletics Are Outside HEW's Jurisdiction," 65 *Georgetown L. J.* 49 (1976).) The Civil Rights Act of 1964 specifically excludes employment from the scope of Title VI, except for programs in which the federal government's main purpose is to provide employment (42 U.S.C. sec. 2000d-3), and the HEW regulations follow suit (45 C.F.R. secs. 80.2 and 80.3(c)). Neither Title IX nor Section 504 contains such a statutory exclusion for employment, and the HEW regulations broadly cover employment discrimination (see Sections 3.3.2.3 and 3.3.2.6 above).

On athletics, the Title VI regulations contain no specific provisions, and their application to athletics programs is unclear. On the other hand, both the Title IX and Section 504 regulations broadly prohibit discrimination in athletics programs (see Sections 4.11.2 and 4.11.3).

Critics have asserted that HEW exceeded its statutory authority in applying Title IX and Section 504 to employment and athletics. The major argument is that an institution's employment and athletics programs are not generally subsidized by federal aid and thus cannot be assumed, across-the-board, to be programs receiving federal financial assistance within the meaning of the statutes. In addition, in relation to employment, critics argue that the statutory prohibitions on discrimination are directed to the beneficiaries, not the employees, of subsidized programs and that Congress covered employment discrimination under Title VII of the Civil Rights Act (see Section 3.3.2.1) and did not intend to cover it under the other civil rights statutes. The latter argument does not apply to Section 504 because, unlike race and sex discrimination, discrimination against the handicapped is not covered in Title VII.

Some of these coverage issues are involved in litigation, and more litigation is likely. In the leading opinion thus far, *Romeo Community Schools* v. *HEW*, 438 F. Supp. 1021 (E.D. Mich. 1977), a local school district sued HEW when HEW threatened to cut off funds because of alleged sex discrimination in employment. The court held that Title IX "addresses itself only to sex discrimination against . . . school children," not faculty members. "HEW cannot regulate the practices of an educational institution unless some of those practices result in sex discrimination against the beneficiaries of some federally assisted education program operated by the institution." The court found that broad coverage of employment would exceed HEW's jurisdiction, which is limited to specific programs receiving federal assistance, because school district employment policies cover all employees in the district, not just those working in federally subsidized programs. "Regulation of those policies by HEW will therefore necessarily entail the regulation of employment practices unrelated to the particular programs funded by the Federal government and without regard to whether such practices result in sex discrimination against the beneficiaries of those programs." Although several other lower courts have followed *Romeo*, its reasoning may be unduly narrow and the issue will be satisfactorily resolved only after higher courts have spoken.

7.4.8. Administrative enforcement. Compliance with each of the three civil rights statutes is enforced through a complex system of procedures and mechanisms administered by the federal agencies which provide financial assistance. Postsecondary administrators should develop a sound understanding of this enforcement process so they can satisfactorily pursue both the rights and the responsibilities of their institutions should compliance problems arise.

The Title VI statute delegates enforcement responsibilities to the various federal funding agencies. By Executive Order 11247, 30 Fed. Reg. 12327 (1965), the U.S. Attorney General is responsible for coordinating Title VI enforcement. Justice Department regulations, 28 C.F.R. Part 42, 41 Fed. Reg. 52669-52672 (1976), impose certain requirements on the agencies' enforcement efforts. Each agency must submit proposed enforcement regulations to the assistant attorney general, Civil Rights Division, before publication (28 C.F.R. sec. 42.403). Each agency must issue guidelines on Title VI for each program for which it provides federal financial assistance (28 C.F.R. sec. 42.409). The regulations and guidelines must be available to the public (28 C.F.R. sec. 42.405). The Justice Department regulations require the agencies to collect sufficient data, on such items as the racial composition of the population eligible for the program and the location of facilities, to determine compliance (28 C.F.R. sec. 42.406). All Title VI compliance decisions must be made by or be subject to the review of the agency's civil rights office. Programs found to be complying must be reviewed periodically to assure continued compliance. A finding of probable noncompliance must be reported to the Attorney General (28 C.F.R. sec. 42.407). Each agency must establish complaint procedures and publish them in its guidelines. All Title VI complaints must be logged in the agency records (28 C.F.R. sec. 42.408). If a finding of probable noncompliance is made, enforcement procedures shall be instituted after a "reasonable period" of negotiation. If negotiations continue for more than sixty days after the finding of noncompliance, the agency must notify the Attorney General (28 C.F.R. sec. 42.411). If several agencies provide federal financial assistance to a substantial number of the same recipients for similar or related purposes, the agencies must coordinate Title VI enforcement efforts. The agencies shall designate one agency as the lead agency for Title VI compliance (28 C.F.R. sec. 42.413). Each agency must develop a written enforcement plan, specifying priorities, timetables, and procedures, which shall be available to the public (28 C.F.R. sec. 42.415).

Under HEW's Title VI regulations, fund recipients must file assurances with HEW that their programs comply with Title VI (45 C.F.R. sec. 80.4) and must submit "timely, complete and accurate compliance reports at such times, and in such form and containing such information, as the responsible Department official or his designee may determine to be necessary to enable him to ascertain whether the recipient has complied or is complying" with Title VI (45 C.F.R. sec. 80.6(b)). HEW may make periodic compliance reviews and must accept and respond to individual complaints from persons believing themselves to be victims of discrimination (45 C.F.R. sec. 80.7). If an investigation reveals a violation which cannot be resolved by negotiation and voluntary compliance (45 C.F.R. sec. 80.7(d)), HEW may refer the case to the Justice Department for prosecution (see Section 7.4.9) or commence administrative proceedings for fund termination (45 C.F.R. sec. 80.8). The regulations specify the procedural safeguards which must be observed in the fund termination proceedings—notice, the right to counsel, a written decision, an appeal to a reviewing authority, and a discretionary appeal to the secretary of HEW (45 C.F.R. sec. 81).

Title IX employs the same fund termination procedures as Title VI but also imposes additional compliance responsibilities on institutions receiving federal aid. Recipients must undertake a self-evaluation of their current policies and practices and prepare a remedial plan which shall be available for HEW inspection (45 C.F.R. sec. 86.3). Institutions must appoint at least one employee to coordinate the compliance efforts and must establish a grievance procedure for handling discrimination complaints within the institution (45 C.F.R. sec. 86.8).

Under Section 504, the secretary of HEW coordinates the enforcement efforts of all federal funding agencies (Executive Order 11914, 41 Fed. Reg. 17871 (1976)). HEW's regulations for its own programs impose compliance responsibilities similar to those under Title IX. However, recipients with fewer than fifteen employees need not conform to certain requirements: (1) having a copy of the remedial plan available for inspection (45 C.F.R. sec. 84.6(c)(2)); (2) appointing an agency employee to coordinate the compliance effort (45 C.F.R. sec. 84.7(a)); and (3) establishing a grievance procedure for handling discrimination complaints (45 C.F.R. sec. 84.7(b)). Most postsecondary educational institutions are not excepted from these requirements, since most have more than the minimum number of employees. Section 504 also adopts the Title VI procedural regulations concerning fund terminations.

The federal courts exercise a limited review of federal agencies' enforcement efforts. If a federal agency terminates an institution's funding, the institution may appeal that decision to the courts once it has exhausted administrative review procedures within the agency.[3] If a federal agency abuses its enforcement authority during enforcement proceedings and before a final determination decision, an affected educational institution may also seek injunctive relief from such improper enforcement efforts. On the other hand, if the agency fails to fulfill its enforcement responsibilities, victims of unlawful discrimination may seek judicial enforcement of the agency's affirmative duty to implement the civil rights statute.

In *Mandel* v. *U.S. Dept. of Health, Education, and Welfare*, 411 F. Supp. 542 (D. Md. 1976), HEW commenced fund termination proceedings against the state of Maryland based on alleged Title VI violations in the state's system of higher education. The state sought judicial intervention, claiming that HEW had not in good

---

[3]Such judicial review is specifically authorized by the Title VI and Title IX statutes. (See 42 U.S.C. sec. 2000d-2; 20 U.S.C. sec. 1683.) Section 504 provides no such basis for judicial review. However, the legislative history of the Rehabilitation Act Amendments of 1974, P.L. 93-516, indicates that Congress clearly contemplated judicial review of fund terminations under Section 504 (4 *U.S. Code Cong. and Admin. News,* at 6390–91). The Administrative Procedure Act, 5 U.S.C. secs. 701 *et seq.,* is apparently available to provide a statutory basis for such review.

faith sought voluntary compliance. Maryland complained that HEW delayed review of the state's original desegregation plan, prematurely cut off negotiations, and did not provide guidelines on how to effect desegregation. The state specifically claimed that HEW refused to rule on the importance of statistics in assessing compliance or on the future of traditionally black educational institutions. The court found that HEW did not seek voluntary compliance in good faith. Maryland also complained that HEW failed to "pinpoint" which of the state's programs violated Title VI. The court held that HEW must pinpoint the offending programs before enforcement proceedings are begun:

> It is paradoxical to assume that a recipient of federal funding, such as a state or a large city, could rectify any discriminatory programs within its system without ever being informed which program was considered by HEW to be operating discriminatively. Consequently, a statewide or citywide approach to enforcement of Title VI is, doubtless, not conducive to compliance by voluntary means and, in all likelihood, contrary to Congressional nonvindictive intent.
>   Other reasons come to the fore which, likewise, suggest that plaintiffs' reading of Title VI in this regard is a proper one. As will be developed *infra*, in . . . the State system . . . there are multitudinal programs receiving federal financing which, due to the nonprogrammatic approach assumed, are being condemned by defendants en masse. . . . [In the state system] there is federal funding to programs within twenty-eight institutions of higher education ranging from a unique cancer research center to the student work-study program. To compel all of these programs, regardless of whether or not each is discriminatory, to prepare a defense and endure protracted enforcement proceedings is wasteful, counterproductive, and probably inimical to the interests of the very persons Title VI was enacted to protect. It is far more equitable, and more consistent with Congressional intent, to require program delineation prior to enforcement hearings than to include all programs in enforcement proceedings [411 F. Supp. at 558].

The U.S. Court of Appeals subsequently modified the lower court's ruling to allow HEW to take a systematic approach if it first adopted systemwide guidelines and gave Maryland time to comply voluntarily (562 F.2d 914 (4th Cir. 1977)). A rehearing was scheduled, however, because one judge had died before the court's opinion was issued. On rehearing three appellate judges voted to affirm the lower court and three voted to reverse, and the equally divided vote had the effect of automatically affirming the lower court. 571 F.2d 1273 (4th Cir. 1978).

Some victims of unlawful discrimination sought judicial intervention to compel enforcement of Title VI in *Adams* v. *Richardson*, 356 F. Supp. 92 (D.D.C. 1973), affirmed 480 F.2d 1159 (D.C. Cir. 1973). The plaintiffs accused HEW of failure to enforce Title VI in the southern states. In the part of the case dealing with higher education, HEW had found the higher education systems of ten states out of compliance with Title VI and had requested each state to submit a desegregation plan within four months. At the time of the lawsuit, three years later, five states had not submitted any plan and five had submitted plans which did not remedy the violations. HEW had not commenced administrative enforcement efforts or referred the cases to the Justice Department for prosecution. The district court ordered HEW to commence enforcement proceedings:

> The time permitted by Title VI of the Civil Rights Act of 1964 to delay the commencement of enforcement proceedings against the ten states for the purpose of securing voluntary compliance has long since passed. The continuation of HEW financial assistance to the segregated systems of higher education in the ten states violates the rights of plaintiffs and others similarly situated protected by Title VI of the Civil Rights Act of 1964. Having once determined that a state system of higher education is in violation of Title VI, and having failed during a substantial period of time to achieve voluntary compliance, defendants have a duty to commence enforcement proceedings [356 F. Supp. at 94].

The appellate court agreed with the district court's conclusion but expressed more sympathy for HEW's enforcement problems:

> We agree with the District Court's conclusion that
> HEW may not neglect this area of its responsibility.
> However, we are also mindful that desegregation problems
> in colleges and universities differ widely from those in
> elementary and secondary schools, and that HEW admit-
> tedly lacks experience in dealing with them. It has not yet
> formulated guidelines for desegregating statewide systems
> of higher learning, nor has it commented formally upon the
> desegregation plans of the five states which have submitted
> them. As regrettable as these revelations are, the stark truth
> of the matter is that HEW must carefully assess the
> significance of a variety of new factors as it moves into an
> unaccustomed area. None of these factors justifies a failure
> to comply with a Congressional mandate; they may,
> however, warrant a more deliberate opportunity to identify
> and accommodate them [480 F.2d at 1164].

The appellate court modified the terms of the injunction to give
HEW more time to initiate enforcement proceedings. Future courts
would likely be much less sympathetic to administrative delay as
HEW develops experience in enforcing the civil rights statutes
against postsecondary institutions.

7.4.9. Other enforcement remedies. Administrative negotiation and fund termination are not the only means federal agencies
have for enforcing the civil rights statutes. In some cases the responsible federal agency may also go to court to enforce the civil
rights obligations which educational institutions have assumed by
accepting federal funds. Title VI authorizes agencies to enforce
compliance not only by fund termination but also by "any other
means authorized by law" (42 U.S.C. sec. 2000d-1). HEW's Title VI
regulations explain that "[s]uch other means may include, but are
not limited to, (1) a reference to the Department of Justice with a
recommendation that appropriate proceedings be brought to
enforce any rights of the United States under any law of the United
States (including other titles of the Act), or any assurance or other
contractual undertaking, and (2) any applicable proceeding under
state or local law" (45 C.F.R. sec. 80.9(a)). HEW may not pursue
these alternatives, however, "until (1) the responsible Department
official has determined that compliance cannot be secured by

voluntary means, (2) the recipient or other person has been notified of its failure to comply and of the action to be taken to effect compliance, and (3) the expiration of at least ten days from the mailing of such notice to the recipient or other person" (45 C.F.R. sec. 80.9(d)). The same enforcement alternatives and procedural limitations also apply to HEW enforcement of Title IX and Section 504.[4]

Besides administrative agency enforcement by fund termination or court suit, educational institutions may also be subject to private lawsuits brought by individuals who have allegedly been discriminated against in violation of the civil rights statutes or regulations. In legal terminology, the issue is whether the civil rights statutes afford these victims of discrimination a "private cause of action" against the institution which is allegedly discriminating and, if so, whether any "administrative remedies" must be "exhausted" before such a suit may be brought.[5] Courts have not yet reached any clear resolution of this issue.

In *Lau* v. *Nichols,* 414 U.S. 563 (1974), the Supreme Court permitted a private cause of action under Title VI. The Court

[4]HEW's Title IX and Section 504 regulations each incorporate the enforcement regulations for Title VI (see 45 C.F.R. sec. 86.71; 45 C.F.R. sec. 84.61). The Title IX statute also contains the same "other means authorized by law" language found in Title VI. (See 20 U.S.C. sec. 1682.) Although the Section 504 statute contains no such language, adequate authority for HEW to proceed probably exists without it. (See the *Frazer* and the *Institute of Computer Technology* cases discussed in Section 7.3 above.)

[5]The basic requisites for a private cause of action are outlined in *Cort* v. *Ash,* 422 U.S. 66 (1975): "In determining whether a private remedy is implicit in a statute not expressly providing one, several factors are relevant. First, is the plaintiff 'one of the class for whose *especial* benefit the statute was enacted,'—that is, does the statute create a federal right in favor of the plaintiff? Second, is there any indication of legislative intent, explicit or implicit, either to create such a remedy or to deny one? Third, is it consistent with the underlying purposes of the legislative scheme to imply such a remedy for the plaintiff? And finally, is the cause of action one traditionally relegated to state law, in an area basically the concern of the States, so that it would be inappropriate to infer a cause of action based solely on federal law?" (422 U.S. at 78, citations omitted). For information on the exhaustion-of-remedies doctrine, see Section 3.5.3; and for an application of the doctrine to HEW, see *Barrera* v. *Wheeler,* 441 F.2d 795 (8th Cir. 1971).

briefly reasoned that the defendant school district had a contractual commitment to HEW to comply with civil rights requirements and that the plaintiff school children, as third-party beneficiaries of that contract, could sue to enforce the terms spelled out in HEW regulations and guidelines. And in *Lloyd* v. *Regional Transportation Authority*, 548 F.2d 1277 (7th Cir. 1977), a U.S. court of appeals permitted the handicapped plaintiffs to bring a private cause of action to enforce Section 504. But the *Lloyd* decision was rendered before HEW's Section 504 regulations were implemented, and the court reserved the question whether, once the regulations were in force, a private cause of action could be brought without first pursuing the administrative remedies available under the regulations. And in later Section 504 cases courts have split in results and reasoning on whether handicapped plaintiffs must first resort to HEW administrative mechanisms; see, for example, *Crawford* v. *University of North Carolina*, 440 F. Supp. 1047 (M.D.N.C. 1977). The same question apparently remains under Title VI even after *Lau;* in *Johnson* v. *County of Chester*, 413 F. Supp. 1299 (E.D. Pa. 1976), the court disallowed a private cause of action because the plaintiffs had not utilized the Title VI administrative enforcement machinery. Under Title IX, the leading case broadly rejects the private cause of action concept; in *Cannon* v. *University of Chicago*, 559 F.2d 1063 (7th Cir. 1977), the court refused to follow *Lau*, saying it applies only to suits brought by a large class of similarly situated individuals, and concluded that "no individual right of action can be inferred from Title IX in the face of the carefully constructed scheme of administrative enforcement contained in the Act."

The uncertainty on these issues must be resolved before postsecondary administrators can know the extent to which their institutions are subject to private suits to enforce the requirements of the Title VI, Title IX, and Section 504 statutes and regulations. Even if the uncertainty is resolved against such private causes of action, private litigants could still raise civil rights issues in court by suing under the Constitution's equal protection clause or under various other federal and state statutes prohibiting discrimination (see Sections 3.3 and 4.2.4).

Whenever private litigation can be brought against the

institution under Title VI or Title IX, or directly under the
Constitution, the institution may be liable for the plaintiff's
attorney's fees if the plaintiff wins the suit. Under the Civil Rights
Attorney's Fees Awards Act of 1976, 90 Stat. 2641, 42 U.S.C. sec.
1988, courts have discretion to award "a reasonable attorney's fee"
to "the prevailing party" in actions under Title IX, Title VI, and
several other civil rights statutes. This act, however, does not apply
to Section 504 suits.

Sec. 7.5. Dealing with the Federal Government

7.5.1. Handling federal regulations. In the spring of 1977,
national media attention focused on groups of handicapped
persons staging sit-ins at U.S. Department of Health, Education,
and Welfare offices across the country. The groups were pressuring
HEW's Secretary Califano to sign regulations implementing
Section 504 of the Rehabilitation Act of 1973, 29 U.S.C. sec. 794, as
it applies to recipients of financial assistance from HEW. The sit-
ins reveal the important niche that regulations can fill in
implementing legislation. In the case of Section 504, the regulations fill in the broad form of the statute, itemizing for educational
institutions, as well as other aid recipients, what must be done to
conform to the statutory requirement of nondiscrimination. (See
Section 7.4.4.)

Administrative agencies write regulations either to implement legislation, as for Section 504, or to formalize their own
housekeeping functions. Such "rulemaking lies along the continuum between legislation and executive decision making. A rule
reflects the intent of the statute on which it is based as well as the
manner in which the administrator will exercise the discretion that
the statute grants. The position on the continuum varies from rule
to rule. Where, for example, a rule carries out a statutory direction
to define a term by regulation, subject to explicit legislative history
regarding the definition, the 'legislation' element may be para-
mount. Where the rule sets forth funding criteria in order to fill in
a gap left by the program statute, the rule reflects a greater degree
of executive decision making, the exercise of which is implicit in
the enactment of a program statute leaving details to be supplied

by the administrator" (T. Sky, "Rulemaking and the Federal Grant Process in the United States Office of Education," 62 *Virginia L. Rev.* 1017, 1027 n. 26 (1976)). Proposed and final regulations are published in the *Federal Register,* and final regulations are codified in the *Code of Federal Regulations.*

Postsecondary administrators have complained that the multitude of federal regulations applying to the programs and practices of postsecondary institutions creates heavy financial and administrative burdens for their institutions. A 1975 survey by the American Council on Education indicated that institutions of higher education are spending between 1 and 4 percent of their annual operating budgets on complying with federal regulations. Though the federal government pays subsidies to help meet these expenses, administrators have argued that the subsidies are inadequate. (See K. Winkler, "Proliferating Federal Regulations: Is Government Now 'the Enemy'?" *The Chronicle of Higher Education,* Dec. 13, 1976, p. 3, col. 1.)

The regulatory burdens on postsecondary institutions could likely be lessened if postsecondary administrators and legal counsel took more active advisory roles in the process by which the federal government makes and enforces rules. The following suggestions identify ways in which they can participate in these processes. (See generally C. Saunders, "Regulating the Regulators," *The Chronicle of Higher Education,* March 22, 1976, which discusses many of these suggestions and others.)

1. Appoint someone to be responsible for monitoring the *Federal Register* and other publications for announcements regarding regulations that will affect postsecondary educational institutions. The *Federal Register* publishes "Notice(s) of Intent" (NOIs) to publish rules and "Notice(s) of Proposed Rulemaking," which are invitations for comments from interested parties. In addition, the Department of Health, Education, and Welfare will make draft regulations available for review before the proposed form is published. (See "Memorandum on Regulatory Policies," July 25, 1976, reprinted at 41 *Fed. Reg.* 34881–34812 (Aug. 17, 1976).)

2. File comments and deliver testimony in response to NOIs and notices of proposed rule making when the rules would

have a substantial effect on institutional operations. Support these comments with specific explanations of how the proposed regulations would have a negative impact on the institution. Have legal counsel review the proposed rules for legal and interpretive problems, and include legal questions or objections with your comments when appropriate. Consider filing comments in conjunction with other institutions that would be similarly affected by the proposed regulations.

3. Keep federal agencies informed of your views on and experiences with particular federal regulations. No regulations should be considered so final that they are beyond comment. Complaints and difficulties with final regulations should be communicated to the responsible agency.

4. When the institution desires guidance concerning ambiguities or gaps in particular regulations, consider submitting questions to the administering agency. Make the questions specific and, if the institution has a particular viewpoint on how the ambiguity or gap should be resolved, forcefully argue your view. Legal counsel should be involved in this process. Once questions are submitted, press the agency for answers.

5. Be concerned not only with the substance of regulations but also with the adequacy of the rule making and rule-enforcing procedures. Be prepared to object to situations in which institutions are given insufficient notice of an agency's plans to make rules, too few opportunities to participate in rule making, or inadequate opportunities to criticize or receive guidance concerning already implemented regulations.

7.5.2. *Obtaining information.* Several pieces of federal legislation from the 1970s and a 1972 executive order may be helpful to administrators and counsel of postsecondary institutions as they participate in federal rule making or otherwise deal with the federal government: the Freedom of Information Act (FOIA) Amendments of 1974, the Privacy Act of 1974, the Government in the Sunshine Act of 1976, and Executive Order 11652 (1972).

The Freedom of Information Act Amendments, 5 U.S.C. sec. 552, make available to the public information from federal government files that is not specifically exempted from disclosure by the legislation. Nine categories of information are exempted from disclosure under 5 U.S.C. sec. 552(b), the most relevant to postsecondary institutions being national security information (see the discussion of E.O. 11652, later in this section), federal agencies' internal personnel rules and practices, interagency or intraagency memoranda or letters that would not be available except in litigation, and investigatory files compiled for law enforcement purposes.

The FOIA is useful when it appears that the government holds information which would be helpful to the institution in a certain situation, but informal requests have not yielded the necessary materials. FOIA requests can serve several purposes, such as (1) obtaining information prepared by the agency as a means of better understanding agency ground rules; (2) obtaining information prepared by the agency or someone else that may be helpful in processing a claim or grievance against the government; (3) determining what information the government has that it could use against the institution, for example, in a fund termination proceeding; (4) preparing for a lawsuit against the government or other party. (See Arnold, "Who's Going Fishing in Government Files?" *Juris Doctor* 17, 20–21 (April 1976).)

There are particular procedures to be followed in requesting information under the FOIA. (See "How to Get the Goods," *Juris Doctor* 20 (April 1976), and "A Scholar's Guide to Obtaining Information from the Government," *The Chronicle of Higher Education*, Feb. 14, 1977, p. 7, col. 3.) Persons or institutions whose requests are denied by the agency may file a suit against the agency in a U.S. district court. The burden of proof is on the agency to support its reasons for denial.

Executive Order 11652 establishes the necessary procedures and the schedule for classifying and declassifying government documents related to national security. Classifications can be challenged, and there is an appeals mechanism. The Order becomes important when an FOIA request is refused on national security grounds. (See "How to Use Executive Order 11652," *The Chronicle of Higher Education*, Feb. 14, 1977, p. 7, col. 3.)

The Privacy Act, codified in part at 5 U.S.C. sec. 552(a), is discussed above in Section 4.12.3, with regard to student records. The point to be made here is that in requesting certain information under the FOIA, the requester may find an obstacle in the Privacy Act. The FOIA itself exempts "personnel and medical files and similar files the disclosure of which would constitute a clearly unwarranted invasion of personal privacy" (5 U.S.C. sec. 552(b)(6)).

The Privacy Act provides an even broader protection for information whose release would infringe privacy interests. While the act thus may foil a requester of information, it may also protect the postsecondary institution and its employees and students when the federal government has information concerning them in its files. (For a discussion of the FOIA, the privacy exemption, and the Privacy Act, see Comment, "The Freedom of Information Act's Privacy Exemption and the Privacy Act of 1974," 11 *Harvard Civil Rights–Civil Liberties L. Rev.* 596 (1976); and M. Hulett, "Privacy and the Freedom of Information Act," 27 *Administrative L. Rev.* 275 (1975).)

The Government in the Sunshine Act, 5 U.S.C. sec. 552(b), assures the public that "meetings of multimember Federal agencies shall be open . . . , with the exception of discussions of several narrowly defined areas" (H.R. Rep. No. 880, 94th Cong., 2d Sess. 2 (1976), reprinted at 3 *U.S. Code Cong. and Admin. News* 2184 (1976)). Institutions can individually or collectively make use of this act by sending a representative to observe and report on agency decision making that is expected to have a substantial impact on their operations.

Selected Annotated Bibliography

Sec. 7.1 (Federal Constitutional Powers over Education)

1. Nowak, J., Rotunda, R., and Young, J. N., *Handbook of Constitutional Law* (West, 1978), provides, in chaps. 3–5, 10, and 17, a comprehensive overview of federal commerce power, taxing and spending powers, civil rights enforcement power, and the doctrine of federal preemption of state authority.

Sec. 7.2. (Federal Regulation of Postsecondary Education)

1. Burke, G., "Federal Taxation of State Colleges and Universities: Recent Developments Call for Reconsideration of Theories of Exemption," 4 *J. of College and University Law* 43

(1977), considers the legal bases on which public institutions may seek federal tax exemption and the differences in the ways such institutions may be treated under each legal basis.

2. Cardozo, M., "To Copy or Not to Copy for Teaching and Scholarship: What Shall I Tell My Client?" 4 *J. of College and University Law* 59 (1977), analyzes the 1976 General Revision of the Copyright Law as it applies to the teaching and scholarship functions of postsecondary institutions and provides useful guidance on how to cope with the new act.

3. Comment, "Proprietary Vocational School Abuses: Can the FTC Cure Them?" 24 *Catholic University L. Rev.* 603 (1975), discusses the jurisdiction and powers of the Federal Trade Commission and its proposed trade regulation rule on proprietary schools.

4. Stedman, J., "The New Copyright Law: Photocopying for Educational Use," 63 *AAUP Bulletin* 5 (1977), describes the 1976 General Revision of the Copyright Law and analyzes its impact on photocopying practices of educational institutions; can be usefully read in conjunction with the article in entry no. 2 of Sec. 7.2.

5. Stein, W., "Employee Benefit Reporting After ERISA," 36 *Louisiana L. Rev.* 867 (1976), discusses the reporting requirements in the ERISA statute and regulations as they apply to all types of employee benefit plans. (See also entry no. 3 in Sec. 2.2.)

6. Sullivan, L., *Handbook of the Law of Antitrust* (West, 1977), provides a comprehensive general survey of federal antitrust law.

7. Symposium, "Federal Taxation and Charitable Organizations," 39 *Law and Contemporary Problems* 1 (1975), is a sophisticated collection of articles on federal tax policy and law concerning charitable organizations; includes J. H. Levi on "Financing Education and the Effects of the Tax Law," which discusses the impact of the Internal Revenue Code's charitable deduction provisions on postsecondary institutions, and J. F. Kirkwood and D. S. Mundel on "The Role of Tax Policy in Federal Support for Higher Education," which examines federal tax policy regarding higher educa-

tion and compares tax programs with expenditure and regulatory programs.

8. Symposium, "Federal Tax Issues Confronting Institutions of Higher Education," 3 *J. of College and University Law* 1 (1976), is a series of articles discussing major tax issues confronting postsecondary institutions; includes a selected bibliography.

9. Symposium, "Occupational Safety and Health," 38 *Law and Contemporary Problems* 583 (1974), is a collection of articles discussing legal problems arising from the Occupational Safety and Health Act, federal administration and enforcement of the act, and the role of the states in occupational safety and health.

10. Wang, W., "The Unbundling of Higher Education," 1975 *Duke L. J.* 53, discusses the legal doctrines and policy considerations relevant to the application of federal antitrust laws to private, nonprofit postsecondary institutions; argues for a broad application of antitrust laws.

11. See the Selected Annotated Bibliography for Chapter Three, Sec. 3.3, for references on federal employment discrimination legislation.

Sec. 7.3 (Federal Aid-to-Education Programs)

1. Des Marais, P., *How to Get Government Grants* (Capitol, 1977), is a guide for administrators on how to qualify for, obtain, and manage government grants; includes checklist of information sources regarding government funding and several case histories of institutions that successfully obtained grants.

2. Fauntleroy, J. (ed.), *Federal Education Program Guide* (Capitol, 5th ed., 1977), is a quick-reference guide to 256 federal aid-to-education programs, covering the Office of Education, National Institute of Education, Public Health Service, National Endowments for the Arts and Humanities, National Science Foundation, Veterans' Administration, and other federal agencies; includes names, addresses, and telephone numbers for the managers of each program covered.

3. *Federal Grants and Contracts Weekly* (Capitol), a weekly newsletter, lists new grant application opportunities, contains
   summaries and detailed explanations of new requests for
   proposals (RFP's), describes new grant programs, and analyzes the workings of the grant and contract processes.
4. Lacovara, P., "How Far Can the Federal Camel Slip Under the
   Academic Tent?" 4 *J. of College and University Law,* in
   press, is a constitutional analysis, in the postsecondary education context, of the federal government's spending power
   and potential First Amendment and due process limitations
   on that power.
5. O'Neil, R. M., "God and Government at Yale: the Limits of Federal Regulation of Higher Education," 44 *University of
   Cincinnati L. Rev.* 525 (1975), is an analysis of both constitutional and nonconstitutional issues regarding the extent of
   federal authority to regulate higher education.
6. *School Law Register* (Capitol, issued and updated periodically)
   is an information service containing the complete texts of
   federal education laws and implementing regulations;
   updated twelve times a year to cover new and revised laws
   and regulations.
7. Sky, T., "Rulemaking and the Federal Grant Process in the
   United States Office of Education," 62 *Virginia L. Rev.* 1017
   (1976), is a comprehensive, practical review and analysis
   written by the HEW Assistant General Counsel for Education. It includes discussion of the General Education Provisions Act and the Administrative Procedure Act.
8. Wallick, R., and Chamblee, D., "Bridling the Trojan Horse:
   Rights and Remedies of Colleges and Universities under
   Federal Grant-Type Assistance Programs," 4 *J. of College
   and University Law,* in press, describes the legal nature and
   policy impact of federal assistance to postsecondary institutions, and analyzes steps legal counsel might take to protect
   the interests of institutions in grant programs.

Sec. 7.4 (Civil Rights Compliance)

1. Comment, "Implementing Title IX: The HEW Regulations,"
   124 *University of Pennsylvania L. Rev.* 806 (1976), is an
   overview and legal analysis of the Title IX regulations;

includes extensive citations to legislative history of Title IX, sex discrimination cases, and periodical literature.

2. *Equal Opportunity in Higher Education* (Capitol, biweekly) is a newsletter on recent developments regarding race, sex, age, and handicap discrimination; includes up-to-date information on federal civil rights compliance efforts, especially in HEW's Office for Civil Rights.

3. *Guide to the Section 504 Self-Evaluation for Colleges and Universities* provides suggestions and technical assistance for complying with Section 504 (discrimination against the handicapped) and HEW's implementing regulations. Prepared under contract to the HEW Office for Civil Rights and recommended to institutions by OCR.

Sec. 7.5 *(Dealing with the Federal Government)*

1. Bender L., *Federal Regulation and Higher Education* (American Association for Higher Education, ERIC/Higher Education Research Rpt. No. 1, 1977), considers the problem of federal infringement on college and university autonomy, the regulation writing process, the cost to institutions of implementing regulations, and strategies for reform.

2. Rosenblum, V., "Dealing with Federal Regulatory Agencies," in D. H. Blumer (ed.), *Legal Issues for Postsecondary Education II* (American Association of Community and Junior Colleges, 1976), Chap. 5, is a concise, practical, "how to" guide written for administrators of postsecondary institutions.

3. Summerfield, H., *Power and Process: The Formulation and Limits of Federal Educational Policy* (McCutchan, 1974), provides description and analysis of the process by which federal education policy is made; considers the roles of the education lobbying groups, the Congress and its education subcommittees, the President and the President's staff, and the federal administrative agencies.

4. See entry no. 7 and entry no. 8 in bibliography for Section 7.3.

Chapter VIII

❧❧❧❧❧❧❧❧❧❧❧❧❧❧❧❧❧❧

The College
and the Accrediting
Agencies

Sec. 8.1 Accreditation System

Besides dealing with government agencies at local, state, and federal levels, postsecondary administrators must cope with a substantial external force in the private sector: the educational accrediting agencies. Educational accreditation, conducted by private associations rather than by a ministry of education or other government agency, is a development unique to this country. As the system has evolved, the private accrediting agencies have assumed an important role in the development and maintenance of standards for postsecondary education and have become able to

exert considerable influence on individual institutions and programs which seek to obtain and preserve the accreditation which
only these agencies can bestow.

There are two types of accreditation: institutional (or
general) accreditation and program (or specialized) accreditation.
Institutional accreditation applies to the entire institution and all
its programs, departments, and schools; program accreditation
applies to a particular school, department, or program within the
institution, such as a school of medicine or law, a department of
chemistry, or a program in medical technology. Program accreditation may also apply to an entire institution if it is a free-standing,
specialized institution, such as a business school or technical
school, whose curriculum is all in the same program area.
Institutional accreditation is granted by six regional agencies—
membership associations composed of the institutions in each
region that have obtained accreditation. Since each regional agency
covers a separate, defined part of the country, each institution is
subject to the jurisdiction of only one agency. Program accreditation is granted by a multitude of "specialized" (or "professional"
or "occupational") accrediting agencies which may or may not be
membership associations and are often sponsored by the particular
profession or occupation whose educational programs are being
accredited. The jurisdiction of these specialized agencies is
nationwide. Overseeing and speaking for both the regional and
specialized agencies at the national level is the Council on
Postsecondary Accreditation (COPA), a private organization created in 1975 with offices in Washington, D.C.

Being private, accrediting agencies do not derive their power
directly from public law, as do federal, state, and local governments. They owe their existence and legal status basically to state
corporation law and to the common law of "voluntary (or private)
associations" (see Section 8.2), and they have whatever general
powers are set forth in their articles of incorporation or association
and the accompanying bylaws and rules. These powers are
enforced through private sanctions embodied in the articles,
bylaws, and rules, the primary sanctions being the withdrawal and
denial of accreditation. The force of these private sanctions is

greatly enhanced, however, by the extensive public and private reliance on accrediting agencies' decisions.

The federal government relies in part on these agencies to identify the institutions and programs eligible for a wide range of aid-to-education programs, particularly those administered by the U.S. Office of Education. (See Section 8.3.) The states demonstrate their reliance on the agencies' assessments when they exempt accredited institutions or programs from various licensing or other regulatory requirements. (See Section 6.3.) Some states also use accreditation to determine students' or institutions' eligibility under their own state funding programs, and the state approving agencies operating under contract with the Veterans' Administration depend on accreditation in approving courses under veterans' programs (38 U.S.C. sec. 1775(a)(1)). State professional and occupational licensing boards also rely on the accrediting agencies by making graduation from an accredited school or program a prerequisite to obtaining a license to practice in the state. Private professional societies may use professional accreditation in determining who is eligible for membership. Students, parents, and guidance counselors may employ accreditation as one criterion in choosing a school. And postsecondary institutions themselves often rely on accreditation in determining the acceptability of transfer credits.

Because of this extensive public and private reliance on accrediting agencies, accreditation is very important for postsecondary institutions. Administrators usually consider both institutional and program accreditation to be necessary for successful operation. Thus, administrators usually cannot avoid meeting these standards and requirements by foregoing accreditation; needing this "stamp of approval," they must deal with the multitude of accrediting agencies having jurisdiction over their campuses. Consequently, administrators and counsel need to understand the legal limits on the agencies' powers and the legal leverage they might apply if an agency threatens denial or withdrawal of accreditation.

This is not to suggest that institutions should consider accrediting agencies to be adversaries. Usually accreditation depends on mutual help and cooperation, and the dynamic between institution and agency can be very positive. Therefore, institutions and programs willing to cooperate and expend the necessary effort usually can obtain and keep accreditation without serious threat of loss. But serious differences can and do arise, particularly with institutions which are innovating with curricula, the use of resources, or delivery systems. Such institutions may not fit neatly into accrediting standards or may otherwise be difficult for accrediting agencies to evaluate. Similarly, institutions which operate in more than one state (see Section 6.4), which contract for the delivery of educational services with nonaccredited outside organizations,[1] or which are organized as proprietary entities (see Section 8.2.2), may pose particular problems for accrediting agencies. When these or other circumstances involve the institution in accreditation problems, they can be critical because of accreditation's importance to the institution. Administrators should be prepared to deal, in an adversary way if necessary, with the difficulties such situations may create for the institution.

Sec. 8.2. Accreditation and the Courts

There are few reported judicial opinions on the powers of accrediting agencies. The first case arose in 1938 after the North Central Association had threatened to withdraw the accreditation of North Dakota's State Agricultural College. The state's governor sought an injunction against North Central. Using traditional legal analysis, the court denied the governor's request, reasoning that "in the absence of fraud, collusion, arbitrariness, or breach of contract, . . . the decisions of such voluntary associations must be accepted in litigation before the court as conclusive" (*North Dakota* v. *North Central Association*, 23 F. Supp. 694 (E.D. Ill.), affirmed, 99 F.2d 697 (7th Cir. 1938)). Another case did not arise until 1967, when Parsons College sued the North Central Association. That case, along with the *Marjorie Webster* decisions

[1]COPA and some of the regional accrediting agencies have adopted or are preparing policy statements on the accreditation of off-campus and multistate programs and on educational contracting.

in 1969 and 1970 and the *Marlboro Corporation* case in 1977, provides the core of the contemporary law of educational accreditation.

8.2.1. Parsons College case. In 1963 Parsons College was placed on probation by the North Central Association. This probation was removed in 1965 with the stipulation that the college's accreditation status be reviewed within three years. In 1967 the Association conducted a two-day site visit of the college, after which the visiting team issued a report noting that "some improvements . . . had not been realized, and that other deficiencies persisted." After a meeting at which the college made statements and answered questions, the association's accrediting committee reported to the executive board, which recommended that Parsons be dropped from membership. This recommendation was accepted in a subsequent vote of the association's full membership. The college then appealed to the board of directors, which sustained the disaccreditation decision on the basis that the college was not "providing an adequate educational program for its students, especially those of limited ability." 271 F. Supp. at 69.

When the college sought to enjoin the association from implementing its disaccreditation decision, the federal district court denied its request (*Parsons College v. North Central Association of Colleges and Secondary Schools,* 271 F. Supp. 65 (N.D. Ill. 1967)). The court rejected the college's claim that the association must comply with the due process requirements of the federal Constitution, reasoning that "the Association stands on the same footing as any private corporation" and is not subject to "the constitutional limits applicable to government." (See Section 1.4.) The court then engaged in a much more limited review of the association's procedures and rules. After deciding that the "law applicable to determine the propriety of the expulsion of a member from a private association is the law which he agreed to when he voluntarily chose to join the Association, that is, the rules of the Association itself," the court found that the college had neither charged nor proved any violation of association rules.

The college did argue, however, that the association's action should be invalidated, even though consistent with its own rules, if the action was "contrary to rudimentary due process or grounded in arbitrariness." Without admitting that this more stringent legal requirement would apply to accrediting agencies, the court did provide a useful analysis of the association's action under the common law concept of "rudimentary due process." The court defined rudimentary due process to include (1) an adequate opportunity to be heard, (2) a notice of the proceedings, (3) a notice of the specific charges, (4) sufficiently definite standards of evaluation, and (5) substantively adequate reasons for the decision. After reviewing the entire process by which the association reached its disaccreditation decision, the court concluded that "the College has failed to establish a violation of the commands of any of the several rules."

The court found that the college had been afforded the opportunity to speak and be heard at almost every stage of the proceedings and that the opportunity afforded was adequate for the type of proceeding involved:

> The nature of the hearing, if required by rudimentary due process, may properly be adjusted to the nature of the issue to be decided. In this case, the issue was not innocence but excellence. Procedures appropriate to decide whether a specific act of plain misconduct was committed are not suited to an expert evaluation of educational quality. . . .
>
> Here, no trial-type hearing, with confrontation, cross-examination, and assistance of counsel would have been suited to the resolution of the issues to be decided. The question was not principally a matter of historical fact, but rather of the application of a standard of quality in a field of recognized expertise [271 F. Supp. at 72–73].

The court further found that the college had ample notice of the proceedings because "after a long history of questionable status, the visit of the Examining Team was adequate notice without more."

The requirement of specific charges, (3), was satisfied by the examining team report given to the college. The court found that this report, "supplemented by the evidence produced by the College itself, contained all the information on which all subsequent decisions were made. No fuller disclosure could have been made."

The court also found the evaluative standards of the association to be sufficiently definite to inform the school of what was expected of it. Disagreeing with the college's claim that the standards were "so vague as to be unintelligible to men of ordinary intelligence," the court reasoned as follows:

> The standards of accreditation are not guides for the layman but for professionals in the field of education. Definiteness may prove, in another view, to be arbitrariness. The Association was entitled to make a conscious choice in favor of flexible standards to accommodate variation in purpose and character among its constituent institutions, and to avoid forcing all into a rigid and uniform mold [271 F. Supp. at 73].

Finally, the court refused its own invitation to explore the substantive adequacy of the reasons for withdrawing accreditation. While courts are well equipped to handle problems of procedural fairness, according to this court, they can hardly claim professional expertise in evaluating educational quality:

> In this field, the courts are traditionally even more hesitant to intervene. The public benefits of accreditation, dispensing information and exposing misrepresentation, would not be enhanced by judicial intrusion. Evaluation by the peers of the college, enabled by experience to make comparative judgments, will best serve the paramount interest in the highest practicable standards in higher education. The price for such benefits is inevitably some injury to those who do not meet the measure, and some risk of conservatism produced by appraisals against a standard of what has already proven valuable in education [271 F. Supp. at 74].

In other words, the court assumed that the association had relied on its expertise in making its accreditation decision and deferred to this assumed expression of expertise.

8.2.2. Marjorie Webster case. In 1966, Marjorie Webster

Junior College, a proprietary (for profit) junior college, applied to the Middle States Association for accreditation. The association refused to consider the application because the college was not a nonprofit organization. The college sued, and the lower court held that the nonprofit criterion was invalid under the federal antitrust laws, the "developing common law regarding exclusion from membership in private associations," and the federal Constitution's due process clause (*Marjorie Webster Junior College* v. *Middle States Association of Colleges and Secondary Schools,* 302 F. Supp. 459 (D.D.C. 1969)). The lower court ordered the association to consider the college's application and to accredit the college "if it should otherwise qualify for accreditation under Middle States' standards." The court of appeals reversed, finding that in the circumstances of the case the association's reason for refusing to consider the application (the proprietary character of the college) was valid (432 F.2d 650 (D.C. Cir. 1970)). Unlike the *Parsons College* opinion, however, the court of appeals opinion (and the lower court's opinion) clearly departs from the traditional judicial reluctance to examine the internal affairs of private organizations.

In relation to the antitrust claims, the appellate court held that the "proscriptions of the Sherman Act were 'tailored for the business world,' not for the noncommercial aspects of the liberal arts and the learned professions," and that since the "process of accreditation is an activity distinct from the sphere of commerce," going "rather to the heart of the concept of education," an accreditation decision would violate the act only if undertaken with "an intent or purpose to affect the commercial aspects of the profession." Since no such "commercial motive" had been shown, the association's action did not constitute a combination or conspiracy in restraint of the college's trade.

Regarding the common law claims, the appellate court agreed with the lower court that, under a developing exception to the general rule of judicial nonintervention in private associations' affairs, an association possessing virtual monopolistic control in an area of public concern must exercise its power reasonably, "with an even hand, and not in conflict with the public policy of the jurisdiction." To the court of appeals, however, the scope of judicial review under this exception depended on the amount of "deference" which courts should accord to the accrediting agency's action, and deference varied "both with the subject matter at issue and with the degree of harm resulting from the Association's action." Since the subject matter was the "substantive standards" of the association, the court accorded more deference to the association than it would if the subject were "the fairness of the procedures by which the challenged determination was reached." With respect to the degree of harm, while "lack of accreditation may be a not insignificant handicap to the college," the court found that "denial of accreditation . . . is not tantamount to exclusion [of the college] from operating successfully as a junior college." Having thus weighed the "subject matter" and the "degree of harm," the court concluded that "substantial deference" should be accorded the association's judgment "regarding the ends that it serves and the means most appropriate to those ends." The appellate court then looked to the basis for the association's nonprofit criterion—that the profit motive is inconsistent with educational quality. The lower court had held that the "assumption that the profit motive is inconsistent with quality is not supported by the evidence and is unwarranted." The court of appeals "neither disregard[ed] nor disbelieve[d] the extensive testimony . . . regarding the values and benefits" of proprietary institutions. But in light of the substantial deference it accorded the association in setting its criteria for accreditation, the appellate court held that it had not "been shown to be unreasonable for [the association] to conclude that the desire for personal profit might influence educational goals in subtle ways difficult to detect but destructive, in the long run, of that atmosphere of academic inquiry which . . . [the association's] standards for accreditation seek to foster."

Regarding the due process claims, the court of appeals also held that the association's nonprofit criterion was not unreasonable and therefore was valid. The significant point here, however, is that the court in fact engaged in a constitutional due process analysis. The lower court had found that the association's accreditation activities were "quasi-governmental" in nature and thus could be considered "state action" subject to federal constitutional restraints. The court of appeals "assume[d] without deciding" that state action did exist. Thus, unlike the court in *Parsons College,* which specifically rejected the state action argument, the lower court in *Marjorie Webster* accepted the argument and the appellate court left the question unanswered.

8.2.3. Marlboro Corporation case. The Marlboro Corporation operated the Emery School, a private proprietary business school, which was subject to evaluation by the Accrediting Commission of the Association of Independent Colleges and Schools. Emery applied for renewal of its accreditation in April 1975 as required by the commission's rules, and an inspection team visited the school. The team filed a negative evaluation, to which the school responded in writing. The commission then ordered a temporary extension of the school's accreditation through December 1975 and ordered the school to submit, by June 30, 1975, evidence of compliance with association criteria in twelve specified areas of weakness. An audited financial statement, evidence of adequate library holdings, and a catalog meeting association standards were among the requirements. Rather than complying, the school admitted its deficiencies and indicated its plans to correct them. In accordance with its published rule that "a letter of intent will not be accepted" as evidence of the correction of deficiencies, the commission voted in August to deny accreditation. When the school appealed, the commission held a hearing at which the school was given thirty minutes to present its case and respond to questions, including questions concerning its method of accounting and the use to which it had put federal student aid money. The school was unable to specifically account for this money. After the hearing, the commission reaffirmed its refusal to renew Emery's accreditation.

The lower court denied the school's request for an injunction requiring the association to grant accreditation, and the court of appeals affirmed (*Marlboro Corporation* v. *The Association of Independent Colleges and Schools,* 556 F.2d 78 (1st Cir. 1977)). The school contended that the association had violated its rights to due process under the Constitution and under common law principles and that the denial of accreditation deprived it of rights protected by the rules and regulations of the U.S. Commissioner of Education. (See Section 8.3.) The court of appeals held that none of the school's procedural rights had been violated, that the commission's decision was not "arbitrary and capricious" because "the irregularities in Emery's financial statement alone . . . justified the Commission's decision," and that the rules of the Office of Education were not violated by the association's internal appeal procedure.[2]

First the court considered whether the commission's procedures should be scrutinized under common law due process standards or under the more exacting standards of the U.S. Constitution's due process clause. The lower court had held that the Constitution did not apply because the commission's action was not "state action." The court of appeals, however, found it unnecessary to decide this "close question" since, "even assuming that constitutional due process applies," none of Emery's procedural rights had been violated. To reach this conclusion, the appellate court did review the commission's procedures under the constitutional standard, stating that "under either constitutional or common law standards . . . procedural fairness is a flexible concept" to be considered case by case. The court held that "due process did not . . . require a full-blown adversary hearing in this context." The court noted that the commission's inquiry concerned a routine reapplication for accreditation and was "broadly evaluative" rather than an accusatory inquiry with specific charges. "Emery was given ample opportunity to present its position by written submission and to argue it orally," and more formalized proceedings would have imposed too heavy a burden on the commission.

The court then considered Emery's claim that the decision to deny accreditation was tainted by bias because the chairman of the Accrediting Commission was the president of a school in direct competition with Emery. While it emphasized that a "decision by

[2]The procedures and standards of this same accrediting commission were also at issue in *Rockland Institute* v. *The Association of Independent Colleges and Schools,* 412 F. Supp. 1015 (C.D. Cal. 1976). In relying on both *Parsons College* and *Marjorie Webster* to reject Rockland's challenge to its disaccreditation, the court ruled that the accrediting commission followed its own rules, that the rules provided sufficient procedural due process, and that the commission's evaluative standards were neither vague nor unreasonable.

an impartial tribunal is an element of due process under any standard," the court found that the chairman took no part in the discussion or vote on Emery's application and in fact did not chair, or participate in, the December hearing. Recognizing the "local realities"—the prolonged evaluation process, the large number of people participating in the decision at various levels, and the commission's general practice of allowing interested commissioners to remain present without participating—the court viewed the question as "troublesome" but concluded that "Emery has [not] shown sufficient actual or apparent impropriety."

Lastly, the court found that (1) the commission's decision was substantively justified by the record, and (2) the Office of Education rules had not been violated. Although these issues were in the last paragraph of the opinion and only briefly discussed, their mention is significant. In *Parsons College* the court refused to consider the first issue at all, and the second issue raises the novel question whether the Office of Education's rules can be enforced by court suits by individual schools. (See Section 8.3.)

8.2.4. Lessons from the cases. The cases discussed in Sections 8.2.1 through 8.2.3 make clear that the courts will impose some constraints on accrediting agencies in their dealings with postsecondary institutions. Though the accrediting agencies ultimately won all three cases, each court opinion suggests some limits on the authority to deny or withdraw accreditation. It is equally clear, however, that the courts still view accrediting agencies with a cautious eye and do not subject them to the full panoply of controls which state and federal governments impose on their own agencies. Though the law on accreditation is too sparse to permit a precise description of the rights of postsecondary institutions in dealing with accrediting agencies,[3] the cases do provide valuable guidelines.

At the very least, it is clear that courts will require an accrediting agency to follow its own rules in withdrawing

---

[3]For an extended analysis of judicial review in a related area of the law, which can be used to predict available rights in accreditation, see W. Kaplin, "Professional Power and Judicial Review: The Health Professions," 44 *George Washington L. Rev.* 710, 716–750 (1976).

accreditation (as in *Parsons College*) or refusing to renew accreditation (as in *Marlboro Corporation*). It is less clear whether courts will require an agency to follow its own rules in considering an initial application for accreditation. There is no accreditation case on this point, and some judicial pronouncements in related areas suggest that the right to be judged by the rules only accrues after the applicant has been admitted to membership or otherwise approved by the association. The better view, however, is that an applicant can also require that the agency follow its own rules.

Beyond following its own rules, an accrediting agency apparently must act fairly and reasonably under the particular circumstances of the case. The primary requirement seems to be that the agency must provide institutions with procedural due process before denying, withdrawing, or refusing to renew their accreditation. The institution appears to have a right to receive notice that its accreditation is being questioned, to know why, and to be heard on the question. *Parsons College* and *Marlboro Corporation* provide useful analyses of the extent of these protections. Apparently, the less broadly evaluative and the more accusatory an action is, the more extensive the due process protections must be. A disaccreditation would thus occasion the highest level of due process protection, perhaps including a formal hearing with the right to counsel, witnesses, and cross-examination.

It is not clear from the cases whether the courts will consider an accrediting agency's decisions to be "state action" subject to the federal Constitution. Such a holding would provide postsecondary institutions with further protection from unfair or unreasonable accrediting decisions. Under *Marjorie Webster*, the federal antitrust laws could also provide additional protections in particular circumstances indicating some commercial or economic reason for the accrediting decision.[4]

---

[4]The viability of the antitrust approach is strengthened by the Supreme Court's decision in *Goldberg* v. *Virginia State Bar*, 421 U.S. 773 (1975), the first case in which the Court clearly indicated that the antitrust laws apply to professional associations.

Sec. 8.3. Accreditation and the U.S. Office of Education

The Office of Education (OE) plays an important role in the accrediting process. Numerous federal aid-to-education statutes specify accreditation "by a nationally recognized accrediting agency or association" as a prerequisite to eligibility for aid for the institution or its students. (See, for example, the Higher Education Act of 1965, 20 U.S.C. sec. 1141(a)(5).) The statutes authorize or require the Commissioner of Education to "publish a list of nationally recognized accrediting agencies which he determines to be reliable authority as to the quality of education or training offered." Most postsecondary institutions and programs attain eligibility for federal funds by obtaining accreditation from one of the accrediting bodies recognized by the commissioner.

Most of the federal aid statutes provide for alternative means to attain eligibility besides accreditation, the primary method. The alternatives available vary with the aid program. Under many aid programs an unaccredited institution may become eligible if it attains "three letter certification," that is, certification by three accredited institutions that they accept the nonaccredited institution's credits on transfer. Another alternative is "preaccreditation status," under which an unaccredited institution or program may be eligible for funds if "the Commissioner has determined that there is satisfactory assurance" that it will meet the accreditation standards of a nationally recognized agency within a reasonable time. Sometimes approval by a recognized state agency is an alternative, as is the case for public vocational education and nursing education institutions under the student financial aid programs. Thus, for most institutions and programs, accreditation is not invariably necessary in order to be eligible for federal funds. The primary exception appears to be proprietary institutions under the student loan programs, which must be accredited by a nationally recognized accrediting agency in order to be eligible.

Pursuant to his statutory authority, the commissioner periodically publishes in the *Federal Register* a list of nationally recognized accrediting agencies and associations. The criteria and procedures for listing are also published in the *Federal Register* and codified in the *Code of Federal Regulations* at 45 C.F.R. Part

149. In addition, the commissioner periodically publishes a pamphlet containing a current list of recognized agencies, the criteria and procedures for listing, and background information on accreditation.[5] The listing process and other aspects of institutional eligibility for federal aid are administered within the Office of Education by the Division of Eligibility and Agency Evaluation in the Bureau of Postsecondary Education.

To be included in the commissioner's list of nationally recognized agencies, an agency must apply to the commissioner for recognition and must meet the commissioner's criteria for recognition. Agencies are reevaluated and their listings are renewed or terminated at least once every four years (45 C.F.R. sec. 149.5). The criteria for recognition concern the agency's functional aspects, responsibility, reliability, and autonomy. For each of the four categories there are specific standards the agency must meet to obtain recognition. The standards cover such matters as the agency's organization, its procedures, and its responsiveness to the public interest. Though these provisions give the commissioner substantial influence over the accrediting process, the commissioner has no direct authority to regulate unwilling accrediting agencies. Agencies must apply for recognition before coming under the commissioner's jurisdiction. Moreover, recognition only gives the commissioner authority to assure the agency's continued compliance with the criteria; it does not give the commissioner authority to overrule the agency's accrediting decisions on particular institutions or programs.

Postsecondary administrators who deal with accrediting agencies will find it beneficial to understand the relationship between the agency and OE, because many of the requirements in the commissioner's criteria for recognition redound to the benefit of the individual institutions and programs. The criteria require,

---

[5] U.S. Department of HEW, *Nationally Recognized Accrediting Agencies and Associations: Criteria and Procedures for Listing by the U.S. Commissioner of Education and Current List* (March 1977 and subsequent editions). The pamphlet may be obtained from the Division of Eligibility and Agency Evaluation, Bureau of Postsecondary Education, U.S. Office of Education, Department of Health, Education, and Welfare, Washington, D.C. 20202.

for example, that an accrediting agency provide specified due process safeguards in its accrediting procedures (45 C.F.R. sec. 149.6(b)(3)) and that an agency's decision-making body be free from conflicts of interest (45 C.F.R. secs. 149.6(b)(2) and 149.6(c)(4)). Because recognition is vitally important to an accrediting agency's influence and credibility in the postsecondary world, agencies will be disinclined to jeopardize their recognition by violating the commissioner's criteria in their dealings with individual institutions. Institutional administrators therefore have considerable leverage to insist that accrediting agencies comply with the commissioner's criteria.

While it is clear that an institution may complain to the commissioner concerning an agency's violation of the recognition criteria, it is unclear whether the commissioner's criteria are enforceable in the courts upon suit by an individual institution. The prevailing judicial view is that government regulations are to be enforced by the government agency that promulgated them, unless a contrary intention appears from the regulations and the statute which authorized the regulations. Since there is no indication that the commissioner's criteria are to be privately enforceable, the courts would likely leave problems concerning compliance with the criteria to the commissioner. The commissioner could require an immediate reevaluation of the agency, withdraw recognition, or do nothing if he believed that no plausible violation existed. Thus, even though the *Marlboro* case discussed in Section 8.2.3 suggests that courts may review accrediting agency actions for compliance with the commissioner's criteria, institutional administrators should not assume that their institution could go to court and nullify any agency action not in compliance with the commissioner's criteria.

Even if the commissioner's criteria are not privately enforceable, that does not mean they would be irrelevant in any suit by an institution against an accrediting agency. Since the judicial standards applying to accrediting agencies are not fully developed (see Section 8.2), courts may look to the commissioner's criteria as evidence of accepted practice in accreditation or as a model to consult in formulating a remedy for an agency's violation of legal standards.

Sec. 8.4. Dealing with Accrediting Agencies

A postsecondary administrator dealing with an accrediting agency should obtain from the agency information concerning its organization and operation. The Commissioner of Education's criteria (Section 8.3 above) require that a USOE-recognized accrediting agency have a clear definition of the scope of its activities (45 C.F.R. sec. 149.6(a)(1)(ii)), clear definitions of each level of accreditation status and clearly written procedures for making accreditation decisions (45 C.F.R. sec. 149.6(a)(3)(i)), clearly defined purposes and objectives (45 C.F.R. sec. 149.6(b)(1)(ii)), published evaluative standards (45 C.F.R. sec. 149.6(b)(2)(ii)(A)), and written procedures for reviewing complaints about institutional or program quality (45 C.F.R. sec. 149(b)(2)(iv)). The commissioner's criteria also require that the accrediting agency make available the names and affiliations of the members of its policy and decision-making bodies; the names of its principal administrative personnel; and a description of its ownership, control, and type of legal organization (45 C.F.R. sec. 149(b)(2)(ii)(D) and (E)). Administrators may insist on receiving any or all of this information from the accrediting agency. Administrators may also insist, backed up by the court cases (Section 8.2), that the agency scrupulously follow its own rules in dealing with the institution.

Most important, an administrator should have copies of the agency's evaluative standards, procedures for making accrediting decisions, and procedures for appealing adverse decisions. An understanding of the standards and procedures can be critical to an effective presentation of the institution or program to the agency. In particular the administrator should take advantage of all procedural rights, such as notice and hearing, which agency rules provide in situations where accreditation is in jeopardy. If agency rules do not provide sufficient procedural safeguards to meet the requirements of the court cases and the commissioner's criteria, administrators may insist on additional rights. The commissioner's criteria, which are more specific than the court guidelines, require that the agency (1) provide an opportunity for the institution to comment on the site-visit report of the agency's evaluation team and to file supplemental materials responding to the report, (2) provide the institution with a specific statement of the reasons for any adverse accrediting action and a notice of the right to appeal, (3) provide an opportunity for a hearing before the appeal body, and (4) provide a written decision of the appeal body with a specific statement of the reasons for its action (45 C.F.R. sec. 149.6(b)(3)).

If the institution should be subjected to an adverse accrediting decision which appears to violate the agency's own rules or the requirements of the court cases or the commissioner's criteria, or to be otherwise unreasonable or unfair, the first recourse is to exhaust all the accrediting agency's internal appeal processes. Simultaneously, it is likely that constructive negotiations can take place with the agency concerning the steps the institution might initiate to reverse the accreditation decision. Should negotiations and internal appeals fail to achieve a resolution satisfactory to the institution, outside recourse to the courts or to the Commissioner of Education is possible. The developing law on accreditation (Section 8.2) provides significant bases for court challenges to accrediting decisions. The commissioner's criteria, while not providing any basis for the commissioner to reverse an individual accrediting decision, may provide a basis for the commissioner and the Division of Eligibility and Agency Evaluation to use their good offices in disputes regarding compliance with the criteria. But court actions and complaints to the commissioner should be last resorts, pursued only in exceptional circumstances and only when reasonable prospects for resolution within the accrediting agency have ended.

Thus the process for resolving accreditation issues parallels the process for most other legal issues in this book. Courts have a presence, and government agencies have a presence—both of which have increased in recent years. But in the end it is usually in the best interests of education for institutions and private educational organizations to develop the capacity for internal resolution of legal disputes. So long as affected parties have meaningful access to the internal process, and the process works fairly, courts and government agencies should allow it ample breathing space to permit educational expertise to operate. It is the challenge of the remainder of this century for courts, agencies, and postsecondary institutions and organizations to work such constructive accommodations in the interests of all participants in the postsecondary community.

Selected Annotated Bibliography

General

1. Kaplin, W., and Hunter, J. P., "The Legal Status of the Educational Accrediting Agency: Problems in Judicial Supervision and Governmental Regulation," 52 *Cornell Law Quarterly* 104 (1966), is a comprehensive legal analysis of accreditation and the authority of courts, the U.S. Office of Education, and state legislatures to constrain or channel the operations of accrediting agencies.

Sec. 8.1 (Accreditation System)

1. Selden, W., and Porter, H., *Accreditation: Its Purposes and Uses* (Council on Postsecondary Accreditation, 1977), an "occasional paper" from a series sponsored by the Council on Postsecondary Accreditation, explains the historical derivation of private accreditation, the current purposes and uses of accreditation, and emerging pressures on the accreditation system.

Sec. 8.2 (Accreditation and the Courts)

1. Kaplin, W., "Judicial Review of Accreditation: The *Parsons College* Case," 40 *J. of Higher Education* 543 (1969), explores considerations regarding accrediting relevant to judicial review of accrediting decisions, analyzes the *Parsons College* case, and evaluates its impact on accreditation.
2. Kaplin, W., "The Marjorie Webster Decisions on Accreditation," 52 *Educational Record* 219 (1971), analyzes the antitrust law, common law, and constitutional law aspects of the *Marjorie Webster* case and evaluates its impact on accreditation.
3. Tayler, C. W., and Hylden, T., "Judicial Review of Accrediting

Agency Actions: *Marlboro Corporation d/b/a The Emery School* v. *The Association of Independent Colleges and Schools*," 4 *J. of College and University Law* 199 (1978), analyzes the *Emery School* case in the context of the developing law of educational accreditation; discusses the scope of judicial review and the legal standards courts will apply in accreditation cases.

Sec. 8.3 (Accreditation and the U.S. Office of Education)

1. Finkin, M., "Federal Reliance and Voluntary Accreditation: The Power to Recognize as the Power to Regulate," 2 *J. of Law and Education* 339 (1973), provides an overview of the accreditation process and the role of the federal government in that process; emphasizes the evolution—through the various federal aid-to-education statutes—of the relationship between private accrediting agencies and the U.S. Office of Education, the present status of the relationship, and the legal basis for the Office of Education's recognition function.

2. Kaplin, W., *Respective Roles of Federal Government, State Governments, and Private Accrediting Agencies in the Governance of Postsecondary Education* (Council on Postsecondary Education, 1975), another COPA "occasional paper," examines the current and potential future roles of federal and state governments and the accrediting agencies, particularly with regard to determining eligibility for federal funding under U.S. Office of Education programs.

Sec. 8.4 (Dealing with Accrediting Agencies)

1. Fisk, R., and Duryea, E. D., *Academic Collective Bargaining and Regional Accreditation* (Council on Postsecondary Accreditation, 1977), another COPA "occasional paper," analyzes the potential impact of collective bargaining on regional accreditation and on the relationship between the institution and the agency that accredits it; provides helpful perspective

for administrators who must deal with accrediting agencies in circumstances where their faculty is unionized.

2. Heilbron, L., *Confidentiality and Accreditation* (Council on Postsecondary Accreditation, 1976), another COPA "occasional paper," examines legal and policy considerations concerning confidentiality of an accrediting agency's records and other information regarding individual institutions; discusses the kinds of information the accrediting agency may collect, the institution's right to obtain disclosure of such information, and the accrediting agency's right to maintain the confidentiality of such information as to federal or state agencies, courts, or other third parties seeking disclosure.

Appendix

Constitution of
The United States
of America:
Provisions of
Particular Interest to
Postsecondary Education

Article I

Section 1. All legislative Powers herein granted shall be vested in a Congress of the United States, which shall consist of a Senate and House of Representatives.

* * *

Section 7. All bills for raising Revenue shall originate in the House of Representatives; but the Senate may propose or concur with Amendments as on other Bills.

Every Bill which shall have passed the House of Representatives and the Senate, shall, before it become a Law, be presented to the President of the United States; If he approves he shall sign it, but if not he shall return it, with his Objections to that House in which it shall have originated, who shall enter the Objections at large on their Journal, and proceed to reconsider it. If after such Reconsideration two thirds of that House shall agree to pass the Bill, it shall be sent, together with the Objections, to the other House, by which it shall likewise be reconsidered, and if approved by two thirds of that House, it shall become a Law.

Section 8. The Congress shall have Power To lay and collect Taxes, Duties, Imposts and Excises, to pay the Debts and provide for the common Defence and general Welfare of the United States;

* * *

To regulate Commerce with foreign Nations, and among the several States, and with the Indian Tribes;

To establish a uniform Rule of Naturalization, and uniform Laws on the subject of Bankruptcies throughout the United States;

* * *

To promote the Progress of Science and useful Arts, by securing for limited Times to Authors and Inventors the exclusive Right to their respective Writings and Discoveries;

* * *

To provide for calling forth the Militia to execute the Laws of the Union, suppress Insurrections and repel Invasions;

To provide for organizing, arming, and disciplining, the Militia, and for governing such Part of them as may be employed in the Service of the United States, reserving to the States respectively, the Appointment of the Officers, and the Authority of training the Militia according to the discipline prescribed by Congress;

* * *

To make all Laws which shall be necessary and proper for carrying into Execution the foregoing Powers, and all other

Powers vested by this Constitution in the Government of the United States, or in any Department or Officer thereof.

* * *

Section 10. No State shall . . . pass any Bill of Attainder, ex post facto Law, or Law impairing the Obligation of Contracts.

* * *

Article II

Section 1. The executive Power shall be vested in a President of the United States of America.

* * *

Section 3. He shall from time to time give to the Congress Information of the State of the Union, and recommend to their Consideration such Measures as he shall judge necessary and expedient; . . . he shall take Care that the Laws be faithfully executed.

Article III

Section 1. The judicial Power of the United States, shall be vested in one supreme Court, and in such inferior Courts as the Congress may from time to time ordain and establish.

Section 2. The judicial Power shall extend to all Cases, in Law and Equity, arising under this Constitution, the Laws of the United States, and Treaties made, or which shall be made, under their Authority; . . .—to Controversies to which the United States shall be a party;—to Controversies between two or more States;— between a State and Citizens of another State;—between Citizens of different States,— . . . and between a State, or the Citizens thereof, and foreign States, Citizens or Subjects.

* * *

Article IV

* * *

Section 2. The Citizens of each State shall be entitled to all Privileges and Immunities of Citizens in the several States.

*   *   *

Article VI

*   *   *

This Constitution, and the laws of the United States which shall be made in Pursuance thereof; and all Treaties made, or which shall be made, under the Authority of the United States, shall be the supreme Law of the Land; and the Judges in every State shall be bound thereby, any Thing in the Constitution or Laws of any State to the Contrary notwithstanding.

*   *   *

Amendment I

Congress shall make no law respecting an establishment of religion, or prohibiting the free exercise thereof; or abridging the freedom of speech, or of the press; or the right of the people peaceably to assemble, and to petition the Government for a redress of grievances.

*   *   *

Amendment IV

The right of the people to be secure in their persons, houses, papers, and effects, against unreasonable searches and seizures, shall not be violated, and no warrants shall issue, but upon probable cause, supported by oath or affirmation, and particularly describing the place to be searched, and the persons or things to be seized.

Amendment V

No person shall be held to answer for a capital, or otherwise infamous crime, unless on a presentment or indictment of a Grand Jury . . . ; nor shall any person be subject for the same offence to be twice put in jeopardy of life or limb; nor shall be compelled in any criminal case to be a witness against himself, nor be deprived of life, liberty, or property, without due process of law; nor shall private property be taken for public use, without just compensation.

Amendment VI

In all criminal prosecutions, the accused shall enjoy the right to a speedy and public trial, by an impartial jury of the State and district wherein the crime shall have been committed, which district shall have been previously ascertained by law, and to be informed of the nature and cause of the accusation; to be confronted with the witnesses against him; to have compulsory process for obtaining witnesses in his favor, and to have the assistance of counsel for his defence.

* * *

Amendment X

The powers not delegated to the United States by the Constitution, nor prohibited by it to the States, are reserved to the States respectively, or to the people.

Amendment XI

The Judicial power of the United States shall not be construed to extend to any suit in law or equity, commenced or prosecuted against one of the United States by Citizens of another State, or by Citizens or Subjects of any Foreign State.

* * *

Amendment XIII

Section 1. Neither slavery nor involuntary servitude, except as a punishment for crime whereof the party shall have been duly convicted, shall exist within the United States, or any place subject to their jurisdiction.

Section 2. Congress shall have power to enforce this article by appropriate legislation.

Amendment XIV

Setion 1. All persons born or naturalized in the United States, and subject to the jurisdiction thereof, are citizens of the United States and of the State wherein they reside. No State shall make or enforce any law which shall abridge the privileges or immunities of citizens of the United States; nor shall any State deprive any person of life, liberty, or property, without due process of law; nor deny to any person within its jurisdiction the equal protection of the laws.

* * *

Section 5. The Congress shall have power to enforce, by appropriate legislation, the provisions of this article.

* * *

Amendment XXVI

Section 1. The right of citizens of the United States, who are eighteen years of age or older, to vote shall not be denied or abridged by the United States or by any State on account of age.

Section 2. The Congress shall have power to enforce this article by appropriate legislation.

Amendment XXVII (Proposed)

Section 1. Equality of rights under the law shall not be denied or abridged by the United States or by any State on account of sex.

Section 2. The Congress shall have the power to enforce, by appropriate legislation, the provisions of this article.

Section 3. This amendment shall take effect two years after the date of ratification.

Case Index

467

Subject Index

A new book in
THE JOSSEY-BASS SERIES
IN HIGHER EDUCATION

The Law of Higher Education

The involvement of courts and governmental agencies in campus affairs is one of the most important changes in higher education over the past decade. Law has become intertwined with the structure and policies of all postsecondary institutions; today, more than ever before, academic administrators must consider the legal implications of the decisions they make. William Kaplin's new, up-to-date volume is the first comprehensive sourcebook on law for administrators and their legal counsel. The book, which includes detailed discussions of the *Bakke* and *Horowitz* cases, cites and clearly summarizes the laws, regulations, and court decisions pertaining to higher education. Kaplin addresses today's most important legal issues and developments, from affirmative action and faculty collective bargaining to federal aid-to-education programs and civil rights compliance. For each issue, Kaplin clarifies basic legal principles, points out future trends, and gives advice to administrators for handling the issues in a way that is both legally sound and in the best interests of the institution.